MW01138513

TRANS HISTORICAL

GENDER PLURALITY BEFORE THE MODERN

EDITED BY GRETA LAFLEUR,
MASHA RASKOLNIKOV, AND
ANNA KŁOSOWSKA

CORNELL UNIVERSITY PRESS

Ithaca and London

Copyright © 2021 by Cornell University

Support for the publication of this book was provided by
the Hull Memorial Publication Fund of Cornell University
and by the Frederick W. Hilles Publication Fund of Yale
University.

All rights reserved. Except for brief quotations in a review,
this book, or parts thereof, must not be reproduced in any
form without permission in writing from the publisher. For
information, address Cornell University Press, Sage House,
512 East State Street, Ithaca, New York 14850. Visit our
website at cornellpress.cornell.edu.

First published 2021 by Cornell University Press

Library of Congress Cataloging-in-Publication Data

Names: LaFleur, Greta, 1981– editor. | Raskolnikov, Masha,
    1972– editor. | Kłosowska, Anna, 1966- editor.
Title: Trans historical : gender plurality before the modern /
    edited by Greta LaFleur, Masha Raskolnikov, and Anna
    Kłosowska.
Description: Ithaca [New York] : Cornell University Press,
    2021. | Includes bibliographical references and index.
Identifiers: LCCN 2021016397 (print) | LCCN 2021016398
    (ebook) | ISBN 9781501759505 (paperback) |
    ISBN 9781501759086 (hardcover) | ISBN 9781501759512
    (epub) | ISBN 9781501759529 (pdf)
Subjects: LCSH: Gender nonconformity—History—To
    1500. | Gender nonconformity—History—16th century.
    Gender nonconformity—History—17th century. |
    Gender nonconformity—History—18th century.
Classification: LCC HQ77.9 .T74125 2021 (print) |
    LCC HQ77.9 (ebook) | DDC 306.76/8—dc23
LC record available at https://lccn.loc.gov/2021016397
LC ebook record available at https://lccn.loc.gov/2021016398

CONTENTS

ACKNOWLEDGMENTS

The development of this volume transpired over almost four years, after Kathleen Perry Long brought us together at Cornell University's "Transforming Bodies" conference, under the auspices of the Early Modern Conversions Project in 2017. Her extraordinary intellectual and human generosity profoundly shaped the superb conference she organized, and we are so glad that the event had the collateral effect of bringing the three of us editors together.

We are profoundly grateful to Mahinder S. Kingra at Cornell University Press for taking on this project. We thank the editorial board and the press for their support, and each person on the publication team for their exquisite professionalism and great courtesy.

We want to thank the contributors whose work is featured here: Abdulhamit Arvas, Roland Betancourt, M. W. Bychowski, Emma Campbell, Igor H. De Souza, Leah DeVun, Micah James Goodrich, Alexa Alice Joubin, Scott Larson, Kathleen Perry Long, Robert Mills, and Zrinka Stahuljak. Without their insights and enduring commitment to making their essays the best possible versions of themselves, there would be no volume. Bringing out their important work allowed us, as we hope you will agree, to take concepts and histories of premodern trans lives further than they were a few years ago.

We also want to thank the anonymous reviewers whose incisive and substantial comments helped to strengthen the volume. Their guidance enabled the best aspects of many of the chapters to shine. Colby Gordon graciously shared with all of us his work in progress on the special issue of the *Journal of Early Modern Cultural Studies*—"Early Modern Trans Studies"—that he edited with Simone Chess and Will Fisher. Blake Gutt read and commented on several contributions. Such intellectual generosity is what makes working in trans and queer studies such a wonderful and deeply fun experience.

The experience of developing this volume was made immeasurably more challenging by the onset of the COVID-19 pandemic in early 2020. At a moment when all meetings moved online, we gave up on the idea of working and editing in person, as we had hoped to do over the course of our collaboration. That said, we are immensely grateful for our Friday morning meetings, and for one another's company, support, thoughtfulness, and care as we negotiated this year and this project. We thank, too, our incredibly alert (some might say *too* alert) dogs, astonishingly mischievous children, and other beloveds. May we be able to reciprocate the love and energy they have so liberally bestowed upon us.

We submitted the final version of this book on the last day of June, a time dedicated (at least in the United States) to celebrating the fighting spirit of the trans teachers and leaders who came before us and continue to transform the world today. That season overlapped importantly with protests around the globe demanding an end to anti-Black police violence and the abolition of police, prisons, and detentions. It has been heartening since then to find these demands at the center of queer political organizing (meanwhile, this has *always* been at the center of trans political organizing), instead of taking the form of afterthought or counterprotest. May that energy continue to build! We dedicate this book to those who have come before, those who are leading us righteously in our current moment, and those who have yet to arrive. Your legacies are powerful, and the futures that you promise us all, gorgeous.

Introduction
The Benefits of Being Trans Historical

Greta LaFleur, Masha Raskolnikov, and Anna Kłosowska

In 1782 Deborah Sampson applied for an "invalid's pension"—effectively veteran's pay—from the new United States federal government. Sampson, born in 1760 into a poor family in central Massachusetts, had been hired out as a servant to wealthy families in their community since they were a young child, and had joined the Continental Army under the name of Robert Shurtliff in 1782. While there is much we do not know about Sampson/Shurtliff, records suggest that they enlisted in the Continental Army not once but twice—the first time they enlisted and accepted the enrollment bonus, but then did not report for duty—and continued to live and work as a man for at least a year following their discharge. We also know that, after their time in the military, Sampson went on to live as a woman, marrying and having children, and reassuming the name Deborah Sampson as they waged a public campaign for their veteran's pension. It is unusual that we should know so much about a poor enlisted person who fought in some of the smaller and less storied battles of the Revolutionary War, but Sampson's life has maintained a great deal of staying power, in part because of the attention that they received both during their lifetime and after their death. Herman Mann published a fictionalized memoir of Sampson's life titled *The Female Review* in 1797, and Sampson appears in multiple nineteenth-century biographies of famous American *women*, to this day holding the honor of being the Official State "Heroine" of Massachusetts. Meryl Streep invoked

Sampson's status as an early gender revolutionary in a rally for Hillary Clinton's presidential campaign in 2016, and in 2014, Sampson was the subject of yet *another* fictionalized memoir, this time by their distant descendant Alex Myers (who is himself trans), who rewrote their story as a narrative of sexual and trans awakening set against the backdrop of the Revolutionary War. It would be difficult to argue that Sampson's historical notoriety is not due to the widespread knowledge of their life as a person who lived as both a man and a woman. But does this mean that Sampson was transgender? Are they part of transgender history? What do we make of the fact that Sampson seems to have chosen to live openly as both a woman and a man during their lifetime?

In his 2004 biography of Sampson, Alfred Young demurred on this point, writing simply that when it came to whether Sampson was a feminist or a lesbian, "we are in the dark."[1] (Young does not consider whether Sampson might have been transgender.) This volume takes Young's statement as a challenge, a provocation, and an invitation, one that gathers a wide range of questions about the possibilities and limitations that inhere in producing histories of the transgender past. We consider what might be both broadly true and broadly wrong about Young's assessment of the unknowability of a person's political, sexual, or gendered experience before the advent of vocabularies—frequently derived from medicine, race science and pseudoscience, and religious doctrine—for gender nonconformity that would not arrive in North America, Sampson's birthplace, until almost a century after the events described here, with the sexological sciences of the late nineteenth century. Yet while this volume is concerned with the knowability of individual, gendered, and especially gender-nonconforming experience in the presexological period, it also builds on recent work in transgender studies by scholars such as C. Riley Snorton, Susan Stryker, and Jules Gill-Peterson (among many others), who argue for the importance of extending the purview of trans studies and trans histories beyond individual experience to serve as an analytical tool for inquiry into affective flows, structures of power, and burgeoning epistemologies of difference. This volume explores what might be gained by importing some of these emergent frameworks from trans studies— a field that is, by and large, focused on the period after 1950—to earlier periods, when questions about the experience, performance, and meaning of gender were every bit as live as they are today.

The archaeology of knowledge production is central to transgender studies, and archival silences, gaps, and erasures bear a uniquely structuring influence on the landscape of the field, especially when it comes to trans history and historiography.[2] These archival absences, whatever their origins, are also compounded in the medieval and early modern periods in particular by the realities of slavery and colonialism, which actively sought to erase the voices of African and Native peoples who found themselves the target of European and broader settler colonial violence and expropriation.[3] The dynamism of current ways of understanding diversity in gendered presentation and behavior—think of the fact that Deborah Sampson was first claimed as a feminist, then as a lesbian, and then as a trans person—both expands and limits what the past looks like to twenty-first-century readers, and at times makes it more difficult to perceive what medieval and early modern texts have to say about how gendered experience, knowledge, performance, and embodiment were understood in their own times. The trans past cannot be considered without a commensurate reckoning with the politics of historiography.

One of the pleasures of studying historically distant periods is the possibility of being confronted with the deep alterity of the past. In distant periods and geographies, notions of the gendered subject are surprisingly different from that which modern readers find familiar. Some scholars emphasize that alterity, insisting on the radical difference between "now" and "then," "us" and "them." Others cope with that same alterity and strangeness by finding patterns of similarity, seeking universal experiences, or refusing charges of anachronism with claims to excavating what Lillian Faderman called a "usable past."[4] We have collected the essays that follow under the umbrella of trans history, but they also highlight critical differences in the way that gender-nonconforming behavior was embodied, understood, and disciplined, as well as the different ways in which the past might, at times, be simply unknowable.

This volume takes up a widely discussed contemporary category—*transgender*—and looks in a necessarily partial way at both real people and fictional characters from the pre- and early modern periods who might have had something in common with that designation. Does this approach amount to a claim about a universal human experience? Does it show how genuinely different past understandings of human sex and gender were from present ones? A little of both, and also neither. This volume looks at stories about what we might now term gendered experience and at how they are told. It is bound to the utter specificity of long-ago ways of representing heavily racialized terms such as *man* and *woman*, and listens carefully to the way that both fictional works and discussions of historical people and events consider gendered experience that does not fit easily within either category.

What further complicates the project of studying early gendered, gender-nonconforming, and transgender experience is the reality of mediation.

All that we know about early periods comes to us via the interventions of the authors, scribes, and amanuenses who told the stories; by people who recorded and passed down the stories; and by those who either permitted or did not permit the written texts of such stories to survive until the present day. The power of discourse, as Eve Kosofsky Sedgwick cannily reminds us, has always included the power to ignore, trivialize, and indifferently destroy the evidence of lives deemed not worth preserving for the future; as Martha Vicinus put it, "Ignorance now and in prior times can be willed."[5] Given the great powers massed against those who transgress norms—a term whose etymological stem also gives us *normal* and *normative* but that did not bear its modern meaning until the nineteenth century—it is extraordinary how many records of gender plurality we have from early periods.[6]

Trans studies has a history problem, albeit one that scholars from all branches of the field are busy working to address.[7] Because the movement for trans recognition is a development of the last century or so, and because assertions of the putative "newness" of transgender experience have been consistently used to undermine the legitimacy of nonbinary genders, trans people, activists, and scholars have had to fight to claim the historicity of trans lives. Some scholars have argued, and still do argue, that prior to the coinage of the term, transgender experience did not exist. Compounding this issue is the fact that transgender studies, like many other interdisciplinary fields, leans toward the present. And yet, gender-nonconforming and transgender people appear consistently in fiction, religious texts, church and court records, and even in texts authored by trans people themselves from antiquity onward. Furthermore, narratives about gender transition and gender confirmation were told long before any of those terms came into being. While none of these figures had the word *transgender*—not to mention a host of other modern vocabularies—at their disposal as a framework for characterizing their experience, we strongly believe that their stories can and should be united under the mantle of the transgender past.

Medieval and early modern studies also have a trans problem. Because these fields are concerned with historical moments that precede the coinage of *transgender, transsexual,* and related terms, writing about transness can appear to some as the imposition of contemporary concerns upon the past. How could a trans identity have expressed itself prior to contemporary trans rights activism, prior to medical and legal interventions and architectures supporting gender transition and affirmation, prior to the world-making efforts that trans people from across the globe have embarked upon to take space and create protections for trans people, trans communities, and trans futures? While identity itself is a more or less modern framework for understanding the relationship between one's experience and one's role in the social and political world, trans and gender-nonconforming peoples more broadly appear consistently in medieval and early modern records— emphatically so. If trans studies has seemed to be an awkward fit to some scholars of the medieval and early modern periods, perhaps it is not because transgender experience is anachronistic to these periods but rather because medieval and early modern scholarship needs its own trans studies, one responsive to the historical particularities and methodological challenges of studying an era at least seven hundred years behind us. Laying claim to the persistence of gender crossings over historical time and geographical space has been critical for those who seek to historicize and assert the longtime existence of transgender people, and scholars of all genders from medieval and early modern studies now have the unique opportunity to join efforts with current trans political movements in this endeavor.

But how to recognize, identify, or theorize trans peoples, sensoria, or ways of knowing in the past? Furthermore, how might we recognize, identify, or theorize what is *not* trans about the past? While not a self-identical (or even necessarily overlapping) term, the word "queer" has been put to work, in the development of queer theory and in the traction that the word has found in gender and sexuality studies more broadly, to describe a capacious range of subjects and ideological formations that are positioned against the normative. Beyond just describing queer people, the term is usually used to describe politically or socially agonistic (or antagonistic!) relations between peoples, communities, or ideas and hegemonic structures of power. Some scholars have worried, however, that the word or idea of "queer" has become too capacious, broad to the point of risking an emptiness of signification. While this volume is built on a curious, capacious, and extensive sense of what trans experiences, ways of knowing, ways of being, and forms of relating to the world might be, we are also wary of reducing the descriptive, categorical, or ontological powers of trans analytics to a metaphor, if it is to serve real populations who find themselves particularly vulnerable to violence and stigmatization. We want a past replete with trans people and fictions, and we also want a proliferation of trans futures. In that spirit, we hope that this volume indexes the efflorescence of archaeologies of the past: a past that may hold a space for forms of transness that have not yet been fully articulated or imagined, a past that, in the future, may unfold forms of alterity unknown to us at present.

Ultimately, this collection engages but also moves beyond the alterity/ continuity debates that have been so central to scholarship in queer studies and queer historiography in favor of tarrying with the specific methodologies, forms of inquiry, and scholarly conversations at the center of trans studies in our moment and in recent years. It does so in part to emphasize the way that queer theory, sometimes in consort with women's history and feminist theory, has at times overdetermined or made impossible forms of critique that are revealed by trans studies frameworks. Insofar as broad understandings of queerness rely on assumptions of fixed sexual difference—Eve Kosofsky Sedgwick defined this paradigm, that of how homosexuality came to be almost wholly defined by a sexual preference for the "same" sex, as the "Great Paradigm Shift"—there is much that queer critique, and early queer theory in particular, could not "see" about the gender nonconformity of especially early writers and texts, reading this nonconformity as queerness to the exclusion of transness.[8] Queer theory has a symbiotic—some have said parasitic—relationship to trans studies; the inverts and gender-fuckers of the past have done heavy double duty for both fields.[9] While queer theory and trans studies have in many ways experienced similar institutional fortunes, and have at times shared many political and intellectual priorities, there can be, and has long been, active transphobia in queer communities and among queer scholars, and queer and trans people have not always or usually articulated the same (or even overlapping!) scholarly prerogatives or claims for justice.[10]

Some queer studies scholars have, fortunately, begun to ask critical questions not only about what scholarship in queer theory made possible, in terms of the emergence and institutionalization of trans studies, but also about what queer theory's particular optics and analytics *precluded*, in terms of objects of inquiry. In 1995, for example, Ruth Karras and David Boyd published an article in the fourth-ever issue of the flagship journal of queer studies, GLQ, titled "The Interrogation of a Male Transvestite Prostitute in Fourteenth-Century London."[11] The article discusses the now famous medieval arrest of Eleanor Rykener, who may have been assigned male at birth and was arrested for prostitution at the turn of the fifteenth century (1394). In her testimony, Rykener told the court the story of how she had come to be a sex worker, explaining the process by which a number of other sex workers had taught her the etiquette of the profession. Eleanor Rykener's story was important to the then emergent field of queer theory insofar as it seemed to provide evidence that what was then termed "same-sex" sexuality—often understood under the broad rubric of "sodomy" in the Middle Ages—existed and was expressed in that era. Karras's and Boyd's reading of the Rykener case also crucially misses a series of details that, to readers today, would likely seem obvious: that Rykener very intentionally chose to work, and perhaps also to live, as a woman, and, as our contributor M. W. Bychowski points out, to use the name Eleanor to indicate her identity. Rykener, the archival text suggests, may be an important figure to trans history.

Carolyn Dinshaw, a foundational figure in queer medieval studies and one of the co-founders of *GLQ*, returned to the Rykener case in a 2019 issue of *GLQ* celebrating the journal's twenty-fifth anniversary, simultaneously lamenting and praising the use of the medieval case in that 1995 issue. Dinshaw finds a productive tension in the way that the queer reading of the case missed what later critics read as its important testimony for early trans histories, and glosses what she terms the "afterlives" of the Rykener document, with all of its divergent responses from scholars in queer, trans, and medieval studies, as a reading problem: "Most strikingly, to my mind, this range of responses demonstrates the limitations or liabilities of queer analysis: it shows in particular the need for more precision and suppleness regarding gender and embodiment."[12] This collection, then, represents an attempt to move beyond the methodological and analytical limitations that queer theory has inadvertently (or at times intentionally) visited upon antique, medieval, and early modern discussions of gender diversity, and to address precisely the need that Dinshaw enumerates for greater precision, suppleness, and curiosity regarding the possibilities of the trans past.

To further heed Dinshaw's call, one of the many concerns that animates the essays that follow is the fact that trans studies, like queer studies before it, is vulnerable to a form of *historical* scholarship that focuses more heavily on individual people than on the structures, affects, or logics that inform the experience of gender, its social and political performance, and how those structures, affects, and logics are portable for the project of meaning making beyond individual trans lives. Writing from a political moment in which the articulation of individual experience and the recognition of identity can at times both undergird and hinder the goal of crafting more effective structural critiques of gendered (and thus also racial) power, many of the essays in this collection reach beyond individual experience to consider the religious cultures, legal architectures, and other forms of structural power that created the conditions under which certain forms of gendered expression became familiar and knowable, and others obscured.

This is not to say that individual people are unimportant to trans histories—people *are*, precisely, trans histories—but simply to index the fact that one of the hallmarks of thinking in trans studies has been a scholarly willingness, even from the field's inception, to think beyond the unit of the person or the population to evince what we might call a trans metaphysics.[13] Following this scholarly impulse, the essays in this collection are part of an approach to trans studies characterized by expansiveness, rather than contraction, about what and who might be gathered under the auspices of "trans." The volume includes essays on people, figures, historical events, cultural production, and modes of being that we believe have something to tell us about more distant trans pasts that at times seem radically out of sync with, and perhaps even entirely unrelated to, our many trans presents.

This volume writes back against assumptions that trans studies falls under the purview of the modern—assumptions that, in our experience, are far more common in the study of more distant periods, including the antique, medieval, and early modern worlds. While this will be a familiar move to many readers, we make this statement as scholars in medieval studies (Raskolnikov and Kłosowska) and eighteenth-century studies (LaFleur), fields that have familiarized all three of us, at times, with an effect that can at best be characterized as a knee-jerk historicism, and at worst as a thinly veiled form of transphobia, used to refuse, reject, or simply shut down scholarly inquiry into what are often characterized as unnecessarily and/or anachronistically "politicized" pasts. One of the most common iterations of this form of refusal travels under the charge of anachronism; according to this narrative, any inquiry into transgender pasts is motivated by necessarily unscholarly political motivations rather than legitimate intellectual inquiry. This form of refusal implicitly rests on the notion that transgender pasts are not possible; scholarship on trans historicities is supposedly anachronistic, this reasoning goes, because it requires reading into the past what was not already there, always in uncritical service of the political present. While readers coming to this volume from fields that privilege the late nineteenth century onward will not always be familiar with this genre of conservative critique, we also write for readers working in the history of sexuality, the history of race, critical race studies, the history of gender, early queer studies, and of course early trans studies—fields in which the politics of the production of history are bread-and-butter concerns—who are refusing to concede trans lives, affects, logics, and worlds to the modern period, however one might define it. A transgender studies designed for the study of early periods must assume an eclectic approach to both method and the idea of history itself in order to craft a framework for interpretation that is attentive to the regional, cultural, and historical specificities that inform how gender was understood in a given time and place.

As editors, we build on a long tradition of work in women's history and gender and sexuality studies when we insist that *gender*—one in the long list of terms that have been accused by critics of importing anachronistic notions of difference to the distant past—has served as an interpretive methodology that sets up the limits of intelligibility for beings in the world. This has existed as a truism for feminist thinkers coming from many fields at least since the publication of Joan Scott's landmark "Gender: A Useful Category of Historical Analysis" in 1986.[14] But if gender is a useful category of historical analysis, so too is transgender. Furthermore, we also proceed from a position of curious uncertainty, asking: Is *transgender* always gender? If not, what else might it be?

Yet if transgender, as a category or analytic, *is* always gender, then that still does not resolve a series of crucial questions about what gender indexes or does not index. As we assembled the essays that make up this volume, we found ourselves returning, again and again, to a series of key concepts that, despite changing a great deal over time, nonetheless fundamentally inform how we understand gendered experience, gendered knowledge, and the way that social worlds have made sense of gender in the past.

First: language. The essays collected in this volume address histories that occur in many different locations and linguistic traditions, among them Spanish, French, English, Turkish, Polish, Greek, and Latin. Many languages gender concepts, expressions, and aesthetics, such that it is not only a story's protagonist that is gendered, but frequently their cat, desk, and shoes as well. Because some form of gendering is often the verbal marker of anthropomorphism, even when referencing personifications or inanimate objects, languages without masculine and feminine noun gender might offer a different experience of the world to their speakers.[15]

Second: terminologies, old and new. One of the most challenging aspects of working on the history of gendered experience is that the vocabularies for describing that experience vary immensely over time and space, even within the same language. Far from there being a paucity or impoverishment of language to describe gendered experiences that appear to fall outside the realm of cisgender, during the medieval and early modern periods and the eighteenth century there was a simply enormous range of terms that signified different aspects of gender presentation and performance. Indeed, at times the analytical challenge of working on early trans studies is less excavating ancient trans people from some long-lost or forgotten archive than just figuring out which terms, specific to their historical, cultural, and linguistic context, were used to describe the social, political, and personal meaning of gender, and listening carefully. To borrow a slogan from the early LGBT rights movement in the United States, "we are everywhere"; wherever and whenever structures of meaning existed for making sense of gendered experience, we will find people who were, in whatever way, outliers to those structures.

One of the problems of discussing those outliers in a twenty-first-century collection, however, is that the words they use to describe themselves—and that their contemporaries used to define, describe, and often discipline them—are words that still land hard on our twenty-first-century ears. Words and ideas such as "hermaphrodite" and "monster" were common sites for the discussion of genders, bodies, and even entire cultures that were unfamiliar to those observing and describing them. Language and expressions that we know to have been not merely common but at times not even necessarily derogatory in the periods we study can seem hurtful, offensive, and transphobic in the gendered idioms of our current moment. The essays in this collection explore many such terms, while including explanations of these words and ideas and justifications for reproducing them, in the spirit of offering a little extra context for contemporary trans readers and trans studies scholars who may be encountering pre- and early modern language in situ for the first time. Scholars such as Saidiya Hartman have explored the political and ethical complexities of reproducing violent and racist representations of Black people in scholarly writings, even in scholarship explicitly intended to combat racism and white supremacy.[16] We believe that a range of related ethical and historiographic questions are also live in scholarship on trans histories, and some of the essays that follow, such as Scott Larson's "Laid Open," are organized around precisely these complicated methodological issues.

Third: racial and ethnic differences have always structured gendered knowledge. Cultural beliefs about the meaning of race, religion, and ethnicity, as well as histories of labor and labor exploitation, have all significantly inflected ideas and experiences of gender. Scholars in Black studies, for example, such as Hortense Spillers, Saidiya Hartman, and C. Riley Snorton, have explored at length the alienation from work, state, and kin wrought by the Atlantic slave trade, and how this alienation, in turn, both shaped Black engenderment and further alienated Black people from dominant structures of gendered meaning.[17] Highly particularized historical *and present-day* structures of racism, xenophobia, and classism also inflect the way that gender is understood, disciplined, and rewarded. To extend the logic of Cathy Cohen's landmark essay "Punks, Bulldaggers, and Welfare Queens" (1997), race, class, or sexual preference and practices—among other things—can also foreclose the inclusion of some people or populations, even those who identify as cisgender, in normative structures of gender.[18]

The scholars whose work is featured in this collection consider specific histories of the racialization of gender or the sexualization of labor to situate these ideas in particular regions and periods. For example, with the heightened scrutiny aimed at people of color and non-Christians in Europe both before and after the Spanish Inquisition came the emergence of idioms for the explanation of difference that used gender expression as a way to shore up taxonomies of human variety, and with them racial, religious, and ethnic hierarchies.[19] As Geraldine Heng has demonstrated, these structures had already emerged during the period of the Crusades, with its defining anti-Semitism and other religious and ethnic intolerance, and the early rumblings of statecraft that characterized the Middle Ages.[20] Similarly, the work of scholars such as Hannah Barker have tracked the way that racial, religious, or ethnic difference structured the idiom of enslavement, sexual subjection, bondage, or servitude such that, for example, words like *sudan* could, in the medieval period, describe the origin of a person (Africa), their appearance, their unfree status, or a combination of these meanings.[21] Consider, too, the function, in medieval Arabic, of the word *sqâliba*, which means a person of Slav origin, an enslaved person, or a eunuch (the eunuchs themselves being one example of the lived complexities of premodern understandings of gender in some regions and cultures). These structures and terminologies were the foundations of the concepts and institutions of bondage and unfreedom that often combined racial as well as gendered and sexualized meaning to reinforce weaponized hierarchies of human difference. This history has some continuity as well as profound differences from what Spillers has theorized as the "ungendering" of Black women, in particular, in the United States, and the ways in which survivors of slavery and descendants of enslaved peoples might find themselves denied the simultaneously harmful and potentially freeing legibility of normative gender.[22]

Fourth: the putative "newness" of trans lives and identities. It can be difficult to renounce the seduction of progressive historical narratives which imagine that gender nonconformity, or even the concept of gender itself, is a recent development that distinguishes the modern from what came before it. This narrative, which ascribes a *different* kind of novelty to trans people and politics than the form discussed earlier, implicitly assumes that antique, medieval, and early modern peoples built consensus around terms like *man* and *woman*, or that they had some sort of confidence surrounding their knowledge about what gender *is* or *was*. The essays in this volume describe a plurality of modes for the representation of gendered experience that exist outside of the tight bifurcation of *male* and *female* that proliferated before the consolidation of gender expansiveness into, among other things, the idiom of *transgender*.

While we absolutely believe that the essays collected in this volume all point to different features, moments, and theorizations of trans histories, we are also committed to guaranteeing the figures at the center of the essays that follow the freedom *not* to "be" transgender. It is not the responsibility of the medieval personage of Silence, for example—the centerpiece of Masha Raskolnikov's essay—to evidence or materialize the existence of trans people in the past. This is not to say that Silence is not themself one possible figure in the great expanse of trans history, but rather to insist on the fact that Silence cannot *only* be defined by a vocabulary that arrived several hundred years after the eponymous *roman*. As editors of this volume, we understand our task to be, as much as anything else, remaining open to what the texts, historical figures, and events at the center of the essays that follow might teach us about gender in their time and place. We aspire to be close readers, and even closer listeners. Indeed, maintaining a sense of intellectual curiosity about how trans pasts might diverge from, or appear radically out of sync with, some of the common sense about trans experience in the present is one of the overarching goals of the volume. To this end, the essays in this collection refuse any teleological understanding of trans histories. They do not offer any kind of account of a linear or progressive march forward, from a past characterized by trans obscurity to a modernity in which trans life is knowable in advance, or in which trans logics, affects, or possibilities for critique bear a kind of transparency unavailable prior to the rise of the sexological sciences, the rise of a widespread vocabulary for describing them, or the advent of modernity itself. This is also not to imply that every person who identifies as other than *male* or *female* uses the term "transgender," but merely to point to the global traction of the term itself. Gender-nonconforming people also use a host of other terms and frameworks for describing gendered experience that cannot be accounted for with terms like *male* or *female*, or *man* or *woman*, but that, at times, nonetheless *do* travel under the umbrella of those terms. Some Native and Indigenous scholars, in particular, have expressed consternation over the increasing ubiquity of *transgender* frameworks, especially within social services contexts, that inadvertently or intentionally seek to replace Native and Indigenous ways of theorizing, knowing, explaining, and experiencing nonbinary gender.[23]

As scholars seeking to illuminate trans and gender-nonconforming lives in the distant past, we ask: How do we conceive of "gender" relative to "sex" in the medieval and early modern periods? Did it exist? If so, what was it? Were there normative forms of gender, and if so, how were they imposed and policed? To build on the insights of Karma Lochrie in *Heterosyncracies*, if the very idea of homo- and heterosexuality had not yet fully emerged or solidified in the medieval or early modern periods, then how could normative sex and gender systems have functioned? And if there was, as Lochrie argues, no "normal" during the periods that this collection covers, then what possibilities for the flourishing of trans subjects might those periods have permitted?[24] Insofar as our work as critics is partly to "unmake common sense," we have to ask ourselves both what culturally and historically specific senses of "men" and "women" consisted of, and what possibilities may have existed "outside the natural" when it came to gender.

Throughout this introduction we have refrained from using the language of normativity to describe the trans and gender-expansive subjects at the center of this collection. This was intentional. Because the essays in this volume focus on periods at least several hundred years prior to the advent of the "normal" as a statistical concept in the nineteenth century, we also ask whether normativity or non-normativity provides an adequate framework for considering the many forms of gendered embodiment, experience, and knowledge in these distant periods. This collection proceeds, furthermore, from the understanding that gender normativity today is an impossible and frequently dangerous ideal. The essays that follow suggest that there is neither a present nor a past existence of some sort of totalizing gender normativity.

If gender normativity is in fact a fiction, then it has centuries of fictions that refuse it too. Many works discussed in this volume qualify as "fictions" in some way; they tell stories that do not necessarily claim to be true, and in which magical or miraculous events provide occasion or explanation for the flourishing of trans lives. Fiction, as a space of experimentation, has always allowed for the imagining of worlds yet to come. At times these fictions are happy ones, calling forth realities not yet available, and at other times they end badly, serving as a warning or articulating a prohibition. As Leah DeVun's and Emma Campbell's essays on the wonderful and unfamiliar organisms featured in many medieval bestiaries and travel narratives illustrate, these stories can be unrepeatable and extraordinary, and even their ugliest predictions about disciplinary forms of gender nonetheless testify to the fact that other worlds were imagined to be possible.

One of the many goals of building collective memory about the distant past is to infuse present-day individual and collective consciousness with historical power and to support the development of thicker and more meaningful connections between resilient trans pasts and current trans lives. Genealogy, history, and origins can be strategically instrumentalized to shore up beliefs about authenticity, nature, norm, and legitimacy. Historical and literary scholarship thus constitutes a strategy of holding space for trans lives in the present, in our relations to people and institutions, in our classrooms, and in the longest reaches of our lives. The legitimacy of trans lives today does not depend on early modern historical precedents, but to have these early modern examples at hand helps us when we have to constantly counter persistent and violent rhetoric that aims to undermine trans people's claims to recognition, support, solidarity, and justice. Furthermore, trans history exposes the incredible precarity of binary understandings of gender, revealing how fragile they are and how very possible it is to refuse and undo them. This volume contributes to the recent effort to assemble, analyze, and make easily accessible the collective memories—especially autobiographies and fictions, but also documents and traces of institutional symptoms—of trans lives in the antique, medieval, and early modern periods.[25]

At the same time, however, we hope that the essays in this volume will also point to the variety and expansiveness of gendered experience in the antique, medieval, and early modern periods, before the coagulation of gender ideologies that gave rise to the hegemony of a binary understanding of gender. While we have no interest in wading into the question of when a binary understanding of gender—that is to say, a notion of *male* and *female* in which these figures represent the poles of a continuous spectrum of experience that is directly reflected by genital embodiment—emerged or came to some sort of dominance, we do want to insist on the fact that binary approaches to theorizing gender have a history and are not unchanging transhistorical universalisms. Indeed, this volume testifies to the wonderful heterogeneity of gender experience across time, space, and positionality, to a diversity of gendered and transgendered experience that may, in fact, be what renders trans pasts so difficult to think. We hypothesize that one of the less insidious reasons why trans experience may be assumed to be a "modern phenomenon" (both terms that, together and separately, work to denaturalize trans lives and undermine trans historicities) is actually precisely the lack of a consolidated, widespread understanding of any gender at all. Without a polarized and siloed understanding of *man* and *woman*, it is difficult to assert some sort of categorical difference because of the lack of a categorical understanding of terms like *male* and *female* to begin with.

Furthermore, with the advent of, for example, the global sexological sciences throughout the nineteenth century and into the twentieth and twenty-first came the development of vocabularies both hegemonic and liberatory for gender experience and expression that could not be captured by the ideological bifurcation of human bodies into two sexed types, especially in North America and Europe. As trans studies scholars have explored at length, these vocabularies were weaponized by institutions bent on eradicating trans people, bodies, and communities, and they were also wrested from precisely those institutions by trans people themselves. Regardless of one's relationship to heavily medicalized terms such as *invert*, *transsexual*, or *transgender person*, however, it would be difficult to deny the cultural traction of these terms, especially by the turn of the twenty-first century in the United States, the vantage point from which we write. Today there are trans people in communities all over the world who describe themselves using the term *transgender*; the term has achieved a certain form of global aggregation that has brought trans people together but also consolidated a wide range of experiences under that nominal umbrella.

It has been argued that all the terms—*gender, sexuality, transgender,* and others—that organize the complex identities structuring this volume are rooted in globalized taxonomies of gender that threaten to erase other modalities. The words *trans* and *transgender* appear in many languages across the world, evidencing the realities of soft imperialism and cultural hegemony, despite the fact that these terms do different work, and bear a myriad of divergent meanings, for the many people who use them. While this volume sought contributions beyond the "usual suspects" of European premodernity, the lion's share of essays in this collection are concerned with European (as well as some North American) sources and archives. It is also true that, most likely by the time this volume is in the hands of its readers, some of the terminology that we make use of today will already have become outdated and stale. The field of trans studies is undergoing rapid and enormously exciting changes, and while we cannot predict the future landscape of the field, we hope that its directions will include a continued interest in historically distant archives of trans lives. At heart, this is a trans history oriented toward trans futures—futures we hope to amplify by cataloguing a host of divergent visions of what transness was or might have been, or might someday be. It is a project that we hope, in due time, will become outdated and surpassed by the work of those who come after us, whose vision of what it is to be trans historical will be broader, deeper, and more precise than our own.

We designed the volume as a series of explorations into legal documents, literary texts, and images that represent trans lives, fictions, and frameworks before 1800, intended to showcase the plurality of gender from antiquity to the cusp of the modern era. In the opening section, "Archives: Revisiting Law and Medicine," Leah DeVun's essay, "Mapping the Borders of Sex," examines twelfth- through fifteenth-century medieval "Wonders of the East" narratives and their accompanying illustrations. DeVun explores the trans aesthetics of fictional "monstrous races," called "hermaphrodites," whose societies allegedly existed on the margins of the climate zones. Medieval "geographers" describe "hermaphrodites" as beings with fanciful anatomy who switch back and forth between male and female sexual and social roles.

DeVun argues that these heavily racialized figures index an expansive under-standing of sexed embodiment in the premodern period.

Following this first essay, the other articles in this section are organized around the histories of specific individuals whose genders were questioned by juridico-medical authorities. In "Elenx de Céspedes: Indeterminate Gen-ders in the Spanish Inquisition," Igor H. De Souza focuses on the deposition of Elenx de Céspedes (b. 1546) to examine how gender plurality was some-times subsumed under accusations of sodomy in depositions conducted by the Spanish Inquisition. Inquisitorial attempts to define and control prac-tices defined as "sodomy," De Souza argues could in fact be attempts to regulate the presentation of gender. Kathleen Long's essay, "The Case of Marin le Marcis," focuses on a seventeenth-century French case that trans-pired around the perceived undecidability of Marin le Marcis's sex, and the architecture of legal and empirical medical knowledge that was used to decide it. Long's essay reveals that early modern medical and legal texts acknowledged variations in what today we might term "biological sex" as well as lived gender.

In "The Transgender Turn: Eleanor Rykener Speaks Back," M. W. Bychowski analyzes a 1394 London court deposition, to this day one of the most oft-discussed medieval texts in both queer and trans studies. Bychowski reflects on the deposition, which had been construed exclusively as a text documenting same-sex desire in earlier queer scholarship, to the detriment of its trans meaning. Bychowski does so to argue that "most scholarship is, effectively, cisgender scholarship, not only because it is mostly cisgender scholars who have claimed the education and tools to publish it but also because most scholarship assumes the cisgender status of any character or historical figure who is presented to readers."

In "Wojciech of Poznań and the Trans Archive, Poland, 1550–1561," Anna Kłosowska translates a 1561 Polish court deposition previously available only in Polish and German, which describes the life of an individual who had been publicly designated a woman despite a previous period of living as a man. The deposition narrates a decade in a trans person's life, including three marriages and many sexual partners. Kłosowska points out that an archival record for one trans person in effect documents the existence of a commu-nity of trans and queer allies at a time and place that might be imagined as less than hospitable to such a social formation.

The subsequent section, "Frameworks: Representing Early Trans Lives," examines how trans and genderqueer lives are imagined in visual arts, performance, and fiction from the premodern period. The essay by Rob-ert Mills analyzes visual representations of Saint Wilgefortis/Liberata/

Uncumber, who is usually portrayed as a crucified bearded person wearing a dress. Wilgefortis was worshipped by wives who wished to be rid of their husbands: the saint's legend describes how Wilgefortis, assigned as female, miraculously grew a beard to repulse a pagan suitor. Mills cautions against identifying Wilgefortis as trans and reflects how art history may respond to Jack Halberstam's idea of a "politics of transitivity" in which trans studies becomes "a site of possibility rather than diagnosis."

Abdulhamit Arvas's chapter, "Performing and Desiring Gender Variance in the Early Modern Ottoman Empire," draws on the eighteenth-century poet Enderunlu Fazıl's *Defter-i Aşk* (Book of Love). Its third volume describes the *köçek*, a term used in the sixteenth through eighteenth centuries for dancers assigned male at birth famous for their traditionally feminine attire and performances (earlier scholars inaccurately describe *köçek* as cross-dressing). Arvas's essay argues that *köçek* are part of the genealogy of modern trans identity in Turkey that was suppressed in favor of the production of a binary gender system aligned with Western prerogatives.

In "Without Magic or Miracle," Masha Raskolnikov analyzes *Le Roman de Silence*, a thirteenth-century French text by "Heldris de Cornouaille." The protagonist, Silence, is assigned female at birth and brought up as a boy in order to legally inherit. Silence had not chosen to live as a man but excels at it; their choice is a pragmatic one. Transness is often held up as an expression of an inner truth, but a queer reading critiques the possibility that an inner truth is ultimately knowable or desirable. According to modern conventions, one assumes a necessary sex despite any obstacles, which is simply not the case here. Can Silence still be considered a trans ancestor?

In an instance of corrective translation of Vasco da Lucena's *Deeds of Alexander the Great*, Zrinka Stahuljak focuses on censorship, humanistic textual criticism, and manuscript illumination in her essay, "Transgender Translation, Humanism, and Periodization." The essay examines two moments of censorship surrounding the legacy of Alexander the Great that erased the queer potential of Alexander's male lovers as the text circulated in the medieval and early modern period.

The concluding section of the volume, "Interventions: Critical Trans Methodologies," imports a series of frameworks from transgender studies to showcase the innovative questions and methodologies uniquely enabled by trans inquiry. Unlike the prior two sections, the essays at the heart of this one do not focus primarily on people or experiences that are readily identifiable as "trans"; instead they model the kinds of insights that become possible when we put trans methodologies to work in service of the analysis of pre- and early modern cultures. Opening the section is Emma Campbell's essay,

"Visualizing the Trans-Animal Body," which focuses on the hyena, an animal understood colloquially even today, at times, as capable of changing sex. The fictional hyena is "an uncomfortable, but significant, source for transgender history." Campbell argues that, on the one hand, French bestiaries show that medieval authors were able to theorize nonbinary gender as a part of the natural world and confirm the presence of transgender concepts in mainstream medieval culture; on the other hand, they show stigmatization of gender nonconformity.

Micah Goodrich's "Maimed Limbs and Biosalvation: Rehabilitation Politics in *Piers Plowman*" deploys disability theory to examine the definition of virtuous versus immoral poverty in the Middle English allegory. Goodrich demonstrates how the medieval poem anticipates today's legal policies relevant to trans lives. The poem raises the question of whether someone has the right to modify their own body to use it in the ways they want, including in ways that contradict, subvert, or exploit laws and social regulations. Medieval concepts of bodily mutilation and alteration in theology, fiction, and the law expose the workings of institutional biopolitics already operative in the Middle Ages.

Roland Betancourt's "Where Are All the Trans Women in Byzantium?" focuses on the gender politics of the late antique and Byzantine world (fifth to ninth centuries). At the confluence of Greek, Syriac, and Coptic traditions, Betancourt analyzes the Byzantine *Lives of Saints* and other texts such as rhetorical treatises, letters, and medical textbooks to excavate an emergent vocabulary for different modalities of nonbinary and non-cisgendered women.

In "Performing Reparative Transgender Identities from *Stage Beauty* to *The King and the Clown*," Alexa Alice Joubin analyzes the role of trans characters in two films set in the early modern period: *The King and the Clown* (2012), a Korean blockbuster featuring an openly trans heroine, and *Stage Beauty* (2004), a British movie that portrays Edward (Ned) Kynaston, the last "boy actor" of the Elizabethan period. Joubin explores how both films expand the "repertoire of trans performance," including the final scene where the transfeminine protagonist hopes to be reborn in exactly the same body.

Scott Larson's essay concludes this section with a meditation on the methodological politics of trans historical analysis. "Laid Open: Examining Genders in Early America" offers a critically important warning to scholars in trans studies, and especially those who work on historical archives, to err away from reproducing the empirical violence done to our own trans bodies here and now in our relationships to our objects of inquiry. If, as Larson suggests, "laying open" the trans body is not only not the point but also perhaps inimical to the prerogatives of trans inquiry and trans justice, then what methods might better enact a careful and ethical relationship to our forebears?

This volume seeks to bring together fields that do not always speak to one another: trans studies and early modern studies, medieval and early American studies. But while these fields might not speak to one another or come together at conferences very often, the people in these fields certainly do. This volume comes out of a discovery of shared interests between its editors, and it comes out of friendship, and the extension of that friendship into space and time, into the making of a book out of a conversation. This volume also comes out of the simple realization that many scholars work on the intersection of trans studies and antique, medieval, and early modern cultural studies, but that there have heretofore been very few opportunities to bring our bodies and scholarship together to address the unique challenges and intellectual promises that working between these two fields begets.

Notes

1. See Herman Mann, *The Female Review; or, Memoirs of an American Young Lady* (Dedham, MA: Printed by Nathaniel and Benjamin Heatons for the author, 1797); Alfred Young, *Masquerade: The Life and Times of Deborah Sampson, Continental Soldier* (New York: Penguin Random House, 2005); and Alex Myers, *Revolutionary* (New York: Simon & Schuster, 2015). See also Deborah Sampson Gannett, "Address, Delivered with Applause" (Dedham, MA: Mann, 1802); Sandra Gustafson, "The Genders of Nationalism: Patriotic Violence, Patriotic Sentiment in the Performances of Deborah Sampson Gannett," in *Possible Pasts: Becoming Colonial in Early America*, ed. Robert Blair St. George (Ithaca, NY: Cornell University Press, 2000), 380–400; Judith Hiltner, "'Like a Bewildered Star': Deborah Sampson, Herman Mann, and 'Address, Delivered with Applause,'" *Rhetoric Society Quarterly* 29.2 (Spring 1999): 5–24; and Hiltner, "'She Bled in Secret': Deborah Sampson, Herman Mann and *The Female Review*,'" *Early American Literature* 34.2 (1999): 190–220. See also a forthcoming essay on how Sampson's gender nonconformity articulates with disability history: Don James McLaughlin, "A Queer Crip Historiography for Early American Letters," in *Nineteenth-Century American Literature in Transition*, vol. 1, ed. William Huntting Howell and Greta LaFleur (Cambridge: Cambridge University Press, 2021).

2. See the special issue "Trans*Historicities," ed. Leah DeVun and Zeb Tortorici, *TSQ: Transgender Studies Quarterly* 4.5 (November 2018); also the special issue "Archives and Archiving," ed. K. J. Rawson and Aaron Devor, *TSQ: Transgender Studies Quarterly* 2.4 (November 2015); and Susan Stryker, *Transgender History* (New York: Seal Press, 2008). See also Susan Stryker's *Changing Gender: A Trans History of North America* (New York: Farrar, Straus and Giroux, forthcoming).

3. On archival silences, gaps, and erasures that attend, for example, histories of Atlantic slavery, see Saidiya Hartman, "Venus in Two Acts," *Small Axe* 26.12–2 (2008): 1–14; also see the special issue of *History of the Present* that responds to Hartman's

"Venus" (and to which Hartman, in turn, responds), "From Archives of Slavery to Liberated Futures?," ed. Brian Connolly and Marisa Fuentes, *History of the Present* 6.2 (2016).

4. Lillian Faderman, "A Usable Past?," in *The Lesbian Premodern*, ed. Noreen Giffney, Michelle M. Sauer, and Diane Watt (New York: Palgrave Macmillan, 2011), 171–78.

5. See Martha Vicinus, "Lesbian History: All Theory and No Facts or All Facts and No Theory?," *Radical History Review* 60 (1994): 57–75; and Eve Kosofsky Sedgwick, "Axiomatic," in *The Epistemology of the Closet* (Berkeley: University of California Press, 1990), 1–66.

6. Valerie Traub has been working on the history of normality, focusing on the early modern period; see Valerie Traub, "Mapping the Global Body," in *Early Modern Visual Culture: Representation, Race, and Empire in Renaissance England*, ed. Peter Erickson and Clark Hulse (Philadelphia: University of Pennsylvania Press, 2000), 44–97.

7. See, for example, Susan Stryker's *Transgender History* and her forthcoming book *Changing Gender*; the forthcoming special issue of the *Journal of Early Modern Cultural Studies*, "Early Modern Trans Studies," ed. Simone Chess, Will Fisher, and Colby Gordon, on early modern trans histories; the special issue of *Transgender Studies Quarterly* "Trans* Historicities"; Jules Gill-Peterson, *Histories of the Transgender Child* (Minneapolis: University of Minnesota Press, 2018); C. Riley Snorton, *Black on Both Sides: A Racial History of Trans Identity* (Minneapolis: University of Minnesota Press, 2017); Emma Heaney, *The New Woman: Literary Allegory, Queer Theory, and the Trans Feminine Allegory* (Evanston, IL: Northwestern University Press, 2017); and Joanne Meyerowitz, *How Sex Changed: A History of Transsexuality in the United States* (Cambridge, MA: Harvard University Press, 2002).

8. On this, see Benjamin Kahan's introduction to his monograph, *The Book of Minor Perverts: Sexology, Etiology, and the Emergences of Sexuality* (Chicago: University of Chicago Press, 2019).

9. Consider, for example, that Carolyn Dinshaw and David Halperin, a medievalist and a classicist, respectively, founded *GLQ: A Journal of Lesbian and Gay Studies* in 1991, with the first issue being published in 1993. On queer history and historiography, see Michel Foucault, *The History of Sexuality*, vol. 1, trans. Robert Hurley (New York: Verso, 1979); John Boswell, *Christianity, Social Tolerance, and Homosexuality: Gay People in Western Europe from the Beginning of the Christian Era to the Fourteenth Century* (Chicago: University of Chicago Press, 1981); Aranye Fradenburg and Carla Freccero, *Premodern Sexualities* (New York: Routledge, 1996); Carolyn Dinshaw, *Getting Medieval: Sexualities and Communities, Pre- and Post-Modern* (Durham, NC: Duke University Press, 1999); Valerie Traub, *Thinking Sex with the Early Moderns* (Philadelphia: University of Pennsylvania Press, 2016); and Carla Freccero, *Queer/Early/Modern* (Durham, NC: Duke University Press, 2006), to name just a few.

10. We write this with an awareness of the fact that, until the late twentieth century, many queer and trans people did not think of the categories of "queer" and "trans" as mutually exclusive; see, for example, David Valentine, *Imagining Transgender: An Ethnography of a Category* (Durham, NC: Duke University Press, 2007), the introduction to which discusses the fact that in the mid-1990s, most of the gender nonconforming members of the community and advocacy organizations with which he worked (and whom he studied) did not describe themselves with the word "trans" or "transgender," opting instead for "gay" or "queen."

11. David Lorenzo Boyd and Ruth Mazo Karras, "The Interrogation of a Male Transvestite Prostitute in Fourteenth-Century London," *GLQ* 1.4 (1995): 459–65.

12. Carolyn Dinshaw, "Afterlives," *GLQ* 25.1 (2019): 5–6, quotation at 6.

13. A new generation of trans studies scholars have also been using trans studies frameworks to think more broadly about relations between the human, the animal, the machine, and the post-human; the putatively natural or organic world and the inorganic; methods for the production of knowledge; and racialization and the significance assigned to it, to name only a few. Aren Aizura and Susan Stryker playfully refer to this turn as "Transgender Studies 2.0" in their introduction to *The Transgender Studies Reader 2*, "Introduction: Trans Studies 2.0," in *The Transgender Studies Reader 2* (New York: Routledge, 2013), 1–12. For a handful of examples of this turn in trans studies scholarship, see Micha Cárdenas, "Monstrous Children of Pregnant Androids: Latinx Futures after Orlando," *GLQ* 24.1 (2018): 26–31; Mel Chen, "Animals, Sex, and Transubstantiation," in *Animacies: Biopolitics, Racial Mattering, and Queer Affect* (Durham, NC: Duke University Press, 2012), 127–58; Eli Clare, *Brilliant Imperfection* (Durham, NC: Duke University Press, 2017); Kai M. Green, "The Essential I/Eye in We: A Black TransFeminist Approach to Ethnographic Film," *Black Camera* 6.2 (2015): 187–200; Eva Hayward, "More Lessons from a Starfish: Prefixial Flesh and Transspeciated Selves," *Women's Studies Quarterly* 36.3–4 (Winter 2008): 64–85; and Paul Preciado, *Testo Junkie: Sex, Drugs, and Biopolitics in the Pharmacopornographic Era* (New York: Feminist Press, 2013).

14. Joan W. Scott, "Gender: A Useful Category of Historical Analysis," *American Historical Review* 91.5 (1986): 1053–75. Note how this influential article returns as Afsaneh Najmabadi's question "Are Gender and Sexuality Useful Categories of Historical Analysis?," the subtitle to her article "Beyond the Americas: Are Gender and Sexuality Useful Categories in Historical Analysis?," *Journal of Women's History* 18.1 (2006): 11–21. There Najmabadi considers what it would mean to look at the history of gender and sexuality without presuming modern categories for "women" and "men," asking, "How has sex become sex?" (14) and "Remember the debates over the question, were there any lesbians (or lesbian-like women) in medieval Europe? Without replaying that discussion, I want to use it as a way of returning that question to gender: Were there any women in medieval Europe?" (18). See also Chandra Mohanty, "Under Western Eyes: Feminist Scholarship and Colonial Discourses," *Boundary 2* 12.3 (Spring–Fall 1984): 333–58, which was later expanded and republished in *Feminist Review* 30 (Autumn 1988): 61–88, which advanced another early critique of the putative universality of gendered experience.

15. Middle and modern English experienced a unique historical confluence that resulted in historical noun genders being largely done away with, and so Anglophone shoes, desks, and cats are less anthropomorphized than Francophone, Hispanophone, Germanic, and Lusophone objects. Once the Norman Conquest had changed English forever, authors writing in that language could avoid gendering the world—which required that English writers make more or less conscious choices about when to indicate the gender of a given depiction. See chapter 3 of Masha Raskolnikov, *Body against Soul: Gender and Sowlehele in Middle English Allegory* (Columbus: Ohio State University Press, 2009).

16. Hartman, "Venus in Two Acts."

17. See Hortense Spillers, "Mama's Baby, Papa's Maybe: An American Grammar Book," *Diacritics* 17.2 (Summer 1987): 64–81; and Snorton, *Black on Both Sides*. In

Scenes of Subjection, Hartman seems to be arguing not with Spillers but with *readings* of Spillers, arguing, "What I am attempting to explore here is the divergent production of the category woman rather than a comparison of black and white women that implicitly or inadvertently assumes that gender is relevant only to the degree that generalizable and universal criteria define a common identity. Can we employ the term 'woman' and yet remain vigilant that 'all women do not have the same gender'? Or 'name as "woman" that disenfranchised woman whom we strictly, historically, geopolitically, *cannot imagine* as a literal referent' rather than reproduce the very normativity that has occluded an understanding of the differential production of gender? By assuming that woman designates a known referent, an a priori unity, a precise bundle of easily recognizable characteristics, traits, and dispositions, we fail to attend to the continent and disjunctive production of the category. In other words, woman must be disassociated from the white middle-class female subject who norms the category." Saidiya Hartman, *Scenes of Subjection* (New York: Oxford University Press, 1997), 99–100.

18. Cathy Cohen, "Punks, Bulldaggers, and Welfare Queens: The Radical Potential of Queer Politics?," *GLQ: Journal of Gay and Lesbian Studies* 3.4 (1997): 437–65.

19. See María Elena Martínez, *Genealogical Fictions: Limpieza de Sangre, Religion, and Gender in Colonial Mexico* (Palo Alto, CA: Stanford University Press, 2011).

20. Geraldine Heng, *The Invention of Race in the European Middle Ages* (Cambridge: Cambridge University Press, 2018).

21. See Hannah Barker, *That Most Precious Merchandise: The Mediterranean Trade in Black Sea Slaves, 1260–1500* (Philadelphia: University of Pennsylvania Press, 2019).

22. Spillers, "Mama's Baby, Papa's Maybe."

23. See, for example, Aren Z. Aizura et al., "Introduction," *TSQ* 1.3 (2014); Tom Boellstorff et al., "Decolonizing Transgender," *TSQ* 1.3 (2014): 419–39; Louis Esme Cruz and Qwo-Li Driskill, "Puo'Winue'L Prayers: Readings from North America's First Transtextual Script," *GLQ* 16.1–2 (2010): 243–52; Deborah A. Miranda, "Extermination of the Joyas: Gendercide in Spanish California," *GLQ* 16.1–2 (2010): 253–84; Scott Morgensen, "Settler Homonationalism," *GLQ*, special issue, "Sexuality/Nationality/Indigeneity" 16.1.2 (2010): 105–31; and Saylesh Wesley, "Twin Spirited Woman: Sts'iyóye smestíyexw shhá:li," *TSQ* 1.3 (2014): 338–51.

24. See Karma Lochrie, *Heterosyncrasies: Female Sexuality When Normal Wasn't* (Minneapolis: University of Minnesota Press, 2005). See also Traub, "Mapping the Global Body"; and Michael Warner, *The Trouble with Normal: Sex, Politics, and the Ethics of Queer Life* (New York: Free Press, 1999).

25. See, for example, Saqer A. Almarri, "'You Have Made Her a Man among Men': Translating the Khuntha's Anatomy in Fatimid Jurisprudence," *TSQ* 3.3–4 (2016): 578–86; Blake Gutt and Alicia Spencer-Hall, eds., *Trans and Genderqueer Subjects in Medieval Hagiography* (Amsterdam: Amsterdam University Press, forthcoming); and Joan Cadden, *Meanings of Sex Difference in the Middle Ages* (Cambridge: Cambridge University Press, 1993). See also Domitilla Campanile, Filippo Carlà-Uhink, and Margherita Facella, eds., *TransAntiquity: Cross-Dressing and Transgender Dynamics in the Ancient World* (New York: Routledge, 2017); Simone Chess, *Male-to-Female Crossdressing in Early Modern English Literature: Gender, Performance, and Queer Relations* (New York: Routledge, 2016); Howard Chiang, ed., *Transgender China*

(New York: Palgrave Macmillan, 2012); Leah DeVun, "Heavenly Hermaphrodites," *Postmedieval* 9.2, special issue, "Medieval Intersex: Language and Hermaphroditism," ed. Ruth Evans (2018): 132–46; Leah DeVun, "Erecting Sex: Hermaphrodites and the Medieval Science of Surgery," *Osiris* 30.1 (2015): 17–37; Leah DeVun, *Prophecy, Alchemy, and the End of Time: John of Rupescissa in the Late Middle Ages* (New York: Columbia University Press, 2009); Leah DeVun, "The Jesus Hermaphrodite: Science and Sex Difference in Premodern Europe," *Journal of the History of Ideas* 69.2 (2008): 193–218; Carolyn Dinshaw, *Getting Medieval;* Gary Ferguson, "Early Modern Transitions: From Montaigne to Choisy," *L'Esprit Créateur* 53.1 (2013): 145–57; Jules Gill-Peterson, "Technical Capacities of the Body: Assembling Race, Technology, and Transgender," *TSQ* 1.3 (2014): 402–18; Emma Heaney, *The New Woman: Literary Modernism, Queer Theory, and the Trans Feminine Allegory* (Chicago: Northwestern University Press, 2017); Cary Howie, "On Transfiguration," *L'Esprit Créateur* 53.1 (2013): 158–66; Scott Larson, "'Indescribable Being': Theological Performances of Genderlessness in the Society of the Publick Universal Friend, 1776–1819," *Journal of Early American Studies* 12.3 (2014): 576–600; Karma Lochrie, "Medieval Masculinities without Men," in *Beyond Heteronormativity: New Directions in Medieval Masculinity and Gender*, ed. Ann Marie Rasmussen and J. Christian Straubhaar (South Bend, IN: University of Notre Dame Press, 2018); Karma Lochrie, "Gower's Transgender Riddles in 'Iphis and Ianthe,'" in *Ovidian Transversions: "Iphis and Ianthe," 1350–1650*, ed. Patricia Badir, Peggy McCracken, and Valerie Traub (Edinburgh: University of Edinburgh Press, 2018); Karma Lochrie, "Presumptive Sodomy and Its Exclusions," *Textual Practice* 13.2 (1999): 295–310; Karen Lurkhur, "Medieval Silence and Modern Transsexuality," *Studies in Gender and Sexuality* 11.4 (2010): 220–38; Robert Mills, *Seeing Sodomy in the Middle Ages* (Chicago: University of Chicago Press, 2015); Deborah A. Miranda, "Extermination of the *Joyas*: Gendercide in Spanish California," *GLQ: A Journal of Lesbian and Gay Studies* 16.1–2 (2010): 253–84; "Transgender France," ed. Todd Reeser, special issue of *L'Esprit Créateur* 53.1 (2013); Emily Rose, "Keeping the Trans in Translation: Queering Early Modern Transgender Memoirs," *TSQ* 3.3–4 (2016): 485–505; and Valerie Traub, *Mapping the Global Body* (Philadelphia: University of Pennsylvania Press, 2000).

Part I

Archives

Revisiting Law and Medicine

CHAPTER 1

Mapping the Borders of Sex

Leah DeVun

The medieval text *Marvels of the East* shares fantastic tales of monsters—giant ants, cannibal *donestres*, headless *blemmyes*, among others—that live in the "East." The work survives in three well-known illuminated manuscripts created between the tenth and twelfth centuries, each stocked with illustrations so arresting that they nearly upstage the written text.[1] In the visual images within the manuscripts, monsters seem to project themselves toward the viewer, extending beyond the bars of their illuminated frames and breaching the bounds of standard portraiture.[2] Among the monsters featured in one manuscript copy of *Marvels* is a nonbinary-sexed figure: a standing nude, starkly drawn against a deep red background (fig. 1.1).

The figure is depicted as half-male and half-female, with a flat "masculine" chest on one side and a prominent "feminine" breast on the other. This drawing, encased in its own intact rectangular border, might seem more static than its frame-transgressing neighbors. But if other monsters breached the line between subject and object, viewer and viewed, this figure traversed perhaps even more crucial boundaries. As I'll suggest, this *Marvels* dual-sexed figure—like other contemporary images of similar subjects—crossed key borders in the Middle Ages, "traveling" between the sexual domains of male and female, and setting in contrast the geographic domains of "West" and "East." I offer a few observations about the nonbinary-sexed figure of

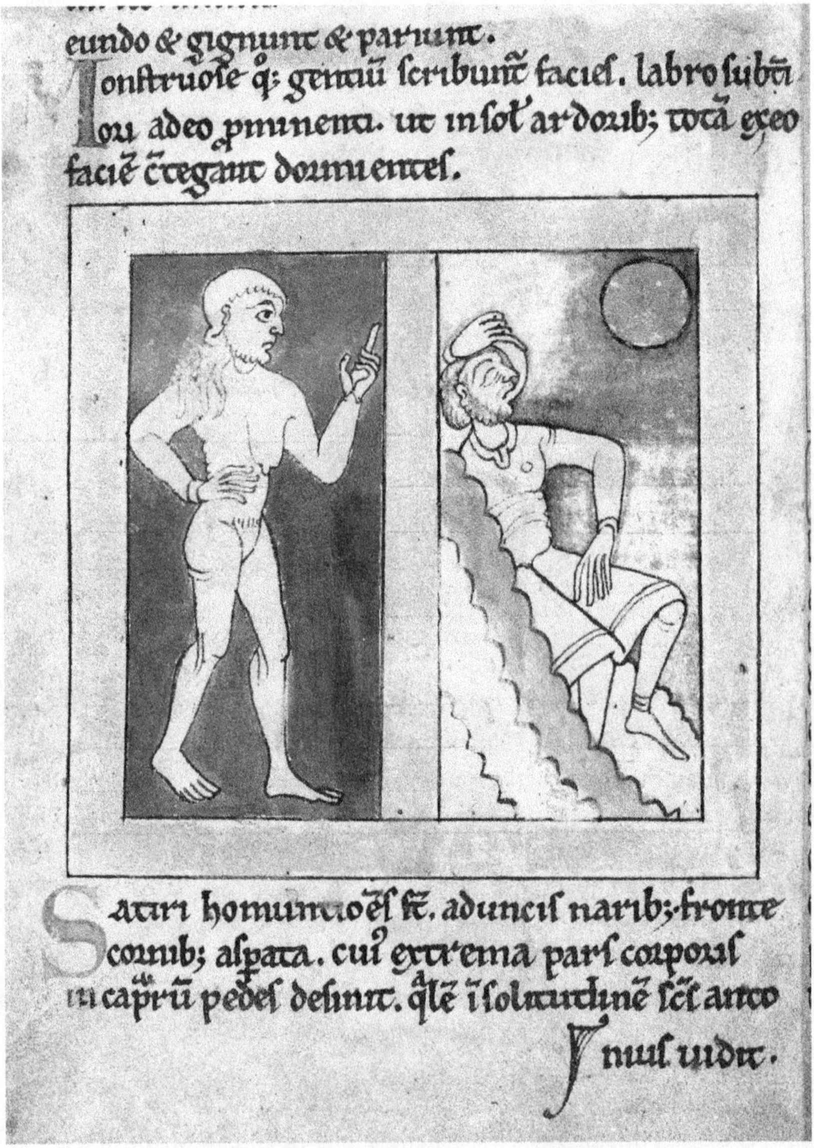

FIGURE 1.1. Nonbinary-sexed figure (at left), in *Marvels of the East*, University of Oxford, Bodleian Library, MS Bodley 614, fol. 50v (twelfth century). With permission of the Bodleian Libraries.

Marvels of the East in this short essay, focusing on the figure's role in establishing medieval boundaries of sex and space.

The twelfth-century Anglo-Latin version of *Marvels of the East*—MS Bodley (the image does not appear in the other two related recensions of the text)—describes this bifurcated half-male/half-female figure as a "hermaphrodite" (*ermafrodite*).[3] The word "hermaphrodite" is generally viewed today as an outdated and stigmatizing term, and the terms "DSD" (an abbreviation for "disorders" or "differences of sex development") and "intersex" (which I use in this work) are widely preferred to describe modern individuals whose bodies are perceived to be neither typically male nor female.[4] I use the term "hermaphrodite" here when quoting medieval texts, and I hope readers will accept my use of it as I critically engage with my original primary sources. In the course of that engagement, I try to avoid reifying derogatory language and concepts while also remaining attentive to historical specificity.[5] To that end, I prefer the term "nonbinary-sexed" to refer to the medieval illustrated figures on which I focus here, although I am aware that many intersex people today do not identify as nonbinary.

I argue here that we might productively read this particular strain of medieval nonbinary imagery not only through the lens of "intersex" but also through that of "transgender."[6] Intersex people—that is, those born with bodies that are judged to be neither typically male nor female, and transgender people, that is, in simple terms, those born with bodies that do not fit their gender identity, or whose practices defy gender norms in some way—are distinct groups. In the modern world, intersex and transgender communities have different concerns and identities, although their political and intellectual movements, as well as their gendered experiences, have been in certain respects linked by scholars and activists.[7] As I suggest here, the medieval nonbinary-sexed figure from *Marvels of the East*, along with other similar images, invoke simultaneously the potential of intersex and transgender histories without necessarily conflating them.

Marvels of the East was one of many premodern texts concerned with the "monstrous races"—mythical humanoid creatures with extraordinary anatomies and customs, imagined by Europeans to live in Africa, Asia, or at the very eastern edges of the earth.[8] Myths about the monstrous races were widespread in ancient and medieval sources: they appear in well-known works by Pliny the Elder, Augustine of Hippo, and Isidore of Seville, as well as in *Mandeville's Travels*, *The Book of Monsters*, and, of course, *Marvels of the East*.[9] Monstrous-race literature was escapist entertainment for European audiences; as historians have noted, however, such literature conveyed serious information too, sorting sexual practices into the proper and improper, and dividing bodily traits into the human and nonhuman. As the scholar Dana M. Oswald observes, in such texts, the "gendered bodies of the monstrous both disrupt and reaffirm the social hierarchy: that is, monsters reveal and enforce the standards for appropriate human appearance and behavior. They demonstrate the boundaries beyond which humans should not proceed."[10]

Although *Marvels of the East* graciously names at least some of its subjects "men," its emphasis on monstrosity and human-animal hybridity undercuts any certainty that its subjects are truly human. By including nonbinary-sexed characters among the monstrous races—a motley crew of (at best) dubiously human beings—*Marvels of the East* indicated that sex and gender variance had important roles to play in the definitional limits of humanity.

Marvels of the East explained that in the "East," there existed a society in which all members were "hermaphrodites." These individuals switched between male and female roles in generation, playing the "father" in one instance and the "mother" in another. The individuals' unusual anatomies facilitated this behavior: "Hermaphrodites are so called because both sexes appear in them. . . . These, having a male right breast and a female left breast, in sexual intercourse sire and bear children in turn."[11] Other writings too suggested that members of this nonbinary monstrous race switched back and forth between male and female social roles; each had "a right breast like a man for performing work, and a left breast like a woman for nourishing children," as the seventh-/eighth-century Anglo-Latin *Book of Monsters (Liber monstrorum)* pointed out.[12] Such details highlighted the supposedly cyclical nature of monstrous nonbinary activities: these individuals labored as men at work, and they labored as women at child rearing. Other texts too repeated the myth of the monstrous nonbinary race, sometimes illustrating it with a bilaterally split figure much like the one we see in *Marvels of the East*. A later English source, the famous Hereford World Map (ca. first decade of the fourteenth century), for instance, includes a bifurcated male/female figure, alongside the claim that the individual represented "a race of both sexes, unnatural in many of their customs."[13] Another illumination of the monstrous races in the English Westminster Abbey Bestiary (ca. 1270–1280) features yet another bifurcated nonbinary figure, this one holding a sword in one hand and a pair of scissors in the other.[14] Such symbols signaled the divergent behaviors of the figure's two halves: the masculine side clutches a weapon while the feminine side prefers a tool of domesticity.[15] These figures' gendered pursuits, along with the presence of physical markers such as breasts or genitals, made visible the body's dueling allegiances to two ostensibly opposed sexes.

Scholars have discussed medieval nonbinary images within a number of historical contexts, including histories of intersex, disability, and queer sexuality—all important approaches that have enriched our understanding of them.[16] As I suggest here, looking at such figures through the additional lens of "transgender" offers yet further insights. "Transgender" is a term of recent origin, linked to twentieth- and twenty-first-century understandings of sex and gender, and rooted in subjective experiences of self-identification.[17] We might therefore think it anachronistic to include medieval phenomena within a history of "transgender," both because the period entailed very different notions of sex and gender, and because we have little access to medieval individuals' self-ascribed identifications, which, in any case, would hardly conform to our own modern definitions and categories. Moreover, the *Marvels of the East*'s nonbinary-sexed figure, with a hyperbolic bifurcated body, did not reflect the morphology of any "real" individuals living in the medieval world, and hence we might find the image an especially problematic example of sex and gender variance in historical context.[18]

Scholars have indeed been reticent about extending the category of transgender, in particular, to gender-crossing figures from the distant past.[19] Projecting our modern identities backwards in time, as these scholars rightly note, could divest past gender practice of what made it meaningful in its own time and place, imposing a monolithic category on people who were just as variable and uncategorizable in the past as are those in our own present time.[20] Jack Halberstam has argued that "rather than taking knowledge from our current context and using it as a template for the past, we must recognize how much we do not know about gender variability now and use that as a tool for withholding the imposition of knowledge onto vastly different cases from the past."[21]

Some scholars have suggested that we allow "transgender" to operate as an open-ended analytic for viewing categories rather than as a rigid label that we project backwards onto specific historical characters.[22] Following this approach, we can dismiss arguments about whether or not nonbinary-sexed members of the monstrous races were "really" transgender and instead consider how they illuminated medieval categories of sex and gender, as well as how those categories intersected with other kinds of difference. Because medieval authors described monstrous-race nonbinary figures as switching from "male" to "female" (and back again), we might reasonably conclude that they enacted "transgender" or "transgender-like" transitions, even if our modern terms are, as the art historian Robert Mills has suggested, "necessarily partial and provisional."[23] The gendered inversions in monstrous-race texts thus provide us with a lens through which to view medieval systems of maleness and femaleness, as well as to observe how such texts raised questions about the logic of such binaries. That is, however much they adhered to stereotyped notions of masculinity and femininity, monstrous-race nonbinary figures also raised the possibility of different modes of gender that might exist elsewhere, perhaps in the "East."

It is for this reason that dual-sexed figures such as the one pictured in *Marvels of the East* were, by most medieval accounts, "monsters." The word for "monster," *monstrum*, was sometimes thought to derive from the Latin word *monstrare*, meaning "to show."[24] Medieval audiences often understood "monster" to signal that God "showed" divine messages to humanity through the creation of such creatures.[25] I suggest that, in the case of monstrous nonbinary figures, such images also "showed" audiences what it meant to be male or female. They moreover warned against any confusion of categories that could prompt a loss of human status. The nonbinary image in *Marvels of the East*, like those in other similar monstrous-race texts, "showed" that men and women were incommensurate sexes, divided not only by a somatic but also by a behavioral line (represented visually by a vertical bisection of the body). In such discourse, men were defined by their aptitude for "masculine" tasks and women for "feminine" ones, despite the existence of many other medieval texts that praised at least certain gender-inverting characteristics, whether among maternalistic male abbots or virile female "viragos," who were nevertheless accepted as indubitable men or women.[26] In monstrous-race literature, in contrast, confusing the boundary between male and female was a clear indicator of monstrosity, so much so that a whole range of monsters tapped into the theme of nonbinary sex to make clear their departure from the natural.[27] Asa Mittman and Susan Kim, for instance, view the headless blemmyes of *Marvels of the East* as confounding any male-female genital dichotomies. Donestres, another *Marvels* monster, were known more for their cannibalism than for any gendered transgression, but they too were multiply sexed, as Amanda Lehr suggests.[28]

Bifurcated figures such as the one in *Marvels of the East* were "both sexes," as the text stated, not only because they confounded sexual dimorphism, but also because they flouted binary divisions of social and reproductive labor. Such imagined individuals shifted between maleness and femaleness by occupying malleable roles; yet their morphologies, even if bifurcated, remained firmly static. The theorist Gayle Salamon notes that in the modern world, sex is created not by the physical attributes that a body has but by its social relationships, by its "intentionality toward the *other* and toward the *world*."[29] Indeed, in medieval monstrous-race discourse, sex emerges through the body's encounter with the outside world, through its acts and affiliations, which made it legible to readers. Sex was not an endpoint in this discourse, then, not a result of inert biology, but an open-ended process or activity, and one shored up more by sociality than by any single destiny of the flesh.

It is just this intentionality toward the *other* and the *world* that I would like to turn to in closing. In text after text, monstrous-race discourse placed its subjects far outside the territorial bounds of Europe. *Marvels of the East* located its nonbinary figure in the "East"; the Hereford Map presented a similarly drawn figure in Africa; and yet another medieval map, the *Mare historiarum*, placed comparable figures in Africa or Asia.[30] This mapping of monstrosity, which grafted nonbinary sex onto distant, non-European spaces, demonstrates how texts conflated sexual difference with geographic and cultural difference.[31] While monstrous-race literature acknowledged that monsters were born occasionally in Europe as rare anomalies, they imagined whole regions outside of Europe, whether in Africa or Asia, as producers of divergent sexual shapes and cultural practices, not as aberrations but as routine phenomena. This placement of unusual—even "unnatural" (as the Hereford Map called them)—sexes at a spatial remove from Europe demonstrates how images of nonbinary-sexed individuals functioned to draw divisions not only between incommensurate sexes but also between incommensurate regions and peoples.

As scholars have pointed out, the very prefix of *transgender* (from the Latin for "across, beyond or over") connotes a sense of mobility and boundary-crossing. Scholars of modern transgender studies have recently capitalized on this etymology to consider how transgender might encompass movements not only across gender categories but also across geographic space.[32] As Aren Z. Aizura has documented, modern transgender biographies often use the tropes of travel, and geographic metaphors (as well as Orientalist fantasies) continue to populate contemporary narratives of gender transition.[33] The topos of spatiality and mobility within modern transgender literature resonates with how medieval monstrous-race literature focused on intersections of gender and geographical position, and hence medieval sources were already making parallel creative use of gender and spatial mobility in a much earlier period. Within medieval monstrous-race discourse, the proper expression of sexual difference in Europe was placed in contrast to an improper one in the "East." In such sources, sex at the level of the individual came to bear on a larger model of civilizational organization: sex was one thing inside Europe and another "outside" it.

In regions deemed exotic by European authors and readers, inhabitants need not be merely male or female; instead, all residents of a foreign place might be between or beyond two sexes. Texts such as *Marvels of the East* defined Europe in opposition to an imagined "non-Europe," where sexual and gendered standards were relatively more flexible and varied.[34] According to such texts, parts of the East were the homelands of mythical, quasi-human creatures with unnatural bodies and customs. Europe, in contrast, generated only binary-sexed humans operating within the bounds of binary behavior, except in rare and unfortunate cases. Through this contrast, binary sex became enshrined for readers as a human ideal. Moreover, because

Europeans remained uncertain about the ontological status of monstrous peoples, the inhabitants of regions identified with monsters became themselves tainted by the stigma of inhumanity. A number of texts and images justified repressive or even violent measures against purportedly foreign peoples or religions by invoking their link to monstrosity.[35] Monstrous-race literature hence mapped out distinctions not only between men and women but also between Europe and non-Europe, between "here" and "elsewhere." These spatial dislocations of the *trans*geographical and *trans*cultural were therefore indispensable for what nonbinary-sexed figures meant not just for sex and gender but for the hierarchical organization of peoples and places as well.

A nonbinary-sexed monster, such as the one pictured in *Marvels of the East*, worked across visual and textual traditions to define geographical and sexual boundaries, communicating what it meant to be male, female, and—ultimately—human. Individuals who supposedly swung between "male" sexual activity and "female" passivity, between "male" labor and "female" caretaking, both disrupted and reaffirmed the sexual hierarchy.[36] Not only did such images interrogate the purported boundaries between the sexes, but also they questioned the humanity of those who crossed such boundaries. As a result, we see how images of mapping and travel were at the heart of how readers and viewers imagined territorial and corporeal coherence. There is much more to be said about these complicated nonbinary images (and their relation to new and long-standing iconographical trends, to interreligious relations, to shifting notions of embodiment and racial difference, and to a host of other factors).[37] But placing these medieval images within a historical narrative of sex and gender variance can direct us to think more carefully about the different kinds of crossings they encompassed.

These examples from the Middle Ages also help us situate modern cartographies of gender and space within a much broader chronological framework. As I have written elsewhere, allowing the strangeness of the past to resonate across a temporally expansive, historicized framework can prompt us to view with new skepticism the seemingly natural categories of "man" and "woman." It can also prevent us from assuming that our own modern debates about sex and gender are wholly new and unique.[38] Thinking through deep histories of sex and gender variance can aid us in appreciating how individuals come to belong to a sex or gender, as well as how such belonging fits into a larger hierarchized order. It can moreover reveal how incorporating the insights of modern critical intersex and transgender studies into our premodern histories can inform our analyses of cross-geographic imaginaries in new ways.

Yet we must also acknowledge that the particularity of medieval discourse—which mixed real peoples and places with those that existed only in the imagination, and which operated in the context of idiosyncratic religious and textual traditions—means that we cannot write any linear history of sex or gender variance, one in which medieval forms develop in a straightforward fashion into what we now recognize as "intersex" or "transgender." As mythical characters, members of the nonbinary-sexed monstrous races did not share in the self-directed identitarian and political impulses of our present period, nor do medieval systems of sex and gender map perfectly onto our own modern categories. In addition, although some modern scholars of intersex and transgender studies have expressed a cross-temporal sense of kinship with the "hermaphrodites," "eunuchs," and "monsters" of the distant past, others have worried that placing present communities within these past conceptual frameworks might cause real harm to living people now.[39] These divergent views should signal that any history of medieval sex and gender variance can provoke a host of responses. Some might experience a comforting realization that sex- and gender-variant figures populated even the very distant past; others might wonder at the incredible diversity of past thinking about sex and gender, which was much more varied and flexible than we often acknowledge; and yet others might experience only confusion in the face of such alien imagery. Perhaps our view of the medieval past resembles nothing so much as medieval Europeans' visions of foreign lands in *Marvels of the East*, a mirror that reflects back a distorted image of ourselves, one that is both strange and familiar.[40]

Notes

1. The text, also known as *Wonders of the East*, was a classically based work that survives in three famous English illustrated manuscripts: London, British Library, Cotton MS Vitellius A. xv (ca. 975–1025); London, British Library, Cotton MS Tiberius B. v, part 1 (eleventh century); and University of Oxford, Bodleian Library, MS Bodley 614 (twelfth century). The first text is in Old English, the second in bilingual Latin/Old English, and the third in Latin only; each represents a different recension. On the content and the dating of the manuscripts, see Andy Orchard, *Pride and Prodigies: Studies in the Monsters of the Beowulf-Manuscript* (Cambridge: D. S. Brewer, 1995); Asa S. Mittman and Susan M. Kim, eds., *Inconceivable Beasts: "The Wonders of the East" in the Beowulf Manuscript* (Tempe, AZ: ACMRS, 2013); A. J. Ford, *Marvel and Artefact: The "Wonders of the East" in Its Manuscript Contexts* (Leiden: Brill, 2016); Dana M. Oswald, *Monsters, Gender and Sexuality in Medieval English Literature* (Woodbridge, Suffolk: D. S. Brewer, 2010), 27–65.

2. This is particularly true of the Vitellius and Tiberius manuscripts; see John Block Friedman, *The Monstrous Races in Medieval Art and Thought* (Cambridge, MA: Harvard University Press, 1981), 153; Simon C. Thomson, *Communal Creativity in the Making of the "Beowulf" Manuscript: Towards a History of Reception for the Nowell Codex* (Leiden: Brill, 2018), 124–26; Mittman and Kim, *Inconceivable Beasts*, 31–33, 138–46, 150–51.

3. See note 11.

4. The nomenclature is controversial, and both "intersex" and "DSD" have long been the subjects of much criticism. See Ellen K. Feder, "Imperatives of Normality: From 'Intersex' to 'Disorders of Sex Development,'" *GLQ: A Journal of Lesbian and Gay Studies* 15.2 (2009): 225–47; see also the statement of the Intersex Society of North America (ISNA) on their shift to the term DSD, http://www.isna.org/node/1066 (accessed June 15, 2020). In this essay I use "intersex" when referring to affected individuals and communities because it is the least pathologizing term, and it is the one favored in social science literature. For an overview of intersex studies, see Hil Malatino, *Queer Embodiment: Monstrosity, Medical Violence, and Intersex Experience* (Lincoln: University of Nebraska Press, 2019); David A. Rubin, *Intersex Matters: Biomedical Embodiment, Gender Regulation, and Transnational Activism* (Albany: SUNY Press, 2017); Lisa Downing, Iain Morland, and Nikki Sullivan, *Fuckology: Critical Essays on John Money's Diagnostic Concepts* (Chicago: University of Chicago Press, 2015); Georgiann Davis, *Contesting Intersex: The Dubious Diagnosis* (New York: NYU Press, 2015); Julie A. Greenberg, *Intersexuality and the Law: Why Sex Matters* (New York: NYU Press, 2012); Elizabeth Reis, *Bodies in Doubt: An American History of Intersex* (Baltimore: Johns Hopkins University Press, 2009); Morgan Holmes, ed., *Critical Intersex* (Aldershot: Ashgate, 2009); Iain Morland, *Intersex and After*, special issue of *GLQ: A Journal of Lesbian and Gay Studies* 15.2 (2009); Katrina Karkazis, *Fixing Sex: Intersex, Medical Authority, and Lived Experience* (Durham, NC: Duke University Press, 2008); Sharon E. Sytsma, ed., *Ethics and Intersex* (Dordrecht: Springer, 2006); Anne Fausto-Sterling, *Sexing the Body: Gender Politics and the Construction of Sexuality* (New York: Basic Books, 2000); Suzanne Kessler, *Lessons from the Intersexed* (New Brunswick, NJ: Rutgers University Press, 1998); Alice Domurat Dreger, *Hermaphrodites and the Medical Invention of Sex* (Cambridge, MA: Harvard University Press, 1999); Alice Domurat Dreger, ed., *Intersex in the Age of Ethics* (Hagerstown, MD: University Publishing Group, 1999); Cheryl Chase [now Bo Laurent], "Hermaphrodites with Attitude: Mapping the Emergence of Intersex Political Activism," *GLQ: A Journal of Lesbian and Gay Studies* 4.2 (1998): 189–211; as well as the information collected by ISNA (http://www.isna.org/) and Accord Alliance (http://www.accordalliance.org).

5. See "What's the History behind the Intersex Rights Movement?," ISNA, http://www.isna.org/faq/history (accessed June 15, 2020); April Herndon, "Getting Rid of 'Hermaphroditism' Once and for All" (2005), http://www.isna.org/node/979 (accessed June 15, 2020); Thea Hillman, *Intersex (for Lack of a Better Word)* (San Francisco: Manic D Press, 2008), 25–29. A number of affected individuals in Europe now identify themselves as "hermaphrodites" or "herms," but this terminology remains pejorative in the United States. C. G. Costello, "Intersex and Trans* Communities: Commonalities and Tensions," in *Transgender and Intersex: Theoretical, Practical, and Artistic Perspectives*, ed. Stefan Horlacher (New York: Palgrave Macmillan, 2016), 85.

6. For some definitions of transgender, see Jack Halberstam, *Trans*: A Quick and Quirky Account of Gender Variability* (Oakland: University of California Press, 2017), 1–21; Paisley Currah and Susan Stryker, eds., "Postposttranssexual: Key Concepts for a Twenty-First-Century Transgender Studies," special issue of *TSQ: Transgender Studies Quarterly* 1.1–2 (2014); Susan Stryker, *Transgender History* (Berkeley, CA: Seal Press, 2008); David Valentine, *Imagining Transgender: An Ethnography of a Category* (Durham, NC: Duke University Press, 2007). I am aware that the definitions I offer here are, by

necessity, simplifications. Both "intersex" and "transgender" are umbrella terms for a spectrum of complex bodies, identities, and practices.

7. See Thea Hillman's memoir *Intersex*, 76, 129–37, which describes complicated engagements between queer, trans, and intersex communities. Trans and intersex studies constitute distinct fields, but trans studies often seeks to engage intersex studies, historical studies of intersex have recently engaged trans studies, and some prominent works of theory discuss both trans and intersex. On the two fields' interaction, see Rubin, *Intersex Matters*, 74–76; Stefan Horlacher, "Transgender and Intersex: Theoretical, Practical, and Artistic Perspectives," in Horlacher, *Transgender and Intersex*, 1–27; Malatino, *Queer Embodiment*, 62, 79–89, 140–50. Among other recent examples, see Kathleen P. Long, "Intersex/Transgender," in *The Bloomsbury Handbook of 21st-Century Feminist Theory*, ed. Robin Truth Goodman (London: Bloomsbury, 2019), 121–41; Paul B. Preciado, *Countersexual Manifesto*, trans. Kevin Gerry Dunn (New York: Columbia University Press, 2018), 106–19.

8. The "East" was a nebulous category: it could encompass the Near or Middle East, as well as parts of Asia and Africa. The "South" could also be an "other," and encyclopedic texts often favored a tripartite division of the world into Europe, Asia, and Africa, which overlapped with East-West binaries. For the "East," see Asa S. Mittman and Susan M. Kim, "Monsters and the Exotic in Early Medieval England," *Literature Compass* 6.2 (2009): 335–37; for the interrelation of binary, ternary, and quaternary divisions, see Suzanne Conklin Akbari, *Idols in the East: European Representations of Islam and the Orient, 1100–1450* (Ithaca, NY: Cornell University Press, 2009), 20–66; Suzanne Conklin Akbari, "From Due East to True North: Orientalism and Orientation," in *The Postcolonial Middle Ages*, ed. Jeffrey Cohen (New York: St. Martin's Press, 2000), 19–34. On monsters and the "monstrous races," see Friedman, *Monstrous Races*; Debra Higgs Strickland, *Saracens, Demons, and Jews: Making Monsters in Medieval Art* (Princeton, NJ: Princeton University Press, 2003); Asa S. Mittman, *Maps and Monsters in Medieval England* (New York: Routledge, 2006); Asa S. Mittman and Peter Dendle, eds., *The Ashgate Research Companion to Monsters and the Monstrous* (Aldershot: Ashgate, 2013); Jeffrey J. Cohen, ed., *Monster Theory: Reading Culture* (Minneapolis: University of Minnesota Press, 1996); Sherry Lindquist and Asa S. Mittman, *Medieval Monsters: Terrors, Aliens, Wonders* (New York: Morgan Library and Museum and D Giles, 2018).

9. Scholars in recent years have reinterpreted travel literature in a new light, focusing on how its cartographic content reflected complex global connections. See, for instance, Shirin A. Khanmohamadi, *In Light of Another's Word: European Ethnography in the Middle Ages* (Philadelphia: University of Pennsylvania Press, 2014); Kim M. Phillips, *Before Orientalism: Asian Peoples and Cultures in European Travel Writing, 1245–1510* (Philadelphia: University of Pennsylvania Press, 2014).

10. Oswald, *Monsters*, 30.

11. MS Bodley 614, fol. 50v: "Sunt homines ermafrodite nuncupati eo, quod eis uterque sexus appareat. . . . Hii dexteram mammam virilem sinistram muliebrem habentes. Vicissim coeundo et gignunt et pariunt." This text borrows from Isidore of Seville, *Isidori Hispalensis Episcopi Etymologiarum sive originum*, ed. W. M. Lindsay, 2 vols. (Oxford: Clarendon Press, 1911), vol. 2, 10.3.11; see Orchard, *Pride and Prodigies*, 22.

12. *Liber monstrorum*, in Orchard, *Pride and Prodigies*, 270: "Et in his incredibilibus quoddam genus utriusque sexus describitur, qui dexteram mammam uirilem pro

exercendis operibus et ad fetus nutriendo sinistram habent muliebrem. Quos inter se uicibus coeundo ferunt alternis generare."

13. Hereford Mappamundi: "Gens uterque sexus innaturales multimodis modis." See Naomi Reed Kline, *Maps of Medieval Thought: The Hereford Paradigm* (Woodbridge, Suffolk: Boydell & Brewer, 2001), 143; for more on this image, see M. W. Bychowski, "The Isle of Hermaphrodites: Disorienting the Place of Intersex in the Middle Ages," *postmedieval: a journal of medieval cultural studies* 9.2 (2018): 161–78.

14. Westminster Abbey Bestiary, Westminster Abbey Library MS 22, fol. 3r.

15. An image of a bearded woman in a thirteenth-century manuscript of Gerald of Wales's *Topographia Hibernica* affirms the subject's female sex by picturing her with a distaff for spinning; here too gendered pursuits are key to establishing sex. See Asa S. Mittman, "The Other Close at Hand: Gerald of Wales and the 'Marvels of the West,'" in *The Monstrous Middle Ages*, ed. Bettina Bildhauer and Robert Mills (Toronto: University of Toronto Press, 2003), 100.

16. See, for instance, Ruth Evans, ed., "Medieval Intersex: Language and Hermaphroditism," special issue of *postmedieval: a journal of medieval cultural studies* 9.2 (2018); Cary J. Nederman and Jacqui True, "The Third Sex: The Idea of the Hermaphrodite in Twelfth-Century Europe," *Journal of the History of Sexuality* 6 (1996): 497–517; Robert Mills, *Seeing Sodomy in the Middle Ages* (Chicago: University of Chicago Press, 2015), 106–7; Glenn W. Olsen, *Of Sodomites, Effeminates, Hermaphrodites, and Androgynes: Sodomy in the Age of Peter Damian* (Toronto: Pontifical Institute of Mediaeval Studies, 2011), 65; John Boswell, *Christianity, Homosexuality, and Social Tolerance* (Chicago: University of Chicago Press, 1980), 185; Irina Metzler, *Disability in Medieval Europe: Thinking about Impairment during the High Middle Ages, c. 1100–1400* (London: Routledge, 2006).

17. Instructive here is Michel Foucault's understanding of homosexuality as a purely modern phenomenon, inseparable from the formation of modern concepts of sex and selfhood. If we extend Foucault's logic to issues of gender variance, as some scholars have suggested, one cannot write a history of "transgender" phenomena before the advent of the very vocabulary that generated its subjects. See, for instance, the cautions of Peter Boag, "Go West Young Man, Go East Young Woman: Searching for the Trans in Western Gender History," *Western Historical Quarterly* 36.4 (2005): 479–80; and Genny Beemyn, "A Presence in the Past: A Transgender Historiography," *Journal of Women's History* 25.4 (2013): 113. Historical scholarship on transgender has nevertheless flourished in recent years.

18. For the "truth" of wonders literature, see Susan M. Kim and Asa S. Mittman, "Ungefraegelicu deor: Truth and the *Wonders of the East*," *Different Visions: A Journal of New Perspectives on Medieval Art* 2 (June 2010), https://differentvisions.org/wp-content/uploads/sites/1356/2020/03/Issue-2-Kim-and-Mittman.pdf (accessed June 15, 2020); for wonders and the sensation of wonder, see Caroline Walker Bynum, "Wonder," in *Metamorphosis and Identity* (New York: Zone Books, 2001), 37–75.

19. For a summary of parallel approaches to queer history, see Laura Doan, *Disturbing Practices: History, Sexuality, and Women's Experience of Modern War* (Chicago: University of Chicago Press, 2013).

20. For the limits of the category of transgender to describe modern identities and practices, see, for instance, Valentine, *Imagining Transgender*; Yv E. Nay, "The Atmosphere of Trans* Politics in the Global North and West," *TSQ: Transgender Studies*

Quarterly 6.1 (2019): 64–79; Cole Rizki, "Latin/x American Trans Studies: Toward a *Travesti*-Trans Analytic," *TSQ: Transgender Studies Quarterly* 6.2 (2019): 145–55.

21. M. W. Bychowski et al., "Trans*historicities: A Roundtable Discussion," *TSQ: Transgender Studies Quarterly* 5.4 (2018): 677.

22. Susan Stryker uses "transgender" to signify any "movement across a socially imposed boundary from an unchosen starting place," regardless of whether or not an individual has explicitly identified as transgender. Stryker, *Transgender History*, 1. See also Susan Stryker, Paisley Currah, and Lisa Jean Moore, "Introduction: Trans-, Trans, or Transgender?," *WSQ: Women's Studies Quarterly* 36.3 (2008): 11–22; Paisley Currah and Susan Stryker, eds., "Postposttranssexual: Key Concepts for a Twenty-First Century Transgender Studies," special issue of *TSQ: Transgender Studies Quarterly* 1.1–2 (2014). Robert Mills notes that scholars of the Middle Ages have rarely used "transgender" as a category of analysis, despite the fact that medieval vocabulary is not always sufficient to capture the gender configurations of the period. Mills, *Seeing Sodomy*, 81–84. Recent scholarship has demonstrated that this convention is quickly changing. See, for instance, Valerie Traub, Patricia Badir, and Peggy McCracken, eds., *Ovidian Transversions: "Iphis and Ianthe," 1300–1650* (Edinburgh: Edinburgh University Press, 2019); M. W. Bychowski and Dorothy Kim, eds., "Visions of Medieval Trans Feminism," special issue of *Medieval Feminist Forum* 55.1 (2019).

23. On "transgender-like" as a way of describing medieval gender inversions, see Ruth Mazo Karras and Thomas Linkinen, "John/Eleanor Rykener Revisited," in *Founding Feminisms in Medieval Studies: Essays in Honor of E. Jane Burns*, ed. Laine E. Doggett and Daniel E. O'Sullivan (Woodbridge, Suffolk: Boydell & Brewer, 2016), 111–21. Robert Mills, however, warns against the teleology implicit in "trans-like," which might suggest that medieval behaviors were mere precursors, incomplete gestures that find full expression only in modern forms. Mills, *Seeing Sodomy*, 86–87, quotation at 22. See also Kadin Henningsen, "'Calling [Herself] Eleanor': Gender Labor and Becoming a Woman in the Rykener Case," *Medieval Feminist Forum* 55.1 (2019): 249–66.

24. Isidore of Seville, *Etymologiarum*, vol. 2, 11.3.3–4.

25. On monsters as portents, see Lorraine Daston and Katharine Park, *Wonders and the Order of Nature, 1150–1750* (New York: Zone Books, 1998); Lisa Verner, *The Epistemology of the Monstrous in the Middle Ages* (New York: Routledge, 2005), 20–36 and passim. Medieval notions of monstrosity were complex and diverse.

26. Many medieval texts attest to the existence of males who preferred "feminine" pursuits and females who preferred "masculine" ones but who were inarguably male or female. Among many examples, see Joan Cadden, *Meanings of Sex Difference in the Middle Ages* (Cambridge: Cambridge University Press, 1993), 201–9; Barbara Newman, *From Virile Woman to WomanChrist* (Philadelphia: University of Pennsylvania Press, 1995); Caroline Walker Bynum, "Jesus as Mother and Abbot as Mother: Some Themes in Twelfth-Century Cistercian Writing," in *Jesus as Mother: Studies in the Spirituality of the High Middle Ages* (Berkeley: University of California Press, 1982), 110–69.

27. Asa S. Mittman and Susan M. Kim, "The Exposed Body and the Gendered *Blemmye*: Reading the *Wonders of the East*," in *Sexuality in the Middle Ages and Early Modern Times: New Approaches to a Fundamental Cultural-Historical and Literary-Anthropological Theme*, ed. Albrecht Classen (Berlin: Walter de Gruyter, 2008), 171–201.

28. Amanda Lehr, "Sexing the Cannibal in *The Wonders of the East* and *Beowulf*," *postmedieval: a journal of medieval cultural studies* 9.2 (2018): 179–95. See also Oswald, *Monsters*, 53–63.

29. Gayle Salamon, *Assuming a Body: Transgender and Rhetorics of Materiality* (New York: Columbia University Press, 2010), 50, emphasis added. See also Susan Stryker, "(De)subjugated Knowledges: An Introduction to Transgender Studies," in Susan Stryker and Stephen Whittle, eds., *The Transgender Studies Reader 1* (New York: Routledge, 2006), 1–17.

30. Chet Van Duzer, "A Neglected Type of Medieval *Mappamundi* and Its Reimaging in the *Mare Historiarum* (BNF MS Lat. 4915, Fol. 26v)," *Viator* 43.2 (2012): 277–302.

31. As A. J. Ford points out, divisions between East and West were never absolute, as some material in *Wonders* transposed local phenomena onto foreign places and vice versa. Ford, *Marvel and Artefact*, 138–40.

32. A. Finn Enke, "Introduction: Transfeminist Perspectives," in *Transfeminist Perspectives in and beyond Transgender and Gender Studies*, ed. A. Finn Enke (Philadelphia: Temple University Press, 2012), 7–8; Susan Stryker and Aren Z. Aizura, *The Transgender Studies Reader 2* (New York: Routledge, 2013), 8, 471–540; Keja Valens, "Excruciating Probability and the Transgender Jamaican," in *Trans Studies: The Challenge to Hetero/Homo Normativities*, ed. Yolanda Martínez-San Miguel and Sara Tobias (New Brunswick, NJ: Rutgers University Press, 2016), 69.

33. Aren Z. Aizura, *Mobile Subjects: Transnational Imaginaries of Gender Reassignment* (Durham, NC: Duke University Press, 2018).

34. For the "East" as an opposite of Europe that aided in European identity formation, see Mary Baine Campbell, *The Witness and the Other World: Exotic European Travel Writing, 400–1600* (Ithaca, NY: Cornell University Press, 1988); Michael Uebel, *Ecstatic Transformation: On the Uses of Alterity in the Middle Ages* (New York: Palgrave, 2005); Akbari, *Idols in the East*, 280. Much of this work is quite nuanced, admitting to middle areas and ambiguous contacts between regions. See also Phillips, *Before Orientalism*; Albrecht Classen, "Introduction: The Self, the Other, and Everything in Between: Xenological Phenomenology of the Middle Ages," in *Meeting the Foreign in the Middle Ages*, ed. Albrecht Classen (New York: Routledge, 2002), xi–lxxiii; Paul Freedman, "The Medieval Other: The Middle Ages as Other," in *Marvels, Monsters, and Miracles: Studies in the Medieval and Early Modern Imaginations*, ed. Timothy S. Jones and David A. Sprunger (Kalamazoo, MI: Medieval Institute Publications, 2002), 1–24.

35. For religion, race, and the monstrous races, see Geraldine Heng, *The Invention of Race in the European Middle Ages* (Cambridge: Cambridge University Press, 2018); Cord J. Whitaker, *Black Metaphors: How Modern Racism Emerged from Medieval Race-Thinking* (Philadelphia: University of Pennsylvania Press, 2019), 163–70; Akbari, *Idols*, 67–75, 140–54 and passim; Debra Higgs Strickland, "Monstrosity and Race in the Middle Ages," in Mittman and Dendle, *Ashgate Research Companion to Monsters and the Monstrous*, 365–86; Strickland, *Saracens, Demons, and Jews*.

36. See the quotation from Dana Oswald, *Monsters*, 30, cited in note 10; see also Mills, *Seeing Sodomy*, 12.

37. I consider these additional links to religious and racial difference in detail in Leah DeVun, *The Shape of Sex: Nonbinary Gender from Genesis to the Renaissance* (New York: Columbia University Press, 2021).

38. Leah DeVun and Zeb Tortorici, "Trans, Time, and History," *TSQ: Transgender Studies Quarterly* 5.4 (2018): 518–39.

39. See, for instance, the comments of M. W. Bychowski and Marcia Ochoa in "Trans*historicities: A Roundtable Discussion," 658–85. On queer community across time, see Carolyn Dinshaw et al., "Theorizing Queer Temporalities: A Roundtable Discussion," *GLQ: A Journal of Lesbian and Gay Studies* 13.2–3 (2007): 177–95; Carolyn Dinshaw, *Getting Medieval: Sexualities and Communities, Pre- and Postmodern* (Durham, NC: Duke University Press, 1999); Elizabeth Freeman, *Time Binds: Queer Temporalities, Queer Histories* (Durham, NC: Duke University Press, 2010).

40. I paraphrase here Jeffrey J. Cohen, *The Postcolonial Middle Ages* (New York: Palgrave Macmillan, 2001), 5; Freedman, "Medieval Other," 1–24.

CHAPTER 2

Elenx de Céspedes

Indeterminate Genders in the Spanish Inquisition

Igor H. De Souza

Elena or Eleno de Céspedes was born in 1546, a mixed-race freed slave, and in the course of this essay I call them Elenx, in order to avoid singularizing de Céspedes's gender identity. Elenx claimed to the Inquisition that they were a "hermaphrodite," meaning someone with a "double nature."[1] There is a vast literature on various facets of Elenx's life.[2] There is also a vast literature on the repression of sodomy by the Spanish Inquisition and in early modern Spain in general.[3] This essay brings together those two scholarly conversations by focusing on an aspect of Elenx's story that has received little attention: the relationship between their conceptualization of hermaphroditism, on the one hand, and sodomy, on the other. Richard Cleminson and Francisco Vázquez García are among the few scholars to have looked closely into the accusation of sodomy against Elenx, and this essay elaborates on their analysis.[4] Much of this essay will delve into the implications of the initial accusation brought against the presumptively heterosexually married, male-presenting Eleno—that they were guilty of sodomy—and how that accusation led to an investigation of their sex and gender by the Spanish Inquisition.

Early modern conceptions of sodomy relied on a presumption of what today we might term binary gender—male or female.[5] What counted as sodomy depended not only on the participants' conduct but also on their social presentation and sexual genitalia. Hence, determinations of sodomy relied on the congruence of two kinds of "sex": the sex you allegedly have and the sex you allegedly are. Although Elenx was initially accused of sodomy, their actual crime(s) were indeterminate—perhaps permissible, perhaps not—because Elenx's sex was indeterminate. The case illustrates that the Inquisitorial preoccupation with sodomy was not restricted to sexual behavior. While ostensibly targeting a sexual practice, the criminalization of sodomy in the Inquisitorial context presupposed control over gender expression.

The Inquisitorial Repression of Sodomy

The Spanish Inquisition is infamous for its repression of non-Catholic practices, in particular those with real or imagined links to Judaism, Islam, and Protestantism. In 1492 Jews were officially expelled from Spain, except for those who chose to convert to Christianity, and Muslims were to meet the same fate in successive waves, culminating in the general and final expulsion of 1609. In the wake of the Counter-Reformation, moreover, any sign of Protestantism was seen not only as a betrayal of Catholic values but also as a threat to the political hegemony of Spain. In this environment, the Inquisition was ostensibly deployed to ferret out heresy from the body Catholic. Among those seen as particularly susceptible to heresy were the descendants of converted Jews, now known as "New Christians"; the descendants of converted Muslims, now known as "Moriscos"; and any present foreigners from a Protestant nation (and occasionally also foreigners from Catholic lands, especially Italy and France). By the late sixteenth century, substantial numbers of New Christians and Moriscos, several generations removed, found themselves accused by their neighbors and prosecuted by the Inquisition for allegedly relapsing into the religion of their ancestors.[6]

After the first century of its existence, the Inquisition in Spain turned its gaze toward populations that were not ostensibly heretics but Catholics: the so-called "Old Christians," Spaniards who claimed to have neither Jewish nor Muslim ancestry.[7] These prosecutions turned on transgressions of the moral and sexual order. As an extension of the preoccupation with rooting out heresy, the Inquisition came to function as an organ of social-moral control.[8] It began to prosecute charges such as adultery, bigamy, blasphemy, and sodomy. Adultery and bigamy were interpreted as heresy because they implied a heretical attitude toward the sacrament of marriage. But sodomy as a manifestation of heresy was more difficult to articulate, and also more controversial.

In early modern Spain, sodomy was a secular legal transgression. Spanish secular laws, however, were phrased in terms of preexistent religious discourse on sodomy. The earliest systematic code of Spanish law, the Siete Partidas (thirteenth century), stands out for its clear declaration of sodomy as a crime against nature, a theological-philosophical notion, and a crime that would bring divine punishment upon the entire community and not just upon sodomites—a notion of biblical origin. (It is a reference to the divine punishment of Sodom, when a rain of fire destroyed the entire town.)[9] The royal decree termed *Pragmática de los Reyes Católicos acerca de los reos de pecado nefando*, issued in 1497, doubles down on the earlier Siete Partidas by emphasizing the appropriate punishment for sodomy: fire. It introduced capital punishment for sodomy in the form of a public burning (auto-da-fé).[10] Sodomites were thus routinely met with the threat of the death penalty in much of Spain.

The first problem with the regulation of sodomy by the Inquisition in Spain is jurisdictional. As a religious body that stood apart from secular law, the Inquisition was meant to target behavior that was offensive to God, that is, breaches of divine law—not of secular law. Indeed, in the Spanish Inquisitorial tribunals that did prosecute sodomy charges—primarily those in Zaragoza, Valencia, and Barcelona—the cases were frequently characterized by power struggles between the Inquisition and local authorities over jurisdiction in the case.

The second problem inherent to Inquisitorial oversight over sodomy is that it was unclear how sodomy could constitute heresy, even if indirectly. How did the Inquisition justify its repression of sodomy? We might imagine that sodomy is heresy in the sense that it amounts to neglect of marriage as a Catholic sacrament. A good number of those arrested by the tribunal for sodomy, however, were in fact married, including Elenx. Sodomy was already punishable under secular law. On what basis should the Inquisition attempt to prosecute anyone for this crime? Certain voices emerged that sought to justify this moral crusade in theological terms, insisting that sodomy and heresy were closely related.[11] Heretics, such as presumed Jews, were painted as sodomites (for example, in the anti-Jewish satire by Francisco de Quevedo), and the ambassador of the Aragonese Inquisition to Rome, the Duke of Sessa, argued that sodomy was the "sin of the Muslims," thus justifying the Inquisitorial jurisdiction over sodomy in order to stamp out heretical practices.[12] Sodomy was assimilated to heresy, and António Gomez argued in 1550 that it was even "worse than heresy" and "as such the maximum offense against God and nature."[13] Sodomites, it was claimed, were considered heretics because they defied the divinely created order of nature: dictates that genitalia be used in the proper way, to wit, penetration of a vagina with internal vaginal ejaculation.[14] All other uses of genitalia are read theologically as statements of atheism, or as a denial of divine control over the world and a denial of the "natural order." Genital misuse is both heretical and sodomitical.

The preoccupation of the Inquisition with sodomy cases went beyond "genital misuse." In the case of people assigned male, it was semen and its location that determined what kind of sodomitical act had transpired. Reminiscent of earlier configurations of sodomy, the Inquisition instituted a gradient of sodomitical crimes and of the punishments that accompanied them, all calibrated by the semen's location. The Inquisition concentrated primarily on what was called "perfect" sodomy—defined as seminal ejaculation inside a male anus. In some rare cases the Inquisition also prosecuted seminal ejaculation inside a female anus.[15] Other forms of same-sex genital contact, including ejaculation outside the anus, masturbation, or intercrural copulation, were deemed "imperfect" sodomy, or *mollices*, and such cases were turned over to secular authorities; they were of no concern to the Holy Office.[16] Significantly for Elenx's case, same-sex female genital contact with an instrument used for physical penetration also fell under the category of "perfect" sodomy, but such cases rarely came to the attention of Inquisitorial authorities.[17] The Inquisitorial concern with sodomy, in the case of men and of heterosexual coupling, was regulated by the physical placement of semen; in the case of women, it was regulated by whether penetration had occurred with an ersatz phallus (as the Inquisition saw it).[18]

In the context of this chapter, I must emphasize that sodomy as the placement of semen or penetration with an instrument relies on an underlying clear and unambiguous identification of sex. Only men were supposed to emit semen; only women were thought to penetrate one another with an instrument. In light of these criteria, the Inquisitorial determination of Elenx's sex becomes problematic to the extent that they report to have had "abundant pollution" with their female partners, but no instrument was found, and they reported possessing a penis at different stages of their life. Yet Elenx was gendered and sexed female in socially visible ways: raised as a girl, Elenx had married a man and given birth to a child. This contradiction undermined the reliability of Inquisitorial categories of gender and sodomy.

To return to the Inquisitorial regulation of sodomy, the two factors that made sodomy problematic were political (shared jurisdiction with secular authorities) and gendered/sexual (where semen was ejaculated, and by/in what sex). A third factor is sociological-theological: for the public, repression of sodomy is evidence of the occurrence of sodomy. Harsh widespread and public punishment intimates that Spain—the "tip of the spear" of the

Catholic sword—harbors sodomites. Furthermore, public Inquisitorial proclamations concerning sodomy announce to "closeted" sodomites that they are not alone. A similar concern regarding the perpetuation of sin by publicly proscribing it arose centuries earlier in the ecclesiastical environment of the confessional. According to some penitential manuals, a priest should not ask a confessant about sodomy in particular, lest the confessant comes to believe that such a sin is common and that others share in this kind of sin.[19]

These three factors, political, gender/sexual, and theological-sociological, help to explain why the Inquisition initially hesitated to prosecute sodomy. Was it under the jurisdiction of the state or the Inquisition? On what basis could it be prosecuted under the Inquisition? Would public condemnation signal that it was a common practice? Those three factors also help explain why the number of sodomites arrested was relatively low when compared to other offenders (such as New Christians), and why the various tribunals that prosecuted sodomy decided to switch from public to private sentencing. In Elenx's case, as they were initially arrested by the secular authorities for sodomy, the claim of Inquisitorial jurisdiction over the case turned a potential public punishment for sodomy into a focused investigation that resulted in other charges and was concluded in private.[20]

The recursive problem (perpetuating sodomy by proscribing it), with its theological overtones, illuminates why the Inquisition was hesitant to prosecute sodomy. Any involvement with the so-called "nefarious" sin, even prosecutorial, entailed disrepute and shame. Some Inquisitorial authorities were openly concerned about involvement with such a heinous crime (against nature); they thought it best prosecuted by the state and punished by death. It bears mentioning that the Inquisition itself never put its victims to death; those who were found to deserve capital punishment were handed over to the state ("relaxed" to the state, in Inquisitorial parlance). But the concerns over the nefariousness of sodomy remained. In Castile, where Elenx's story takes place, the Inquisition did not extend its formal jurisdiction over sodomy. Nonetheless, the tribunals located in Aragón (Valencia, Barcelona, and Zaragoza), in Mexico City, and in Portugal asserted judicial prerogative over individuals accused of sodomy. The moves by certain tribunals to prosecute sodomy led to a period of some two and a half centuries when sodomites were subject to a double threat of persecution, secular and Inquisitorial, both in parts of Iberia and in its colonies. Sodomy was repressed in other early modern European countries and in the New World, in both Catholic and Protestant lands, but only in Iberia and its colonies was there a dual system of repression with secular law on the one hand and the Inquisition on the other.

Because the Inquisition did not ordinarily prosecute sodomy in Castile, its interest in Elenx is all the more intriguing.

Life Narrative

In 1587 a sodomy-related case came to the attention of the Castilian Inquisition. Acting on an allegation, a royal official (*corregidor*) abruptly arrested Eleno de Céspedes, who had been living outside Toledo for about a year with their young wife, María del Caño. The basis of the accusation was not that Eleno and "his" wife had engaged in heterosexual sodomy. Rather, it was that Eleno was in fact a woman, and that two women were engaging in sodomitical practices.

For reasons explored in the course of this chapter, the Toledo tribunal of the Inquisition claimed jurisdiction over the case. As Richard Kagan remarks, had de Céspedes been punished by secular authorities, they would have likely met a gruesome end at the stake.[21] This means that secular authorities could probably have convicted Elenx for sodomy on the basis of witness testimonies. But in the context of the Inquisition, a prosecution for sodomy had to clear a higher bar: for two women, that bar was penetration with the use of an object (along with corroborating witness testimony of that act).[22] But was the male-presenting Eleno indeed a woman, Elena?[23] A clear answer to the question was crucial to the case: If Elenx was a male, no charges of sodomy would apply. If Elenx was a woman, further inquiries would be necessary. A medical examination arranged by the secular authorities at the time of the initial arrest, finding that Elenx had no penis, determined them to be a woman.

Elenx, however, was at that time married to a woman, which made the medical findings ambiguous. The Inquisitorial interest in the case turned to Elenx's formal sacrament of marriage to María del Caño. Had a church-endorsed same-sex marriage occurred? In Elenx's narrative, they reported having married a man earlier in their life: Was bigamy at stake? A third possibility aimed at resolving the ambiguity surrounding sex and gender was also relevant to Elenx's gender presentation: Were they really a man, or a sorcerer who tricked people into believing that they were a man? It bears remembering that none of these charges were major crimes nor directly linked to heresy.[24] While all these questions were pertinent to the Inquisition, they only emerged in the course of the trial, after Elenx was transferred from secular to Inquisitorial jurisdiction. But why was the Inquisition interested in Elenx in the first place?

I argue that Inquisitorial interest in the case was in all likelihood tied to Elenx's transgression of gender codes. Their transgression of gender norms came to light before they became involved with the Inquisition. It first occurred when Elenx was faced with the accusation of sodomy, because the allegation implied that Elenx was unambiguously a woman, although they presented as a heterosexually married man. Without the allegation of sodomy, Elenx might have lived quietly as a married man. Once the allegation was made, it was impossible to ignore the underlying premise: that the male-presenting Eleno and their wife were of the same sex. The allegation of sodomy, then, was significant in bringing to light a disconnect between what we would today call biological sex and lived gender—an unusual situation in early modernity. Interest in the case shifted entirely to gender policing. The allegation itself was quickly laid aside and not brought up again during the course of the trial. That is curious because the Inquisition ultimately found Elenx to be a woman, and there was some precedent that would have allowed the Inquisition to transfer Elenx back to the secular sphere for a sodomy trial. But the shift to gender policing allowed the local Inquisitorial tribunal to retain jurisdiction over the case, which would not have happened for an ordinary accusation of sodomy.

That is an important point, as it reveals something about early modern repression of sodomy in general: gender policing was a necessary prerequisite for prosecuting a sodomite. It was necessary for someone, at some point, to determine the sex as well as the gender of the subject in order to consider whether sodomy had been committed. Elenx's transgression of gender codes and their investigation by the Inquisition illuminates how gender policing, along with sex, traveled under the auspices of sodomy: an allegation of sodomy could set the stage for an investigation of the subject's gender if there was reason to believe it did not correspond to their sex. Thus, what Elenx's case makes clear is that an accusation of sodomy was never merely a claim that some sex act had occurred. In early modernity, it was also a claim regarding the sex and gender of the parties involved.

The Inquisitorial procedure was to solicit newly arrested defendants to retell their own life narrative, the *discurso de su vida*, an early form of autobiography retold orally, before the Inquisitors in an adversarial setting, and therefore under conditions that made it advantageous for a defendant to lie, embellish, or stretch the truth.[25] The Inquisition did not inform the defendant of their crimes beforehand, and it exploited gaps or contradictions in the life narrative to uncover new charges.

Elenx's story was far more complicated than it seemed at first. As they narrated to the Inquisition, they were born an enslaved person in Valencia, the result of a mixed union of a enslaved Moorish mother and her Christian master, and they were freed from slavery as a child. At age sixteen, Elenx married a man, Cristóbal Lombardo, who abandoned them while they were pregnant with their first child. Regarding the whereabouts of the husband, Elenx reports, "I think Cristóbal Lombardo died in Baza a short time after he married me," which was vague enough to raise Inquisitorial suspicions of bigamy, and led to that eventual charge at the end of the trial. After child-birth, Elenx left their baby with friends and moved around Spain. As I will detail shortly, in their travels they adopted different gender expressions, took up variously gender-restricted careers, and had affairs with women. They called themself Céspedes or Eleno when wearing men's clothing and Elena, the name they took as a teenager, when in women's clothing. They married a cis woman, María del Caño, in a church ceremony in 1586.

At this point in their life narrative, Elenx might have been liable for sod-omy, since one previous medical examination revealed that they did not have a penis, and Elenx had just admitted to having relations with women. But the Castilian Inquisitors could not charge Elenx with sodomy, and they were not satisfied with just a potential bigamy charge. The Inquisitors wanted to ferret out just how Elenx, apparently female, was able to convince scores of people (priests, medical and non-medical examiners, María del Caño herself, and past female lovers), presumably familiar with their genitalia, that they were in fact a man. Thus, the trajectory of Elenx's gender presentation in relation to their genitals became, in the eyes of the Inquisition, the crux of their life narrative. Elenx was pressed for details about how they were able to marry María del Caño. They told the Inquisition:

> When I asked for María del Cañõ's hand in marriage, and it was given to me, I went to Madrid to ask the vicar for a license to marry and post banns. The vicar, who saw that I was beardless and hairless, asked me if I was a capon [i.e., a "castrated" man]. I told him I wasn't, and that he should look at me to see that I wasn't. To this end, they took me to a nearby house, where three or four men looked at me from the front, though I didn't let them look at me from the back, so they wouldn't see my woman's parts. The men testified that they'd seen me and that I wasn't a capon.[26]

But the vicar who was to marry Elenx was not satisfied. There was a public rumor that Elenx was, as they put it, "both male and female."[27] In light of that rumor, and before finally gaining approval to marry, Elenx was once again subjected to an examination. Before the second examination took place, Elenx made use of their surgical knowledge—they had apprenticed as a surgeon in years prior—"to prepare certain remedies with wine and alco-hol, and many other remedies and potions to see if I could close my woman's part. . . . With all the remedies I prepared, my woman's part wrinkled up and got so narrow that nothing could be put inside it."[28] When the appointed ten men came to examine Elenx, they "felt a hard wrinkled spot which was the result of my remedies. When they asked me what it was, I told them it was a hemorrhoid I'd gotten, which I'd cauterized and which had left behind this hard knot. By this ruse, all ten men, including the physicians and the others who'd seen me, declared, said, and affirmed to the *alcalde* [the mayor of a town or village, who was also head of the town council] that I didn't have a woman's part and that I did have a male member."[29]

The vicar who was to marry Elenx was nonetheless unconvinced and had them once more examined by two surgeons of the royal court, including Dr. Francisco Díaz, a renowned urologist.[30] Elenx reported to the Inquisition that when the doctors tried to insert a probe, and asked Elenx what they "had there," Elenx claimed to have a hemorrhoid. The two royal doctors then reported that Elenx didn't have a "woman's part." Elenx was given permission to marry.

Many witnesses, then, examined Elenx and found them to either possess a penis and/or lack a vagina. Unfortunately for Elenx, when they moved to the town of Ocaña with María del Caño over a year after the marriage, Elenx was recognized by a figure from the more distant past. A town official claimed to have met Elenx when they had both served as Spanish soldiers against the Morisco uprising known as the Rebellion of Alpujarras, which took place in 1568–1571, about fifteen years before Elenx's marriage. Furthermore, the town official testified that "it had been said by some that [Elenx] was a woman and by others that [Elenx] was male and female."[31] This rumor, which questioned Elenx's sex, was mentioned in the course of the initial accusation that Elenx had committed sodomy and may have served as corroborating evidence.

Natural or Unnatural Desire?

How did Elenx address the charge of sodomy? They claimed to be a man, not a woman, and as such they had neither deceived María del Caño nor committed sodomy. Elenx was asked if they had committed sodomy with any of their past lovers; they answered that they had had "relations with other women naturally, as a man, not unnaturally."[32] Thus, from the outset of their trial, Elenx relied on an unspoken notion of heterosexual privilege—a man was presumed not to commit sodomy with a woman—in order to frame their conception of their own gender and sexuality. The revindication of that conceit as a strategy for Elenx to empower themself would come up throughout the course of the trial.[33]

Pressed now by the Inquisitors, who asked how Elenx, "being a woman," was able to convince witnesses and physicians that they were a man, Elenx gave a more extensive self-definition:

> In reality I am and was a hermaphrodite. I have and had two natures, one of a man and the other of a woman. What happened is that when I gave birth, I did so with such force in my [woman's] part, that a piece of skin broke out above my urethra and a head emerged about half the size of a thumb, like so, which resembled the swollen head of a male member, which, when I had *natural* passion and desire, came out, as I said. When I felt desire it got bigger. I gathered the member up and put it back in the place where it had come from so that the skin wouldn't break.[34]

We see in these words the underlying claim that Elenx could not have committed sodomy because they experienced only "natural" desire. That desire can be said to be natural in that it mimics putatively "male" heterosexual desire: possessing a penis implies desire for a woman. The penis that emerged during the birth of their child served as legitimation of Elenx's sexual desire. It mattered less what their own gender identification might be, or that they might have two sets of genitalia, and mattered more that their genitalia absolved them *ab initio* from charges of unnatural desire and sodomy. Indeed, once the penis emerged, and even after it had fallen away (discussed momentarily), Elenx never again had sexual relations with a man.[35] This fact, coupled with the fact that Elenx sought a bona fide Christian marriage with a woman, makes Elenx's perspective appear to be deeply if strangely conservative. At every turn, they claim to have sought to reproduce and appropriate the naturalness of heterosexual desire and privilege: now with a man, when they were a woman; then with women, when their penis emerged. Elenx is not trying to overturn or question dominant early modern notions of sexuality, and this is what makes their perspective "conservative." Rather than contesting such notions, Elenx deploys them to naturalize their unconventional sex and gender configuration. In their rhetoric and reported practices, Elenx takes for granted the early modern Spanish cultural equivalence of genitals with gender and sexuality, and they try to seize the legitimation that an ostensibly heterosexual orientation provided.[36]

But this binary repertoire fails to capture the full complexity of Elenx's experience. In a letter that Elenx submitted to the Inquisition in their own defense, as an appendix to their testimony, they explain their "hermaphroditic anatomy" in greater detail:

> I have never pretended to be a man in order to marry a woman as some have impugned. What has happened is that in this world we have often heard of people who are androgynous, or who, by another name, are also called hermaphrodites, who have two sexes.[37] I am and have been a hermaphrodite, and at the time I married [Maria del Caño] the masculine sex prevailed in me. I was *naturally* a man and had all the necessary parts of a man in order to marry, as had been proven through examinations by doctors and surgeons licensed in their arts, who saw and touched me and swore legal oaths that I could marry as a man. . . . I have *naturally* been a man and a woman, and though this may be a prodigious and rare thing that is not often seen, hermaphrodites, as I am and have been, *are not unnatural*. . . . I married first as a woman to a man, then as a man to a woman, because when I married a man, the feminine sex heated up and prevailed in me. Then, when my husband died, the masculine sex heated up and I could marry a woman.[38]

Here, once again, we see Elenx's appeal to physiological nature to legitimate and to safeguard desire; the heterosexuality of their desire distances Elenx from the possibility of sodomy. Even though the Castilian Inquisition did not punish sodomy, Elenx took pains to emphasize the naturalness of their desire and its concomitant legitimate expression through official religious channels (the sacrament of marriage). In their testimony, furthermore, Elenx did not hide the fact that they had taken lovers outside the bonds of marriage; simple fornication was not a major Inquisitorial preoccupation. In fact, Elenx proffered their sexual history to affirm the naturalness of both their genitalia and their sexual desire. In their own words, Elenx was not, as the Inquisition feared, a *burladora*, a trickster. Nor did they conceive of or express any potential disjunction between their genitalia and their gender expression: Elenx was not claiming to have female genitalia while dressing as a man.[39] Rather, Elenx's conception of their sexuality relies on the dictates of "nature," under the assumption that changes occurring in their body were not unnatural but teleological. In that sense, Elenx's natural teleology shares some affinities with that of Aristotle.[40]

Elenx's view of their hermaphroditic condition as a natural phenomenon was in line with early modern scientific thought. The ancient philosophers Aristotle and Galen were considered the main authorities on sexuality and hermaphroditism in early modern Iberia. While their views diverged sharply on where the "hermaphrodite" fit within the natural world, both agreed that "hermaphroditism" was a real phenomenon, not self-delusion. For both thinkers, the evaluation of "hermaphroditism" is anchored in an investigation of genitalia. Elenx's views were closer to Galen on that point. For Galen, male and female genitalia are structurally identical; the only distinction is placement in the body: the penis is a vagina that extrudes outward; the vagina is a penis that grows inward. The two sets of genitalia are mirror images of each other, the so-called "one-sex" model.[41] The Galenic approach, therefore, allows for a number of possible natural configurations of genitalia that are situated at various points between a "fully formed" vagina and a "fully formed" penis. The Aristotelian "two-sex" model, by contrast, proposed a radical distinction between a vagina and a penis. Those who followed Aristotle over Galen considered "hermaphrodites" to be aberrations of nature, prodigies or monsters.[42] In that classification, just as in Galen, prodigies or monsters were considered part of nature: there was nothing inherently wrong with them, since they were natural.

Neither the Galenic nor the Aristotelian school of thought denied the reality of hermaphroditism. In both cases it was a "natural" phenomenon. "Hermaphrodites" existed as a social category of their own.[43] What this means is that the Inquisition had philosophical-scientific evidence suggesting that Elenx's account was true. The account was anchored in scientific sources that agreed on the reality of "hermaphroditism" as a historical phenomenon. Nonetheless, in line with current Christian doctrine, the Inquisition also held that the devil was real and that he could create deceitful illusions. By those lights, Elenx could have been, and eventually was, sentenced as a sorcerer, one who colluded with the devil. In addition, there were sociocultural reasons for the Inquisition to be skeptical of Elenx's account of their sexuality, which are explored in the next section.

Along with Galen and Aristotle, other ancient sources on "hermaphroditism" were available. In fact, we have evidence that Elenx had direct knowledge of them. In the aforementioned letter written by Elenx in support of their testimony, they had referenced Pliny, Cicero, and Augustine on the subject. Sections of Pliny's *Natural History* describe what were then called "curiosities," monsters, marvels, or aberrations of nature, a favorite topic among Spanish and other European early modern scholars in the late sixteenth through seventeenth centuries.[44] In Pliny's view, the female body was essentially unstable and susceptible to transformation into a male body as a result of extreme physical activity, although Pliny—consistent with the belief that bodies tend toward greater "perfection"—offers no cases of "male" bodies transformed into "female" bodies.[45] Elenx's account of a penis emerging precisely during childbirth accords well with the notion of physical exertion leading to a change in genitalia.

Elenx's argument that hermaphroditism is a real condition, and that it occupies a niche within nature, is a crucial part of their defense against charges of sodomy. Should the Castilian Inquisition have found that sodomy was committed, Elenx likely would have been turned over to the secular authorities, possibly after also having been convicted for the minor moral offenses of bigamy or sorcery.[46] Since the early modern Spanish conception of sodomy was that it was against nature, however, Elenx's argument that their hermaphroditic sexual self existed fully *within* nature—authenticated by ancient and contemporaneous authorities—made them safe from the charge of sodomy.

That the Inquisition chose to pursue the case nonetheless and to maintain its jurisdiction over Elenx indicates incredulity—to say the least—toward the argument that "hermaphrodites" did exist within the natural world. This skepticism overlaps to some degree with a broader incredulity as to whether Elenx really was who they claimed to be—a "hermaphrodite"—or whether they were resorting to trickery in gender presentation and during sexual relations, with the use of an inserted object in order to commit sodomy.

In a broader sense, the conundrum was: How might one determine what is real and what is illusory? On what basis should Elenx's account be evaluated? Which experts should be believed? Should the Inquisitors accept the results of their own medical examinations, which found Elenx to be female, and thus possibly also a sodomite? Or should they believe that some individuals could, at some points in their life, possess a vagina and a penis, as was so amply documented in the scientific literature of the day—in Aristotle, Galen, Pliny, and other authorities? What about the examinations immediately preceding Elenx's marriage to María del Caño, which assigned Elenx as male, not as a hermaphrodite?[47] Even if scientific sources agreed that hermaphroditism was real, was Elenx really a hermaphrodite? Might they instead be a female sodomite sorceress, one who was able to deceive experts and witnesses by using powers of diabolical origin? How was the Inquisition to go about determining the truth of this case? As we shall see, those questions were voiced from a place of broader cultural unease.

The Reality of Gender: Between Truth and Illusion in Golden Age Spain

Early modern Spanish society was gripped with anxiety over the boundaries between reality and unreality, a conceptual ambiguity over what constitutes a fact and who determines it to be a fact. There was a "fascination with reality and illusion . . . rooted by the disconcerting realization that their relationship was dialectical."[48] It is a significant theme in a number of cultural registers and different institutions: in literature, theater, visual arts, dioramas, and optical devices. The fascination with the dialectic of reality and illusion is reflected, too, in the social and Inquisitorial anxiety over the "real" religious allegiances of New Christians and Moriscos. It appears in the institutional requirements of genealogical certificates attesting to "purity of blood," which certify that one's ancestry is purely "Old Christian," untainted by Jewish and Muslim blood. Such certificates were frequently manipulated through bribery, giving rise to suspicions about the "real" origins of individuals. Finally, as Elenx's case indicates, the reigning confusion between reality and illusion also manifests itself in the construction of sex and gender. What might constitute a "real" man and a "real" woman? Can an individual be both, or neither?[49]

This social disquiet is visible in the artistic productions of the so-called Spanish Golden Age, roughly from the late sixteenth to the late seventeenth centuries. Works of literature dating to Spain's Golden Age often thematize the conceptual blurriness of boundaries that characterized the century. Cervantes's *Don Quixote*, for example, is the narrative of a figure who refuses or is unable to see reality as it is. He insists on approaching the world as colored by his individual perspective and resists yielding to "facts," such as in the incident in which he attacks the windmills that he imagines to be giants. Should the Inquisitors treat Elenx as a Don Quixote, one who imagines things that do not exist? Or as a characteristic literary figure of the period, the trickster (*pícaro*)?[50] Recall the Inquisitorial suggestion that Elenx is a trickster (*burladora*).[51] In a number of literary works, especially in the flourishing genre of theater, authors played with the idea that appearances and reality were both subjective, two sides of the same coin, whose boundaries were porous. Crafty individuals—tricksters—were understood as able to bend and mold the fine line that divides deception from truth.[52]

In this environment, the search for one's "true" self constitutes a source of anxiety. What constitutes the self? Is it essential or constructed? What is the true self versus the illusory world of appearances? Elenx's scientific explanation for their sexuality is a symptom of the then-prevalent social anxiety over the nature of the self. Elenx's strategy embodies the desire to find purportedly objective categories with which one can explain one's nature and one's place in the world. In this sense, it represents an effort to distinguish the real self from the illusory self, the self that *is* versus the self that appears to be. The Inquisition shares in that anxiety: Who, or what, is the real self of Elenx?

In the broader early modern Spanish context, the problem of the real versus the illusory self appears in several domains. It is revealed in the search for ethnic origins in the form of purity of blood statutes.[53] It drives Inquisitorial ethnic-religious persecution, which focuses on Christian individuals of Jewish or Muslim ancestry, and exploits the fear that some Christians were secretly the Other—*not* Christian. The problem of the real self is also revealed in the increasingly absolutist concepts of masculinity and femininity that emerge at this time.[54] In this period, the paradigmatic man embodied the national values of veneration for religious practices and for Spain's Christian past, and the heroic virtues represented by military victories over Muslims. More important for our purposes, the figure of the ideal Spanish man is one that is a partner with God in the work of Creation, through his reproductive power and especially through his semen, which was held to contain the potential for new beings.[55]

Hence we return to Elenx de Céspedes. To be a Spanish man, as Elenx claimed to have been at certain times in their life, meant possessing several concurrent traits, ranging from the proper ancestry to a shared masculine national vision.[56] It included, too, having the proper social rank and occupation, and a certain configuration of sexuality whereby semen was discharged in the proper manner and in the proper place, which excluded sodomy. Elenx's claim to masculinity was not reducible to the configuration of their sexual organs, and Elenx could point to different ways in which they functioned as a man. (In addition to having been a soldier, Elenx had also worked as a tailor and a surgeon, which were eminently masculine occupations.) Nonetheless, their sexual organs were reportedly fluid: sometimes the "female" nature predominated and sometimes the "male." Their gender presentation was likewise fluid: they had, after all, birthed a child early in life and married a woman in a Catholic ceremony. The problem of Elenx is not that they could not fit into preexisting categories. Rather, the problem is that the so-called "hermaphroditic" Elenx fit in too well, ultimately rendering male-female categories illusory rather than real.[57]

Therefore, in order to determine Elenx's "real self"—which became its own question, with the allegation of sodomy still in the background—the Inquisition could look into Elenx's gender presentation in terms of social status: their profession, their social standing in the community, their spouse, their lineage and religious allegiances, their mode of dress. It was presumed that these would match a certain biological configuration. Since Elenx was found to be orthodox in those aspects, the investigation turned to sexual organs and the emission of semen. Elenx was asked if they had presently, at the time of the interrogation, a penis, to which Elenx replied, "The male member that emerged from me has just recently come off in jail, while I was a prisoner. . . . I'd hurt myself while riding horseback and the root of my member became weak. The member became spongy and I went cutting it bit by bit, so that I've come to be without it. It just finished falling off about fifteen days ago, or a little more, as I've said."[58] Elenx was asked about testicles, since some of the previous medical examinations had found Elenx to have had testicles. Elenx replied that they had them in a "particular form" and attempted to clarify through hand gestures, but the Inquisitors did not understand what Elenx meant. Elenx added that had a physician been present, they would understand the "form and way" of their testicles.[59] Elenx was asked if, during relations with their wife and other women, they had experienced "pollution," that is, ejaculation, to which Elenx replied, "Yes, I had pollution and completed the act with them as my husband had completed the act with me. There was abundant pollution."[60]

On the afternoon of July 17, 1587, Elenx was "told that what she [sic] said here regarding the male member was fiction and trickery." Despite Elenx's having presented abundant evidence as to the reality of their "hermaphroditic" status, including the testimony of medical examiners, of scholarly sources, of priests, and of the several women with whom they had had intimate relations, the Inquisition tribunal determined that "she [sic] had never been anything but a woman, which is how she was born and was at present," and that "she" was therefore obligated to "tell how the trickery was accomplished, and the ways in which she fooled the witnesses who testified in her favor."[61]

The fact that the Inquisition found Elenx to be a trickster should be understood in light of the broader cultural focus on illusion and reality in early modern Iberia. One the one hand, the tribunal accepted as a fact that the numerous corroborating accounts of Elenx's gender and sex by witnesses unknown to one another, from uneducated examiners to eminent doctors, from strangers to intimate partners, were the product of large-scale, consistent deception. On the other hand, the tribunal dismissed the claim of "hermaphroditism," even though it was corroborated by scientific sources and numerous precedent cases listed in the relevant literature. The finding that Elenx was deceitful raised the possibility of sorcery. The large scale of the deceit, involving witnesses unknown to one another, over many years, and significant markers such as childbirth and a Catholic wedding, were difficult to explain through human effort alone. A charge of sorcery provided a convenient if controversial answer to the problem of Elenx as a trickster.[62] Elenx was found to be one of those crafty individuals who could shift the fine line that divides deception from reality.[63]

A parallel ambiguity surrounding the reality of Elenx's hermaphrodit-ism bedevils contemporary research on Elenx de Céspedes. Scholars have approached the case with pre-formed notions about what constituted the truth of Elenx's self, including the pivotal question of Elenx's sex. While Elenx themself defended the notion that they had a hermaphroditic nature, some current scholars have doubted that Elenx was, in the terms of their day, a "hermaphrodite" at all. Some have raised the possibility that the "male member" was a fiction, "endorsed by members of the Madrid or Toledo medical communities whom Elena had befriended or bribed, or both."[64] Others have implicitly treated Elenx as a woman, considering them primar-ily a "she."[65] Yet others have described Elenx as a "man caught in a wom-an's body," brandishing Elenx as a proto-transgender fighter for freedom of expression, a precursor to identitarian social movements;[66] or they have seen Elenx as having led a "heterodox" life, which nonetheless can be placed in an anthology about women.[67] For yet others, Elenx ought to be understood within the context of "lesbian erotics."[68]

I would suggest caution, however, before making such pronouncements regarding Elenx's "real" self as man, woman, or transgender individual. To do so would be to follow in the footsteps of the Inquisition itself, which did not accept Elenx's account of "hermaphroditism" as valid. If Elenx was a trick-ster, and hence not what the Inquisition would have termed a "hermaphro-dite," it is difficult to suppose that Elenx would have been inclined to submit to medical examinations or, for that matter, to have sought church sanction for their marriage to María del Caño. To determine or presume Elenx's "real" sex apart from their words is to agree implicitly with the Inquisitorial claim of trickery and to disbelieve Elenx, elevating one account to the realm of reality while necessarily relegating the other to the realm of illusion.[69]

The Persistence of Sodomy

In conclusion, I return to sodomy. In Elenx's case, control of over gender became a proxy for control over sodomy. The Castilian Inquisition had no jurisdiction over sodomy, but as it turns out, its concern with gender polic-ing resulted in other charges with which to impugn Elenx. The Inquisition could have allowed the original charges of sodomy to have worked their way through the secular courts, and Elenx would no doubt have suffered a far worse fate.[70] Some have claimed that this amounts to a measure of "mercy." With respect to all individuals accused of sodomy, even in areas where the Inquisition could and did convict them, it is said that the Inquisition attacked sodomy itself with vigor, but when it came to the treatment of individual sodomites, it showed clemency, imposing hard labor or fines, rather than exile or allowing what they termed "relaxation," that is, extradition to the secular arm for capital punishment, and choosing to announce sentences in private rather than in public.[71] Recalling the motto of the Holy Office, "Justice and Mercy," Luiz Mott writes that the Inquisition judged sodomites with severity but sentenced them with mercy.[72]

We could likewise read the Inquisition's interest in Elenx, and the eventual light penalty applied to their case, as a manifestation of mercy. Elenx's sentence came in the form of corporal punishment and ten years of unpaid labor at a hospital. By claiming jurisdiction over certain aspects of Elenx's case that were clearly within the Inquisitorial purview, such as Elenx's two marriages, the Inquisition elided the more problematic and heavier charges of sodomy and "rescued" Elenx from a secular power willing to burn convicted sodomites.

In my reading, the Inquisitorial interest in the case is a manifestation of an underlying concern with gender expression in the regulation of sodomy. The repression of sodomy depended on a determination of sex. Elenx's case makes it clear that where the Inquisition was not able to prosecute sodomy, it still managed to use the determination of gender as a basis for detention. Recall that Elenx was first arrested for sodomy by secular authorities, and it was only later that the Inquisition stepped in and claimed jurisdiction over the case. If Elenx had presented as unambiguously female, they likely would not have come to the attention or under the jurisdiction of the Castilian Inquisition at all. In order to determine if sodomy had been committed— and therefore who was going to have authority over the case—it was central to assign a particular gender to the accused. Sodomy prosecutions, then, did not occur in a vacuum separate from gender policing. The Inquisitorial interest in Elenx makes this *sine qua non* visible. Where sodomy could not be prosecuted, as was the case for the Castilian Inquisition, gender policing took its place.

It was only because of an accusation of sodomy that Elenx gained attention. There would have been no case without the charge: Elenx could not have been prosecuted merely for their gender expression, as that did not constitute a crime in itself. Sodomy was a crime. Transgressive gender presentation was not; but gender policing becomes necessary for the sake of ferreting out potential sodomites. Elenx's case, then, and perhaps early modern hermaphroditism as a whole, cannot be understood apart from sodomy.

Notes

1. For a cultural reading of hermaphroditism and of legal / medical cases concerning hermaphrodites, see Michel Foucault, *Abnormal: Lectures at the Collège de France,*

1974–1975 (New York: Picador, 2003), 66–74. Foucault's focus is on later periods, but his lecture raises useful metrics for approaching Elenx's case, such as whether a hermaphrodite is a mixture of the sexes or something apart from them, and a switch to viewing hermaphrodites as a "monstrosity of conduct rather than a monstrosity of nature" (73).

2. See primarily the studies by Israel Burshatin: "Written on the Body: Slave or Hermaphrodite in Sixteenth-Century Spain," in *Queer Iberia: Sexualities, Cultures, and Crossings from the Middle Ages to the Renaissance*, ed. Josiah Blackmore and Gregory S. Hutcheson (Durham, NC: Duke University Press, 1999), 420–56; "Elena alias Eleno: Gender, Sexualities, and 'Race' in the Mirror of Natural History in Sixteenth-Century Spain," in *Gender Reversals and Gender Cultures: Anthropological and Historical Perspectives*, ed. Sabrina Petra Ramet (New York: Routledge, 1996), 105–22; "Interrogating Hermaphroditism in Sixteenth-Century Spain," in *Hispanisms and Homosexualities*, ed. Sylvia Molloy and Robert McKee Irwin (Durham, NC: Duke University Press, 1999), 3–18. See also Lisa Vollendorf, *The Lives of Women: A New History of Inquisitorial Spain* (Nashville: Vanderbilt University Press, 2005), 11–31; Guillermo Folch Jou and María del Sagrario Muñoz Calvo, "Un pretendido caso de hermafroditismo en el siglo XVI," *Boletín de la Sociedad Española de Historia de la Farmacia* 93 (1973): 20–33; Marie-Catherine Barbazza, "Un caso de subversión social: El proceso de Elena de Céspedes (1587–1589)," *Criticón* 26 (1984): 17–40. This is a not an exhaustive list.

3. Principally the foundational study by Rafael Carrasco, *Inquisición y represión sexual en Valencia: Historiade los sodomitas (1565–1785)* (Barcelona: Laertes S.A. de Ediciones, 1985); William Monter, *Frontiers of Heresy: The Spanish Inquisition from the Basque Lands to Sicily* (Cambridge: Cambridge University Press, 1990), 276–302; Bartolomé Bennassar, *Inquisición española: Poder político y control social* (Barcelona: Editorial Crítica, 1981), 295–320; Cristian Berco, *Sexual Hierarchies, Public Status: Men, Sodomy, and Society in Spain's Golden Age* (Toronto: University of Toronto Press, 2007); and the sources mentioned in the notes that follow (especially François Soyer, *Ambiguous Gender*). For the Portuguese and Latin American Inquisitorial contexts, see for now Harold Johnson and Francis A. Dutra, *Pelo Vaso Traseiro: Sodomy and Sodomites in Luso-Brazilian History* (Tucson, AZ: Fenestra Books, 2007); Zeb Tortorici, ed., *Sexuality and the Unnatural in Colonial Latin America* (Oakland: University of California Press, 2016); and Zeb Tortorici, *Sins against Nature: Sex and Archives in Colonial New Spain* (Durham, NC: Duke University Press, 2018).

4. Richard Cleminson and Francisco Vázquez García, *Sex, Identity and Hermaphrodites in Iberia, 1500–1800* (London: Pickering & Chatto, 2013), 49–51.

5. Hermaphrodites could be charged with sodomy, but that depended on their clearly being identified with either one sex or the other. Those who displayed characteristics of both sexes in equal measure "should choose one of these and swear before a bishop that they would remain true to this identity in order to ensure their heterosexuality for the rest of their lives." Cleminson and Vázquez García, *Sex, Identity and Hermaphrodites*, 49. Neither of these outcomes took place in Elenx's case.

6. In many cases it is clear that the accused practiced so-called Jewish or Muslim rituals as an ethnic element of their identity rather than out of religious conviction. What complicates this narrative is evidence that some New Christians and Moriscos did continue with at least some Jewish and Muslim religious practices in private while taking on a public Christian persona, a sort of religious "closet." See L. P. Harvey,

Muslims in Spain: 1500 to 1614 (Chicago: University of Chicago Press, 2005); David M. Gitlitz, *Secrecy and Deceit: The Religion of the Crypto-Jews* (Albuquerque: University of New Mexico Press, 1996); and António José Saraiva, *The Marrano Factory: The Portuguese Inquisition and Its New Christians, 1536–1765* (Leiden: Brill, 2001).

7. The status of "Old Christian" was a fluid rather than a fixed category. Genealogies could be falsified or fabricated. Certificates attesting to "purity of blood," that is, untainted by Muslim or Jewish blood, were required for entry into important institutions such as universities, military orders, and the Inquisition itself. But those certificates could be bought, and one institution might not accept the certificate issued by another. This instability is part of the overall early modern Spanish phenomenon of confusion between reality and illusion, what is real and what is not. See the section of this chapter titled "The Reality of Gender" and María Elena Martínez, *Limpieza de Sangre, Religion, and Gender in Colonial Mexico* (Stanford, CA: Stanford University Press, 2008). Elenx harnessed these categories to their own defense, claiming paradoxically that their mother was of "Old Christian" blood, allowing only that she was "probably a Gentile." In fact Elenx's mother had been either Muslim or Morisca. Elenx also admits their mother had been both a "slave and black" (all these categories are incompatible with the notion of "Old Christian"). Elenx then goes on to describe themself as an "Old Christian." The Inquisition always interrogated the accused about their genealogy, and Elenx knew that any trace of Jewish or Muslim ancestry would be seen negatively.

8. Traditional scholarship on the Inquisition has painted it as a major instrument of social control. This thesis was questioned by Henry Kamen in *The Spanish Inquisition: A Historical Revision*, 4th ed. (New Haven, CT: Yale University Press, 2014).

9. See the relevant passage of the seventh *partida* in John Boswell, *Christianity, Social Tolerance, and Homosexuality* (Chicago: University of Chicago Press, 1980), 289.

10. Federico Garza Carvajal, *Butterflies Will Burn: Prosecuting Sodomites in Early Modern Spain and Mexico* (Austin: University of Texas Press, 2003), 42.

11. The idea that the Inquisition, whose purpose was to stamp out heresy, should also have jurisdiction over sodomy, which is, strictly speaking, not a sin of heresy, was controversial. While the Inquisition in Aragón was given jurisdiction over the crime by Pope Clement VII, "irrespective of the presence of heresy," Inquisitorial involvement in what was an unspeakable offense was thought to bring shame to the institution itself. Thus the head court of the Inquisition in Spain (the Suprema) warned the Barcelona office, which had begun to prosecute sodomites, that Inquisitorial prosecution of such crimes would lead to "loss of reputation, since this is not a business that concerns you," and it enjoined the Barcelona office to turn sodomites over to the secular authorities for punishment. Hence the theological arguments identifying sodomy with heresy played an important role in buttressing the jurisdiction of the Inquisition over sodomy. Kamen, *Spanish Inquisition*, 289; Monter, *Frontiers*, 278.

12. Fernanda Molina, "La herejización de la sodomia en la sociedad moderna: Consideraciones teológicas y praxis inquisitorial," *Hispania Sacra* 62.126 (2010): 539–62. See also François Soyer, *Ambiguous Gender in Early Modern Spain and Portugal: Inquisitors, Doctors, and the Transgression of Gender Norms* (Leiden: Brill, 2012), 33–34.

13. Garza Carvajal, *Butterflies Will Burn*, 52.

14. Ibid., 53–54.

15. Soyer writes that heterosexual anal intercourse was practiced as a means of birth control or as a result of sexual preference, but married women arrested for such an offense, as well as prostitutes, would often claim that they had submitted unwillingly. Soyer, *Ambiguous Gender*, 47.

16. Soyer, *Ambiguous Gender*, 32–33; see also Luiz Mott, "Justitia et Misericórdia: The Portuguese Inquisition and Repression of the Nefarious Sin of Sodomy," in Johnson and Dutra, *Pelo Vaso Traseiro*, 68–69.

17. To date, Inquisitorial archives have yielded no cases of the death penalty as a response to lesbian sexual activity, even with the use of an instrument. The best-known case of sodomy between women with an instrument is that of Catalina Ledesmo and Inés de Santa Cruz, studied by Federico Garza Carvajal in *Las cañitas: Un proceso por lesbianismo a principios del XVII* (Palencia: Simancas Ediciones, 2012).

18. As Cleminson and García put it, "As it was believed that the semen that was spent in these cases did not have any consequences for procreation, divine creation was not undermined and the disorder caused was far less important than was supposed by similar male activity." Cleminson and García, *Sex, Identity and Hermaphrodites*, 51. Elenx was questioned by the Inquisition on this issue and reported "abundant pollution" in their relations with women (see the discussion that follows in the text).

19. Mark Jordan, *The Invention of Sodomy in Christian Theology* (Chicago: University of Chicago Press, 1997), 103–7.

20. At the end of their trial Elenx was sentenced to two hundred lashes, to be administered in public, but I disagree with Marie-Catherine Barbazza that the Inquisition was concerned with applying "public and exemplary punishment that would reach the largest possible number of people." A far more public punishment would ensue if it had handed Elenx back to the secular authorities with a recommendation for a public burning. As for the second part of their punishment, Elenx was also sentenced by the Inquisition to serve for ten years without pay as a surgeon at a hospital, where they became famous and sought after as a miracle worker. As Barbazza notes, the publicity worked in Elenx's favor rather than against them. The hospital sentence, however, was not meant to ensure publicity for the case; it was an undesirable consequence. The hospital's director complained to the Inquisition when too many patients came searching for treatment by Elenx, and the Inquisition then had Elenx transferred to another hospital, which arguably is evidence that the Inquisition did not wish Elenx to be a public figure. Barbazza, "Un caso de subversión," 38.

21. Richard Kagan and Abigail Dyer, ed. and trans., *Inquisitorial Inquiries: Brief Lives of Secret Jews and Other Heretics* (Baltimore: Johns Hopkins University Press, 2011), 81. Kagan and Dyer's volume contains an abridged transcript of Elenx's trial (64–87). Elenx's trial transcript is over 150 folios long and has yet to be published in full. The original is in *legajo* 234, *expediente* 24, Sección Inquisición, Archivo Histórico Nacional, Madrid.

22. Federico Garza Carvajal points out that while many early modern Spanish moralists acknowledged that both men and women could commit sodomy, they deemed sodomy between women "inauthentic, imperfect, devoid of scattered or wasted semen," which reinforces my earlier point on the proper use of semen as the locus of control over sodomy. Garza Carvajal, *Butterflies Will Burn*, 56.

23. Elenx is sometimes called Eleno, and sometimes Elena, in the transcript of their Inquisitorial trial. There is a more consistent switch to Elena in the transcript once the authorities decide on the gender of the prisoner. Elenx's name was in flux throughout their life. As a teenager they called themself Elena in honor of their former master's wife. At the time of their arrest, Elenx was using the name Eleno, under which they had married María del Caño. When telling their life narrative to the Inquisitorial authorities, Elenx testified that one of the names they took initially was Céspedes (their last name), but, Elenx specified further, "without saying Pedro, Eleno, or Juan" (which in Spanish are male-identified names). Elenx said they went by Céspedes again when they became a soldier ("calling myself only Céspedes"). Elenx's strategy of naming, specifically in devising a nonbinary name, is early evidence of a trend that would become more visible only centuries later. The Inquisition also had Elenx moved from the men's side of the prison, where they had been initially placed, to the women's side, while their then-wife, María del Caño, was moved to a separate room in the women's section. In Israel Burshatin's interpretation, "the prisoners['] relocation captures the vehemence—as well as the futility—of official attempts to peg Eleno's protean genders according to the ruling model of dimorphic sex and gender." Kagan and Dyer, *Inquisitorial Inquiries* 69; Burshatin, "Elena alias Eleno," 106.

24. Kagan and Dyer, *Inquisitorial Inquiries*, 82.

25. Unlike modern autobiographies, early modern autobiographies do not necessarily entail a presumption of truth. This is even more so for prisoners of the Inquisition, who were more interested in saving their own property and lives than in an attachment to facts. James Amelang, *The Flight of Icarus: Artisan Autobiography in Early Modern Europe* (Palo Alto, CA: Stanford University Press, 1998); Kagan and Dyer, *Inquisitorial Inquiries*, 4, 6.

26. Kagan and Dyer, *Inquisitorial Inquiries*, 71. It's unclear why Elenx thought that viewing their genitals from the back would reveal that they were female.

27. Ibid., 72.

28. Ibid.

29. Ibid., 73

30. Emilio Maganto Pavón, "La intervención del Dr. Francisco Díaz en el proceso inquisitorial contra Elena/o de Céspedes, une cirujana transexual condenada por la Inquisición de Toledo en 1587," *Archivos Españoles de Urología* 60.8 (2007): 873–86.

31. Kagan and Dyer, *Inquisitorial Inquiries*, 73. Elenx served as a soldier in the rebellion, presenting as male.

32. Ibid., 74

33. It is also possible that Elenx answered the sodomy question with a more immediate goal in mind—to escape potential punishment or torture by the tribunal—not to give a statement that reflected the truth of their experience. Nevertheless, Elenx's account to the Inquisition as a whole is extremely detailed and cites a number of learned sources on hermaphroditism, which suggests that their testimony was the fruit of much thought and reflection, and matched the truth to some degree.

34. Ibid., emphasis added.

35. Among ancient and early modern scholarly sources on hermaphroditism, some of which were known to Elenx, the example of a sex change was almost

invariably that of a woman becoming a man (that is, growing a penis), and much more rarely that of a man becoming a woman (growing a vagina). See, e.g., Pliny, *Natural History* 7.3; Jacques Duval, *Traité des hermaphrodits* (Rouen, 1612), 322.

36. Elenx's conception of their sexuality recalls Judith Butler's heterosexual matrix and Adrienne Rich's compulsory heterosexuality. Judith Butler, *Gender Trouble: Feminism and the Subversion of Identity* (New York: Routledge, 1990); Adrienne Rich, "Compulsory Heterosexuality and Lesbian Existence," *Signs* 5.4 (1980): 631–60.

37. At the margin of the text here the Inquisitor wrote, "Cicero, Pliny, and Augustine." Kagan and Dyer, *Inquisitorial Inquiries*, 74.

38. Ibid., 74–75, emphasis added.

39. Elenx did have a vagina, but as they reported regarding the second medical examination, it narrowed and became a hard knot.

40. In Aristotle's view, nature "acts for something," and that something is the best (or most ideal) outcome for the individual. Biological changes such as Elenx's physical changes after childbirth, and the desires that follow from those changes, could be understood to be as morally neutral as the fact that nature causes front teeth to grow "sharp and suitable for biting" and that back teeth function better for chewing. In other words, instead of seeing hermaphroditism as an aberration of nature or otherwise outside nature, as it was generally considered in early modern Spain, Elenx preferred to interpret these biological-psychological changes simply as the normal manifestation of their individual constitution. Aristotle, *Physics* 2.8.198b, in *A New Aristotle Reader*, ed. J. L. Ackrill (Princeton, NJ: Princeton University Press, 1987), 106–7.

41. On the one-sex model, see Thomas Laqueur, *Making Sex: Body and Gender from the Greeks to Freud* (Cambridge, MA: Harvard University Press, 1990), 63–113.

42. Soyer, *Ambiguous Gender*, 53.

43. Loraine Daston and Katharine Park, "The Hermaphrodite and the Orders of Nature: Sexual Ambiguity in Early Modern France," *GLQ* 1 (1995): 419–38, examines how hermaphrodites fit (and don't fit) into the socially constructed category of "natural."

44. Ibid. Among the works that focused on hermaphroditism as a subject in its own right, and alongside other monstrous and supernatural phenomena, I should emphasize the manual by Antonio de Torquemada, *Jardin de flores curiosas* (1570), which gained a broad audience and was placed in the Inquisitorial index of forbidden books in Spain in 1632.

45. Pliny, *Natural History*, 7.3; Burshatin, "Written on the Body," 447.

46. Neither the Spanish nor the Portuguese Inquisition typically pursued charges of witchcraft and sorcery. With the exception of the Basque witch hunts of 1609–1611, witch hunts in Spain never took on the dimensions found in other European countries at the same time. See Brian Levack, *The Witch-Hunt in Early Modern Europe*, 4th ed. (New York: Routledge, 2015), 113. The Inquisitorial reluctance to become involved with such cases makes the verdict against Elenx for sorcery seem all the more suspicious.

47. One of those examinations was conducted by none other than King Phillip II's own personal surgeon, Dr. Francisco Díaz, who also wrote the first-ever treatise in the field of urology. He retracted his assignation of Elenx as male after the Inquisitorial examination assigned Elenx as female. It has been claimed that Elenx "deceived" Dr. Díaz, although it is hard to believe that the preeminent authority on

urology in early modern Spain (perhaps in all of Europe) could be so easily fooled. See Maganto Pavón, "La intervención," 874. See also Burshatin, "Interrogating Hermaphroditism," 16, on the significance of Elenx's assignation as male.

48. María Elena Martínez, *Genealogical Fictions: Limpieza de Sangre, Religion, and Gender in Colonial Mexico* (Stanford, CA: Stanford University Press, 2008), 76.

49. As Elma Dassbach puts it, "Baroque society is comfortable in a world of reality and appearance, which disturbs the contemporary society that is always pursuing certainty. For the seventeenth-century man, the answer to all inexplicable phenomena was simpler: it was either magic or miracle. The truth was not that important because, as Don Quixote reminded, everything seems to be the work of enchanters." Elma Dassbach, "Las artes mágicas y los sucesos milagrosos en las comedias de santos," *Hispania* 82.3 (1999): 433.

50. The *pícaro* is a literary figure, generally an orphan, low-born and self-sufficient, whose activities are often criminal, and who taken on a variety of disguises in order to "move up in the world through any means possible." Always on the move, either by necessity or by choice, the *pícaro* is solitary and "devoted to none other than himself or herself." Christina H. Lee, *The Anxiety of Sameness in Early Modern Spain* (Manchester: Manchester University Press, 2016), 56–57. See also Burshatin, "Written on the Body," 422.

51. *Burlar* is one of the reprehensible strategies employed by *pícaros* to deceive or trick others so as to "move up in the world." *Burlar*, however, also had a more specific sense of "gender deviation as well as a man taking sexual advantage of a woman." The latter meaning is clear from the well-known literary figure Don Juan, the main character in Tirso de Molina's play *El burlador de Sevilla*, whom Elizabeth Rhodes interprets as embodying femininity as well as masculinity. *Burlador(a)*, then, essentializes the *pícaro* as a gender deviant. *Burlar* can refer "specifically to the performance of a gender in defiance of one's biological identity, or a refusal to limit oneself to the performance of the Male or the Female." Elizabeth Rhodes, "Gender and the Monstrous in 'El burlador de Sevilla,'" *MLN* 117.2 (2002): 275–76.

52. On the tension between gender as reality or illusion in the theater of the Spanish Golden Age, see the editors' introduction to *Gender, Identity, and Representation in Spain's Golden Age*, ed. Anita K. Stoll and Dawn L. Smith (Lewisburg, PA: Bucknell University Press, 2000), 9–22. On the perception of the hermaphrodite as miracle workers, "an individual equipped with redemptory and fantastic powers," see Cleminson and Vázquez García, *Sex, Identity and Hermaphrodites*, 51.

53. For the purposes of proving "pure" blood (that is, untainted by Jewish or Muslim ancestry), a requirement for admission, official genealogy certificates were offered by important institutional bodies in Spain: universities, some military orders, and the Inquisition itself. Such certificates add to the insecurity over what is real and what is illusory: they could be manipulated through bribery or fabricated; and a certificate from one institution was not necessarily acceptable at another. Thus an individual could be considered an Old Christian for a university but a Jew for a military order. Hence, rather than defining one's ethnic/social status, the blood purity certificate augmented the lack of clarity over one's "real" origins. See Martínez, *Genealogical Fictions*, 70–84.

54. Elizabeth A. Lehfeldt, "Ideal Men: Masculinity and Decline in Seventeenth-Century Spain," *Renaissance Quarterly* 61.2 (2008): 464, 466; Dian Fox, *Hercules and the*

King of Portugal: Icons of Masculinity and Nation in Calderón's Spain (Lincoln: University of Nebraska Press, 2019), 12. See also Mar Martínez-Góngora, *El hombre atemperado: Autocontrol, disciplina y masculinidad en textos españoles de la temprana modernidad* (New York: Peter Lang, 2005). Pointing to works such as *The Education of a Christian Woman* (1523) and *The Perfect Wife* (1583), which promoted a "rigid definition of the roles of men and women in society," François Soyer explains that "in spite of such widespread gender stereotypes, or perhaps because of them, many individuals did find themselves transgressing gender roles." Soyer, *Ambiguous Gender*, 17–18

55. Garza Carvajal, *Butterflies Will Burn*, 45.

56. This view of Spanish masculinity helps to explain why Elenx defines themself to the Inquisition as an "Old Christian" even though they were of mixed Morisco-Christian parentage, and it sheds light on Elenx's choice to become a soldier at one point in their life.

57. Aurelia Martín Casares and Magdalena Díaz Hernández, "Nuevas reflexiones sobre 'Elena, alias Eleno de Céspedes,' transgénero, redes sociales y libertad en la España del siglo XVI," *Bulletin for Spanish and Portuguese Historical Studies* 41.1 (2016): 28 ("Céspedes did not reject norms, turning instead to constructing a zone of autonomy within them").

58. Kagan and Dyer, *Inquisitorial Inquiries*, 77.

59. Elenx may have been suggesting that the testicles were internal rather than external. Ibid., 77n31.

60. Ibid., 78.

61. Ibid.

62. Whether sorcery and witchcraft were "real" or imaginary phenomena divided scholars throughout Europe, and the Inquisition tended to discount their reality. For a clear analysis of the issue, see Levack, *Witch-Hunt*, 12–19.

63. Late on the day when Elenx told their life narrative to the Inquisition, the Holy Office, according to its transcript, "once again accused the aforesaid Elena de Céspedes of having made and continuing to hold a tacit or explicit pact with the devil, since she was a woman and had always been, without its being possible to naturally have the virile member without the favor and help of the devil" (tornó a acusar a la dicha Elena de Céspedes de haber tenido y tener pacto tácito o expreso con el demonio, porque siendo como era mujer y habiéndolo sido siempre sin ser possible naturalmente haber tenido miembro viril con favor y ayuda del demonio). Ignacio Ruiz Rodríguez and Alexander Hernández Delgado, *Elena o Eleno de Céspedes: Un hombre atrapado en el cuerpo de una mujer, en la España de Felipe II* (Madrid: Editorial Dykinson, 2017), 243. The volume by Rodríguez and Delgado contains excerpts of the trial omitted from Kagan and Dyer's abridged version. See also Cleminson and Vázquez García (*Sex, Identity and Hermaphrodites*, 46), who argue that "the only way to understand Céspedes is to appreciate her within a context that was not dominated by this binary model [of sex and gender], and instead to place her in a world that was wrought by tensions between the flexibility of magical natural representations (*mirabilia*) and rigid social and reproductive imperatives (*magicus*).

64. Kagan and Dyer, *Inquisitorial Inquiries*, 71n21.

65. Barbazza, "Un caso de subversión."

66. Rodríguez and Delgado, *Elena o Eleno de Céspedes*, 34–35, 255.

67. Vicenta Maria Márquez de la Plata y Ferrándiz, *Mujeres pensadoras: Místicas, científicas y heterodoxas* (Madrid: Editorial Castalia, 2008), 357.

68. Sherry Velasco, "Interracial Lesbian Erotics in Early Modern Spain: Catalina de Erauso and Elena/o de Céspedes," in *Tortilleras: Hispanic and U.S. Latina Lesbian Expression*, ed. Lourdes Torres and Inmaculada Pertusa (Philadelphia: Temple University Press, 2003), 213–27.

69. Thus Cleminson and Vázquez García affirm all elements of Elenx's narrative and refuse to place Elenx squarely in any one category, as they describe Elenx as "a woman, a hermaphrodite, a man, a wife, a husband" (*Sex, Identity and Hermaphrodites*, 47).

70. Kagan and Dyer, *Inquisitorial Inquiries*, 82.

71. Monter, *Frontiers*, 298–99. I do not agree, however, with Monter's conclusion that the Inquisitors used such pity and mercy that we can designate the Inquisition a "precursor of Gay Liberation."

72. Mott argues that from our point of view, sodomites would routinely receive sentences that were harsher than warranted by their transgressions, so the commutation of a sentence eventually amounted to something more just. From the point of view of the accused, the commutation of sentences also served to "lessen the hatred and possible desire for vengeance against the inquisitors," thereby reducing the "reaction of the most insubmissive victims." Mott, *Justitia et Misericordia*, 96–97. For a contrary view, see Carrasco, *Inquisición y represión*, 65, who rules out any aspect of mercy.

CHAPTER 3

The Case of Marin le Marcis

Kathleen Perry Long

In 1601, a young man wearing the clothing of a woman came to present a request to the local deacon in the town of Monstiervillier, France. He did this at the urging of the woman he had promised to marry, and on the advice of two future in-laws with some standing in the community. Born a Catholic, baptized a girl, converted to Protestantism, and having realized that he was a man, Marin le Marcis requested to be re-baptized as a Catholic man. His fiancée, Jeanne le Febvre, a widow who had been raised a Protestant, also requested to be baptized a Catholic, and supported her future husband's request. Marin dressed in men's clothing to carry the deacon's letters concerning this case to the penitentiary of Rouen, who sent him back with a reply. Upon his return to Monstiervillier, Marin, along with Jeanne, was arrested, and they were both put on trial for sodomy.[1]

Marin and Jeanne both testified. Marin was then examined twice, first by two surgeons and then by a doctor (*médecin*, or practicing physician, as opposed to a *docteur*, or professor of medicine), an apothecary, and two surgeons. They found no sign of "virility" in him ("aucune marque ou signe de virilité").[2] His former masters, for whom he had served as a chambermaid, testified that while he was in their service, he presented only appearances and behaviors that were feminine. Marin was sentenced to be burned alive, and Jeanne to be flogged in public over the course of three days. Marin's sentence was then reduced to hanging, his body to be burned only after he was dead, and Jeanne's was reduced to being flogged only once.[3]

Marin appealed the death sentence, thus bringing the case to the Parliament of Rouen. According to Jacques Duval's account, the most experienced doctors, surgeons, and midwives were called upon to examine Marin; six doctors, two surgeons, and two licensed midwives assembled for the examination. All but one of them simply observed Marin's body from a distance. Duval, one of the doctors, was the only medical expert in this group who performed a clinical examination of his body, finding functional male genitalia, and thus establishing that Marin had the potential reproductive capacity of a man. After sharing this finding and making an argument about how Marin's circumstances affected his body, Duval managed to persuade the court to have yet another examination performed. One of the two doctors called to do this agreed with Duval's conclusion, and the court set Marin free, declaring, however, that he must wear women's clothing for the next four years, until he was twenty-five (the age of majority, when one could marry without parental consent),[4] and not live with anyone of either sex.[5] Duval asserts in his preface that this "womanly man [*gunanthrope*] is at present in a better manly state than he was before, and that, under the name of du Marcis the younger, he practices the profession of tailor, undertakes, does, and completes all activities appropriate to a man, wears a beard on his chin, and has that which is necessary to content a woman so that he might engender in her."[6] He had sought this information on Marin as he was preparing his work for publication ten years after the trial.

This version of the case of Marin le Marcis is not one that is familiar to modern readers of Michel Foucault, who dedicates several pages to it in his lectures on the abnormal;[7] rather, this is how the story is told by Duval in his treatise *On Hermaphrodites, Women's Labor in Childbirth, and the Treatment That Is Required to Lift Them Up Again in Good Health and Raise Their Children Well* (*Des hermaphrodits, accouchemens des femmes et traitement qui est requis pour les relever en santé et bien élever leurs enfans*), published in 1612. This version includes a summary of Marin's own testimony. For a number of years, this version was the subject of a heated published debate concerning the existence of "hermaphrodites" between Duval and Jean Riolan, a member of the medical faculty at the University of Paris. This debate reveals the complex interactions between the rising emphasis on empirical science in medicine and the persistence of more traditional forms of medical practice, based in France on Aristotelian philosophy, interactions that reflect the changing nature of medical authority in this period. Riolan vehemently denies the existence of "hermaphrodites" in his assessment of this case,[8] and Duval responds, defending his view that they do in fact exist.[9] This sustained confrontation kept questions concerning natural variation in bodies and the use of certain categories to classify those bodies—male/female, natural/monstrous—in the mind of the reading public.[10] This debate also offers some insight into the complications that ensue relative to early modern theories of gender when they are deployed to explain intersex individuals while insistently maintaining male and female as the sole definitional categories.

Furthermore, Duval's treatise on "hermaphrodites" is part of a larger body of material that calls into question the distinction between what we call "biological sex" and what we call "binary gender." Recent research on the genetics of sex difference suggests that there may be a significant number of variations on what we have sorted into male and female, because a range of mutations can affect the relatively limited number of genes that dictate development of various parts of the body into what we call male or female.[11] This falls in line with what some early modern and modern (nineteenth-century) theorists of *sexe* (which comprises both what we think of as biological sex and what we think of as gender) seem to convey: even as they try to categorize bodies into male and female (and perhaps because they try), they see a significant number of variations of body types that raise questions about those two categories being (a) distinct and (b) adequate to describe the natural variations in humanity relative to what is really gender rather than sex, since it is a cultural imposition that constrains bodies into types that they do not actually fit into. What is being suggested in the work of Ambroise Paré, Duval, and even Isidore Geoffroy Saint-Hilaire (a nineteenth-century teratologist who tries to taxonomize *sexe* to no avail) is precisely that bodies do not all map onto male and female, or even male, female, and another gender in between these two. Duval makes this idea very clear in his contextualization of the case of Marin le Marcis, and thus adds the notion of quasi-infinite variations on *sexe* to his discussions of Marin as a transgender man.

As Cathy McClive points out in her article "Masculinity on Trial," in early modern France, the trials of Marin le Marcis represent the first of a handful of well-documented cases concerning intersex individuals undertaken for the purpose of legally defining their gender.[12] While Pierre de L'Estoile mentions an earlier case, that of an individual named Daniel who seems to have been intersex, there are no judicial or medical records concerning this person.[13] As for the case of Antide Collas, cited by Foucault in his lectures as an example of someone executed for having a body that did not conform to gender norms, Sophie Duong-Iseler has shown that legal records concerning this case confirm a condemnation for sorcery, not for "hermaphrodism." Rather than having an intersex physiology, Collas was executed in 1599 for having a "devil's mark," a scar that was believed to prove his pact with Satan.[14] There is another trial alluded to in late eighteenth-century collections of judicial records as having taken place in 1603, in which a young male "hermaphrodite" is condemned for sodomy, but documentation contemporary to the case itself is not cited in any scholarship.[15] Later cases involving the determination of gender include those of Marguerite Malaure, tried in 1686 and again in 1691,[16] and Anne Grandjean, tried in 1765, whose case is discussed by Foucault as well.[17] Thus Marin le Marcis's case stands alone at the beginning of the seventeenth century in France as a carefully documented legal and medical determination of gender in an individual who was most likely intersex, but who in his day was eventually understood to have undergone a gender transformation.

Duval's version of this case emphasizes several elements that merit further analysis. First, the individual in question, Marin le Marcis, has agency and is supported in his choices by those closest to him: he is the one who seeks to change his gender status by means of official recognition by the Catholic Church. He has the support of his future wife's relatives to do this. Faced with official condemnation of his actions and imminent execution, he appeals the decision. Jeanne, her relatives, and his own parents, who know his situation best, do not respond to him as a monster. Duval refuses to present him as such, but insists on framing his account with a detailed portrait of Marin and his behavior, both presented as quite natural.[18] This is in sharp contrast to both Foucault, who lists "Marie" le Marcis among his monsters, and Stephen Greenblatt, who calls the le Marcis case "a cheerfully grotesque story."[19]

Second, Duval respects the individual's chosen gender in this account, always using "il" to designate le Marcis, and using his chosen name, Marin, except when he discusses the young man's first baptism and early childhood, when he was thought to be a girl. This insistence on the chosen gender and name is in contrast to much of the modern scholarship on the case, which, in keeping with Foucault's and Greenblatt's accounts, uses the feminine pronoun and the name Marie more often than not. Duval's choice of language may have been strategic, as he aimed to prove that Marin was a man in order to save him from hanging.

Related to this strategic use of language in the presentation of the le Marcis case is the fact that both the defendant and Duval use established medical discourses concerning gender designation in order to legitimize Marin's choice. Duval in particular cites a full range of authors, classical and contemporary to him, and in particular uses Paré's discussions of "hermaphrodites" and women who "degenerate into men" as precedents. He uses these precedents to justify

Marin's gender transformation while maintaining his place in the two-gender system that governs French language, society, politics, and medicine.

Perhaps most important for the purposes of this essay, Duval performs an exploration of the conceptual relationship between gender mobility and gender diversity, and between what we would call transgender and intersex. In this process, he describes a feedback loop between the sexed body and its environment, suggesting that the body itself can be transformed by a number of factors from one gender to another. This in turn naturalizes gender transformation by revealing it as a process that is continually present, potentially in all humans. If the environment shapes the body in this way, the notion of what we sometimes call biological sex becomes complicated. This presentation of gender as a state of being subject to change is set within the context of what we might think of as biological sex, here offered as the most prominent example of the impossibility of adequately taxonomizing natural variation. For in Duval's account, bodily presentations do not map onto the categories of male and female but trouble them, with the potential for infinite variations of diversity in sexed bodies.[20] While we think of there being a lot of possibilities for social gender, historically and today, we don't always imagine there to be a plurality of possibilities in the premodern period for what some people now term "biological sex." The case of Marin, however, provides stark evidence to the contrary.

If bodies must be made intelligible under the regime of binary gender, as Judith Butler suggests ("Gender likewise figures as a precondition for the production and maintenance of legible humanity"),[21] then intersex bodies remain illegible until interpreted in a manner that does not acknowledge their complexity. Since Marin's case is a matter of life and death, Duval must carefully inscribe him within this system. But he reveals the tension between this system and the reality of Marin's body by means of a careful rhetorical balancing act that allows for both natural variation and the gender binary of male and female used to organize or contain this variation.

Early modern science recognized that a wide expanse of divergent bodily types could be included in the realm of the "natural," including bodies that do not fit into masculine or feminine "types." The original meaning of the word *genre* in French is "types," but *genre* was also used in the early modern period in relation to the categories we would designate as gender. Early modern anatomical science also recognized the possibility of a broader understanding of *sexe* (a term that encompasses the two concepts of sex and gender). Duval suggests the possibility of infinite variations on intersex, as well as of men and women; this proliferation of *sexes* reveals the inadequacy of the concepts of male and female to account for bodily experience.

Some warnings must be given about considering gender in a French context, particularly an early modern one. McClive points out in her article on early modern discussions of masculinity in cases brought against "hermaphrodites" that the "French term 'sexe' designates biological sex, gender, and the male and female members."[22] This usage reflects an awareness of the complex interplay between the biological and the cultural/environmental. Also, gender might seem less tethered to bodies and sexuality in French than it is in English, since masculine or feminine gender designations are used for all things, whether they are concrete objects or abstract concepts. But this all-encompassing nature of binary gender as a grammatical mode of categorization also makes it inescapable; everything must be either masculine or feminine. Some early modern authors imagined a world that complicates such gender division. For example, a satirical novel, *The Island of Hermaphrodites* (*L'isle des hermaphrodites*, published in 1605), describes an imaginary language that uses what is known as "common gender," a form of noun in the Latin language that is both masculine and feminine.[23] The inescapability of the categories of masculine and feminine in French grammar is reflected in the constant reference to masculine and feminine as the options for categorizing all bodies, even those described as intersex, in medical and anatomical treatises. This fact distinguishes early modern French theories of gender from those of the Anglophone world. There is some evidence that by the end of the sixteenth century, the concept of grammatical gender is associated with categorization of humans by gender.[24]

This essay focuses largely on the language Duval uses to discuss Marin's case in the context of a well-known precedent both for the case and for Duval's theories concerning it: Ambroise Paré's work *On Monsters and Marvels*. This language deploys the rhetoric of authority in order to justify the young man's request to have his chosen gender officially recognized while offering a precise, and potentially scandalous,[25] description of a body that defies the traditional categories of male and female. By this means, Duval maintains Marin's place in French society, dominated as it is by a two-gender system, even while raising questions about the viability of gender as a means of categorizing humans.

Early Modern Gender Theory: Ambroise Paré

The master barber-surgeon Ambroise Paré serves as Duval's primary model for negotiating institutional discourses, legal and medical, concerning *sexe*. Although he was the surgeon to four French kings, Henri II (1547–1559), François II (1559–1560), Charles IX (1560–1574), and Henri III (1574–1589),[26] he was not a member of the Faculty of Medicine at the University of Paris, and he met with strong opposition by this institution, which attempted to suppress publication of his collected works. What angered the Faculty of Medicine was that Paré, a mere surgeon, had composed and published the most comprehensive medical manual in French of his time, having already published numerous works on a range of subjects.[27] Paré combined knowledge based on classical and contemporary authors with his own experience as a field surgeon and a practitioner in the public hospital (l'Hôtel-Dieu), as well as his royal duties.[28] French versions of his collected works were published six times between 1575 and 1607, and at least another five times after that, until 1652;[29] his publication record, combined with his mentoring of prominent surgeons such as Jacques Guillemeau (who translated his works into Latin), kept his work circulating widely throughout the early modern period. The conflicts with the Faculty of Medicine at the University of Paris over the 1575 edition of his works only further publicized them, giving him the reputation of someone who had taken on the medical authorities of his day in the name of experience-based medical practices.[30] Thus Paré took on a dual identity as a revolutionary clinical practitioner and a medical authority figure; this mixed identity informs his discussions of the categories of "male" and "female" and the bodies that call those categories into question in his treatise *On Monsters and Marvels*. In this treatise, as well as in his works more generally, Paré gathers material from a wide range of existing sources but generally also offers his own interpretation of particular cases and questions.

Paré's chapters in the treatise "On Hermaphrodites or Androgynes, That Is to Say, Which Have Two Sets of Sex Organs in One Body" and of "Memorable Stories about Women Who Have Degenerated into Men," the sixth and seventh chapters of *On Monsters and Marvels* (*Des monstres et prodiges*) in the 1585 edition of his works, serve as significant models for the purposes of Duval's defense of Marin le Marcis. The association of these two chapters in Paré's work provides Duval with a means of gendering the intersex body, creating a narrative that echoes accepted modes of gender variation and transformation. In France during the early modern period, there was a clear tension between the knowledge acquired from clinical observations of bodies and the demands of legal and social systems. Ambroise Paré, in the sixth chapter of his treatise *On Monsters and Marvels*, focuses on the legal necessity of clear gender designation: "Male and female hermaphrodites are those who have both sets of sexual organs well-formed, and they can help and be used in reproduction; and both the ancient and modern laws have obliged and still oblige these latter to choose which sex organs they wish to use, and they are forbidden on pain of death to use any but those they will have chosen, on account of the misfortunes that could result from such."[31] The traits or signs used to read bodies as male or female and thus render them legible to a culture that demanded these categories be imposed on all bodies (and all things) are not limited to genitalia or even to physical presentations. Paré recognizes four different kinds of "hermaphrodites," predominantly male, predominantly female, neuter, and double, yet all of these must be assigned a gender, male or female. Still, Paré does allow for an intersex individual who cannot be classified as male or female: "And if the hermaphrodite is as much like one as another, he will be called a hermaphrodite, or a 'man-and-woman.'"[32] He leaves unclear what the status of this person would be relative to the law.

Early modern doctors or surgeons asked to pronounce upon the gender of a person often refused to perform clinical exams or view that person's unclothed body; this was evidently an issue in the case of Marin le Marcis. Under these circumstances, the most immediately visible or audible signs were used to determine gender. Paré combines the physiological with the behavioral in his advice to doctors and surgeons trying to establish the gender of an intersex individual:

> The most expert and well-informed physicians and surgeons can recognize whether hermaphrodites are more apt at performing with and using one set of organs than another, or both, or none at all. And such a thing will be recognized by the genitalia, to wit, whether the female sex organ is of proper dimensions to receive the male rod [penis] and whether the menstrues flow through it; similarly, by the face and by the hair, whether it is fine or coarse; whether the speech is virile or shrill; whether the teats are like those of men or of women; similarly whether the whole disposition of the body is robust or effeminate; whether they are bold or fearful, and other actions like those of males and females. And as for the genitalia which belong to a man, one must examine to see whether there is a good deal of body hair on the groin and around the seat, for commonly and almost always women have none on the seat. Similarly, one must examine carefully to see whether the male rod is well-proportioned in thickness and length, and whether it can become erect, and whether seed issues from it, [all of] which will be done through the confession of the hermaphrodite, when he will have kept company with a woman.[33]

As we shall see, Duval echoes a number of these traits, the descriptions not only of genitalia but also of hair on the head and on the body, of the voice, and body strength. Paré's inclusion of the perspective and the voice of the individual whose gender is in question in the phrase "which will be done through the confession of the hermaphrodite" also informs Duval's summary of Marin le Marcis's testimony. In echoing Paré fairly closely at some moments, Duval is using a discourse generated by someone who had, by 1612, become a recognized and regularly cited authority on the matter of both intersex and transgender. Both Paré's authority and the familiarity of this discourse concerning gender lend credibility to Duval's and Marin le Marcis's narrative.

Paré's description of women who become men gives a glimpse of social responses to transgender individuals in the early modern period. (For the purposes of this essay, I am referring to individuals like Marin as "transgender.") In the chapter "Memorable Stories about Women Who Have Degenerated into Men," Paré emphasizes that the crucial element for successful gender designation is social acceptance. Here, naming and clothing become signs of this acceptance, an aspect of the narrative of gender transformation that is reiterated in the story of each transgender man. Paré's version of the famous case that generally is referred to under the name of Marie-Germain, rather than the name of the individual, Germain Garnier, is typical of his tales of gender transformation:

Also being in the retinue of the King at Vitry-le François in Champagne, I saw a certain person (a shepherd) named Germain Garnier—some called him Germain Marie, because when he had been a girl he had been called Marie—a young man of average size, stocky, and very well put together, wearing a red, rather thick beard, who, until he was fifteen years of age, had been held to be a girl, given the fact that no mark of masculinity was visible in him, and furthermore that along with the girls he even dressed like a woman. Now having attained the aforestated age, as he was in the fields and was robustly chasing his swine, which were going into a wheat field, [and] finding a ditch, he wanted to cross over it, and having leaped, at that very moment the genitalia and the male rod came to be developed in him, having ruptured the ligaments by which previously they had been held enclosed and locked in (which did not happen to him without pain). . . . And having brought together Physicians and Surgeons in order to get an opinion on this, they found that she was a man, and no longer a girl; and presently, after having reported to the Bishop . . . and by his authority, an assembly having been called, the shepherd received a man's name: and instead of Marie (for so was he previously named), he was called Germain, and men's clothing was given to him; and I believe that he and his mother are still living.[34]

In the original French of this account of Germain Garnier's story, the masculine gender, grammatically speaking, dominates throughout, even when Paré is discussing Germain's life as a girl. Nonetheless, by alternating feminine and masculine nouns to designate Germain in the course of his transition from female to male, Paré complicates any simple understanding of how gender functions.

This complication is dissonantly obvious to French eyes (and to the autocorrect for grammar in my word-processing program) in phrases like "estant fille estoit appellé"—which I had to fight with autocorrect just to quote correctly, as it wanted to give the feminine version of the past participle for *appeler* (to name). Paré is justified in his choice, as he is speaking about Germain, but the lack of a masculine pronoun in the clause confuses the gender of the antecedent; the grammatical default, then, is to assign gender on the basis of the nearest preceding noun. The dissonance in the entire sentence thus underscores this default assignment of gender and its awkwardness in cases of gender ambiguity, as Paré moves from "Germain Garnier" to "Germain Marie" to "fille" (girl) to "appellé Marie, jeune homme" (called Marie, young man) to "lequel . . . avoit esté tenu pour fille" (he who . . . had been held to be a girl) and "en luy ne se monstroit aucune marque de virilité" (in him was found no mark of virility) to "il se tenoit avec les filles en habit de femme" (along with the girls he even dressed like a woman). In part, Paré's rhetoric pre-justifies or presages Germain's masculinity by suggesting that he is always already male, even when he is called Marie.

The emphasis on masculine gender from the beginning of the narrative is consistent with his invocation of the one-sex theory[35] that informs his account of transgender individuals, based on the misogynist belief in female inferiority as an imperfect version of the male: "Now since such a metamorphosis takes place in Nature for the alleged reasons and examples, we therefore never find in any true story that any man ever became a woman, because Nature tends always toward what is most perfect and not, on the contrary, to perform in such a way that what is perfect should become imperfect."[36] Thus Paré naturalizes gender transformation (but only from female to male) and female inferiority in one sentence.

The Case of Marin le Marcis

Duval quotes Paré's account of Germain Garnier's transition from female to male almost word for word in one of the chapters leading up to his discussion of the case of Marin le Marcis.[37] This case is presented as the culmination of a long series of chapters on the physiological nature of intersex individuals, their generation, and descriptions of numerous particular cases that both suggest the wide variation in physiological characteristics and the naturalness of these variations. After twenty-nine chapters on male and female reproductive organs and childbirth, and a transitional chapter about the distinction between men and women, Duval begins his extended discussion of "hermaphrodites" with mythological origins and poetic examples (chaps. 30 and 31, 287–92). He then devotes fifteen chapters to the history and theories of this "genre,"[38] or type, from the Bible to Aristotle and Hippocrates, with examples given to illustrate or refute each theory. He refutes theories based on the influence of the moon (303), the menstrual cycle of women (which he declares "refuted" in the title of his thirty-seventh chapter, 306–8), and the stars (in four chapters on astrology, chaps. 43–46, 330–41), preferring the Hippocratic theory that equal amounts of male and female seed create an intersex child (chaps. 41 and 42, 313–30).

After debunking astrology, he turns to contemporary accounts and theories, citing a number of authorities, including Paré and Realdo Colombo. In the course of these accounts, he introduces three categories of intersex: the man-woman, which he calls Androgyne (chaps. 47–49); individuals who are believed to be men for a number of years but are discovered to be women (chaps. 50–52, 349–60); and individuals who are reputed to be women for a period of time but then are revealed to be men (chaps. 53–56, 360–73). While he interrupts his discussion of this third category with a list of complex cases that are resolved in different ways in chapter 54 (361–64), his main focus is on twenty-four ancient and contemporary cases of people who were thought to have been women but were revealed to be men (chap. 55, 365–71). He explains the physiological reasons for this seeming transformation, which he believes rather to be the revelation of the true sexe (physiology and gender) of the person in question. In the course of this discussion, he rejects a basic tenet of the one-sex theory, that the vagina is merely a reversed penis, explaining the physiological differences that make this impossible. In these cases, then, he is arguing not so much for gender transformation as for revelation of the true category to which the person belongs.

Duval thus prepares some crucial aspects of Marin le Marcis's defense, first naturalizing his change in gendered social status by listing a compelling number of cases, and then by linking this change not so much to a change in physiology but to a better understanding of that physiology and its ambiguity. The one-sex theory is predicated on the assumption that one can have only a penis or a vagina; since Marin le Marcis has both, Duval must replace this theory with another that accounts for the existence of intersex individuals, and yet genders them appropriately according to their lived experiences, their choices, and rigid social system that allows for only one of two choices, male or female. Duval also lists Germain Garnier's case as one of twenty-four from ancient and early modern times in which girls are revealed to be men at the age of puberty; by doing this, he links Marin's case to a well-known precedent, even as he distances himself from the theories that Paré offers to explain this case.

Having established the plausibility of Marin's own narrative by means of these theories and precedents, he then turns to the legal case, deploying his significant mastery of rhetoric in order to suggest that gender variation, particularly intersex, and gender transformation are related to each other yet not the same. In this he echoes Paré yet surpasses Paré's capacities to describe gender complexity and variation. Since Marin has been sentenced to death for usurping the identity of a man, his gender must be established by official recognition as a male. Duval, like Paré before him, makes it clear that this is a demand made by the legal system rather than a biological given.

Duval is very careful with the language he uses to present this case:

> In this category we will also place Marin le Marcis, who having been baptized, named, dressed, raised & educated as a girl, up until the age of twenty years, after which he felt the signs of his virility, changed his clothing, and had himself called Marin instead of Marie, and engaged himself to marry a woman.

> [Sous ceste espece nous mettrons aussi Marin le Marcis, qui ayant esté baptisé, nommé, vestu, nourri & entretenu pour fille, iusques à l'aage de vingt ans: apres qu'il eut senti indices de sa virilité, changea d'habit, & se faisant appeller Marin, au lieu de Marie, se fiança & donna foy de mariage, à une femme.][39]

Duval insistently uses the masculine form of the past participle even as he is describing Marin's childhood as a girl, thus underscoring the dissonance between the official view of his gender as it was assigned at birth and the identity that Marin wants to establish for himself—and that Duval seeks to confirm.

Marin's testimony fits into the typical narrative of the early modern transgender man: he "insists that he is a man; nonetheless he admits that he wore girl's clothing until recently" ("se maintenoit homme, neantmoins qu'il ait porté cy devant l'habit de fille," 385). His rhetoric, as represented by Duval, also matches the doctor's rhetoric in its careful use of masculine gender, even when he is describing the feminine roles he was called upon to perform. His father sent him out to work as a chambermaid when he was eight years old ("Aagé qu'il fut de huict ans, son pere pauvre de biens de fortune, le bailla pour servir de chambriere," 385). Throughout this presentation of his testimony, as reported by Duval, Marin designates himself with masculine pronouns, even when he describes working as a chambermaid. He also gestures toward the eventual revelation of his masculinity. During his employment in the household where he would eventually meet Jeanne le Febvre, he goes to bed with a woman ("il couchoit avec une fille," 386). Servants were often assigned to share beds. It is not clear from the terms used and the context in which they are presented whether he simply shared a bed or had sex with her; this ambiguity both suggests and denies the possibility of masculinity.

He continues to work as a chambermaid until he is twenty-one, when he meets the widow Jeanne le Febvre. Because of a serious illness, he is sent to sleep with her, and in bed he eventually reveals his "virile member" (386). This member had first appeared about five years before he met Jeanne, but it tended to retract into his body until he began living with her, after which it was more or less continuously apparent until his arrest (388). All of these details are reminiscent of the narratives that appear in Paré's discussion of women becoming men, and thus present a case that would be received as plausible, creating an acceptable explanation of Marin's new identity. By framing his case within familiar narratives, Duval once again moves toward naturalizing Marin's physiology and its transformation.

Marin and Jeanne take every step possible to legitimize his status as a man. When they fall in love, he introduces her to his parents, whose only objection to the proposed marriage is the young widow's poverty and two dependent children (387). There is no mention of their reaction to Marin's new gender identity. Marin and Jeanne apply to abjure their Protestant faith and marry within the Catholic Church, openly sharing the story of Marin's newly revealed identity (386–89). Again, this seeking out of recognition by official representatives of the Catholic Church, the deacon of Monstierville lier and the penitentiary of Rouen, reflects the approved mechanisms for creating a new gender identity listed by Paré. Duval's careful framing of this case, then, locates it firmly within the parameters of acceptable narratives of early modern gender transformation such as the case of Germain Garnier, discussed earlier.

Duval's narrative contains an extensive summary of Marin's own testimony and thus claims to represent (at least to some degree) Marin's own version of his story. Duval also claims to have consulted court documents and spoken to Marin himself; thus the voice of the individual himself hovers somewhere in the background of this narrative (384). In fact, a collection of the court documents of this case (*sac de procès*) has been discovered quite recently, which would be likely to contain a transcript of Marin le Marcis's own testimony.[40]

Jeanne's testimony echoes that of Marin, with the added detail that they "fooled around"[41] in bed. When he reveals his secret, she rebukes him for wearing women's clothing for so long.[42] She states that Marin's member is the same size as that of her late husband, and that Marin did not seem at all like a girl to her.[43] Jeanne repeats these two observations, adding that she had sex with Marin in the same way she did with her husband when her children were conceived: "They slept together, and the said confessing woman knew Marin carnally four times, as naturally as her now-dead husband had done, so that she perceived and knew that he was a man, and had a natural male member, of a length and width such as other men have, with such acts as her now-dead first husband had performed in the procreation of their children."[44] The details offered in this passage are significant, as they echo Paré's descriptions of male "hermaphrodites": they can impregnate women,[45] and their penises are "well-proportioned in thickness and length."[46] Jeanne establishes Marin's maleness by comparing his physiology to that of her husband, with whom she conceived children.[47] But also, importantly, by leaning on the criteria of functionality that Paré describes for designating an ambiguously gendered individual as male, Jeanne's testimony complements that of Marin. It also echoes the cases that Duval has cited previously of individuals who were thought to be women, but revealed to be men.

Yet when Marin is arrested and examined, the two surgeons "do not find any sign of masculinity" (ne trouve[nt] en luy aucun signe de verilité).[48] Again, this echoes Paré's description of Marie-Germain, who had "no mark of masculinity" (aucune marque de virilité)[49] before his transformation into a man. So while this phrase indicates the judgment of the six professors of medicine, two surgeons, and two midwives who judge Marin *not* to be a man, it also undermines this judgment by linking him to Paré's transgender men.

Another examination yields the same results. While his wife says that Marin's physiology is much like that of her first husband, all of his former employers testify that he only showed signs of being a girl. Marin is told that "he had offended God and Justice, to have called himself a man, when no one had found any signs of that, but rather all the signs of a girl" (il avoit offencé Dieu & la justice, de s'estre dit homme, veu qu'on n'en avoit trouvé aucuns indices, mais au contraire tous signes de fille).[50] Marin is convicted of taking on the clothing of a man and usurping a man's name, thus engaging in impersonation. He is also convicted of sodomy, but as Duval's marginal note points out, this crime would require having a penis, and the fact that two surgeons "ne trouver en luy aucun signe de verilité" would ostensibly invalidate that particular conviction.[51] As previously mentioned, according to the court documents, "Marie" le Marcis is condemned to be burned alive, Jeanne to be publicly beaten.[52]

Marin's appeal of this sentence leads to Duval's examination. The signs that his body presents seem to offer contradictory versions of gender. He is solidly built: "He had a stocky body, well built, and well put together" (Il avoit le corps trappe, fourni, bien ramassé).[53] Here Duval once again echoes Paré's description of Germain (formerly Marie): "a young man of average size, stocky and very well put together" (jeune homme de taille moyenne, trappe et bien amassé).[54] The order in which Duval chooses to enumerate Marin's physical characteristics complicates any straightforward assignment of gender even as it echoes Paré's criteria for designating gender in an intersex person. Marin has short hair, but this hair is neither wiry nor soft, evoking and complicating one of the signs Paré enumerated in his list of gender characteristics ("la chevelure courte, de qualité entre dure et molle").[55] This characteristic seems indeterminate, and leaves Marin in the domain of gender ambiguity. He has a mustache ("La levre superieure noircissante, par le poil copieux & noir"), but his voice is high and feminine ("la voix claire & fort semblable à la feminine").[56] As he describes in clinical detail every visible aspect, Duval is careful to alternate stereotypically masculine and feminine characteristics, so that Marin's body offers a wealth of contradictory signs and so eludes clear interpretation. Duval emphasizes the ambiguity here in order to support his argument that while Marin might appear to be a woman, in fact he is a man, just as in the many cases he cited previously.

Duval seeks to establish Marin's physical masculinity by describing in detail how his body is that of a man, particularly in relation to reproductive functions. His clinical examination thus supports Jeanne's testimony. This examination saves Marin from execution.[57] Duval criticizes his colleagues for reading only the external signs and not considering what nature had hidden: "In my mind, I began to blame the negligence of those who wanted to judge by inspection of the exterior that which nature had kept and hidden in a more secret room."[58] In Marin's case, the external signs are no longer reliable as markers of gender; for Duval, what can be seen does not indicate an underlying truth. He stays within the realm of empirical inquiry, however, in suggesting that physical examination is a better indicator of *sexe* than visual cues; the body cannot be read, but it can be felt, by Marin himself and by Jeanne, and finally by Duval, who supports their account of what they feel. The contradictory signs on and inside Marin's body cause Duval to call him a *Gunanthrope*, or womanly man;[59] the name implies that both gender identities are present in one person, but while the feminine seems to prevail, in fact it is the masculine that prevails.

In his description of the case, Duval, and perhaps even Marin and Jeanne as well, try to work with established discourses of gender ambiguity. By repurposing Paré's accounts of "hermaphrodites" and women who become men, Duval locates Marin le Marcis within the realm of a host of familiar discourses concerning gender, rendering his particularly sexed body recognizable as a type (*genre*) and therefore natural. Duval also instrumentalizes Paré's treatise in his construction of a delicate equilibrium between offering a putatively faithful representation of Marin's nonbinary gender characteristics and insisting unequivocally on Marin's masculinity. This allows a disjunction to appear between the physical body and social identity. He is a man in a body that cannot be deciphered clearly enough to establish the dominance of one gender over another. His chosen identity is thus neither in opposition to his body nor in accordance with it, and this destabilized relationship between identity and body calls both sex and gender (what early modern French authors combine in the term *sexe*) into question as a useful mode of organizing humanity, at least in this case and potentially in others.

Duval reiterates Paré's dictum that nature tends toward that which is more perfect: "Also, reason wills and requires that the work of nature tend always toward that which is the most perfect, and man is more perfect than woman."[60] But he plays around with this dictum by asking how one might believe that men may become women once more, suggesting that this might be just a case of natural variation.[61] He then turns the discussion toward Marin's actual variable states of gender.

This instability has a temporal dimension as well. Duval's insistence that the signs of gender vary according to the situation of the person being observed suggests that he sees gender and perhaps even what might be called sex as a contingent, not fixed, quality of the body. Thus, when Jeanne gazes at Marin's body, she may see a penis like that of her late husband or of other men, but the doctors, surgeons, and midwives who later gathered around him to determine his gender do not see it. Duval finds it by clinical examination of Marin, an act he describes in technical detail, so as to grant himself the authority of an expert in anatomical terminology.[62] In his conclusions concerning this exam, he asserts that Marin "was a man with a virile member, sufficient for the conception and propagation of his species with a woman."[63] In this statement he confirms Jeanne's testimony.

Duval continually alternates between invocation of medical authority and his own particular ideas concerning *sexe*. He cites by name a range of authoritative accounts of gender variation, from the encyclopedist Conrad

Lycosthenes, to the classicist Caelius Rhodiginus, to the anatomist Jean Fer-
nel, as well as Paré himself, to establish such variation among "hermaphrodites."[64] Duval continues by celebrating the never-ending diversity of nature,
in which we discern some groupings of accidental resemblances ("accidents
communs"),[65] implying that this diversity is natural rather than a collection
of monstrous exceptions.

This praise of natural variation sets the stage for Duval's presentation of
his final, and ultimately persuasive, argument before the court: that gender
is not a fixed identity, and that even the body can be shaped by its environment and circumstances. He points out that when Marin was free, slept well
in a nice bed, had enough food and exercise, and enjoyed frequent sexual
activity, he had the appearance and behavior of a man. Deprived of these
things—now relatively idle, eating little and exercising less, tired and
listless—he seems more like a woman. These distinctions reflect stereotypical characteristics of gender in the period more than they do any bodily
reality, and suggest that the constraints placed on women's freedom of
movement, diet, comfort, and sexuality have much to do with shaping gender differences. With less freedom to move and fewer resources, women are
not merely deemed to be weaker; they are *made* to be weaker. Duval suggests
that Marin's humoral balance is altered by fear, as well as by lack of freedom
of movement. The constraint of women's clothing creates the appearance of
feminization, but other influences may well shape Marin's body.[66] This body
is not only complex in its gender presentations but also fails to conform to
contemporary understandings of sexed morphology, thus bringing Paré's
tales of intersex and transgender individuals together in one person.

The sentence of the court reverses the death penalty, but, as stated at
the beginning of this chapter, requires Marin to live as a woman until the
age of majority (twenty-five years old, when he could enter into a marriage
contract without the consent of his parents), without engaging in any sexual
contact. When Duval visits him, what he sees confirms his argument that
sexe is contextual or situational. The Marin he sees ten years after the trial is
a better man, more capable of performing as a man because he is free to do
so. In his discussion of this case, Duval had navigated the complex demands
of a legal system that required everybody to inhabit either a masculine or
feminine identity, even as he described a body that was not easily identifiable as belonging to either category. His rhetoric conveys an idea of gender
as both capable of transformation and innately complex, thus revealing the
intersections between intersex and transgender experience in the early modern period in France, as well as the problematic nature of the signs used to
confirm "maleness" or "femaleness."

What is striking about Marin's case is his ability in the end to confirm his chosen identity within the strictures proffered by the law and the courts, even if that confirmation is deferred until he reaches the age of majority. The right to appeal a death sentence and the extant authoritative discourses that placed female-to-male transitions in the context of accepted medical knowledge allowed for a different outcome on appeal than that of the original decision, even in the face of strong opposition from the medical establishment. In this case, then, gender identity and designations of monstrosity and criminality, or humanity and innocence, are determined not only by institutions but also by the individuals who interact with them, establishing their own lives and their own power within the framework of these institutional regimes.

Duval and Foucault

Duval's presentation of the case is quite different from Michel Foucault's characterization of it in his lectures on the abnormal.[67] The early modern doctor devotes twenty-nine chapters, over sixty-four pages, to the legal and medical case, at least partly in response to its complexity. He devotes twenty-one chapters, over ninety-six pages, to the historical and theoretical framing of this case. Rather than a matter of sheer volume, the contents of these chapters suggest that Duval brings a more nuanced attention to this case than does Foucault. For Foucault's claim is that in the early modern period the legal status of the "hermaphrodite" changes from one in which the individual is condemned simply for having a non-gender-normative body to one in which the sexual behavior of the individual is the focus. While Foucault is not entirely wrong in this assessment, he has not captured the full arguments Duval makes.

He misrepresents Duval's argument in part by interspersing it with points from Riolan's assessment of the case. Where Duval represented Marin's actions in a way that demonstrated his agency in the case, stating that he went to religious authorities requesting to be re-baptized as male so that he could marry Jeanne LeFebvre, Foucault's account takes that agency away, claiming that Marin was denounced. Where Foucault deadnames Marin (whom he incorrectly calls "Martin" when he refers to Marin's chosen identity), consistently calling him "Marie," Duval consistently uses the name Marin, making an exception only when he quotes others.

Foucault suggests that the Rouen court's verdict was a permanent injunction to live as a woman, and that "it seems that the hermaphrodite's dominant sex was that of a woman,"[68] when in fact the verdict was that Marin had to wear feminine attire and avoid sexual relations with members of either sex only until the age of majority. The court of the Parliament of Rouen, unable to decide with certainty whether he was male or female, left Marin the possibility of eventually determining his own gender, an unusual result that is not duplicated in other cases.

Apparently Duval's detailed description of Marin's complex *sexe* (combining physiological characteristics of male and female with a narrative of gender transformation), as well as his citation of precedents for that transformation, made for a compelling argument. His description of Marin's body lists both stereotypically masculine and feminine characteristics, by the standard of the era, thus suggesting that Marin may have been an intersex individual, but he also insists that Marin is predominantly male. Duval suggests in his description that Marin's gender is capable of changing, depending on the circumstances. Duval thus does not see gender characteristics as necessarily fixed in the clear binary of male and female.

Foucault's conclusion that Marin is predominantly female is linked to his reliance on Riolan's account of the case, which insists on the existence of only two very clearly distinguishable genders, male and female, and on his claim that intersex individuals do not exist. Basing his conclusions on Riolan's text, Foucault states: "The other reason for the importance of this case is that it clearly asserts that a hermaphrodite is a monster. We find this in Riolan's discourse where he says that the hermaphrodite is a monster because he/she is counter to the order and general rule of nature that has divided humankind into two: male and female."[69] What Foucault does summarize from Duval's arguments is largely taken from the part of his treatise that focuses on childbirth.[70] By taking the focus away from Duval's own arguments concerning intersex and transgender, and Duval's own assessment of Marin's *sexe*, and using the account of Riolan, Foucault can represent both the medical and legal systems as focused on the monstrosity of people who do not conform to gender or sexual norms. Yet Duval and the parliamentary court of Rouen offer an alternative view, one that is important to acknowledge. Duval in particular uses the history and theories of "hermaphrodism" to naturalize both Marin's body and his choice.

Duval also naturalizes intersex, placing it in the context of the unlimited variety in nature: "I would say that we can perceive in the generation of Hermaphrodites, that there are very few who resemble each other, since nature takes no intermission in this variation, in which she takes a singular pleasure."[71] This statement also hints at a potentially unlimited number of different variations of intersex experience, thus moving the early modern model of *sexe* from that of male, female, and the exception, to a world where everyone is an exception—or the exception is the rule. Duval links this emphasis on natural variation to an early modern form of self-determination: if there are many different variations on *sexe* that do not clearly fit into the categories of male and female, and yet the law demands that everyone be categorized as one or the other, then leaving the choice to the individual in question is the only reasonable response.

Foucault mostly summarizes Duval's discussion of reproduction and childbirth in order to place the case in the domain of sexuality, and once again he is not wrong, as Marin le Marcis was charged with sodomy. But Duval's focus on the body rather than on sexuality, with the purpose of naturalizing both that body and Marin's choice of how he lives with/in that body, demonstrates the importance of taking the body into account in a different way. If, as he states, there is great diversity not only among intersex individuals but also among all men and women, then the constraining categories of male and female need to be rethought. For "just as such diversity is not specific to all the other men and women, it is not as remarkable and considerable as in those about whose *sexe* we are uncertain, and for whom even the slightest and most common attributes serve as signs to join with those which are deemed to be useful in distinguishing the species [type], and to assure that, in the absence of clear difference, we might be armed, if not with that which is clear, at least with an accumulation of many similar attributes."[72] Given the diversity among intersex individuals, a wider range of attributes must be taken into account in order to understand and assign these individuals to categories. Duval is presenting *sexe* itself as a complexly embodied phenomenon, opening up a larger range of possibilities. In this recognition of a range of *sexes* that exceed the categories of male and female, he anticipates the much later work of Anne Fausto-Sterling.[73]

Foucault is not wrong about the responses of institutions in France to intersex and transgender individuals. Jean Riolan was a respected member of the Faculty of Medicine at the University of Paris, and, as such, represented an important institutional response to le Marcis's case. The representatives of the Catholic Church also played a problematic, if complicated, role in this case, and the king's prosecutor (or his substitute) brought the initial accusation against le Marcis. But the fact that both the accused man and one of the doctors called in to examine him resisted the narrative that these officials wished to impose, and that the court of the Parliament of Rouen, by leaving the final decision to Marin le Marcis, allowed him eventually to choose his gender identity, is a striking departure from the other early modern cases and from Foucault's assessment of this case.

Duval suggests that there are people whose bodies do not map onto the categories of male and female and that these bodies are not defective but a part of natural variation. He also suggests that the law is insufficient to encompass nature, and that in a case such as that of Marin le Marcis, which escapes the limits of the law, it is the law that should be suspended—as it is by the parliamentary court—rather than consigning the individual in question to the realm of the monstrous. In this Duval's account could be read as refusing the premises on which Foucault's arguments about the case are built.

Marin le Marcis is the hero of this story, having risked his life so that he might live it in the way that felt right to him. Both Duval and Marin use the discourses of the law to justify the choice Marin made while seeking to remain inscribed within the constraints of this system. Duval can be seen as an ally to Marin, albeit an imperfect one, as he clearly uses the case to enhance his own reputation. Nonetheless, by describing and discussing corporeal differences that exceed the categories of male and female, and by refusing to see these differences as merely exceptions to these categories, Duval has hinted at the potential for novel and flexible ways of thinking about both early modern *sexe* and postmodern gender.

Notes

1. Jacques Duval, *Des hermaphrodits, accouchemens des femmes et traitement qui est requis pour les relever en santé et bien élever leurs enfans* [On hermaphrodites, women's labor in childbirth, and the treatment that is required to lift them up again in good health and raise their children well] (Rouen: David Geuffroy, 1612), 384–89. All translations of this text in this chapter are my own. This account is presented as Marin le Marcis's own testimony. I am revisiting Jacques Duval's account of Marin de Marcis's case, which I analyzed briefly in my book *Hermaphrodites in Renaissance Europe* (Aldershot: Ashgate, 2006; repr., New York: Routledge, 2016), in my chapter titled "Jacques Duval on Hermaphrodites: Culture Wars in the Medical Profession," 77–108, and once again, in the context of the longer history of gender theory, in my chapter "Intersex/Transgender," in *Bloomsbury Handbook of 21st-Century Feminist Theory*, ed. Robin Truth Goodman (London: Bloomsbury, 2019), 121–41. Note that Duval uses the masculine version of the word "hermaphrodite," in keeping with his assertion that Marin is a male "hermaphrodite," a possibility that is already presented in the work of Ambroise Paré (see the discussion of Paré in the text). This case has also been analyzed by Lise Leibacher-Ouvrard in her chapter "Imaginaire anatomique, débordements tribadiques et excisions: *Le Discours sur les hermaphrodits* (1614) de Jean Riolan fils," in *L'hermaphrodite de la Renaissance aux Lumières*, ed. Marianne Closson (Paris: Garnier, 2013), 111–24; and by Joseph Harris in his article "'La Force du Tact': Representing the Taboo Body in Jacques Duval's *Traité des Hermaphrodits* (1612)," *French Studies* 57.3 (2003): 311–22. Lorraine Daston and Katharine Park summarize and analyze this case in their article "Hermaphrodites in Renaissance France," *Critical Matrix* 1.5 (1985): 1–19. Their account differs in some details from Duval's version.

2. Duval, *Des hermaphrodits*, 394.

3. Ibid., 396–98.

4. As Cathy McClive points out in her article "Masculinity on Trial: Penises, Hermaphrodites, and the Uncertain Male Body in Early Modern France," *History Workshop Journal* 68 (2009): 56: "Ambiguity surrounding the corporeality of men and women under the age of legal majority was a common theme in early modern jurisprudence, highlighting the importance of puberty and the attainment of physical and legal maturity as preconditions for receiving the 'dividends of masculinity.' It is perhaps not a coincidence that many of the cases of hermaphroditism in early modern France occurred when the individual was on the cusp of an important corporeal or civic transition, be it the onset of puberty, menstrual bleeding, or the legal age at which one could marry without parental consent." See also Sarah Hanley, "Engendering the State: Family Formation and State Building in Early Modern France," *French Historical Studies* 16.1 (1989): 9, for a discussion of the series of edicts promulgated in the late sixteenth and early seventeenth centuries regulating marriage without parental consent, and lengthening "minority age from twenty to thirty years for males, from seventeen to twenty-five years for females." The court in Marin's case is thus deferring his freedom to decide his gender until he reaches the age of majority as a woman.

5. Duval, *Des hermaphrodits*, 441: "very clear prohibitions and interdictions against him living with anyone of one or the other sex, on pain of death" (tres-expresses inhibitions & deffences, d'habiter avec aucunes personnes de l'un ou l'autre sexe, sur peine de la vie).

6. Ibid., A7: "Ce gunanthrope est de present rendu en meilleure habitude virile qu'il n'estoit auparavent, & que qualifié du nom de cadet du Marcis il exerce son estat de tailleur d'habits, entreprend, faict, & execute tous exercices à homme appartenans, porte barbe au menton, & à [sic] dequoy contenter une femme, pour engendrer en elle."

7. Michel Foucault, *Abnormal: Lectures at the Collège de France, 1974–1975*, ed. Valerio Marchetti and Antonella Salomoni, trans. Graham Burchell (New York: Picador), 68–71.

8. Jean Riolan, *Discours sur les hermaphrodits, où il est démontré contre l'opinion commune, qu'il n'y a point de vrays hermaphrodits* (Paris: Ramier, 1614).

9. Jacques Duval, *Responce au discours fait par le Sieur Riolan Docteur en medecine et professeur de chirurgie & pharmacie à Paris, contre l'histoire de l'Hermaphrodit de Rouen* (Rouen: Julian Courant, 1614).

10. For the afterlife of Duval's account, see Valerie Worth-Stylianou, *Pregnancy and Birth in Early Modern France: Treatises by Caring Physicians and Surgeons (1581–1625)* (Toronto: Center for Reformation and Renaissance Studies, 2013), 227–28. Worth-Stylianou points out that the number of copies "that survive in libraries throughout France and abroad suggests that it achieved a fairly wide initial circulation" (227). While she asserts that Jean Riolan's subsequent treatise on "hermaphrodites" (1614) "eclipsed" Duval's, in fact Riolan's work is a direct response to Duval's treatise, repeating much of what his rival says concerning the case.

11. For example, research on the SRY gene linked to the protein associated with male sexual development suggests a number of variations on sex development. See R. Queralt et al., "Atypical XX Male with the SRY Gene Located at the Long Arm of Chromosome 1 and a 1qter Microdeletion," *American Journal of Medical Genetics*

146A.10 (2008): 1335–40, doi: 10.1002/ajmg.a.32284. See also M. Shahid et al., "Two New Novel Point Mutations Localized Upstream and Downstream of the HMG Box Region of the SRY Gene in Three Indian 46, XY Females with Sex Reversal and Gonadal Tumour Formation," *Molecular Human Reproduction* 10.7 (July 2004): 521–26; PubMed, May 21, 2004. For a summary of the research and more sources, see https://ghr.nlm.nih.gov/gene/SRY. For decades, feminist critics have questioned the assumption of biological sex as a natural given unaffected by the cultural construction of gender. For example, David A. Rubin points out that Suzanne J. Kessler "figured the concept of a foundational, essential, innate, true, and abiding 'sex' as a backformation or retroactive effect of the cultural construction of gender" in his book *Intersex Matters: Biomedical Embodiment, Gender Regulation, and Transnational Activism* (Albany: SUNY Press, 2017), 52. Rubin's chapter "Intersex Trouble in Feminist Studies" (49–69) provides an excellent review of the critical work feminist scholars and authors published in relation to intersex. See also Kessler's book *Lessons from the Intersexed* (New Brunswick, NJ: Rutgers University Press, 1998).

12. McClive, "Masculinity on Trial," 47.

13. Ibid., 51.

14. Sophie Duong-Iseler, "Lumières sur le prétendu "hermaphrodite" Antide Collas (ou Colas) de Michel Foucault," *Dix-septième siècle* 256 (2012): 545–56. Duong-Iseler includes trial transcripts in her article. E. William Monter, in his book *Witchcraft in France and Switzerland: The Borderlands during the Reformation* (Ithaca, NY: Cornell University Press, 1976), lists Antide Collas as having been tried and condemned to death for sorcery (216). The Jura region of France was well known for its persecution of both heretics and witches, groups that had significant overlap in the period. Religious tension may have been an aspect of Marin le Marcis's case as well, given the double conversion of Marin and Jeanne that accompanies his request to be re-baptized male.

15. Patrick Graille, *Les hermaphrodites aux XVIIᵉ et XVIIIᵉ siècles* (Paris: Les Belles Lettres, 2001), 107. See also Foucault, *Abnormal*, 67–68.

16. McClive, "Masculinity on Trial," 59–62.

17. Foucault, *Abnormal*, 71–74. See also McClive, "Masculinity on Trial," 56–58; and Graille, *Les hermaphrodites*, 129–44, for detailed accounts of the Grandjean case.

18. For the significance of the term "natural" in relation to the modern concept of "normal," see Elizabeth Bearden, "Before Normal, There Was Natural: John Bulwer, Disability, and Natural Signing in Early Modern England and Beyond," *PMLA* 132 (2017): 33–50.

19. Stephen Greenblatt, *Shakespearean Negotiations: The Circulation of Social Energy in Renaissance England* (Berkeley: University of California Press, 1988), 75.

20. For a brief consideration of this view of natural variation in relation to sex/gender in the early modern period, see my essay "Intersex/Transgender." For more early modern views of the problematic nature of taxonomizing gender, see my chapter "The Cultural and Medical Construction of Gender: Caspar Bauhin," in *Hermaphrodites in Renaissance Europe*, 54–55.

21. Judith Butler, *Undoing Gender* (New York: Routledge, 2004), 11.

22. McClive, "Masculinity on Trial," 53.

23. *L'isle des hermaphrodites*, ed. Claude-Gilbert Dubois (Geneva: Droz, 1996), 71.

24. See, for example, *L'isle des hermaphrodites*: "In another room, I saw this same man stretched out all naked on a table, and several around him who had all sort of surgical instruments, and they were doing all that they could to make him a woman; but from what I could discern by what happened after this story, he remained neuter in gender" ("En une autre piece, je voyois ce mesme homme estendu tout nud sus une table, et plusieurs à l'entour de luy qui avoient diverses sortes de ferremens, et faisoient tout ce qui leur estoit possible pour le faire devenir femme; mais à ce que j'en pouvois juger par la suitte de l'histoire il demeurait du genre neutre").

25. For an analysis of the scandalous nature of Duval's account, see Dominique Brancher, "The Finger in the Eye: Jacques Duval's *Traité des hermaphrodites* (1612)," in *Movement in Renaissance Literature: Exploring Kinesic Intelligence*, ed. Kathryn Banks and Timothy Chesters (New York: Palgrave Macmillan, 2017), 133–54.

26. For an account of his career as a royal surgeon, see the introduction to the most recent edition of Ambroise Paré's *Oeuvres*, ed. Evelyne Berriot-Salvadore, Jean Céard, and Guylaine Pineau, vol. 1 (Paris: Garnier, 2019), 9–19.

27. Paré, *Oeuvres*, 26–28.

28. Ibid., 8.

29. Portions of his other works were published repeatedly as well. His collected works were translated into Dutch, German, Latin, and English, and also published repeatedly over the course of the late sixteenth through seventeenth centuries, in English at least five times between 1634 and 1691.

30. Janis Pallister discusses this conflict and its effect on his reputation in the introduction to her translation of Paré's *On Monsters and Marvels* (Chicago: University of Chicago Press, 1982), xix–xx. In spite of what the title of this book might lead modern readers to believe, Paré's aim in all but the most evidently supernatural of cases was to reframe bodies deemed "monstrous" as natural.

31. Paré, *On Monsters*, 27; *Des monstres*, in *Oeuvres*, 2729: "Hermafrodites masles et femelles ce sont ceux qui ont les deux sexes bien formez, et s'en peuvent aider et servir à la generation: et à ceux cy les loix anciennes et modernes ont fait et font encore eslire, duquel sexe ils veulent user, avec defense, sur peine de perdre la vie, de ne se servir que de celuy duquel ils auront fait election, pour les inconveniens qui en pourroyent advenir."

32. Paré, *On Monsters*, 30; *Des monstres*, 2730: "Et si l'hermafrodite tient autant de l'un que l'autre, il sera appellé hermafrodite homme et femme."

33. Paré, *On Monsters*, 27–28; *Des monstres*, 2729: "Les Medecins et Chirurgiens bien experts et advisez peuvent cognoistre si les hermafrodites sont plus aptes à tenir et user de l'un que de l'autre sexe, ou des deux, ou du tout rien. Et telle chose se cognoistra aux parties genitales, à sçavoir, si le sexe feminine est propre en ses dimensions, pour recevoir le verge virile, et si par iceluy fluent les menstrues: pareillement par le visage, et si les cheveux sont deliez ou gros: si la parole est virile ou gresle, si les tetins sont semblables à ceux des hommes ou des femmes: semblablement si toute l'habitude du corps est robuste, ou effeminee, s'ils sont hardis ou craintifs, et autres actions semblables aux masles, ou aux femelles. Et quant aux parties genitales qui appartiennent à l'homme, faut examiner et voir s'il y a grande quantité de poil au penil et autour du siege: car communément et quasi toujours, les femmes n'en ont point au siege. Semblablement faut bien examiner si la verge virile est bien proportionnee

en grosseur et longueur, et si elle se dresse, et d'icelle sort semence: qui se fera par la confession de l'hermafrodite, lors qu'il aura eu la compagnie de femme."

34. Paré, *On Monsters*, 31–32; *Des monstres*, 2733–34: "Aussi estant à la suitte du Roy, à Vitry le François en Champagne, j'y vey un certain personnage nommé Germain Garnier, aucuns le nommoyent Germain Marie, par-ce qu'estant fille estoit appellé Marie, jeune homme, de taille moyenne, trappe, et bien amassé, portant barbe rousse, assez espesse, lequel jusqu'au quinziesme an de son aage avoit esté tenu pour fille, attendu qu'en luy ne se monstroit aucune marque de virilité, et mesmes qu'il se tenoit avec les filles en habit de femme. Or ayant atteint l'aage susdit, comme il estoit aux champs, et poursuyvoit assez vivement ses pourceaux, qui alloyent dedans un blé, trouvant un fossé le voulut affranchir: et l'ayant saulté, à l'instant se viennent à luy desvelopper les genitoires, et la verge virile, s'estans rompus les ligamens, par lesquels au-paravant estoyent tenus clos et enserrez (ce qui ne luy advint sans douleur) . . . Et ayant assemblé des Medecins et Chirurgiens, pour là dessus avoir advis, on trouva qu'elle estoit homme, et non plus fille: et tantost apres avoir rapporté à l'Evesque . . . par son authorité, et assemblee du people, il receut le nom d'homme: et au lieu de Marie (car il estoit ainsi nommé au-paravant) il fut appellé Germain, et luy fut baillé habit d'homme, et croy que luy et sa mere sont encore vivans."

35. The theory, elaborated by Aristotle among others, essentially states that women are merely underdeveloped men. For a review of the history of this theory, see Thomas Laqueur, "Destiny Is Anatomy" and "New Science, One Flesh," in *Making Sex: Body and Gender from the Greeks to Freud* (Cambridge, MA: Harvard University Press, 1992), 25–113.

36. Paré, *On Monsters*, 33; *Des monstres*, 2734: "Or comme telle metamorphose a lieu en Nature, par les raisons et exemples alleguees: aussi nous ne trouvons jamais en histoire veritable, que d'homme aucun soit devenu femme, pour-ce que Nature tend toujours à ce qui est le plus parfaict, et non au contraire faire que ce qui est parfaict, devienne imparfaict."

37. Duval, *Des hermaphrodits*, 371–72.

38. His term, meaning "type," used at the beginning of his discussion of theories of intersex; ibid., 294.

39. Ibid., 383. This text also summarizes the basic steps required to change one's gender officially in early modern France: physical transformation, change of clothing and name, and sexuality that indicates the new gender within the parameters of contemporary definitions of heterosexuality.

40. Mathieu Laflamme, a doctoral student in the Department of History at the University of Ottawa, has been writing about trials concerning "hermaphrodisme" in early modern France, and has seen these documents. His forthcoming essay on these trials is "Le genre au tribunal: L'hermaphrodisme devant la justice de la France d'Ancien Régime," https://www.academia.edu/28557799/Le_genre_au_tribunal_lhermaphrodisme_devant_la_justice_de_la_France_dAncien_R%C3%A9gime."

41. "Aiguillonnoit et rageoit," synonyms for *folastrer*, used by Paré in his description of behavior that instigates the transformation from female to male in the case of Antoine Loqueneux in *On Monsters*, 31; *Des monstres*, 2733.

42. Duval, *Des hermaphrodits*, 390.

43. Ibid., 391: "Sans qu'elle s'apperceust en aucune maniere, qu'il y eust quelque marque de sexe feminine."

44. Ibid., 392: "Ils coucherent ensemble, & cogneut ledit Marin ladicte confessante charnellement par quatre fois, aussi naturellement comme avoit faict ledit defunct son mari, tellement qu'elle appercevoit et cognoissoit qu'il estoit homme, & avoit un membre viril & naturel, de longueur & grosseur telle qu'ont les autres hommes, avec tels actes, qu'avoit ledit defunct son premier mari, en la procreation de leurs enfans."

45. Paré, *On Monsters*, 26; *Des monstres*, 2728.

46. Paré, *On Monsters*, 27; *Des monstres*, 2729.

47. This emphasis on physiology that was functional in terms of reproduction was central to a number of cases concerning "hermaphrodites" in early modern France; for this, see McClive, "Masculinity on Trial," 46.

48. Duval, *Des hermaphrodits*, 393

49. Paré, *On Monsters*, 32; *Des monstres*, 2733.

50. Duval, *Des hermaphrodits*, 394.

51. Ibid., 397: "Nottez l'erreur, car s'il a commis Sodomie, il faut qu'il ait eu un membre virile" (Note the error, since if he committed Sodomy, he would have had to have a virile member).

52. Ibid., 397–98. It should be noted that Duval uses the name Marie only when he is quoting court documents or others' accounts of the young man's life.

53. Ibid., 400.

54. Paré, *On Monsters*, 32; *Des Monstres*, 2733.

55. Duval, *Des hermaphrodits*, 400.

56. Ibid., 400.

57. Ibid., 402–5.

58. Ibid., 405: "Je commençay blasmer à part moy la negligence de ceux, qui vouloient par l'inspection de l'exterieur, juger et decider de ce que nature avoit retenu, & reconcé en un plus secret cabinet."

59. Ibid., 407.

60. Ibid., 412: "Aussi la raison veut & requert que l'oeuvre de nature tende tousiours à ce qui est plus parfaict, l'homme est plus parfait que la femme."

61. Ibid.: "Quelle raison donc nous induira croire, qu'un homme redevienne femme . . . nous remarquons nature s'estre grandement delectee en la varieté."

62. Ibid., 403–5.

63. Ibid., 406: "Il estoit homme muni de membre viril, suffisant pour la generation & propagation de son espece, avec une femme."

64. Ibid., 413.

65. Ibid., 414.

66. Ibid., 436–38; Long, *Hermaphrodites in Renaissance Europe*, 84.

67. Foucault, *Abnormal*, 68–71.

68. Ibid., 68.

69. Ibid., 71.

70. Ibid., 69–70.

71. Duval, *Des hermaphrodits*, 413: "Je diray que nous pouvons appercevoir en la generation des Hermaphrodits, qu'il y en a fort peu qui soyent semblables les uns

aux autres, ne faisant nature aucune intermission de ceste variation, en laquelle elle prent un singulier plaisir."

72. Ibid., 413–14: "D'autant que telle diversité n'est specifique en tous les autres hommes & femmes, elle n'est tant remarquable & considerable, comme en ceux du sexe desquels nous sommes incertains, & ausquels les accidents & mesmement les plus legiers & communs nous servent de signes pour joindre avec ceux qui sont reputez propres à distinguer l'espece, & faire en sorte, que deffaillant la propre difference, nous soyons munis sinon de ce qui depend de la de [*sic*] ce qui est propre à tout le moins de l'amas de beaucoup d'accidents communs." Here the word *accidents* is being used as a philosophical term designating attributes that are not essential to the substance.

73. For example, her chapter "Should There Only Be Two Sexes?," in *Sexing the Body: Gender Politics and the Construction of Sexuality* (New York: Basic Books, 2000), 78–114.

CHAPTER 4

The Transgender Turn

Eleanor Rykener Speaks Back

M. W. Bychowski

Most scholarship is, effectively, cisgender scholarship, not only because it is mostly cisgender scholars who have claimed the education and tools to publish it but also because most scholarship assumes the cisgender status of any character or historical figure who is presented to readers. Some have called this prejudice *cissexism* because it represents the privileging of cisgender perspectives and identities; institutional cissexism, in turn, has made it easier for cisgender scholars to claim and maintain greater academic authority than trans scholars. As a result, the arrival of transgender scholars—especially in fields such as medieval studies—marks a late-arriving turn in the field. Simultaneously, because of the compulsory cisgender assignment of history and historical figures, texts such as Plea and Memoranda Roll A34, m.2[1] from the London Metropolitan Archives, and historical people such as Eleanor Rykener, have already been coded by cisgender norms. As a result, trans readings do not immediately spring to mind as the primary readings, which—if you look critically at this document—is nothing short of astonishing. Nonetheless, cisgender readings of texts and histories have been dominant for so long they are treated as neutral. This can make it difficult for trans readings to enter academic discourse, because transgender studies can be seen as offering modern additions to long-established traditions within cisgender histories and studies. Trans studies is seen as an act of remaking or rewriting history. Neither the text nor the person was necessarily cisgender until cisgender scribes, scholars, and readers marked them as such. This essay names and interrogates the supposed neutrality of cisgender subject positions and the compulsory cisgender assignment of history and historical figures. Comparable to how trans people are typically assumed to be cisgender at birth and raised to be cisgender by parents, so too do scholars of history compulsively assign cisgender assumptions to people and texts in the past without stopping to seriously consider trans potentials. Thus the transgender turn critiques compulsory cisgender identity assignment and history, as well as opens up discursive possibilities for trans histories to begin to be told on their own terms.

Let's take the case of Eleanor Rykener, a trans woman sex worker whose life story appears only in the London Metropolitan Archives' Plea and Memoranda Roll A34, m.2.[2] Rykener's story, in Latin, runs as follows: along a Cheapside road ("vicum regium de Chepe") in medieval London, a woman who called herself Eleanor ("Elianoram Rykener") stands turned toward the street until a cisgender man[3] named John ("Johannes Britby") observes ("detectus") her womanly self, follows ("assecutus") and accosts ("petens") her, a transgender anomaly in his world, and she turns to him and challenges the look that he gives her. She demands money ("argentum") for her labor before she is willing to consent ("consentiebat") to go with him. Together they retreat to a stall ("stallum") on Soper's Lane ("Sopereslane") to engage in what the record calls an unspeakable ("nephandum") act. They are caught ("capti") by officers ("civitatis ministros") and brought to the mayor's court. There the events of the encounter are confessed and recorded by an unnamed scribe. Eleanor's story was further investigated, including the story of her transition, her work, her clients, and their gifts to her, including a golden ring ("anulum aureum").[4] Thus begins the fourteenth-century story of Rykener and Britby. Their respective turns toward each other generates a sexual and narrative intercourse between masculinity and femininity, cisgender experience (meaning the experience of someone whose gender as a man is not challenged) and transgender experience (meaning that of someone whose gender challenges social assignments and categories). Subsequently both are caught by fourteenth-century officers of the law, by the courts of their day, by the scribe of the Plea and Memoranda Roll A34, m.2, and by waves of subsequent medieval studies scholars.

It took decades of medieval cisgender studies before trans scholars got their turn at the case of Eleanor Rykener. This "transgender turn" in medieval studies came just around the same time that *Time* magazine announced

"The Transgender Tipping Point" (2014).[5] The article suggests that that moment—and only from that moment forward—is when trans people could have a turn at social and legal rights. Being told when it is our "turn," our time, troubles me because it presumes that other turns and other times are not ours. Celebrating that "this time is ours" assumes that what came before and what comes after is not ours. We might call this time before the transgender turn a cisgender era (defined by methodologies of cisgender history and theoretical turns). Such a turn is a moment, not a movement, in which we are allowed to do something; the implication is also that, if we do not act quickly, we will lose our turn. To be effective, however, the "transgender turn" has to mean more than a moment in time. Thus I build on the "transgender turn," evident in the past few years' worth of work in medieval studies. While building on the work of trans, crip, and queer scholars, I contend that the transgender turn is not merely a way to mark and order recent time but a critical movement that has been active since Eleanor Rykener turned tricks on Cheapside.[6]

Turn is a term with overlapping definitions, signifying ordering, orientation, sexuality, and violence. A turn is a way to reorder power as well as reorder the body. A turn is a way to order and reorder one's orientations and perspectives. A turn can signal a period, or the ordering of a series of actions, such as taking turns in a game.[7] Similarly, a turn is used to describe a critical movement within a field, such as the linguistic turn.[8] A turn is also an embodied word. A turn can signify a return or reoccurrence, such as returning to the site of a crime.[9] A turn can signify an orientation or reorientation, such as turning to face the woman or toward the defendant.[10] A turn can also be sexual, such as turning tricks.[11] A turn can be violent or treacherous, such as turning on the sex worker in a stall (*stallum*) or on the courtroom docket.[12] A particular action or use of the word "turn" can combine the multiple meanings of turning. Indeed, the transgender turn occurs concurrently with the cisgender turn or era. The transgender turn is active in the reordering of power and perspective in the medieval archive of and by Eleanor Rykener. Britby turns toward Rykener, but at the same time Rykener turns toward Britby.

The first task is to define "the cisgender turn" as the reifying of cisgender perspectives on the case of Eleanor Rykener: we see this cisgender prerogative showcased most strongly in the accounts of the encounter by John Britby and the scribe. The cisgender turn is marked not only by the predominance of cis scholars and viewpoints but also by compulsory cisgender assignments wherein a historical figure is assumed to be cisgender unless proven otherwise. Even trans scholars have at times reified the cisgender turn (e.g., compulsory cisgender perspectives and identifications). Alongside the initial cisgender readers of Rykener's body and case (Britby and the scribe), a brief review of the critical scholarship in the several centuries since highlights the pattern of cisgender histories, or "cistories" (the version of history determined according to compulsory cisgender assignment and perspectives), privileging cisgender authorities and models. These cistories default to cis perspectives and reify traditions of accosting (modeled by Britby) and silencing (modeled by the scribe) trans bodies and histories. Silencing takes the form of perpetuating compulsory cisgender assignments for people such as Rykener, naming her as John (a name introduced by cis authorities) rather than as Eleanor (her self-given name).

The second task is to articulate critical moves of the transgender turn via the ways that trans people turn out toward and speak back to cisgender people and cisgender versions of history. By inviting readers to reconsider the case from Eleanor Rykener's point of view, we may reframe the exchange between her and the cisgender man as well as reorient the sympathies of later historians. What if our instinct were to identify first with the trans woman, giving her a primacy that is automatically given to cisgender men? The Plea and Memoranda Roll A34, m.2 records that before Rykener would give consent, she demanded pay for her labor. As we reflect on Rykener's relationship to Britby as it is narrated in the Roll, three words deserve our attention: consent (*consentiebat*), labor (*labore*), and payment (*argentum*). What does it mean for Britby or later historians to engage consensually with trans subjects? What does it mean for Britby or readers to recognize the value of trans bodies and labor? What does it mean for Britby and scholars to compensate trans people and histories?

The third task is to call Eleanor Rykener back to the stand. With a name that suggests the profession of reckoner or accountant, it is time for Rykener to once again live up to her name. Rykener shows us point for point how to speak back to the cisgender turn and compulsory cisgender assignment (1) by affirming her transgender embodiment and power, (2) by reclaiming her name, and (3) by citing her authority as collaborator and coauthor of her story. Moving forward, these lessons may allow for a more ethical engagement with trans lives, historical and present, by inviting scholars to recognize the discursive moves of various transgender turns that have been occurring for centuries. In the name and critical practices of Rykener, the transgender turn calls for a reckoning in medieval studies that will hold compulsory cisgender assignments and histories to account.

The Cisgender Turn

Before we unpack the transgender turn as a critical movement, it helps to review in what ways it does mark a shift in the field, a shift that comes after what can be called the "cisgender turn." To begin, the story of Eleanor Rykener was made famous by David Lorenzo Boyd and Ruth Mazo Karras in an article titled "The Interrogation of a Male Transvestite Prostitute in Fourteenth-Century London," in *GLQ* (1995),[13] and later in one titled "Ut cum muliere: A Male Transvestite Prostitute in Fourteenth Century London" (1996).[14] In the same year, Karras referenced Rykener in a contribution to the *Handbook of Medieval Sexuality* titled "Prostitution in Medieval Europe" (1996).[15] Subsequently Carolyn Dinshaw approached Rykener in "Good Vibrations: John/Eleanor, Dame Alys, the Pardoner, and Foucault" in *Getting Medieval: Sexualities and Communities, Pre- and Postmodern*, as an unspeakably queer "sodomite" and "transvestite" (1999).[16] The focus of the piece emphasizes the question of sodomy and queerness, yet Dinshaw's reference to transness does lay groundwork for an overlap in the identification and study of Eleanor across multiple categories at once.

Some years later, Jeremy Goldberg made the claim in "John Rykener, Richard II, and the Governance of London" (2014) that "Eleanor" (*qua* Eleanor) did not exist or at least that this specific event did not happen.[17] While admitting that a John Rykener existed in London, Goldberg contends that the Rykener who exists in the record is the literary representation of the falseness of an individual and the moral decay of truth in London: "He [Rykener] is unmanly. Indeed he even wears a dress and performs women's work. Though he engages in heterosexual sex 'as a man,' he also has sex with men 'as a woman,' having been taught by one Anne, who may herself now be dead. He lacks all honesty or trustworthiness."[18] To launch his argument about the falsity of the person and the fictionality of the text, Goldberg writes, "Neither transvestism nor buggery were matters that are otherwise documented in English secular courts and the mayor's court of London would not have been considered competent to exercise jurisdiction at least in respect of sodomy" and observes, "There is no record of a verdict or of punishment."[19] While other scholars have noted how unusual the case is for the secular court and record, most scholars (as Goldberg reminds readers) do not consider unusualness or non-normativity evidence of the impossibility of Rykener's existence and transness (broadly defined). Breaking from the consensus surrounding the case's plausibility, Goldberg represents the unusualness of Rykner (as a person) and the case (as a text) as evidence supporting an interpretation of both the person and text of Rykener as

based in falsity—problematically echoing transphobic accusations and language that have been used for generations to discredit the legitimacy of
trans people and trans history. Repeatedly deadnaming (using a name given
by parents or society but rejected by the person it putatively describes)
Eleanor as "John," Goldberg refers to the narrative of a man committing
"gay sex" and "homosexual" acts with men and "heterosexual" acts with
women. Rykener is described by Goldberg as "a man in a woman's dress."[20]
This again echoes the same transphobic summary that medieval scholars
recently used (almost word for word) to describe myself and another trans
person to organizers of the New Chaucer Society meeting in 2018.[21] His initial reading of Rykener is as a cheater and a liar, echoing many transphobic
descriptions commonly assigned to transgender people.[22] This line of interpretation of cross-dressing and inauthentic gender leads to an argument
about the Rykener case as inauthentic history, a joke cross-dressing itself as
historical record. Speculating that the story was just a farcical tale of "political pornographic rhetoric" that writers invented to amuse and berate one
another, using sex and sexuality to comment on the state of the kingdom
and the king,[23] Goldberg writes:

> I wish now to make an imaginative leap—one that no doubt not all
> will find convincing—and consider the Rykener narrative as political
> satire and what early modern scholars have dubbed 'political pornog-
> raphy.' . . . The text, as a fiction, necessarily incorporates contempo-
> rary understandings of the sex trade that are surely rooted in informed
> knowledge of late fourteenth-century London. . . . This then is a text
> fabricated by the Latin-literate clerks who serviced the mayor's court,
> who had access to and were versed in the diplomatic of the Plea and
> Memoranda rolls, and would have been unusually well informed in
> current events and the affairs of the city.[24]

Certainly Goldberg acknowledges that his speculation will not find universal
agreement. Indeed, his argument about the fictionality of the text is presented as "an imaginative leap." Yet the degree to which this speculation
about the falsehood of the text is connected by Goldberg to the inauthentic-
ity and falsehood inherent in Rykener—who is consistently described by him
as a cross-dressing man who engages in gay sex—echoes a wider pattern of
undermining the legitimacy and veracity of transgender people in the medieval past and today. While Goldberg's argument is distinct in important ways
from the other scholarship mentioned, his article signals (one might say
"dog-whistles") many problematic patterns in cis scholarship about Rykener

that associates the idea of a medieval trans woman with the impossible, the unspeakable, and the unrealistic.

To best respond to these transphobic patterns of scholarship, it is critical to first be able to name and identify these patterns as symptomatic of generations of the cisgender turn's preeminence in academia. This preeminence has led to the assumption that cisgender perspectives and jokes about trans figures are normal or neutral. The work of naming the cisgender turn as a long-established historical force is thus an extension of the wider work accomplished by naming "cisgender" as an experience. By identifying non-transgender people as cisgender, trans people and trans studies contend that cis people should not and cannot claim a compulsory or universal viewpoint. The irony is that to many cisgender individuals the word "cisgender" may sound like a new thing and yet describes a very old, widespread norm. Yet words are often coined some time after the patterns or traits they describe have existed. That is why, despite the prominence of arguments by Michel Foucault that "the homosexual" (the noun, as opposed to the adjective) came into being in modernity, I would contend that the development of language is only one way to mark moments and movements that predate the subjugated claiming their subjectivity. Homosexuals have been turning toward, looking at, and gazing upon one another and heterosexuals long before they were called homosexual and heterosexual. Likewise, trans people were labeled thus by cis people before so-called transvestites and transsexuals had the language to mark their experience of difference. Compulsory cisgender assignment has likewise operated to make cis identification not just neutral but necessary, much in the way that Adrienne Rich argues that compulsory heterosexuality is the pre-determinate identity and training of all individuals.[25] One critical contribution of the transgender turn is even simply to identify that the cisgender turn has existed for some time, and to critique its traditions. It is a truth experienced by trans people today, and, I will argue, by Eleanor Rykener, that cis people often do not know how they are looking, staring, or taxonomically gazing at us until we turn our gaze back on them. It would be a mistake to assume that the cisgender turn did not exist until trans scholars named it and that our silence until that point excuses the many histories of cis people accosting trans people. Indeed, the fear of transphobic rhetoric and other forms of accosting helps to explain why scholars (and even transgender scholars) for so long have been unspeaking and un-trans-ing transgender.

To understand how cisgender subjectivities have turned on trans bodies since the Middle Ages, we may continue to consider the Plea and Memoranda

Roll A34, m.2 as a document that reflects and reifies the cisgender turns of John Britby. On December 11, 1394, John Britby (Johannes Britby) claims to have been walking down Cheapside between 8:00 and 9:00 p.m., where and when he turned on and accosted (*petere*) a local person, Eleanor Rykener.[26] He (Britby) affirms that she (Rykener) presented as a woman and indeed affirms that he considered her a woman. Britby solicited Rykener for sex. He paid her, and they went to a stall in Soper's Lane (Sopereslane) to complete the transaction. Soon after, they were both accosted by local law enforcement, then brought to court.[27] There, Britby told his story for the scribe. This is the narrative that would effectively become the story of Eleanor Rykener, and it is told first from John Britby's perspective. Importantly, Britby's actions and story both come before Rykener's turn in response. He is the one to pursue and accost her before she can turn toward him or even turn back toward herself to set limits and costs for her body. It is also important to recognize that, narratively, before Rykener is allowed to tell her own history, the cisgender man was able to speak.

The first interaction between Britby and Rykener is the man's "accosting" of the trans woman. In Latin, the word describing Britby's actions is *petens*.[28] This is an adjective form of the word *pĕto*, *petere*, or *petitus*, meaning "to attack, to aim at, to desire, to beg, to entreat, to ask (for), to reach towards."[29] According to Britby's story, it was the cisgender man who turned first, setting the rest of the events into motion. He sees her. He approaches her. He talks to her. He offers money. He brings her to a private place. He reaches toward her body in ways not disclosed. He is then the first person allowed to speak in the courtroom.

How, then, may this cisgender man's turn on the medieval trans woman be qualified? If we are to take Britby's account seriously, his cisgender turn here takes the form of accosting. Unpacking the adjective *petens* and its active forms demonstrates the way that cisgender turns can take the form of the approach, the act of reaching out toward, or the act of attacking or even begging. There is a slippage between the interpretation of accosting that comes into play in present-day debates over sexual assault and rape culture, where one party may view the encounter as a mere approach or request while the other party may view the encounter as an assault or attack. Certainly, asymmetric power relationships between employers and/or employees, compounded by age, gender, sexuality, and racial identity, can further split the interpretation of events. Given a power differential between a cis man and a trans woman, the potential for *petere* to mean "to attack" is worth considering as well. The cisgender subject incites discussion with his question to the trans person (i.e., Rykener): Who are you (in relation) to me? As a result of his narration of the encounter, this cis man is the one who sets the terms and premises of the exchange with the trans person. Britby is the one who seeks out Rykener.[30] It is also true that later generations might never have known the story of a medieval trans woman without a medieval cis man seeking her out. Britby's actions are defined by this, *petens*, and his desire. Even if the cis man approached her with all due respect and politeness, the exchange he proposes between them underlines that he has power that she does not have. He gets to be the desiring subject, empowered to act first on Cheapside and to speak first in the Plea and Memoranda Roll.

Speaking first in a courtroom or the academy can establish trends in how events are interpreted. For instance, scholars have described Rykener's gender in various ways in part because of their different critical investments in Rykener's sexuality. Dinshaw repeatedly refers to the presence of the "John" element of Eleanor's story—despite the fact that the equal billing of genders espoused by calling her "John/Eleanor" has become the standard among scholars for naming her—emphasizing the sodomy claims in her queer reading of the case.[31] Yet Alexander Baldassano argues that Britby emphasizes Eleanor's female identity in order to undermine such claims, staving off the accusation that Britby had committed sodomy.[32] Reading these scholarly debates in the age of social media reminds us that this issue is still very much alive; consider, for example, the transphobic and homophobic online trend in which (mostly young straight male) Internet personalities debate whether or not engaging in sexual activity with a trans women makes them gay. Academic and online debate evidence the way that a person's perceived gender influences whether sexual encounters are considered sodomitical, gay, or queer.

Indeed, online commentators are protected somewhat from scrutiny for transphobic comments by the anonymity of screen names or pseudonyms, much as the scribe of the Rykener case can fade into the background despite how much influence he has over the narration of events. On December 11, 1394, the scribe of the Plea and Memoranda Roll A34, m.2 observed and transcribed the interrogation of Eleanor Rykener and John Britby, who stood accused of engaging in the unspeakable vice *nephandum*, sodomy.[33] Unlike Britby in his brief turn toward Rykener, the scribe maintains a longer gaze and records multiple turns in her story. Considering the scribe's examination of Rykener more deeply reveals ways in which he is not simply recording a neutral, ungendered history. Whether or not the scribe is cisgender, his text adheres to cisgender presumptions, such as reinforcing the compulsory cisgender assignment of Rykener. The trans woman calls herself Eleanor, but the cis scribe calls her John. Following the scribe's appellation, generations of scholars call her John too, illustrating how the word of a cis scribe is taken more seriously than that of a medieval trans woman. Cisgender assessments of history (such as calling Eleanor "John") are usually more likely to be accepted as neutral history. The lack of a byline or other identifier for the scribe leaves readers to infer his existence from the document he produced, further illustrating how cis perspectives are rendered "invisible" or transparent (in the sense that they are not seen as a frame, a choice, a methodology) or assumed to be neutral.

Even though medieval scribes and modern scholars have plenty to say on the issue, there are centuries-old traditions in cistory that mark medieval sodomy and people operating within non-normative sexual identities (e.g., those labeled as sodomites) as unspeakable, what the scribe calls *nephandum*. *Nephandum* comes from *infandus, infanda, infandum*, meaning "abominable, monstrous" and "unspeakable, unutterable."[34] Ironically, both premodern writers and modern scholars have made medieval transgender identity unutterable by speaking of potential trans subjects almost exclusively under the terms of sodomy and queer identity. Consequently, even for scholars such as Dinshaw who note (however briefly) that a figure such as Rykener may be considered a "transvestite," this potential identification with transness and womanhood are sidelined to make room for an argument about queerness and sodomites.[35] It may be speculated that as Eleanor as a (trans) woman becomes more visible, then the (cross-dressing) gay-like figure of John becomes less visible, and thus the claims about queer sodomy become more complicated. Of course, medieval sodomy and modern queer identity are expansive enough to include trans erotics; the particulars of transgender sex and sexuality, however, would add another level of complexity to such arguments. In short, scholars such as Dinshaw may sideline Eleanor in order to tell a more cisgender-friendly history of a queer sodomite. In 1999, telling the story of a queer male cross-dresser is unspeakable enough within academic discourse without working to give voice to a trans woman. This may also have been the case for the medieval scribe who told the story of "John" the cross-dressing male sex worker in place of the trans woman who called herself Eleanor. And indeed, the scribe participates in un-trans-ing or unspeaking Rykener. Although she introduces herself into the record as Eleanor ("Elianoram"), the scribe choses to name her as John ("Johannes") twenty-five times.[36] The scribe may be compelled to do so by social norms yet still insists on using a deadname. This alone points to how cistory distorts facts to bring them in line with compulsory cisgender assignment. Cisgender history is not neutral but comes into being as much through what it excludes as what it includes; cistory insists on an un-transing of history.

In line with the cisgender turn, subsequent scholars generally follow the conventions of the scribe, renaming Rykener "John" despite her recorded act of self-naming. Boyd and Karras open their article on a "male transvestite" by referring to Rykener as "John."[37] Dinshaw opens her article telling the story of Eleanor but moves to using "John/Eleanor," creating an equivalence between the names.[38] Later, when revisiting Rykner in the wake of trans studies, Karras again refers to "John/Eleanor" when creating a collaborative piece with Tom Linkinen which nonetheless explores Rykener as a transgender or at least "transgender-like" figure.[39] Jeremy Goldberg, by contrast, simply calls Rykener "John" in his article, dismissing Eleanor as part of the case's compounded falsity and fictionality.[40] The insistence on using the name "John," over or alongside "Eleanor," suggests that cistory prefers to follow the patterns laid down by cis authorities rather than those offered by trans subjects. This compulsory cisgender assignment not only affects Rykener scholarship but also reveals the cisgender narration of history to be highly constructed and definitively not neutral. Only by denaturalizing the cisgender turn can we retrain our understanding, practices, and sympathies to include the critical revelations of the transgender turn.

The Transgender Turn

In recent years, Eleanor Rykener's case has begun to be revaluated as a result of the arrival of the transgender turn to medieval studies. In the 2014 novel *A Burnable Book*, Bruce Holsinger reimagined Rykener as a "swerver," a term he invented as ersatz medieval vernacular that locates Rykener somewhere between a gender-fluid person and a trans woman in transition.[41] The Plea and Memoranda Roll became an important part of the plot, outshining in some ways the significance of Rykener herself in the sequel, *The Invention of Fire* (2016).[42] Around this time Karras recounted in "John/Eleanor Ryekener Revisited" (2016) why she found it necessary to re-turn to Rykener. Karras admits that if she were to rewrite her initial study, she would consider identifying the figure as "transgender" rather than as "transvestite."[43] In the wake of this admission, the article then describes how Karras's coauthor, Tom Linkinen, was inspired by Karras to create a puppet show reimagining Rykener as transgender. Subsequently the two came together to explore if and how one could re-turn to the figure as "transgender-like," informed by recent scholarship in transgender studies.[44] In this same year, at the 2016 convention of the Modern Language Association in Austin, Texas, an out trans scholar, Kadin Henningsen, presented a paper on the need to identify Rykener both as Eleanor and as transgender, not merely as "transgender-like." This paper was later adapted into an article—"Calling [herself] Eleanor"—for "Medieval Trans Feminisms" (2019), a special issue of *Medievalist Feminist Forum*.[45] That essay is important because it refers to Rykener as a trans woman named Eleanor, but also because it emphasizes the role of women's labor as foundational for Eleanor's expressed identity.[46] Each of these studies exemplify how the transgender turn works to re-turn transgender subjectivities to trans bodies and histories; to rename, rearticulate, and remobilize erased modes of trans life and activism.

The work of the transgender turn is not merely to import insights from the present into the past. The long-standing existence of trans people, and centuries of transgender turns, is precisely what makes new interventions and reclamations possible. As part of this movement, this essay also labors not merely to force a premodern trans woman to perform modern tricks, but rather to highlight the critically trans ways that she already turned tricks in the streets, sheets, and courtrooms of medieval London. Resisting Rykener's compulsory cisgender assignment returns us to a Middle Ages that always already was transgender.

In this spirit, Eleanor's actions and discourse can guide our understanding of the transgender turn. It is worth noting that the document contains eighteen instances of Rykener saying something (five instances of "dictus" and thirteen instances of "quod" connected to her), whereas Britby has only two instances of confessing ("fatebatur"). This emphasizes the degree to which the testimony is first and foremost a record produced about and by Rykener. The record states that on December 11, 1394, Eleanor Rykener ("Elianoram Rykener") told the story of how she had been standing on Cheapside between 8:00 and 9:00 p.m., where and when she turned back toward and negotiated with a man, John Britby. According to the record, "Requesting money for [her] labor, Rykener consented" (Qui ab eo argentum pro labore suo petens sibi consentiebat). She was on this day, as she had been on many days previously, presenting as a woman and calling herself Eleanor. She had learned to perform sex work from a woman, Anna. Responding to Britby's accosting, Rykener demanded to be paid before performing sexual acts with him. This exchange was one of a series of such exchanges; Rykener described the fact that she had negotiated sex from men for pay or gifts, such as a golden ring ("anulum aureum"), and from women, including several nuns ("quampluribus monialibus") and many other women ("quampluribus mulieribus"), married and otherwise, seemingly without pay. Finally, she consented to sex with Britby. She proceeded to a stall in Soper's Lane ("Sopereslane") and completed the transaction for which Britby had accosted and paid her.[47] Soon after, they were caught by local law enforcement, then brought to the court. There, Rykener consented to give the scribe her name—Eleanor—and told her story as Eleanor.

This is the story of Eleanor Rykener from Eleanor Rykener's perspective. This version of the story is important to consider, given the way that the cisgender turn in scholarship has refused or redacted such a trans perspective. In particular, the fact that the record includes Rykener's demand for payment ("argentum") for her labor ("labore") and that this was a prerequisite for consent ("consentiebat") evidences the fact that this trans woman is not a passive body on which cisgender men act. While Britby pursued and accosted her, the mention of Rykener's consent highlights that Rykener was at least somewhat active in the exchange. The sexual encounter is not something a cisgender man does to a trans woman but something the two of them do together. He did not just turn toward her—she also turned toward him, a transgender turn to meet the cisgender turn in a moment of negotiation that proved to be (and should be to us) pivotal. The insistence on payment before Rykener would consent tells readers that the trans woman did not merely submit to the cis man's desires. He may have desired her body, but she had desires of her own: silver, *argentum*. The cisgender turn toward the transgender subject was going to cost the cisgender subject. The record says that Rykener asked for money for her "labor," signaling that she understood this encounter—that of a cisgender subject with her body—to be a form of work that demands recognition and compensation. Why would we imagine that this same trans woman—who recognized the value of her body, time, and labor—would not also recognize the value of sharing her name ("Elianoram"), her appearance, and the authority of her story with the court?

Eleanor Rykener's Turn

The goal of this transgender turn as I invoke it here is to call Eleanor Rykener back to the stand, to let her speak back to cisgender medieval studies by heeding her demand for consent and payment. Inspired by her demands, I conclude this essay by making three of my own, demanding an overturning of three mistakes of cisgender medieval studies: (1) I demand that we reclaim her body by turning from accosting her gender to affirming the beauty and dignity of her trans identity; (2) I demand that we reclaim her name by turning away from the practice of repeatedly deadnaming her as "John" to a privileging of her self-given identity as Eleanor; and (3) I demand that we reclaim her story by turning away from an analysis that imagines Rykener as a trans body subjugated to cisgender subjectivities and embracing one that recognizes her narration of events with Britby as a collaboration between trans and cis subjects.

The first step toward developing a more consensual scholarly relation with Rykener may simply be to look at the trans woman in order to glimpse what she showed Britby: that transgender is beautiful. In "The Transgender Look," Jack Halberstam plays with the double meaning of the word *look* to explore how the appearance and gaze of trans people function. Pushing beyond cis assumptions, Halberstam calls readers to see the unexpected beauty of trans lives, arguing, "The transgender character surprises audiences with his/her ability to remain attractive, appealing, and gendered while simultaneously presenting a gender at odds with sex."[48] The transgender turn is thus the power not only to turn heads out of surprise but also to compel second looks that are driven by a response to trans beauty. The disability studies scholar Rosemarie Garland-Thomson puts it another way: "Beauty is a perceptual process and a transitive action: it catches interest, prompts judgment, encourages scrutiny, creates knowledge."[49]

Although there is no record of how Rykener looked beyond the fact that she appeared to Britby to be a woman, we have evidence that she turned heads. From her confession, we know that Britby was not the first man or woman to turn and give Rykener a second look. Not only did she make them look twice, but also she could hold their look long enough to receive sexual advances, gifts, and payment. To see the beauty of Rykener is to recognize the power of trans bodies to engage actively in the power dynamics of sexual exchanges. Britby objectifies her body; but she expresses her attractiveness and exploits his desire for her. Furthermore, Rykener rejects sexual passivity by demanding to be paid for her collaborative labor. That exchange of money insists that sex is not something that a man simply does to a trans woman but rather is something he might do *with* her, pending her consent. Yet given these particular power dynamics, the sex they have is not a collaboration between equals. The trans woman is being objectified and exploited, yet she demands compensation for that exploitation, reclaims ownership over her body, and demands acknowledgment of her beauty and collaborative labor.

The second step toward cultivating a more consensual scholarly relation with Rykener and her narrative begins by allowing the trans woman at the center of this story to educate us about how to see her better, just as she tried to educate the scribe. How Rykener turns in response to Britby's act of accosting her and how the scribe unspeaks her story centers on the trans woman's demand for consent, *consentiebat*.[50] This is a modification of the Latin word *consentio/consensus*, which means "to assent to, favor, fit, be consistent/in sympathy/in unison with, agree."[51] By demanding that their exchange be premised upon payment and consent, Rykener reclaims some agency over her body and story. Britby may see her, but she turns his head. He approaches her, but she receives him. He asks for sex, but she demands payment. He engages with her sexually, but she consents. He touches her, but she touches him back. He speaks first in the courts, but she gets the final word. Thus, although Rykener insists on pay ("argentum") before she will consent ("consentiebat") only one time in the narrative, her numerous turns of body, agency, and story enact the praxis of visual activism defined by Garland-Thomson wherein staring turns from a one-sided act into an active, consensual collaboration.[52]

Scholars can likewise engage in a more consensual and ethical relationship with Rykener by calling her Eleanor. By repeating "John" throughout the record, the scribe reifies what the court sees and how it allows or fails to allow gender to unfold in time and space. John Britby consents to tell his story in the persona of John Britby. Because this name and identity match his given name and gender—not stated otherwise, because he is cisgender—the scribe and, later, historians affirm the story of John Britby as John Britby's story. Sara Ahmed writes that through repeated affirmations of who may be present, seen, and heard within a particular space, "spaces become straight, which allow straight bodies to extend into them."[53] Expanding upon this idea, we might also argue that that time, like space, can become cisgender, allowing cis bodies to extend into them. Yet in the face of a cisgender time and place that insist she is "John," Rykener seeks to reclaim her name and educate onlookers by calling herself Eleanor: "Se Elianoram nominans veste muliebri detectus" (Discovered in women's attire, she named herself as "Eleanor").[54] Although the word "transgender" did not yet exist in the fourteenth century, by asserting the truth of her name and person, she lays the foundations for later readers, arriving at her narrative in the wake of the transgender turn, to see her trans womanhood and reclaim her name. The name that Eleanor Rykener gives the court is *Eleanor*. The story she tells is Eleanor's story, mostly concerning her life as Eleanor. The scribe and cistory do not honor the conditions of her agency and self-identification. The scribe and cistory use Eleanor's life story but sideline her from it by calling her "John," or equivocating between "Eleanor" and "John," calling her "John/Eleanor."[55] Even in these cases of "John/Eleanor," the name "Eleanor" comes second.

Yet Rykener did not consent to tell her story as "John" or as "John/Eleanor." She demands, in the record, to tell her story as "Eleanor." The story logged in the court record is the story of Eleanor Rykener, wherein "John" is but a footnote.

Finally, a third step toward creating a more ethical scholarly relation to Rykener is in honoring the sense of obligation she inspires in readers who *are* conscious of her trans subjectivity in the Plea and Memoranda Roll A34, m.2. An important response to the labor performed by Eleanor Rykener and by her story can be to mark her as a collaborator and coauthor in the text's construction. Without the class status or cis male identity that would have better enabled her to purchase control over her words, Rykener's story is taken, used, and retold without the author's ever being paid. No payment is mentioned. In fact, although no specific court decision or sentence is noted, Rykener may have been punished for sharing her body, her life, and her words. What can be determined is that throughout the whole proceeding, Rykener was accosted in various forms and her story un-transgendered.

The violation of Rykener's consent and the appropriation of her story may be partially rectified by naming Eleanor Rykener as an author of her text. Critics may reply that Rykener did not physically pen her story and that the Plea and Memoranda Roll recounts a narrative in excess of only her perspective. In some respect, all writing requires a confluence of voices. Nonetheless, without Rykener to provide the particularities of her trans body, story, and name to the proceedings, the account would not exist. Take Eleanor *qua* Eleanor out of the equation and the subsequent histories are not written. For these reasons, I argue that Eleanor Rykener should be listed as an author or coauthor (alongside John Britby, who is also not usually listed, and the unnamed scribe). Only by remunerating Rykener through citation and a byline can the transgender turn establish and commit to a truth that is as important for medieval trans lives as for modern trans lives: if you wish to use trans stories and trans bodies, you should pay trans subjects, or in this case, at the very least offer the credit of authorship over their bodies, names, and stories. Toward the goal of holding scholarship accountable for every Eleanor subject to compulsory cisgender assignment and histories, the transgender turn empowers these trans lives to speak back against the appropriation and erasure of trans subjectivities in medieval cisgender studies. May Rykener, whose very name means "the reckoner," teach us to be accountable to our trans histories. Time and again, Eleanor calls us to return and take another look.

Notes

1. David Lorenzo Boyd and Ruth Mazo Karras, "The Interrogation of a Male Transvestite Prostitute in Fourteenth-Century London," *GLQ* 1.4 (1995): 459–65, https://doi.org/10.1215/10642684-1-4-459.

2. London Metropolitan Archives, Plea and Memoranda Roll A34, CLA/024/01/02/035, m.2, https://lmaweb.minisisinc.com/scripts/mwimain.dll/144/LMA_OPAC/web_detail?SESSIONSEARCH&exp=refd CLA/024/01/02/035.

3. The wider goal of this argument is that we would one day pause to consider before automatically assigning a cisgender identity for John Britby. For the purposes of this study, however, John Britby is identified as a cisgender man. There are significant differences between the ways that Britby and Rykener are treated by the document, with the former being given the cisgender (or passing) privilege of not having his gender interrogated, whereas the latter is extensively described in gendered terms, scrutinized for her life history, and deadnamed. Naming these differences between cisgender and transgender historical and literary patterns are important for unpacking critical issues in the past and the ways that stories are told. Regardless of whether Britby is cisgender or not, his story is told as cisgender.

4. Plea and Memoranda Roll A34, CLA/024/01/02/035, m.2.

5. Katy Steinmetz, "The Transgender Tipping Point," *Time*, May 29, 2014, http://time.com/135480/transgender-tipping-point.

6. Jack Halberstam (published under "Judith"), *In a Queer Time and Place: Transgender Bodies, Subcultural Lives* (New York: NYU Press, 2005); Rosemarie Garland-Thomson, *Staring: How We Look* (New York: Oxford University Press, 2009); Sara Ahmed, *Queer Phenomenology: Orientations, Objects, Others* (Durham, NC: Duke University Press, 2006).

7. *OED Online*, s.v. "turn, n. 8c," https://www.oed.com/view/Entry/207668?rskey=vjN61k&result=1&isAdvanced=false (accessed June 2019).

8. Ibid., "turn, v. 3b."

9. Ibid., "turn, v. 21a."

10. Ibid., "turn, n. 1a."

11. Ibid., "turn, v.; turn on, 3a."

12. Ibid., "turn, v. 51."

13. Boyd and Karras, "Interrogation."

14. David Lorenzo Boyd and Ruth Mazo Karras, "Ut cum muliere: A Male Transvestite Prostitute in Fourteenth-Century London," in *Premodern Sexualities*, ed. Louise Fradenburg and Carla Freccero (New York: Routledge, 1996), 99–116.

15. Ruth Mazo Karras, "Prostitution in Medieval Europe," *Handbook of Medieval Sexuality*, ed. Vern L. Bullough and James A. Brundage (New York: Routledge, 1996), 251.

16. Carolyn Dinshaw, "Good Vibrations: John/Eleanor, Dame Alys, the Pardoner, and Foucault," *Getting Medieval: Sexualities and Communities, Pre- and Postmodern* (Durham, NC: Duke University Press, 1999), 100–142.

17. Jeremy Goldberg, "John Rykener, Richard II, and the Governance of London," *Leeds Studies in English*, n.s., 45, ed. Alaric Hall (2014): 49–70, https://www.academia.edu/12677622/John_Rykener_Richard_II_and_the_Governance_of_London.

18. Ibid., 69.

19. Ibid., 53.

20. Ibid., 65.

21. M. W. Bychowski and Dorothy Kim, "Visions of Medieval Trans Feminism: An Introduction," *Medieval Feminist Forum: A Journal for the Society of Medieval Feminist Scholarship* 55.1, ed. Dorothy Kim and M. W. Bychowski (2019): 6–41, https://ir.uiowa.edu/mff/vol55/iss1/2/.

22. Goldberg, "John Rykener, Richard II, and the Governance of London," 50.

23 Ibid., 67.

24 Ibid., 66–69.

25. Adrienne Rich, "Compulsory Heterosexuality and Lesbian Existence," in *Blood, Bread, and Poetry* (1985; repr., New York: W. W. Norton, 1994).

26. Plea and Memoranda Roll A34, CLA/024/01/02/035, m.2.

27. Ibid.

28. Ibid.

29. *Latdict: Latin Dictionary and Grammar Resource*, ed. Kevin Mahone, s.v. "peto, verb," ed. Kevin Mahoney, http://latin-dictionary.net/definition/30326/peto-petere-petivi-petitus (accessed June 2019).

30. Plea and Memoranda Roll A34, CLA/024/01/02/035, m.2.

31. Dinshaw, "Good Vibrations."

32. Alexander Baldassano, "Bodies of Resistance: On (Not) Naming Gender in the Medieval West" (PhD diss., City University of New York, 2017), 34.

33. Plea and Memoranda Roll A34, CLA/024/01/02/035, m.2.

34. Mahoney, *Latdict: Latin Dictionary and Grammar Resource*, s.v. "infandus, adj.," http://latin-dictionary.net/definition/23585/infandus-infanda-infandum (accessed November 1, 2018).

35. Dinshaw, "Good Vibrations."

36. Plea and Memoranda Roll A34, CLA/024/01/02/035, m.2.

37. Boyd and Karras, "Interrogation."

38. Dinshaw, "Good Vibrations," 100–101.

39. Ruth Mazo Karras and Tom Linkinen, "John/Eleanor Ryekener Revisited," in *Founding Feminisms in Medieval Studies: Essays in Honor of E. Jane Burns*, ed. Laine E. Dogget and Daniel E. O'Sullivan (Woodbridge, Suffolk: Gallica, 2016), 114.

40. Goldberg, "John Rykener, Richard II, and the Governance of London," 49.

41. Bruce Holsinger, *A Burnable Book* (New York: HarperCollins, 2014).

42. Bruce Holsinger, *The Invention of Fire* (New York: HarperCollins, 2016).

43. Karras and Linkinen, "John/Eleanor Ryekener Revisited," 111.

44. Ibid.

45. Kadin Henningsen, "Calling [herself] Eleanor: Gender Labor and Becoming a Woman in the Rykener Case," *Medieval Feminist Forum: A Journal for the Society of Medieval Feminist Scholarship* 55.1, ed. Dorothy Kim and M. W. Bychowski (2019): 249–66, https://ir.uiowa.edu/mff/vol55/iss1/9/.

46. Henningsen, "Calling [herself] Eleanor," 250.

47. Plea and Memoranda Roll A34, CLA/024/01/02/035, m.2.

48. Halberstam, *In a Queer Time and Place*, 76.

49. Garland-Thomson, *Staring*, 187.

50. Plea and Memoranda Roll A34, CLA/024/01/02/035, m.2.

51. Mahoney, *Latdict*, s.v. "consentio, verb," http://latin-dictionary.net/definition/13306/consentio-consentire-consensi-consensus (accessed November 1, 2018).

52. Garland-Thomson, *Staring*, 193.

53. Ahmed, *Queer Phenomenology*, 92.

54. Plea and Memoranda Roll A34, CLA/024/01/02/035, m.2.

55. Boyd and Karras, "'Ut cum muliere,'" 101; Dinshaw, "Good Vibrations," 100–101; Karras and Linkinen, "John/Eleanor Ryekener Revisited," 111.

CHAPTER 5

Wojciech of Poznań and the Trans Archive, Poland, 1550–1561

Anna Kłosowska

The document translated in this chapter is a 1561 court deposition of Wojciech of Poznań, arrested and interrogated before a tribunal in Kazimierz (now part of Kraków). The text does not mention the accusations, the cause of the arrest, or the reasons for sentencing (the last word is "burned"). It is the only record we have of Wojciech, who lived as a man and a woman. Until now, the deposition was available only in Polish and German.[1]

Wojciech is a common, exclusively masculine name in Polish.[2] Only masculine pronouns are used to refer to Wojciech in the text (on gender in Polish, see the discussion later in this chapter). I refer to Wojciech in what follows with the pronoun "they," but there is no explicit statement regarding Wojciech's preferred expression of gender. The record does not state why Wojciech is deposed as a man, a surprising omission since the deposition reveals that they were publicly ordered to live as a woman sometime around 1550 and lived as one for a decade. The tribunal's questions and reactions to the deposition are not recorded. A few dialogue tags—words like "said" and "confessed"—allow some speculation, but their interpretation is debatable.

One aspect of the text that makes it difficult to follow is the large cast of characters—more than twenty people in a dozen locations. Poznań is likely Wojciech's city of birth (ca. 1530–1535 or earlier), located about five hundred kilometers northwest of Kraków.[3] Of Wojciech's three marriages to men, two were contracted in Kraków, but they resided with their husbands in Poznań. It helps to summarize the content of the document. We know from the deposition that Wojciech lived in Poznań for six months sometime around 1550 as a monk in a monastery. While living as a monk, Wojciech was sexually active with two women while sharing a bed with a man, an organist in the church. One of the women, "Clara the German," the text implies, had sex with the organist and with Wojciech in that bed.[4] Clara and Wojciech had a sexual relationship again later when Wojciech returned from Kraków and was living in Poznań for two years as a married woman.

After six months of living as a monk, for unknown reasons Wojciech left the monastery, and "the lords aldermen ordered him to be examined by women at the town hall in front of the men," implying the aldermen and the mayor.[5] There is no explanation why the order was issued. Wojciech's mother was then publicly sworn at the town hall in front of the aldermen and the mayor, under the threat of death, to present/clothe them as a woman. The word used in the deposition is "nosić," to behave/comport/carry oneself, present/clothe/dress someone/oneself, for example, as a woman or man.[6] This episode suggests that Wojciech did not present as a woman—or at least not exclusively—prior to this.

After Wojciech was ordered to present and dress as a woman in Poznań circa 1550, the record states that they lived as such for a decade: as a maiden for a year, a married woman in Poznań for two years, a married woman with another husband for an unspecified period, and then as a widow at the time of the deposition in Kazimierz in 1561. The two-day deposition focuses on their valuable personal assets (day one)[7] and illicit sex acts (day two).[8]

In addition to marriages to men, Wojciech listed many female-identified sexual partners and described rather standard ways of making a living as an impoverished urban single woman: renting rooms, selling the sex work of other women, brewing beer, embroidery, theft, and fraud. The deposition listed their significant possessions and examined their provenance: sums of money, two expensive dresses, and some ten pieces of jewelry and silver.

This chapter tests two hypotheses: One, that while we know nothing about Wojciech's chosen name and preference, they resemble today's trans or genderqueer people in that they seem to have actively created and curated their gender and sexual expression. Two, that the presence of one trans or genderqueer person reveals the existence of a historically documented queer and trans community in urban centers of mid-sixteenth-century Poland, which valued them and depended on their experience. The deposition at least gestures to a series of coalitions, if not a community, with areas of collaboration in spite of major differences.

The Deposition

Feria s[ecunda] post do[min]icam Oculi. Anno 1561 [Monday after the third Sunday in Lent, i.e., March 10, 1561].

Wojciech of Poznań, son of Szymon[9] Skwarski. When he was called before the tribunal,[10] he confessed that he was a monk in Poznań[11] from Michaelmas to Lent [approximately six months],[12] and when he left the monastery, the Lords aldermen ordered him to be examined by women at the city hall in front of the men. And Lord Lipczyński, the mayor, was there on that occasion, and observed. Then the aldermen ordered the mother under the threat of death and infamy[13] to dress/present [*nosić*] him as a woman, and there, at the city hall, took the mother's overskirt and ordered him to be attired. And the mother bought a maiden's dress,[14] brought it to the city hall and he was ordered to be clad in it, and thus he dressed in such clothes for ten years.

Item[15] [also] he confessed that when he was going to enter the monastery, he took ten *złotych*[16] and two silver spoons from his mother and gave them to the elder monk.

Item in Kraków, at the [house?] of Wojciech the carpenter he married Sebastyjan [Sebastian] the brewer and he lived with him in Poznań for two years, and he allowed this Sebastian to keep a woman, and he himself kept company with another one. Later, it so happened that in a quarrel over a woman whom Sebastian had for his use, he hit that Sebastian in the head with a brick and he was promptly healed, and then he died, but he doesn't know whether from that wound or not.

Item in Kazimierz, he married Wawrzyniec [Lawrence], farm worker,[17] and he said in front of him that he had fifteen hundred *złotych* payable in Poznań, and he [Wawrzyniec] was tempted by it.

Item that little chain,[18] with which he was apprehended, [about which] he said that some landowner/nobleman gave it to him for the night's lodgings, and that Wojciech hid away with it, and then that landowner/nobleman departed.

Item he confessed that he also took money from other people for the night's lodgings, and hid [from them].

Item when he was marrying Wawrzyniec, he took two strings of beads[19] and two silver spoons that he had borrowed from people, and pawned them with the Jew Jeleń [Hirsch][20] for nine *złotych* and the decorative knife sheath [*nożenki*] for two red *złotych*.[21]

Item when he traveled from Opatow to Szydlow, to the guesthouse,[22] John the smith was drinking there, and there, with that smith, they were handfasted/shook hands[23] in front of good people and were married in church, and the next morning after that he left town with the Jews.

Item when he worked with pearls and gold, he kept the leftover materials and did not return them.

Item he took a silver ring from the lords of Górka.

Item a silk summer dress,[24] [which] he said that his mother made for him. But the damask [brocade] one he bought himself from a Jew in Poznań, he paid off half, but not the other half yet.

Item he confessed that he bought a stolen silver cup from a boy, which the boy stole from a certain Countess Ostrowska, who stayed with his mother,[25] and he bartered it for a belt, for which he paid an extra four *talars*.[26]

Item on the second day, Wojciech freely confessed without any torture that when he was a monk in the monastery in Poznań, he had relations with a married woman, Rybitka [Fishwife?].[27]

Item in that monastery as well that Wojciech and the organist of that church would lie in the same bed with Clara the German and they both had sex with her.

Item when he left the monastery, then and there, in Poznań, learning embroidery, and already wearing women's clothing, he had sex with Anuchna, who was learning [apprenticed?] at the same place.[28]

Item he dressed as a maiden through the summer/for a year,[29] living at old Madam Spławska's in Poznań, where he was with the young girl, Annuchna [*sic*], whom Madam Spławska was raising, who later married a tailor in Środka.

Item when he lived at Madam Królikowska's two miles from Żnin, he courted a Maiden, and he had sex with a [female] gardener.

Item when he lived in Poznań with Sebastian the brewer, whom he had married in Kraków, he allowed that Sebastian to keep a woman, and he himself had sex with another one, that first Clara.

Item in Poznań, after the death of that Sebastian, he sold beer, kept loose women, had sex with them himself, and allowed others to have sex with them.[30]

Item in Kraków, in one place he had relations with a cook and he gave her white boots, so that she would not tell on him.

Item in Środa, also in women's clothing, he had relations with a [feminine grammatical gender] cook.

Item in the little town of Dolsko in the same clothing he consorted with a [feminine grammatical gender] cook.

Item he did that a lot elsewhere.

Item he confessed that, in those women's clothes, he had his way with both unmarried and married women, and used his[31] bodily attributes [body] with them, and named them in detail; their names are not described in this writ because they are defamatory. Burned.[32]

Coalitions and Communities

In this section I look more closely at Wojciech's work in creating their own gender. While I read their deposition against the grain in order to excavate the evidence of queer and trans communities, I do so while acknowledging that this person and their associates were trying to function in an environment defined by lethal levels of destructive hostility. Wojciech likely died as a result of these proceedings. I read the record in the service of a trans political past, insisting that those who came into contact with Wojciech can be interpreted as relying on, or responding to, Wojciech's gender creativity and were therefore aware of the possibility of nonbinary gender and nonheteronormative sex acts.

The deposition evokes a communal urban landscape: public buildings and institutions (town hall, guesthouse), meeting a future husband at the house of an acquaintance, joining a group of travelers on a journey. Wojciech was a desirable partner to a great many people identified as men (three husbands) and women (a dozen sexual partners named individually and "many more" unspecified others). While the number and variety of Wojciech's sex and business partners and husbands imply that Wojciech was remarkably socially successful and erotically desirable, that number is not exceptionally high in the context of other, similar depositions.[33]

Only two people—the husband who died and the woman extortionist—among Wojciech's fairly numerous partners and contacts seem to have come into conflict with Wojciech.[34] This low reported incidence of violent conflict or extortion in the deposition could imply that the gender-creative, nonbinary subculture was for the most part collaborative and mutually supportive.

All the events in the deposition are set in an urban landscape. What if this indicates a subculture that thrived in an urban context? The deposition gestures toward the possibility that this urban subculture brought together people from the country and the city, who crossed status boundaries that we find marked in the deposition by the use of different forms of personal names and titles. Landowners are called by their title to the land (the lords of Górka), others by their profession (cook), given name ("that first Clara"), family relationship (mother), or surname (Madam Splawska).³⁵ Communal designations are based on religion and language (German Clara; Jew Jelen [deer/Hirsch]).

The most important name of all, that of Wojciech, is at the center of this deposition's work on gender. The name is a masculine one, although we are never told that Wojciech was in contempt of the previous order to present as a woman. It may have been Wojciech's preference to use the masculine name. But it should also be noted that legal standing as a man promised a better outcome to the trial. Impoverished urban single women with no male relatives had little chance of successfully defending themselves against accusations. Perhaps both the fact that Wojciech's father was named in the deposition and that Wojciech used a masculine name and pronouns were part of their strategy and would not necessarily represent Wojciech's preference without the pressure of defending themself in a tribunal.

While the deposition uses only masculine forms and a masculine given name for Wojciech, Polish has three genders for nouns, pronouns, and adjectives (masculine, feminine, and *niejaki*/none) and seven (these three plus four others) for the remaining parts of speech (verbs, participles, etc.).³⁶ Rather than gender, a Polish sentence often conveys more complex nuances: animate or inanimate? human or not? signifier or signified? respectful or scornful?³⁷ Nouns can change gender for stylistic or affective reasons, especially nouns that designate humans and animals. For example, one *niejaka* (none) form of the noun "boy" is *chłopię*, versus a masculine form of the same noun, *chłopak*; one *niejaka* form of the noun "young woman" is *dziewczę*, versus a feminine noun, *dziewczyna*. These distinctions may be used to produce an arch, elevated, poetic, or archaizing style. A somewhat similar effect can be obtained in English by personification or attributing gender to genderless objects, for example calling the moon "she."

We mentioned that Polish has gendered adjectives, pronouns, and verb forms, but they are not always aligned with one of the three genders that a noun like "boy" can have. The logic of these associations is perfectly clear to a Polish speaker. Take, again, the case of the noun "boy." The *niejaka* noun form *chłopię* and the feminine diminutive noun form *chłopczyna* both convey pity or affection. In the expression "this boy," the *niejaka* noun form is associated with the *niejaka* form of adjective: to *chłopię*; but the feminine noun is associated with the masculine adjective: ten *chłopczyna*. None of that sheds any further light on the deposition, which maintains strictly masculine forms for Wojciech.

The choice of female social gender by the women who examined Wojciech in Poznań can be interpreted as an approximation: a "binary" gender designation for a nonbinary reality.[38] By "binary" I mean only that the women and aldermen of Poznań (ca. 1550) as well as the tribunal of Kazimierz (in 1561) reverted to one of the two labels—"woman" or "man"—in specific circumstances where it suited them. We can ask what personal experience with gender creativity led these women and men to force Wojciech's mother to designate Wojciech as a woman and then, ten years later, to designate them as a man. The reality they were describing was much more complex than their limited means for categorizing it. Wojciech appears to have lived as simultaneously female and male.

For Wojciech, presenting as a woman for a decade was not only a question of gender, marital status, sexual desirability, the type of work Wojciech performed, or their social status. Consider the type of women's dresses listed among Wojciech's personal valuables at the time of arrest and the detailed descriptions of their provenance. Recall that Wojciech trained as an embroidery apprentice and was found in possession of small amounts of money, jewelry, and other precious objects. The deposition describes not only the expensive fabrics of the dresses—silk and damask—but also states in detail the manner in which Wojciech acquired these expensive items, betraying the interrogators' interest in tracking fraudulent transactions such as theft and defaulting on a debt. For example, from the trial record: "*Item*, a silk summer dress,[39] [which] he said that his mother made for him. But the damask one he bought himself from a Jew in Poznań, he paid off half, but not the other half yet."

Note the verb "said" (*powiedział*), used three times in the deposition, once when Wojciech is creating an appearance of wealth to lure a marriage prospect ("he [Wojciech] said in front of him [Wawrzyniec] that he had fifteen hundred *złotych* . . . and he [Wawrzyniec] was tempted by it") and another time to suggest that Wojciech is lying about the provenance of an object suspected of having been illegally acquired ("said that some landowner/nobleman gave it to him"). The last use of "said," about the silk summer dress ("he said that his mother made for him") might be a part of that pattern, used to imply that Wojciech was again lying. In contrast, the deposition regularly uses the word "confessed" (*zeznał*) when Wojciech's statement is an open admission of guilt: for example, "freely confessed without any torture."

In discussing the limits and functioning of premodern women's agency, the feminist Marxist historian Martha Howell considers "the goods of her body," a woman's valuable personal possessions, which are the "private" property to which women are understood to have unalienable rights.[40] That type of legal and linguistic concept making is also reflected in the evolution

since the late fourteenth century of the late medieval Latin legal term "individual" (*individuum*, meaning indivisible inherited property), borrowed from
mathematics ("indivisible"), and later progressively becoming what the word
means today.[41] In these two examples, basic structures of the law and vocabulary forge links between the idea of privacy; agency predicated on the right
to individual property and personhood; indivisible, unalienable possessions;
the emerging concept of personhood and the individual; and the body. If we
consider "her body" and "the goods of her body" as a continuum, we can
see more clearly why, for women, expensive clothes and jewelry are part of a
specifically feminine social gender expression, perhaps in contrast with men,
who have greater access to other forms of agency and property. The use of
the commonplace Polish verb "to present as/dress as" (*nosić*) to describe the
actions of a person who is actively creating their social gender expression is
consistent with the legal tradition and semantics of women's agency examined by Howell. Howell's analysis helps us appreciate that, when asked about
their possessions and ways of making a living, Wojciech is also being interrogated about their gender expression and agency: the twofold structure of
the interrogation being reflected in the two-day deposition.

One of the striking features of the deposition is that both days examine Wojciech's life before and after the gender assignment. On the first day,
Wojciech describes the gender assignment, lists three marriages, travels,
transactions involving money and valuables. On the second day, Wojciech lists
illicit sex acts, training in embroidery, and typical sources of income of poor
urban single women. Roughly, the first day presents Wojciech as a relatively
propertied and well-connected woman, part of a family—a father, a mother,
three husbands. The two deposition days are not split before and after gender
assignment but rather before and after relative prosperity.

In the deposition, strands of irreconcilably different projects are enmeshed
and fused, testing our ability to separate them. On the one hand, in some
instances Wojciech reveals precise details ("in those women's clothes, he had
his way with both unmarried and married women, and used his bodily attributes with them, and named them in detail"). On the other hand, the deposition is also crafted to avoid punishment for illicit acts like sodomy. Although
identifying or identified in the deposition as male, Wojciech lived as a woman
and was married to men during the previous decade. The authorities could
decide to punish them for same-sex acts: having sex with women while living
as a woman, or marrying men "as" Wojciech, the person identified as male.
Since they had been presenting as a woman allegedly on the order of the
aldermen and mayor of Poznań, charges of sodomy leveled at Wojciech as
a person living as a woman who had been married to men might have been

weaker. Wojciech carefully avoids saying that they ever had sex with men, including husbands or the men with whom they shared a bed ("he allowed that Sebastian to keep a woman, and he himself had sex with another one"). The attempted self-representation of their sexual activities as licit (deposing as a man, they list many women sexual partners) seems to unravel on the second day of the deposition, when the record states three times in quick succession, with what I would suggest is an accusatory insistence, that they had sex with women while wearing feminine clothing.

Cultural rituals and performances of belonging, whether founded on gender expression, religion, "class," community membership, or citizenship, are rarely innocent. They separate, close out, and make vulnerable some, even as they bring others together and strengthen them. The intersecting planes of commonality described herein form a complex interplay of publics, addressees, and beneficiaries, even as the deposition cuts through that commonality in the interest of finding the deposed guilty of illicit behavior. Queer and trans studies as an analysis of self-fashioning in a hostile environment are inherently reading against such external scripts and across multiple modalities.

The actions of one gender-creative person constitute only one visible area of a network of social interactions that traverses an entire collectivity. Wojciech is not an isolated trans or gender-creative individual, negotiating an ostensibly binary world. They are a link in a trans, queer, gender-nonconforming network—connected, hybrid, heterogeneous—of people whom they marry, with whom they have sex or engage in manifold business dealings. Some of these people may depend on Wojciech's status and experience as a trans or gender creative person. The document reveals widespread accommodation and tolerance, and even a preference—including sexual preference—for trans and gender creative people, and it may even hint at the existence of a self-aware and vibrant trans and genderqueer collectivity in mid-sixteenth-century Polish cities. Wojciech was publicly forced to conform to one gender, but they lived a trans or genderqueer life, engaged in sex and sex work, and participated in other business transactions for over a decade until their arrest and execution.

Polish Trans Past

Tomasz Nastulczyk and Piotr Oczko discuss Wojciech's case in *Homoseksualność Staropolska: Przyczynek do Badań* (Premodern Polish homosexuality: A prolegomenon to research, 2012).[42] Taking up Michel Foucault's phrase "sodomy, that utterly confused category," they use the term "uncategories" to emphasize that premodern texts often group forms of gender expression and sex acts in ways different from how they are grouped later on.[43] The category of sodomy in the Middle Ages combined practices that are today divided into separate categories: bestiality, pedophilia, avarice, gluttony, oral sex, anal sex, and same-sex acts, among others. By contrast, the heterosexual binary separates into two categories what is today part of a continuum of sexual preference intersecting with a spectrum of gender. The deposition reflects the premodern concept of heterosexual binary as it tries to separate Wojciech and their partners of the "opposite" sex into two discrete categories, "male" and "female," but that is impossible because these two categories were not kept apart in premodern trans and genderqueer experience. Modern readers easily see that the deposition's narrative, which cleaves to a binary and heterosexual model, uneasily hides a more complex reality.

An interesting observation made by Nastulczyk and Oczko concerns the affect of the tribunal where Wojciech makes their deposition, an affect that these two modern readers describe as *bezradna*, "bewildered," a quality explicit in the very confusing deposition. When binary premodern paradigms clash with trans and nonbinary realities they cannot articulate, they produce an affect palpable in the documents they bequeath us: clueless, adrift, hopeless, lost. Perhaps looking for that clueless affect will help us find more trans source texts, expanding our understanding of premodern trans people as well as our awareness of nonbinary and trans collectivities beyond the most visible, exceptional accounts.

Trans theory and terminology are works in progress. The terminology, concepts and theory are only an approximation of experience, both in the premodern era and today. While it frustrates our attempts to excavate a detailed portrait of a trans individual and their community, Wojciech's deposition grips us with a force that a historical *longue durée* study may not possess. The details specific to Wojciech's case, including personal names, private possessions, and Wojciech's public gender assignment as a woman make us take notice. The rich landscape of towns, people, material objects, their interactions and movements help define what we know about premodern trans Poland and Europe. Even though Wojciech's case lacks an interpretive lens or stable indications of a hermeneutics, that lack may be a promise of as yet unconceived possibilities—we can call them trans futurities—that may later be revealed, informing and illuminating the lives of today.

I do not have the expertise needed to situate the Polish deposition in the context of other legal records, but let us for a moment hypothetically assume that it is fictional. That would render this document even stronger evidence of the existence and visibility of trans people in 1550s Poland. A court deposition documents the existence of one trans person and all their contacts. A fictional narrative, in turn, documents the existence of an entire broad readership and an audience for oral transmission in a network of towns and cities inhabited by trans people and their knowing families, contacts, co-workers, and sex partners. A fiction may imply even more mainstream visibility and sexual desirability of trans people in 1550s Poland than a court document.

The court deposition of Wojciech of Poznań can play a positive role as proof of the existence of premodern trans and queer communities in Poland. It is a small chapter in the trans-friendly Polish history, especially valuable now that state-sponsored transphobia is on the rise. LGBTQ+ rights and safety are experiencing setbacks worldwide in democracies under pressure from the political alliance between conservatism, populism, and fascism. Reactionary alliances oppose what they term "gender ideology,"[44] using a broad appeal to "traditional family values" and mobilizing their base around the issues of religion and sovereignty.[45] As a counter to state-sponsored homophobia that claims it is a return to Polish "traditions," this chapter shows that there had always been awareness and performance of queer and nonbinary gender in premodern Poland, ever since Poland was a state. Wojciech's deposition offers today's LGBTQ+ people a positive way to participate in national mythmaking and includes them in our stories of origins. Given the historical record of existence of queer, nonbinary, gender-creative, and trans people in premodern Poland, we can dismiss the conservative alliance's claim that Polish queer and trans people are a product of modernity, a foreign import, a denial of Polish sovereignty, or an attack on traditional Polish values. The communities in the background of Wojciech's deposition are rich with trans lives.

Notes

All translations are mine unless otherwise indicated. The chapter was written in conversation with Blake Gutt, Masha Raskolnikov, Greta LaFleur, and Jack Roberts, without whose expert and generous help the nuances of trans experience in the Polish text would have been lost. Masha Raskolnikov's and Greta LaFleur's unfailing encouragement and incisive comments on four earlier drafts were priceless and transformative. Blake Gutt read and made extensive, major comments on an earlier draft. Ideas for this chapter also came from the other contributors to the volume.

   1. My translation is based on two editions of the Polish text available online and the 1911 German translation. Described by Leon Jan Wachholz as a "clean copy

of the 1561 document," the manuscript is Kraków, Archiwum Narodowe, Księgi Miasta Kazimierza, K266, fols. 52–56. See partial citation/edition, Tomasz Nastulczyk and Piotr Oczko, "'Tradycyjni' czy 'nowocześni'? O metodologicznych dylematach wspǫłczesnych badaczy staropolszczyzny, część druga: Queer Theory oraz Gay and Lesbian Studies," *Terminus* 15.3.28 (2013): 383–400, quotation at 97–398, doi: 10.4467/20843844TE.13.023.1580, www.ejournals.eu/Terminus, and slightly different, Katarzyna Pękacka-Falkowska, "Bawarski obojniak z 'Efemerydow,' czyli o tajemnicy płci," https://www.wilanow-palac.pl/bawarski_obojnak_z_efemerydow_czyli_o_tajemnicy_plci.html. See Wachholz, "Obojniak przed sądem w Kazimierzu w R.P. 1561: Przyczynek do dziejøw obojnactwa," *Przegląd lekarski* 10 (1911): 139–42 (I was unable to consult this source), and Wachholz, "Ein Zwitter von Gericht im Jahre 1561: Beitrag zur Geschichte des Zwittertums," *Vierteljahrsschrift für gerichtliche Medizin und öffentliches Sanitätswesen* 3, 41.2 (1911): 316–23, https://polona.pl/item/ein-zwitter-vor-gericht-im-jahre-1561-beitrag-zur-geschichte-des-zwittertums,NDU 0NzM0MDU/7/#info:metadata.

2. In German or English, the corresponding saint's name is Adalbert, a common name, since Wojciech is a patron saint of Poland. The feminine form would be Wojciecha, quite rare. Wojciech is listed as "of Poznań," and the text also gives the name and surname of Wojciech's father, Szymon Skwarski. I don't use the father's surname because it is not used for Wojciech in the deposition. It is gendered masculine in Polish (the feminine form would be Skwarska), and therefore no different for our purposes from Wojciech.

3. Poznań was the gateway to Germany and an earlier royal capital of Poland in the western part of the country, and since 1320 Kraków had been the southern royal capital in the foothills of the western Carpathian Mountains. The town of Kazimierz, where Wojciech was deposed before a tribunal, was on an island separated from Kraków by a branch of the Wisła (Vistula) River. It was the site of the most prominent Jewish community in Poland-Lithuania.

4. To extrapolate from David C. Mengel's illuminating study of the landscape of sex work in Prague and its countryside nearly two centuries prior, in the 1380s, if Clara presented as German, she could have charged more if she was paid for sex work; but the record does not specify sex work for money in her case. See David C. Mengel, "From Venice to Jerusalem and Beyond: Milíč of Kroměříž and the Topography of Prostitution in Fourteenth-Century Prague," *Speculum* 79.2 (2004): 407–42. Venice and Jerusalem are the names of Prague neighborhoods. Mengel's insightful and comprehensive study is an excellent starting point for anyone who wants to become more familiar with the landscape of sex, sex work, and women's employment and income patterns in central and eastern Europe in the 1380s.

5. The aldermen were the townspeople forming the municipal council who met at the town hall to exercise their civic functions, not related to the monastery.

6. *Nosić*: (1) to dress, clothe someone; (2) to suffer, accept, bear; (3) to persist, to be, behave, maintain; (4) to turn, swivel, weasel out of; (5) to gossip, malign; (6) to consider, understand as, take for; *nosić się przeciw komu*: to behave, comport oneself, take steps; *nosić się za kogo*: to be considered as, accepted as, taken for.

7. The objects are "ten *złotych* [silver coins] and two silver spoons; fifteen hundred *złotych*; little chain; money; two strings of beads, two silver spoons, and a silver

knife sheath pawned for nine *złotych* and two red [i.e., gold] *złotych*; pearls and gold; silver ring; silver cup and four *talars* [silver coin] traded for a [silver] belt."

8. The second day lists sex acts with "a married woman, Rybitka; Clara the German; already wearing women's clothing, he had sex with Anuchna; dressed as a maiden . . . he was with the young girl, Annuchna [whether "Anuchna" and "Annuchna" are the same person or two different women is unknown]; he courted a Maiden, and he had sex with a [female] gardener; when he lived in Poznań . . . married . . . he . . . had sex with . . . that first Clara; [after the husband died] kept loose women, had sex with them himself, and allowed others to have sex with them; he had relations with a cook; also in women's clothing, he had relations with a [word gendered feminine] cook. Item, in the little town of Dolsko in the same clothing he consorted with a [word gendered feminine] cook. Item he did that a lot elsewhere; in those women's clothes, he had his way with both unmarried and married women."

9. English: Simon.

10. "When he was called before the tribunal." *Urząd* in Old Polish can mean sentence, decree, will (God's will, *urząd Boży*); duty; and collectively the persons who administer law or governance. See Antoni Krasnowolski and Stanisław Niedźwiedzki, *Michala Arcta Słownik Staropolski: 2600 wyrazow i wyrażen używanych w dawnej mowie Polskiej* (Warsaw: Michal Arct, ca. 1920).

11. German: Posen.

12. September 29–February or March.

13. *Nad gardłem i nad imieniem.*

14. *Zapaśnica* (skirt, apron) is an exclusively feminine garment, an overskirt or apron that consists of an elongated rectangular piece or long strip of cloth attached at/*za* the waist/*pas*, whence the name *zapaśnica*. The dress that the mother buys is described, literally, as a "young woman's dress." As in English, "dress" and "robe" may designate attire worn by any gender, e.g., formal dress, coronation robes.

15. For clarity I inserted paragraph breaks at "*Item*"; the original is continuous.

16. The circulating currency, the *złoty* (golden) was, in spite of its name, a silver coin, usually about 2 to 6 grams of silver and equivalent to the standard gold coin, 3.5 grams of gold. A silver *grzywna*, 197 grams, was divided into forty-eight *groszy*, or pennies, of 4.1 grams each. The red *złoty*, mentioned earlier, was gold currency, for example a *floren* or a *ducat*, 3.5 grams of gold. The gold coins were mostly out of circulation and were used to store capital; see Andrzej Jezierski and Cecylia Leszczynska, *Historia gospodarcza Polski* (Warsaw: Key Text, 2003), 61–64.

17. *Włoczek* (ploughman), the person who leads the plow animal; the term that also designated the category of farm workers who did not own land. Wachholz, "Ein Zwitter," translates the term as "fisherman."

18. Obviously a precious metal chain necklace.

19. *Pacierz*: a string of beads, bead necklace, or rosary.

20. Hirsch is the German or Yiddish and Jeleń is Polish for "deer," and both are the secular equivalents (*kinnui*, expression of *kinah*) of Hebrew Zvi, the nickname of Naphtali, son of Jacob, and consequently the name of the Naphtali tribe. That is because Jacob compares Naphtali to a "swift deer" in his blessing.

21. The Jewish population of Poland-Lithuania (inception, 1556) in the 1550s is estimated at fifty thousand people. Their governing body and tribunal, the Council

of Four Lands, Va'ad Arba' Aratzot, met twice annually during the fairs in Lublin in Lesser Poland and Jarosław to the east. The Va'ad provided continuous, autonomous tax and judicial governance from the 1520s until 1764. Jewish communities are documented in the 1550s in nearly every town mentioned in the deposition. For example, there were eighty-nine Jewish families in Poznań in 1549, and a first synagogue was built in Szydłów in 1534. Kazimierz, where Wojciech was deposed, was home to the most prominent Jewish community. Competing with the more traditional Jewish refugee destinations in North Africa (today's Tunisia, Morocco, and Egypt) and Italy, Poland became increasingly significant after the massacres in the Rhine Valley (Worms, Mainz) during the First Crusade of 1096 and subsequent Crusades, as well as repeated expulsions of Jewish communities from England (ending in 1290), France (1182, 1306, 1322, 1394), Spain (1391, 1492), Portugal, and elsewhere. A royal decree of Bolesław the Pious (1264) prohibited blood libel. It was followed by subsequent royal legislation of 1531, 1556, 1564, 1576, 1633 and protections issued by local communities, but it is important to understand that, just like the royal grants and communal protections in other parts of Europe, these laws, intended to stem the tide of growing anti-Semitism, also document the rising persecutions. The rise of anti-Semitism in the premodern period is clearly mapped out in Halina Wegrzynek, "Blood Libel Accusations in Old Poland (Mid-16th–Mid-17th Centuries)," *Proceedings of the World Congress of Jewish Studies, Division B: History of the Jewish People* (1997): 121–27.

22. Usually located on the market square, the guesthouse provided lodgings for traveling merchants.

23. *Dali ręce*, "gave hands," which may mean either "were betrothed or wed" or "agreed to," that is, shook hands on a contract.

24. *Letnik kitajski*, a "Chinese" (*kitajski*), that is, silk summer garment (*letnik*).

25. The sentence allows for ambiguity. Ostrowska stayed with either the boy's mother or her own mother. The former is more likely.

26. *Talars* are silver coins, twenty-three to twenty-four grams of silver, and one suspects the belt was silver as well.

27. *Rybitwa* is "fisherman" in Old Polish, so perhaps this means fishwife, fisherwoman, or the fisherman's wife, a name of a trade used as a proper name. Nastulczyk and Oczko, "'Tradycyjni' czy 'nowocześni'?," give the name as "Rybicka." Following the basic standard of scientific publications at the time, Wachholz published two versions of his article including the translation and commentary on Wojciech's deposition in Polish and German (cited earlier), and he translates "Rybitka" into German as the name of a trade used as a proper name, "Fishwife."

28. Wachholz's German translation reads, "who served there." The "Annuchna" mentioned in the next item may be the same name spelled differently or may refer to a different person.

29. Polish has one word for "summer" and "year."

30. As sex work historians show, the two trades, barkeep and pimp, were frequently combined; see Mengel, "From Venice to Jerusalem."

31. *Z niemi cielesności swej używal* (enjoyed their body with them). *Cielesny* is embodied, *ciało*, a body, and *cieleśnik* (a person) is a voluptuary. In Polish, the possessive agrees with that which is possessed. *Cielesność* is feminine, as is the possessive *swej*.

32. *I mianowicie ony powiedział, których imiona dla ich zelżywości tym listem nie są opisane.*

33. See Ulinka Rublack, *The Astronomer and the Witch: Johannes Kepler's Fight for His Mother* (Oxford: Oxford University Press, 2015). I thank Surekha Davies for this reference. While the German mass witch trials were almost a century later (1620–1630), they can provide a measure of comparison: this was not an unusually long list of illicit sexual partners. Witch trials are relevant here because they often secured depositions from impoverished urban single women without families and those we would today see as genderqueer or trans persons; the interrogators specifically examined their sexual histories.

34. In one case exploitation is explicit: one of Wojciech's women sexual partners leverages the relationship by threatening to "tell on" them (we don't know what), and Wojciech pays her off. In the second case, while Wojciech is married to a man and living as a woman for two years, both Wojciech and their husband agree to maintain women sexual partners. At some point they quarrel over one of the women, a violent dispute eventually followed by the husband's death.

35. The document opens by naming Wojciech's father, who has no active role in the court proceedings, but does not name the mother, who is mentioned twice ("mother") and has an important role; it names the mayor who looks on, but not the women who examine Wojciech in the presence of an equally nameless group of aldermen, leading the officials to assign Wojciech's social gender as female. To sum up, Wojciech's three husbands and father are named, as are three people with whom Wojciech lodged, one man identified by the first name and two women by their surnames. Two women are identified by family relationship (mother, guardian), but most are listed by trade, even if it has no relevance to the story: lodger, gardener, embroiderer, cook, brewster, sex worker, and, possibly, fishwife, although that may be a surname. Three women of Poznań with whom Wojciech allegedly had sex are mentioned by the given name and a qualifier if they are single or by a surname if married: Clara the German; a married woman, Rybitka/fishwife; and the young fellow embroidery apprentice Anuchna/Annuchna (who may be the same person or perhaps two different people). Landowners and nobles are called by the name of their property.

36. *Niejaki:* The third gender designates children and young animals but is not limited to them; the heavens/sky and the sun are also that gender. *Niejaki* roughly translates as "none" and does not have the binary or ternary sense conveyed by the frequent English translation, "neuter."

37. I rely on descriptions and examples from Jacek Perlin and Agnieszka Mielczarek's article on gender in Polish, "Kategoria płci w języku polskim," *Linguistica copernicana* 11 (2014), http://dx.doi.org/10.12775/LinCop.2014.041. As noted by Perlin and Mielczarek, there are three basic "genders" (masculine, feminine, neither/*niejaki*) for nouns and adjectives. Other parts of speech (pronouns, numerals, verbs, and participles) have seven "kinds": in addition to the three "genders," there are four other categories—animate, inanimate/thing, person, and *pluralia tantum* or "plural only" words, such as *scissors*. To give an example, numerals *dwa, dwaj, dwoje,* and *dwie* mean "two": thus *dwa domy, dwaj panowie, dwoje dzieci, dwie panie,* and *dwoje nożyc,* two houses (M), men (M), children (N), ladies (F), and scissors (*pluralia*

tantum), respectively. Grammatical "gender" and "kind" are the same word (*rodzaj*); its etymological root is *ród* (birth/clan). A sentence can juxtapose two different "genders/kinds," one for the signifier and one for the signified, which are ruled by different paradigms. For example, in the sentence "What did you do, children?" the noun *children* is the gender "none" (*niejaki*), while the participle can be gendered masculine or feminine, depending on the perceived gender of the children. This is just in the nominative; there are seven cases of declension, just as in Latin, and several declension groups in each of the three genders (five declension groups for feminine, etc.). Rather than convey gender, it would be more accurate to say that a Polish sentence choreographs a refined ballet of "kinds."

38. I thank Blake Gutt for this important point.

39. *Letnik kitajski*, a "Chinese" (*kitajski*), i.e., silk summer garment (*letnik*).

40. "What many customs referred to as the 'goods of her body,' thus making valuable assets such as clothing and jewels [women's] private property." Martha Howell, "The Problem of Women's Agency in Late Medieval and Early Modern Europe," in *Women and Gender in the Early Modern Low Countries*, ed. Sarah Joan Moran and Amanda Pipkin (Leiden: Brill, 2019), 21–31, quotation at 23.

41. Anna Kłosowska, "Individual, 1377–1650: From Mathematics to Self, after Carla Mazzio," *Anuario de Estudios Medievales* 45.1, special issue, ed. Marion Coderch (2015): 263–97.

42. Tomasz Nastulczyk and Piotr Oczko, *Homoseksualność Staropolska: Przyczynek do Badań* (Kraków: Collegium Columbinum, 2012).

43. Michel Foucault, *The History of Sexuality*, vol. 1, *An Introduction*, trans. Robert Hurley (New York: Vintage, 1980).

44. "Gender ideology" includes UN- and EU-recommended instructional materials created to assist teachers in the public education system, for example, "gender kits" (French *malette de genre*).

45. See Lucas Ramón Mendos, *State-Sponsored Homophobia, 2019* (Geneva: ILGA, March 2019), including Marion Beury and Yury Yoursky, "Europe—Increased Visibility, Populist Backlash and Multiple Divisions," 149–54, esp. 149, https://www.ecoi.net/en/file/local/2004824/ILGA_State_Sponsored_Homophobia_2019.pdf. As a former Soviet satellite that recently gained autonomy and inclusion in the EU, Poland is acutely concerned with sovereignty. The long history of Russian dominance and the ever-present threat of Russian invasion make Poland traditionally pro-West and anti-Putin. It may therefore seem contradictory that a Polish conservative government and political majority take a pro-Putin and anti-West stance on LGBT+ rights. Nevertheless, the foundations of Polish sovereignty movements are also conservative, aligned with right-wing Western politicians and Catholic leaders fighting the spread of communism during the cold war.

PART II

Frameworks

Representing Early Trans Lives

Chapter 6

Recognizing Wilgefortis

Robert Mills

The point of departure for this essay is a triptych by Hieronymus Bosch, which is currently exhibited in the Gallerie dell'Accademia in Venice (figures 6.1 and 6.2).

During the work's five hundred years or so of existence, the crucified saint in the central panel has been called by a variety of names. More than a century ago, during the painting's eighty-year sojourn in Vienna, the panel was identified by German and Austrian art historians as Saint Julia.[1] Julia was an early Christian virgin martyr, who was tortured and crucified in Corsica for refusing to sacrifice to pagan gods; she was reputedly abducted from Carthage to Corsica by a merchant called Eusebius, who, according to this explanation, is depicted swooning at the foot of the cross to the left of Bosch's painting.[2] The triptych's side wings have sometimes been interpreted as contributing to the Julia identification, especially the right-hand panel, which shows an exotic-looking port in the background, replete with sinking ships, and two men in the foreground, one of whom is armed with a club and a sword. The landscape possibly represents the port in Corsica to which Julia was taken, while the men have sometimes been construed as slave traders.[3]

Much more recently, in 2006, Larry Silver made a case for interpreting the martyr in question as Saint Eulalia of Barcelona, another maiden similarly tormented and crucified for refusing to recant her Christian faith. Other

FIGURE 6.1. Hieronymus Bosch, triptych of crucified saint, ca. 1495–1506. Oil on panel. 105.2 × 27.5 cm (left panel), 105.2 × 62.7 cm (central panel), 104.7 × 27.9 cm (right panel). Venice, Gallerie dell'Accademia.
Source: Bosch Research and Conservation Project, http://boschproject.org.

fifteenth-century panels and manuscript illuminations show Eulalia being stripped to the waist and crucified, albeit tied with ropes to an X-shaped Saint Andrew's cross rather than to the tau or T-shaped cross shown in Bosch's picture.[4] But Silver cites details such as close trading ties between Spain and the Netherlands, as well as the "Oriental" dress of some spectators within the painting, as evidence that Bosch was catering to a Spanish patron.[5]

Alternative identifications were made by earlier commentators. A statement in a series of notes on Venetian art by a sixteenth-century nobleman, which some scholars have treated as a possible reference to the triptych, describes a large canvas depicting "Saint Catherine above the wheel in the countryside."[6] In the seventeenth century the work is clearly documented by the painter and engraver Marco Boschini as being displayed in the Doge's Palace in Venice. Boschini identifies the martyr in question simply as "una Santa in Croce," that is to say a female saint on a cross, as well as noting

FIGURE 6.2. Detail of central panel, Hieronymus Bosch, triptych of crucified saint, ca. 1495–1506. Venice, Gallerie dell'Accademia.
Source: Bosch Research and Conservation Project, http://boschproject.org.

the swooning figure and ascribing the work to one Girolamo Basi.[7] In 1733, however, the critic and engraver Antonio Maria Zanetti published a guide to paintings in Venice based on Boschini's text, in which the artist's name is corrected to "Bolch," as seen in the white Gothic script at the base of the crucifixion panel. Zanetti says the picture shows not the martyrdom of a female saint but that of a "Santo coronato"—in other words a crowned *male* saint.[8] Meanwhile, the second edition of Zanetti's guide, published by his nephew and namesake in 1771, affirms that it represents the crucifixion of either a "Santo" or a "Santa," thus equivocating over the martyr's gender identity.[9] One factor potentially contributing to the confusion is the fainting figure, who parallels the Virgin Mary in conventional images of Christ's Passion:

Bosch effectively reverses the gender polarity in such images by depicting a man swooning at the foot of the cross in a pose reminiscent of Christ's mother at the Crucifixion.[10]

The seeds of doubt cast by seventeenth- and eighteenth-century Venetian art historians concerning the saint's "true" gender have led many modern commentators, in turn, to assume that the saint in question is in fact the bearded female martyr Wilgefortis, otherwise known as Ontcommer, Uncumber, Kümmernis, Liberata, Livrade, Débarras, Virgeforte, or some other variant.[11] In 2016 Bosch's triptych featured in two hugely popular exhibitions held to mark the fifth centenary since the painter's death, one in his hometown of 's-Hertogenbosch in the Netherlands, called *Visions of Genius*, and the other, at the Prado in Madrid, called simply *Bosch*. On both occasions the work was labeled the *Saint Wilgefortis Triptych*, while interpretation panels in the Accademia in Venice, where the painting is currently displayed, call it the *Santa Liberata Triptych*.[12] What's in a name?

The cult of this crucified virgin martyr seems to have sprung up in the fourteenth century, emerging with particular vigor in German-speaking lands before spreading across many regions of Europe in the course of the 1400s, from Iberia to the Netherlands and from Italy to Scandinavia; the first references to Wilgefortis images in England date to the very end of the fifteenth century.[13] Although it was only documented in the later Middle Ages in Europe, however, the cult appears to be rooted in earlier religious writings and iconography. Notably, there was a miracle-working cross in the Tuscan town of Lucca known as the *Volto Santo* (figure 6.3), which itself echoes the *Christus triumphans* tradition representing Christ as alive, bearded, and dressed in a long robe.

The *Volto Santo*, thought for many years to be a twelfth-century copy but recently confirmed by radiocarbon dating as the eighth-century original, was believed to be based on the impression left by Christ's actual face and body on the Holy Shroud. According to a widely disseminated hypothesis, however, the image was subsequently misinterpreted as representing a female figure. This is perhaps understandable in view of the statue's adornment on feast days with additional vestments including a golden crown and collar, an embroidered skirt bedecked with gold, and a pair of silver shoes (figure 6.4).[14]

But such arguments betray a desire to explain Wilgefortis's existence away on the basis of semantic confusion, rather than asking if sexually ambiguous images of crucified humans—whether the victims were Christ in a robe or a female saint with a beard—fulfilled a distinct demand on the part of devotees, especially women, for androgynous intercessors and

FIGURE 6.3. *Volto Santo* (Holy Face), late eighth century. Walnut, paint, and canvas. Statue 2.5 m from head to toes, cross 4.34 × 2.65 m. San Martino Cathedral, Lucca. Photo ca. 1890.
Source: Archivi Alinari, Florence.

divinities. If, as a number of medievalists have argued, accounts of Christ's Passion were themselves sometimes imbued with sexual ambiguity, then the cult of Wilgefortis may not simply be rooted in the misinterpretation of a particular image type, an elaborately robed figure based on the *Volto Santo* prototype. Instead, it could represent a deliberate strategy on the

Figure 6.4. *Volto Santo* (Holy Face), late eighth century, with crown, collar, necklace, petticoat, slippers, and other decorative paraphernalia from the seventeenth century and later. Walnut, paint, canvas, velvet, precious metals and stones. Statue 2.5 m from head to toes, cross 4.34 × 2.65 m. San Martino Cathedral, Lucca. Photo ca. 1890.
Source: Archivi Alinari, Florence.

part of patrons and artists to cater to popular tastes and psychic needs.[15] To what extent, though, can the self-consciously "gender-inclusive" dimensions that some scholars perceive in Wilgefortis's cult and image be discovered in Bosch's triptych?

Written *vitae* from the fifteenth and sixteenth centuries record how Wilgefortis (or one of the other names assigned to the saint) was the beautiful and noble daughter of a pagan king in Portugal.[16] Deciding in adolescence to convert to Christianity, Wilgefortis takes a vow of celibacy, promises herself to Christ, and subsequently refuses to be married off to a pagan king in Sicily. The father has his daughter imprisoned and, according to some accounts, tortured. Wilgefortis prays to God that, to protect her virginity, she be rendered physically unattractive to her prospective husband. The princess's prayers are answered and she miraculously grows a mustache and beard.[17] The king of Sicily no longer wishes to marry Wilgefortis, which angers her father. Accusing her of using magic, the father has his daughter nailed—or in some versions tied with rope—to a cross. Wilgefortis prays on the cross for deliverance for anyone who remembers her death. Hence the numerous variants on the saint's name (itself a corruption of the Latin phrase *virgo fortis*, that is, "strong virgin" or "valiant maid"). Monikers such as Liberata or Uncumber play on the belief that anyone invoking the martyr will be liberated or unencumbered from their burdens; depending on which version of the tale is being narrated, these difficulties range from mental or physical suffering to imprisonment and unwanted husbands.[18] Significantly, a late fifteenth-century Dutch *vita* harnesses the saint's multiple names as a device to convey her transformation from earthly maiden to sacred intercessor: the text notes that while, during her time on earth, the protagonist's "properen naem" (real name) was Wilgefortis, God bestowed the name Ontcommer on the crucified martyr as a tribute to the virgin's power to release "allen bedructe herten" (all troubled souls) with her prayers.[19] Finally, the Wilgefortis legend generally concludes with an account of the saint's soul being borne aloft by angels and the destruction of her father's palace by fire during a divinely ordained storm.

Arguments in favor of the identification of Bosch's crucified figure with Wilgefortis/Ontcommer include the fact that, whereas Wilgefortis's cult was widespread in the Netherlands during the artist's lifetime, Julia had no significant presence in the region. Bosch's saint also wears a golden crown, which could stand metaphorically for the crown of glory bestowed on a saint by martyrdom but also potentially identifies the protagonist as a princess. Likewise, the themes of the side wings cohere in at least some ways with the general tenor of the Wilgefortis legend. The left-hand panel depicts Saint Anthony being tormented by unchaste demons, while in the background people are shown escaping from a burning city. As already noted, the right-hand panel shows a port with sinking ships but also features a scene of robbery in the middle ground.[20] While there is no direct connection between the imagery in the side panels and Wilgefortis's *vita* (or for that matter Julia's or Eulalia's), the motifs of escape and salvation from physical or spiritual dangers were conceivably designed to resonate with the ability of the saint in the central panel to release worshippers from suffering.

In the last analysis, however, most interpretations of Bosch's saint as Wilgefortis/Ontcommer hinge on whether or not the crucified figure is depicted as a bearded woman (figure 6.2). The martyr is clearly crowned, identifying them as a princess. While the saint's ankles and left wrist are tied securely to the cross, the rope around the right wrist appears to be working itself loose, perhaps an allusion to the virgin's ability to release worshippers from bondage. In late medieval and early modern art, Wilgefortis was typically depicted as having "escaped" from the cords binding them to the cross, or sometimes even holding a piece of rope as a saintly attribute.[21] Bosch's figure wears a billowing crimson-pink gown over a blue skirt embroidered with gold, clothing designed to cover the body almost entirely from head to foot. The only flesh displayed besides the face and hands is the saint's neck and upper chest, both of which are framed and accentuated by the garment's plunging neckline. The shadows and curvature on the saint's upper body are suggestive of breasts, and the martyr sports an exuberant head of auburn hair. Looking at their face, though, leaves it unclear whether there are also traces of a beard.

The beard is a crucial attribute in most surviving images of Wilgefortis/Ontcommer or their namesakes. In works that are roughly contemporary with or predate Bosch's triptych, the beard is usually quite substantial. Miniatures in Netherlandish books of hours show the saint either affixed to a tau cross or occasionally carrying the cross as an attribute, sporting clearly visible and sometimes abundant facial hair.[22] A statue of Uncumber turns up among the ranks of saints that look down upon a Last Judgment scene in Henry VII's chapel in Westminster Abbey, a rare surviving image of the saint in England; again, here the saint's beard is unmistakable.[23] A similar phenomenon is witnessed on a unique tunicle, which is now in the Kaiserliche Schatzkammer in Vienna (figure 6.5).

This garment, a vestment worn by subdeacons at liturgical celebrations, was made in the Netherlands in the first half of the fifteenth century, part of a group of robes belonging to the Order of the Golden Fleece established by Philip the Good, Duke of Burgundy, in 1430. The tunicle features a representation of the bearded virgin in a lineup of other female virgin martyrs such as Saints Cecilia, Christina, Agnes, and Dorothy. Wilgefortis is shown standing upright with a cross, as on the Westminster Abbey statue; but instead of reading a book, as in London, here the saint looks out and upward.

FIGURE 6.5. Saint Wilgefortis. Detail from tunicle with female saints. Liturgical vestments of the Order of the Golden Fleece, Burgundian Netherlands, ca. 1425–1440. Embroidery on linen, metal and silk threads, pearls, velvet. Kaiserliche Schatzkammer, Vienna. Photo: Robert Mills.

In addition, the embroiderer has drawn attention to Ontcommer's ability to unbind or disencumber by fixing raised pieces of thread, which represent the rope used to bind the virgin's hands and feet to the cross, to the silk needlework surface; as elsewhere on this set of vestments, rows of tiny seed pearls have been used to demarcate Ontcommer's crown and halo, enhancing the image's splendor and three-dimensionality. Significantly, although the saint is shown possessing a stereotypically feminine "hourglass" figure, waist bound tightly with a red belt just below the breasts, their forked beard is clearly visible—a marked contrast to the smooth-chinned faces of the other women depicted on the tunicle.[24]

The Hours of Mary of Burgundy, now also in Vienna but completed in Flanders around 1477, features an image of a crowned and haloed martyr that has several features in common with Bosch's painting (figure 6.6).[25] Although the figure's head bends down rather than up, with their eyes closed, they wear a blue dress tied at the waist and feet; here too the ropes binding the wrists are clearly working themselves loose. The saint's hirsute appearance parallels the beards and hair of the two observers, one of whom must be their father. But Ontcommer's waistline and rounded chest suggest that the illuminator set out to represent a body that, despite its beard, bears the anatomical features that are conventionally associated with womanhood. Significantly, the miniature accompanies a verse from the Roman breviary, which describes the wise virgin who brings oil for her lamp as a heavenly bride—a reference to Christ's parable of the wise and foolish virgins in Matthew's Gospel. This signals a theme prominent also in most written versions of the Wilgefortis legend, namely the maiden's self-representation as a virginal bride of Christ. Not only does the saint refer to Christ (or God) as their "bridegroom," but also they want simultaneously to be Christlike in appearance and suffering. This desire both to have and be Christ—conjoining *sponsalia Christi* with the trope of *imitatio Christi*—is typical of other texts recounting the lives of viragos or virile woman saints. The miniature's placement alongside this passage from the breviary effectively draws parallels between the *virgo sapiens*, or wise virgin, as recorded in the text, and the miraculous acquisition of facial hair by the *virgo fortis*.[26]

A few decades after Bosch's death, a chronicle reports that Saint John's Church in the artist's hometown of 's-Hertogenbosch had an altar dedicated to the saint. The altar is described as being adorned with an *Oncummera barbata* (Uncumber with a beard).[27] Although this particular image has not survived, plenty more examples could be cited from the Netherlands to support the view that Wilgefortis/Ontcommer was not, generally speaking, very hard to recognize. Yet in a handful of cases, artists appear to have been more hesitant about depicting a bearded female. Some manuscript illuminators paint a heavily trimmed or wispy set of whiskers.[28] Moreover, it is very rare indeed for them to show hints of a mustache in addition to hair sprouting

Ista e[st]
virgo
sapiens
qua[m] de[us]
vigilante[m]
inue[n]it q[ue]
accepta lam

pade su[m]psit secu[m] oleu[m] et ve
ni[en]te do[m]ino intro[ui]uit ad nu
ptias. ve[rsus] Diffusa est g[rat]ia
in labijs tuis propte[re]a benedi
xit te de[us] in et[er]nu[m]. Oratio
O[mn]ipote[n]s sempit[er]ne
deus miam tuam o[ste]n de
su[pp]lic[ib]z ut qui de merito[rum]
qualitate confidim[us] int[er]ce
dente b[ea]ta o[mn]iu[m] me[m]o[rum] ui[rginum]

FIGURE 6.6. Hours of Mary of Burgundy. Flanders, ca. 1477. 225 × 163 mm. Vienna, Öster-reichische Nationalbibliothek, Cod. 1857, fol. 125v. Photo: ÖNB Vienna.

from the chin. In 1479, Bosch's near contemporary, the Bruges painter Hans Memling, painted Ontcommer on one wing of the Adriaan Reins triptych (figure 6.7).[29] When opened, the altarpiece shows the patron with his namesake Saint Adrian (left), Saint Barbara (right), and the Deposition of Christ (center). When the altarpiece was closed, devotees would have seen Saint Ontcommer (left) and Saint Mary of Egypt (right) on the exterior wings. The pairing of Mary of Egypt and Ontcommer possibly depends on the fact that each

FIGURE 6.7. Exterior wings of Hans Memling, *Triptych of Adriaan Reins*, 1479, showing Saint Ontcommer (left) and Mary of Egypt (right). Oil on oak panel. Whole altarpiece 45.3 × 66.4 cm. Old Saint John's Hospital, Bruges.
Source: Fine Art Images / Alinari Archives, Florence.

represents a contrasting model of sanctity, namely penitence and martyrdom, but presumably also rests on the fact that both saints grew bodily hair to protect their virtue.[30] The facial hair that Memling has given Ontcommer, however, could hardly be described as bushy: viewed from a distance, it might just as easily be interpreted as a shadow. Likewise, Mary's hair does little to cover her own fleshly assets.

The delicate beard Memling assigns to Wilgefortis/Ontcommer may reflect a reluctance on the painter's part to represent an explicitly bearded woman.[31] This taps into a tendency that is also discernible in other images of gender-crossing saints, whereby medieval and early modern artists toned down or turned away from the genderqueer potential of an ambiguously gendered or multigendered body. Elsewhere I have shown this phenomenon at work in visual culture associated with Saint Eugenia, a woman who spends many years dressing and living as a male monk in order to protect her chastity and devote herself to Christ. Whereas textual renditions of the Eugenia legend intermittently draw attention to the saint's status as a gender crosser, image makers tended to maintain an overriding emphasis on Eugenia's femininity, thereby rendering invisible or seriously underplaying her temporary acquisition of male identity and prerogative. While a small number of depictions of Eugenia in art do present alternative perspectives, troubling gender in ways that appear partially to resonate with some modern-day experiences and expressions of gender queerness, as a general rule of thumb artists focused on the narrative's conclusion, when Eugenia's female identity is restored.[32]

Similarly, the threat posed by female facial hair to aesthetic, social, and psychic norms may explain efforts on the part of at least some artists to render Wilgefortis's beard insubstantially. In the Middle Ages, beards often designated, through their presence or absence, some aspect of male social status. The Greek theologian Clement of Alexandria (d. ca. 215) viewed facial hair as an unequivocal sexual signifier: whereas God planned that women be "smooth-skinned," he writes, "man He adorned like the lion, with a beard, and gave him a hairy chest as proof of his manhood and a sign of his strength and primacy. . . . His beard, then, is the badge of a man and shows him unmistakably to be a man."[33] Although the Eastern and Western churches ultimately adopted divergent attitudes toward clerical beards, Clement's conclusion that it is sacrilege to trifle with this "symbol of manhood" was heeded by Orthodox clergy, who were encouraged to grow beards. In western Europe, by contrast, clergymen were expected to be tonsured and clean-shaven, contrasting with the beards sometimes attributed to groups such as Jews, Muslims, and heretics in Christian art.[34] At the same time, however, facial hair was commonly represented as an attribute of God or Christ, as on the *Volto Santo* image; and several male saints were depicted sporting prominent beards, notably early Christian fathers such as Saint Jerome (ca. 340–420), as signs of their wisdom and scholarly attainment.[35] As with these holy figures, kings were commonly (though not inevitably) portrayed with beards; in keeping with the attributes of biblical role models such as King David, beards conventionally communicated a male monarch's maturity and authority.[36] Thus although, as today, beards in the Middle Ages served to demarcate gender difference, their significance was also a product of overlapping and sometimes competing principles. As well as representing embodied maleness, they could be used to communicate ideas of power and intellect, to distinguish between youth and age, or to convey a sense of religious or even ethnic difference.[37]

Images of a bearded holy woman need to be understood in light of these varying associations. Discussing a seventeenth-century image of Elizabeth I as a bearded figure, as well as portraits produced during the queen's lifetime that feature prominent ruffs possibly alluding to her possession of a princely beard, Mark Albert Johnston has drawn attention to the psychological ramifications of representing bearded women in early modern England. If, as Johnston argues, the female beard is a powerfully subversive symbol, a threat to the phallic superiority often ascribed to male facial hair, the spectacle of an explicitly bearded woman may have caused at least some beholders in later medieval or early modern Europe to take offense at the ascription of conventionally masculine privilege and power to a female figure.[38] The perceived affront to social norms of a female beard is put to comic effect in "The Miller's Tale" in Chaucer's fourteenth-century *Canterbury Tales*, which reaches its climax at the moment when, in the hours of darkness, Alisoun jokingly sticks her "hole" out of a window to receive the attentions of her would-be suitor Absolon, who kisses Alisoun's "naked ers . . . ful savourly" before realizing that "a woman hath no berd."[39] Similarly, in written *vitae* of Saint Wilgefortis, the effect that the saint's beard has on the Sicilian king's ardor is emblematic of the broader social stigma—and feelings of disgust or horror—that might be attached to the idea of female facial hair. While names such as Uncumber or Ontcommer seemingly confirm links between the saint's acquisition of a beard and women's defiance of male authority since, as already discussed, the abilities of Wilgefortis/Ontcommer were sometimes believed to extend to relieving wives of an unwanted husband, the rise of popular exhibitions displaying bearded women as physiological wonders to a paying public—a phenomenon Johnston dates to the seventeenth century—coincided with efforts to commodify, contain, and control the female beard's disruptive potential in early modern England.[40]

As to the representation of a seemingly bearded princess in Bosch's painting, it is worth noting that a recent effort to find a resolution to the question of the crucified figure's identity has been staged against a backdrop of intense international competition and conflict concerning the meanings of Bosch's oeuvre. In the lead-up to the *Visions of Genius* exhibition in the Netherlands, the Bosch Research and Conservation Project (a Dutch initiative launched in 2007) focused mainly on microscopic analysis of the artist's drawings and paintings using the very latest techniques in digital imaging. A restoration of the triptych between 2013 and 2015, which included the use of infrared reflectography and ultrahigh-resolution digital macro photography, demonstrated that, in the words of the Dutch curators, "a wispy beard was indeed painted on the martyr's face in a dark colour"—a factor that in their view contributed to the three aforementioned Venetian authors' uncertainty concerning the saint's gender.[41] As they put it in the catalogue raisonné published to coincide with the exhibition: "The feminine physique was decisive for Boschini, while the elder Zanetti probably focused more on the facial hair, which must have been more clearly visible at the time."[42] Furthermore, in a supplementary volume of technical studies, the same team of scholars affirms that while the condition of the painting had previously prevented viewers from resolving the question of the saint's identity, a raking-light micrograph taken during the restoration "shows an irregular feature on her chin that is dissimilar to the surrounding paint," and a visible-light micrograph reveals a "thick, resinous feature there"; furthermore, after the removal of varnishings, retouchings, and non-original residues in this area of the painting in 2014, "remnants of a subtle beard" became visible once again, thereby confirming the identification of the saint as Wilgefortis.[43] When it came to the Prado exhibition, however, the curators remained doubtful. Acknowledging that there has been considerable debate about the "alleged presence" of this detail, the author of the catalogue entry states that, even in the painting's present condition, following the recent restoration, it is "very difficult to establish whether there really are traces of a beard."[44]

Playing out in such statements is a debate about the politics of naming and identification in the history of art. Which group of curators and scholars has the best techniques at its disposal for establishing the "facts" of the artwork in question—namely that it is a painting by Bosch, representing an identifiable subject, that can be dated to a specific point in the artist's career? The Prado catalogue foregrounds the benefits of meticulous documentary research and seemingly "old-fashioned" connoisseurship, while Dutch researchers put their overriding trust in visualization technologies and science. Moreover, the introduction to the Spanish catalogue, written by the chief curator, testifies to the deep rivalries that the 2016 celebrations engendered, claiming the museum as the true "home of Bosch" and describing the exhibition in Madrid as "truly . . . the one that marks the artist's 5th centenary."[45] These tensions also surfaced explicitly in the 2015 documentary *Hieronymus Bosch: Touched by the Devil*, featuring footage of the so-called "Wilgefortis triptych" as it underwent restoration and scientific analysis by the Dutch research team.[46] As a result, answers to the question of whether or not Bosch's crucified figure actually sports a beard have become highly politicized in the context of the anniversary exhibitions. But again, what's in a name?

Perhaps surprisingly, given the lingering questions over the saint's identity, including their gender identity, Bosch's painting—and Wilgefortis imagery more broadly—is rarely filtered through a transgender studies optic by scholars, despite increasing interest in popular culture about the lives, historically and today, of trans people.[47] A hasty Internet search turns up an Instagram post, made a few days after the *Visions of Genius* exhibition opened, which reproduces the picture along with a series of hashtags including #transgender and #intersex (figure 6.8). Wilgefortis also features in various online calendars of queer and LGBT saints.[48] And a 2017 blog post about Wilgefortis by GenderBen!, who identifies themself as a nonbinary trans person, observes, "This particular saint gives some interesting but amusing insight into how gendered cultural signifiers have . . . caused confusion."[49] Such statements are symptomatic of a more widespread and sometimes impassioned desire for representations of trans, queer, and nonbinary embodiment in the historical record. What if anything is to be gained from taking seriously analogies between these identity categories as they are experienced in modernity and premodern expressions of non-normative gender?

Any effort to filter Wilgefortis, Uncumber, Ontcommer, Kümmernis, Liberata, and Co. through the prism of transgender experience needs to contend with the saint's status as a representation, first and foremost. Some medical practitioners have attempted to diagnose the saint's condition with reference to physical or psychological disorders such as anorexia nervosa and Cushing's disease, which sometimes cause spontaneous temporary hair growth in the sufferers.[50] But searching for the "realities" behind the image will ultimately prove elusive: the crucified, bearded female saint is a cultural construction, an accretion formed from multiple layers of text and image.

FIGURE 6.8.   Screenshot of Instagram post by csdickey, February 13, 2016.
Source: www.instagram.com/p/BBulCADjYf_/ (accessed July 2018).

The widespread adoption of the Wilgefortis/Ontcommer legend and image in different regions of western Europe in the Middle Ages might be due to how Wilgefortis's legend and image gave comfort to those women who naturally possessed facial hair that was deemed by society to be excessive, unnatural, or unattractive.[51] Admittedly, this rationale is potentially narrower in scope than the idea that Wilgefortis represents an unwitting "misinterpretation" of the miraculous robed crucifix of Lucca. As discussed at the outset of this essay, one of the common arguments made about the emergence of Saint Wilgefortis's cult is that it represents an error on the part of premodern viewers, who interpreted the *Volto Santo* image as a bearded female on the basis of a simple misreading of the iconography. But what if Wilgefortis also fulfilled a desire on the part of beholders for nonbinary or gender-expansive imagery? What if imagery of a bearded female saint provided a source of inspiration for women, including hairier women?

Another factor that might undermine the saint's easy adoption as a transgender icon is the seemingly limited role that Wilgefortis/Ontcommer plays in the changes that render them physically unattractive to their suitor. Although the saint prays for this outcome, the decision to bestow a beard specifically originates with God. The agency of Wilgefortis in their own transition is thus ultimately diluted, the miraculous growth of facial hair being represented as an act of divine grace. Today, of course, medical practitioners also play a key (and at times, possibly even "godlike") role in facilitating acts such as gender-affirming surgery. But unlike the saint in the story, modern-day trans people who decide to transition are often motivated by a deep-rooted sense of selfhood. As Blake Gutt puts it, in a compelling analysis of the applicability of concepts from transgender theory to medieval literature, "Trans people do not transition because they want to be a man, a woman, or non-binary, but because they already know who they are, and desire congruence between their internal sense of their own identity, their appearance, and the way in which other people relate to them."[52] Accordingly, applying the term "transgender," as we currently understand it, to fictional characters who enact or experience sex/gender transitions or transformations misses the fact that the protagonists' assumption of attributes such as male dress and appearance tends to be conceived as a temporary fix or disguise that enables them to transcend the social barriers they face as women. Likewise, Wilgefortis's beard is presented as a temporary disfigurement, designed to dissuade an unwanted suitor, rather than as an affirmation of the saint's internal and enduring sense of maleness.

It is also worth recalling that Wilgefortis's transition stops at a beard alone. This sets it apart from other narratives of gender transition and transformation, such as the Ovidian tale of Iphis and Ianthe, which circulated in the Middle Ages under various guises and which culminates in the complete bodily transformation of Iphis from female to male.[53] As the fourteenth-century verse *Ovide moralisé* puts it, the protagonist's "feminine nature had completely changed and become masculine. Iphis the daughter had become a son—this was certain and sure!"[54] Conversely, Wilgefortis's bodily change was only ever partial. While the saint's facial hair was usually rendered more or less visible in images, it retained its capacity to provoke, disrupt, disturb, or even offend insofar as it was perceived as being out of kilter with the virgin's otherwise consistently feminine appearance. Imagery of Wilgefortis/ Ontcommer could certainly be interpreted as *queer* in the sense that it dislodges the binary calculus which dictates that only men—or, more specifically, those who identify, appear, and are read as men—can legitimately possess facial hair. The saint's image, however, is not easily aligned with the idea, arguably conveyed in the Iphis story, that gender transformation was culturally acceptable only when it entailed a complete and conclusive shift from one polarity to another. Legends of female virgin martyrs such as Eugenia, who disguised themselves as men to live as monks, validate

crossover or "passing" rather than "cross-dressing" per se: disguise is represented in their *vitae* as being completely convincing, leading the saintly
women to be read as men. But women who retained aspects of their female
identity while adopting particular male attributes (such as clothing or attitude) were often censured or condemned, as was the case in reality with
figures such as Joan of Arc.[55] Wilgefortis arguably has more in common with
this latter group, insofar as the saint's beard coexists with cultural and physical markers that mark them out as enduringly female.

Moreover, the destination our saint finally strives for—marriage to
Christ—is not what most trans people aim for today in the course of their
gendered transitions. Consequently, in many of the images cited thus far,
Wilgefortis's bearded but otherwise conventionally female appearance
does not make the saint a poster child for practices such as hormone treatment or gender-affirming surgery. Nor does their physical transition bear
much resemblance to the vexed concept of "sex change," itself increasingly
being put under pressure as we learn to rethink sex/gender as an ongoing journey rather than as a trajectory with rigidly defined start and end
points.[56] The purpose of staging a dialogue between premodern cultures
and contemporary ideas about transgender is not to look for trans people,
as such (or people who have deliberately and decisively "changed sex" in a
straightforward pathway from female to male or male to female). Rather,
its goal is to foster what Jack Halberstam has termed a "politics of transitivity."[57] Mobilizing the term *trans**, which couples the prefix for transitivity
with the asterisk indicating a wildcard in Internet searches, Halberstam
makes an impassioned plea for the benefits of looking at "how gender
shifts and changes through all bodies"—including historical bodies—and
"how it might be imagined in the future." Berating what he discerns as
"the gender-stabilizing insistence on naming and classification," Halberstam thus gathers together a panoply of experiences of gender variance
under the sign of trans*. With its supplementary asterisk, trans* operates
as a site of possibility rather than diagnosis.[58]

As with other vernacular terms in the ever-evolving ecosystem of gender
terminology, there are arguments both for and against the asterisk in trans*.[59]
It began being adopted in online gender-community spaces around 2010, one
reason being that "trans" alone was felt to represent only transgender men
and transgender women—which is to say, people whose identities are experienced or perceived as placing them to one side or the other of the gender
binary. Proponents of the reformulated term argued that the asterisk signals
greater inclusivity by opposing the prefix itself as the only way to refer to identities and communities invested in gender variability. Notwithstanding these

debates, however, Halberstam's ruminations on the category may allow us to reflect with renewed insight on the issues of naming and recognition that keep bubbling to the surface in images of Wilgefortis. The sheer diversity of names ascribed to the saint speaks to the fact that "she" was always already a "they"—a composite figure whose legend has the capacity to accommodate a considerable variety of meanings and contexts.[60] Hence my decision, in the course of developing this essay, to shift from singular, gendered pronouns—acknowledging how most texts of the Wilgefortis legend consistently refer to the saint as female—to the more provisional and plural "they" and "their." Sticking to a single pronoun will not settle the question of who Wilgefortis/Ontcommer really is or was. Similarly, it might be worth giving up on the project of settling, once and for all, the identity—gendered or otherwise—of Bosch's crucified saint. Instead of simply trying to get the name right, recognizing the figure with reference to a coherent iconographic or interpretive frame, we might be better off accepting the enduring provisionality of such pronouncements and the limits of our taxonomic impulses. The same conclusion arguably applies equally well to art-historical scholarship as it does to gender identity politics.

Notes

This essay originated in a paper presented at a "Meeting of Medievalists" organized by Matthias Meyer at the University of Vienna in July 2018. I'm grateful to Lauren Rozenberg for research assistance during the preparation of that paper, to participants at the conference for their invaluable comments, and to Matthias for the opportunity this event gave me to view the Vestments of the Order of the Golden Fleece firsthand.

1. The triptych was in Vienna between 1838 and 1919, being exhibited in the Kunsthistorisches Museum there from 1893 until it returned to the Doge's Palace in Venice in 1919.

2. See, among others, Hermann Dollmayr, "Hieronymus Bosch und die Darstellung der vier letzten Dinge in die niederländischen Malerei des XV. und XVI. Jahrhunderts," *Jahrbuch des kunsthistorischen Sammlungen des allerhöchsten Kaiserhauses* 19 (1898): 284–343, esp. 289–90; Max J. Friedländer, *Die altniederländische Malerei*, 14 vols. (Berlin: Paul Cassirer, 1924–1937), vol. 5 (1927), 151; and Theodor von Frimmel, *Geschichte der Wiener Gemäldesammlungen* (Leipzig: Georg Heimlich Meyer, 1899), 462. The Saint Julia identification was also subsequently affirmed in Charles de Tolnay, *Hieronymus Bosch* (1937; repr., London: Methuen, 1966), 38–39, 70n135; Paul Lafond, *Hieronymus Bosch: Son art, son influence, ses disciples* (Brussels: G. van Oest, 1914); and Leonard Joseph Slatkes, "Hieronymus Bosch and Italy," *Art Bulletin* 57.3 (1975): 335–45. Slatkes cites the identification as evidence of a hypothesized trip to Italy around 1500, since Julia's cult was particularly popular on the Italian peninsula. In a short monograph cited by Slatkes in support of this argument, D. Bax

prevaricates, weighing up evidence for both Julia and Wilgefortis as the protagonist of Bosch's painting; ultimately, however, while admitting to difficulties with both interpretations, Bax judges the Julia explanation to be more convincing, suggesting among other things that the artist may have created the work for two Italian patrons, whose donor portraits were originally shown on the triptych's wings (now visible only under infrared light) before being overpainted. See D. Bax, *Jeroen Bosch' Drieluik met de Gekruisigde Martelares*, Verhandelingen der Koninklijke Nederlandse Akademie van Wetenschappen, afd. Letterkunde new series 68, no. 5 (Amsterdam: Noord-Hollandsche Uitgevers Maatschappij, 1961), esp. 48–49.

3. Dollmayr, "Hieronymus Bosch und die Darstellung," 289; Tolnay, *Hieronymus Bosch*, 38. The unarmed man dressed in black, who appears to be pointing his right hand toward events in the central panel, could equally be a Christian hermit or a monk, which complicates this interpretation. For a review of arguments connecting the right panel with Julia's *vita*, see Bax, *Jeroen Bosch' Drieluik*, 39–41.

4. For example, Bernat Mortorell's *Martyrdom of Saint Eulalia* panel, dating to 1442–1445, now in the Museu Nacional d'Art de Catalunya in Barcelona.

5. Larry Silver, *Hieronymus Bosch* (London: Abbeville Press, 2006), 208, 211. For parallels between Eulalia and Wilgefortis more generally, see Ilse Friesen, *The Female Crucifix: Images of St. Wilgefortis since the Middle Ages* (Waterloo, ON: Wilfrid Laurier University Press, 2001), 32.

6. "La tela grande della S. Caterina sopra la rota nel paese fu de mano del detto Ioachim" (the large canvas of Saint Catherine above the wheel in the countryside made in the hand of the aforementioned Joachim). Marcantonio Michiel, *Notizia d'opere del disegno nella prima metà del secolo XVI esistenti in Padova, Cremona, Milano, Pavia, Bergamo, Crema e Venezia scritta da un Anonimo di quel tempo*, ed. Jacopo Morelli (Bassano del Grappa: Jacopo Morelli, 1800), 76. The handwritten notes of the Venetian noble Michiel (1484–1552), recording his visit to the Palazzo Ducale in the second quarter of the fifteenth century, are preserved in the Biblioteca Nazionale Marciana, Venice. For arguments against the connection between Michiel's note and the Bosch triptych, see Bernard Aikema and Beverly Louise Brown, *Il Rinascimento a Venezia e la pittura del Nord ai tempi di Bellini, Dürer, Tiziano* (Milan: Bompiani, 1999), 448–49.

7. "V'è un'altro quadro in tre comparti, oue si vede il martirio d'una Santa in Croce, con molte figure, e in particolare uno in terra caduto in suenimétó, sostenuto da diversi e è dipinto da Girolamo Basi" (There is another painting in three parts, in which one sees the martyrdom of a [female] saint on the cross, with many figures, and one in particular falling to earth in a swoon, supported by others, which was painted by Giralamo Basi). Marco Boschini, *Le minere della pittura. Compendiosa informazione di Marco Boschini. Non solo delle pitture publiche di Venezia ma dell'isole ancora circonvicine* (Venice: Francesco Nicolini, 1664), 24.

8. "Il Boschini ne annovera quindici dello stesso autore, e poi vi mette un quadro in tre comparti col martirio di un Santo coronato non d'una Santa, non di Girolamo Bassi, ma di Girolamo Bolch, come vedesi scritto in lettere Tedesche bianche" (Boschini counts fifteen works by the same author, and then he mentions a painting in three parts, with the martyrdom of a crowned [male] saint, not of a [female] saint, [and] not by Girolamo Bassi but by Girolamo Bolch, as may be seen written in white German [Gothic] letters). Antonio Maria Zanetti, *Descrizione di tutte le pubbliche pitture della città di Venezia e isole circonvicine* (Venice: Pietro Bassaglia, 1733), 109.

9. Antonio Maria Zanetti il Giovane, *Della pittura veneziana e delle opera pubbliche de' veneziani maestri*, bk. 5 (Venice: Giambatisa Albrizzi, 1771), 491, describing a work signed by "Jeronimus Bosch" depicting the crucifixion of "un Santo o Santa martire" (a holy martyr, male or female).

10. For a brief comparison between Bosch's painting and fifteenth-century manuscript miniatures of Christ's crucifixion, see Bax, *Jeroen Bosch' Drieluik*, 28–29.

11. The first significant arguments in favor of Wilgefortis as the subject of Bosch's central panel were made by the folklorist Jean Gessler in *De Vlaamsche Baardheilige Wilgefortis of Ontcommer* (Antwerp: Martinus Nijhoff, 1937), 172; see also Jean Gessler, *La vierge barbue: La légende de sainte Wilgeforte ou Ontcommer* (Paris: Picard, 1938), 134. The case for Wilgefortis is assessed in Bax, *Jeroen Bosch' Drieluik*, 30–36. For an overview, see also Friesen, *Female Crucifix*, 55–56; and Ilse Friesen, "Virgo Fortis: Images of the Crucified Virgin Saint in Medieval Art," in *Virginity Revisited: Configurations of the Unpossessed Body*, ed. Bonnie Maclachlan and Judith Fletcher (Toronto: University of Toronto Press, 2007), 116–27, esp. 124–25. Friesen argues that Bosch was possibly aiming to meet the needs of customers in both northern and southern Europe, hence painting a saint that could be interpreted as either Julia or Wilgefortis.

12. In preferring Liberata over Wilgefortis, the Venetian exhibitors follow the Italian art historian Dino Buzzati in *L'opera completa di Bosch* (Milan: Rizzoli, 1966), 96. As noted by several scholars, however, Liberata was equated with Wilgefortis only in the sixteenth century, by the pre-Bollandist hagiographer Joannes Molanus, who in his *Usuardi martyrologium*, published in 1568, proposed that Liberata is simply the Latinized name of Wilgefortis/Ontcommer, despite there being an entirely separate hagiographic tradition surrounding the Spanish martyr Saint Librada. See Gustave Schnürer and Josef Ritz, *Sankt Kümmernis und Volto Santo: Studien und Bilder* (Düsseldorf: Drucken, 1934), 66–67; Martin Wangsgaard Jürgensen, "Altering the Sacred Face," in *Resonances: Historical Essays on Continuity and Change*, ed. Nils Holger Petersen, Eyolt Østren, and Andreas Bücker (Turnhout: Brepols, 2011), 81–110, esp. 90–91; and, on Saint Librada specifically, Cristina Cruz González, "Crucifixion Piety in New Mexico: On the Origins and Art of St. Librada," *Res* 65/66 (2014–15): 89–104.

13. For an overview of the cult in Europe, from the Middle Ages to the present, see Friesen, *Female Crucifix*. Other summaries are provided in Gessler, *De Vlaamsche Baardheilige*; Gessler, *La vierge barbue*; Jürgensen, "Altering the Sacred Face"; and Schnürer and Ritz, *Sankt Kümmernis*. On the Danish cult of Saint Helper, who belongs to the Wilgefortis tradition, see J. K. Hansen, "Sct. Hjælper i Kliplev kirke," *Søndersjyske Årbøger* (1986): 37–55. On evidence for the Wilgefortis/Uncumber cult in England, see Richard Marks, "The Dean and the Bearded Lady: Aspects of the Cult of St. Wilgefortis/Uncumber in England," in *Tributes to Nigel Morgan: Contexts of Medieval Art. Images, Objects and Ideas*, ed. Julian M. Luxford and M. A. Michael (London: Harvey Miller, 2010), 349–63.

14. Connections between the *Volto Santo* cult and Wilgefortis iconography have long been noted. As early as 1507, a woodcut by Hans Burkmair is labeled with a double title identifying the image depicted as either *Volto Santo* or Kümmernis, as discussed in Friesen, *Female Crucifix*, 14, 48, 67, 92; and Friesen, "Virgo Fortis," 117–18. Hippolyte Delehaye was the first scholar to make the connection in modern times, in *Les légendes hagiographiques* (Brussels: Vromant, 1906), 87–88. Delehaye's

view that Wilgefortis represents a mistaken interpretation of images of a bearded, robed Christ crucified has persisted. In addition to Friesen's studies, see especially Schnürer and Ritz, *Sankt Kümmernis*; Gessler, *De Vlaamsche Baardheilige*; Friedrich Gorissen, "Das Kreuz von Lucca und die H. Wilgefortis/Ontcommer am unteren Rhein," *Numaga* 15 (1968): 124–26; and Elizabeth Nightlinger, "The Female *Imitatio Christi* and Medieval Popular Religion: The Case of Wilgefortis," in *Representations of the Feminine in the Middle Ages*, ed. Bonnie Wheeler, Feminea medievalia 1 (Dallas: Academia, 1993), 291–328, esp. 294–96.

15. For critiques of the misinterpretation thesis, see especially Friesen, *Female Crucifix*; Jürgensen, "Altering the Sacred Face"; Richard Trexler, *Religion in Social Context in Europe and America, 1200–1700* (Tempe: Arizona Center for Medieval and Renaissance Studies, 2002), 388–91; David Williams, *Deformed Discourse: The Function of the Monster in Mediaeval Thought and Literature* (Exeter: University of Exeter Press, 1996), 309–22. For a related argument, making the case that devotion to Santa Librada in modern-day Argentina represents a deliberate manifestation of "divine transvestism," see Marcella Althaus-Reid, *Indecent Theology: Theological Perversions in Sex, Gender and Politics* (London: Routledge, 2000), 79–83. The classic study of the feminization of God and Christological imagery in medieval religion is Caroline Walker Bynum, *Jesus as Mother: Studies in the Spirituality of the High Middle Ages* (Berkeley: University of California Press, 1982). Other reflections on the sexual ambiguity of Christ's wounded, tormented body in premodern Europe include Karma Lochrie, "Mystical Acts, Queer Tendencies," in *Constructing Medieval Sexuality*, ed. Karma Lochrie, Peggy McCracken, and James A. Schultz (Minneapolis: University of Minnesota Press, 1999), 180–200; Robert Mills, *Suspended Animation: Pain, Pleasure and Punishment in Medieval Culture* (London: Reaktion, 2005), 177–99; and Richard C. Trexler, "Gendering Christ Crucified," in *Iconography at the Crossroads: Papers from the Colloquium Sponsored by the Index of Christian Art, Princeton University, 23–24 March 1990*, ed. Brendan Cassidy (Princeton, NJ: Princeton University Press, 1993), 107–20.

16. Four fifteenth-century texts originating in the Netherlands, one in Dutch and three in Latin, are provided in Schnürer and Ritz, *Santk Kümmernis*, 14–32. Another late fifteenth-century Dutch text, which Gessler judges to be "more extensive and interesting" than those collated by Schnürer and Ritz, is found in Brussels, Royal Library of Belgium, MS 21875, fols. 10–14. See Jean Gessler, "Une version inédite de la légende de Sainte Wilgefortis ou Ontcommer," *Revue d'Histoire Ecclésiastique* 31.1 (1935): 93–99. Bax deems Gessler's text to be the version most relevant to Bosch's painting, but also summarizes pertinent details in a sixteenth-century French text and seventeenth-century German text. See Bax, *Jeroen Bosch' Drieluik*, 30–32.

17. This motif taps into an older tradition of women saints who pray for disfigurement (and in some cases facial hair) as a means of avoiding marriage or sexual abuse. See further Jane Tibbetts Schulenburg, *Forgetful of Their Sex: Female Sanctity and Society, ca. 500–1100* (Chicago: University of Chicago Press, 1998), 127–75; Schulenburg discusses bearded saints at 152–53.

18. Friesen, "Virgo Fortis," 119; Lewis Wallace, "Bearded Woman, Female Christ: Gendered Transformations in the Legend and Cult of Saint Wilgefortis," *Journal of Feminist Studies in Religion* 30.1 (2014): 43–63, esp. 55–58.

19. Gessler, "Une version inédite," 95, 99.

20. For a detailed discussion of the side panels and their possible connections with the theme of the central panel, see Bax, *Jeroen Bosch' Drieluik*, 9–17, 37–43.

21. Friesen, *Female Crucifix*, 47.

22. Examples include a miniature in the Hours of Charles le Clerc from the second quarter of the fifteenth century (London, British Library, Additional 19416, fol. 145v) and a miniature showing Saint Francis flanked by Mary Magdalene, Saint Dorothea, and Saint Ontcommer in a book of hours of Utrecht usage from circa 1415 (Liège, Bibliothèque de l'Université, fonds Wittert MS 35, fol. 13v).

23. See further Harry S. Lipscomb and Hebbel E. Hoff, "Saint Uncumber or *La Vierge Barbue*," *Bulletin of the History of Medicine* 37 (1963): 523–27, esp. 523; and, for an analysis that places the Westminster carving in the context of other evidence for the saint's cult in England, see Marks, "Dean and the Bearded Lady."

24. Friesen, *Female Crucifix*, 51–52; Friesen, "Virgo Fortis," 124. The tunicle would have been worn by the subdeacon during the celebration of High Mass; a dalmatic from the same set, worn by the deacon, features ranks of male saints and martyrs. See further Katja Schmitz-von Ledebur, "The Vestments of the Order of the Golden Fleece: A Major Work of Burgundian Court Art," in *Splendour of the Burgundian Court: Charles the Bold (1433–1477)*, ed. Susan Marti, Till-Holz Borchert, and Gabriele Keck (Brussels: Mercatorfonds, 2009), 62–71; and Helmut Trnek, "Das Messornat des Ordens vom Goldenen Vlies," in *Kunsthistorisches Museum Wien: Weltliche und Geistliche Schatzkammer, Bildführer*, ed. Rotraud Bauer (Salzburg: Residenz Verlag, 1991), 208–24.

25. See also Friesen, *Female Crucifix*, 54.

26. Wilgefortis's role in modeling a specifically female form of *imitatio Christi* is further discussed in Friesen, *Female Crucifix*, 19–32; Nightlinger, "Female *Imitatio Christi*"; and Wallace, "Bearded Woman, Female Christ," 49–52.

27. Matthijs Ilsink and Jos Koldeweij, *Hieronymus Bosch: Visions of Genius* (Brussels: Mercatorfonds, 2016), 134; Matthijs Ilsink et al., *Hieronymus Bosch, Painter and Draughtsman: Catalogue Raisonné* (Brussels: Mercatorfonds, 2016), 196, citing Wilton Desmense, *Lang leve de Sint-Jan: Een Bossche ode uit de 16e eeuw aan hertog, stad en kerk* ('s-Hertogenbosch: Stadsarchief 's-Hertogenbosch, 1995), 27.

28. As seen in Princeton University Library, MS Garrett 59, fol. 161r, a Dutch book of hours from ca. 1500. For a brief analysis of the miniature, see Martha Easton, "'Why Can't a Woman Be More Like a Man?': Transforming and Transcending Gender in the Lives of Female Saints," in *The Four Modes of Seeing: Approaches to Medieval Imagery in Honor of Madeline Harrison Caviness*, ed. Evelyn Saudinger Lane, Elizabeth Carson Pastan, and Ellen M. Shortell (Farnham: Ashgate, 2009), 333–47, esp. 338.

29. As discussed in Friesen, *Female Crucifix*, 55, the altarpiece was possibly made on the occasion of Adriaan Reins's reception as butler of Saint John's Hospital in Bruges in 1479; hospital patients would potentially have viewed Ontcommer as a source of spiritual sustenance because of the saint's liberating powers.

30. Mary of Egypt was a penitent sinner who withdrew to the desert to atone for her insatiable promiscuity and whose body became covered in a hairy pelt. Her legend was sometimes conflated with that of Mary Magdalene, another penitent figure who features on the main panel of the open triptych and was also sometimes represented by late medieval and early modern artists as a hirsute figure. See further Charles Allyn Williams, "Oriental Affinities of the Legend of the Hairy Anchorite,

Part II: Christian," *University of Illinois Studies in Language and Literature* 11 (1926): 427–93; Ruth Mazo Karras, "Holy Harlots: Prostitute Saints in Medieval Legend," *Journal of the History of Sexuality* 1 (1990): 3–32.

31. When the image is viewed close-up, it is also possible to discern a very fine mustache, itself unusual in Wilgefortis iconography.

32. Robert Mills, "Visibly Trans? Picturing Saint Eugenia in Medieval Art," *TSQ: Transgender Studies Quarterly* 5.4 (2018): 540–64. See also Easton, "Why Can't a Woman Be More Like a Man?," which discerns a similar phenomenon in contemporary illustrations of Joan of Arc showing her as an armored but otherwise securely female figure; and Saisha Grayson, "Disruptive Disguises: The Problem of Transvestite Saints for Medieval Art, Identity, and Identification," *Medieval Feminist Forum* 45.2 (2009): 138–74, which also focuses on Eugenia.

33. Clement of Alexandria, *Christ the Educator*, trans. Simon P. Wood (Washington, DC: Catholic University of America Press, 1954), 214–15.

34. For example, see imagery of beards in the thirteenth-century *Bibles moralisées*, as discussed in Sara Lipton, *Images of Intolerance: The Representation of Jews and Judaism in the "Bible moralisée"* (Berkeley: University of California Press, 1999).

35. One particularly striking story in Jerome's *vita* tells how the saint once wandered into church for mass, having mistakenly donned a woman's dress that had been planted by his bedside by a fellow monk as a joke. As I discuss elsewhere, a unique rendition of the episode in a miniature in the *Belles Heures of Jean de Berry*, a manuscript made by the Limbourg brothers in the early fifteenth century, strikingly represents Jerome's beard not simply as a sign of his sanctity but also as a visible mark of his enduring maleness; the prominence of the saint's lengthy beard serves to accentuate the contrast between Jerome's bodily sex (assumed to be male) and the bright blue dress he ends up wearing (which is coded as unmistakably feminine). See Robert Mills, *Seeing Sodomy in the Middle Ages* (Chicago: University of Chicago Press, 2015), 1–8.

36. See, for example, the near-life-size statues of English monarchs that line the fifteenth-century choir screen in York Minster, where all the kings except Henry VI sport some kind of facial hair. In the thirteenth-century *Bibles moralisées*, bearded men, including kings, were sometimes shown embracing, kissing, or fondling the chins of younger, unbearded males, demonstrating that beards were also used by artists to differentiate youth from age (and in so doing to represent the sexual exploitation of younger by older males). See Mills, *Seeing Sodomy*, 67–69.

37. Hirsutism was also potentially racialized, as in medieval and Renaissance representations of wild men, who were often depicted with lengthy beards as well as furry skin. The excessive hairiness of these mythical creatures highlighted their perceived distance from humanity, as a separate species, but also marked them out as ethnically other—a fiction that preceded and helped inform European responses to the peoples "discovered" and colonized in later centuries. See further Roger Bartra, *Wild Men in the Looking Glass: The Mythic Origins of European Otherness*, trans. C. T. Berrisford (Ann Arbor: University of Michigan Press, 1994).

38. Mark Albert Johnston, "Re-Evaluating Bearded Women," in *Beard Fetish in Early Modern England: Sex, Gender, and Registers of Value* (Farnham: Ashgate, 2011), 159–212. On the suppression of Uncumber imagery during the Reformation, see Carole Levin, "St. Frideswide and St. Uncumber: Changing Images of Female Saints

in Renaissance England," in *Women, Writing, and the Reproduction of Culture in Tudor and Stuart Britain*, ed. Mary E. Burke et al. (Syracuse, NY: Syracuse University Press, 2000), 223–37.

39. Chaucer, "Miller's Tale," ll. 3734–36, in *The Riverside Chaucer*, ed. Larry D. Benson, 3rd ed. (Boston: Houghton Mifflin, 1987).

40. Johnston, "Re-Evaluating Bearded Women," 179–81, 198–201. Johnston quotes Thomas More's 1529 *Dialogue Concerning Heresies*, in which More presents biting commentary on the cult of Wilgefortis, called Uncumber, "bycawse they teken that . . . she wyll not fayle to uncumber them of theyr husbondis."

41. Ilsink and Koldeweij, *Hieronymus Bosch*, 136.

42. Ilsink et al., *Hieronymus Bosch, Painter and Draughtsman*, 190. Memling's panel on the Adriaan Reins Triptych is cited as a precedent for the saint's "light beard."

43. Luuk Hoogstede et al., *Hieronymus Bosch, Painter and Draughtsman: Technical Studies* (Brussels: Mercatorfonds, 2016), 151. A scan of the painting using infrared reflectography can be viewed at http://boschproject.org/#/artworks/Saint_Wilgefortis_Triptych (accessed August 29, 2019).

44. Caterine Virdis Limentani, catalogue entry 32, "Saint Wilgefortis Triptych," in *Bosch: The 5th Centenary Exhibition*, ed. Pilar Silva Maroto (Madrid: Museo Nacional del Prado, 2016), 272–75, esp. 272.

45. Pilar Silva Maroto, introduction to *Bosch*, 15.

46. *Hieronymus Bosch: Touched by the Devil*, directed by Pieter van Huijstee (2015).

47. Rare exceptions include Elisa Heinrich, "Die Ordnung und ihr Anderes? Einige Anmerkungen zum Cross Dressing am Beispiel der Heiligen Kümmernis," *Medium Aevum Quotidianum* 51 (2005): 40–47; Alison Jasper, "Theology at the Freak Show: St. Uncumber and the Discourse of Liberation," *Theology and Sexuality* 11.2 (2005): 43–53; and Wallace, "Bearded Woman, Female Christ." Discussing the cult in general rather than the Bosch triptych specifically, Jasper considers the theological implications of Uncumber's example, notably their potential as a "liberator from the imprisonment of biological essentialisms or normative sex-gender" (52). Wallace usefully maintains a focus on what the saint "*does* rather than what she *is*" (44), suggesting that Wilgefortis's transformations were a key to their popularity. Heinrich argues that Kümmernis's physical transformation sets her apart from other "transvestite" women saints who dress as men to escape marriage or abuse, the term "transgender" being more applicable in her case (44).

48. Friesen, *Female Crucifix*, 3, 128. See, for example, https://qspirit.net/saint-wilgefortis-bearded-woman/ (accessed August 29, 2019).

49. GenderBen!, "How Saint Wilgefortis Came to Be: The Saint of Bearded Ladies," June 19, 2017, https://genderben.com/2017/06/19/how-saint-wilgefortis-came-to-be-the-saint-of-bearded-ladies/ (accessed August 29, 2019).

50. See, for example, F. H. de Jong and W. W. de Herder, "Saint Wilgefortis: Sudden Hirsutism to Prevent an Unwanted Marriage," *Journal of Endocrinological Investigation* 39.12 (2016): 1475; J. Hubert Lacey, "Anorexia Nervosa and a Bearded Saint," *British Medical Journal (Clinical Research Edition)* 285.6357 (December 18–25, 1982): 1816–17; and Lipscomb and Hoff, "Saint Uncumber or *La Vierge Barbue*," citing I. E. Bush and V. B. Mahesh, "Adrenocortical Hyperfunction with Sudden Onset of Hirsutism," *Journal of Endocrinology* 18.1 (January 1959): 1–25. For an overview of these interpretations, which present hirsutism as an "ongoing reality" for some

women, see Friesen, *Female Crucifix*, 121–25. Similar lines of inquiry are pursued in M. A. Katritzky, "'A Wonderful Monster Borne in Germany': Hairy Girls in Medieval and Early Modern German Book, Court and Performance Culture," *German Life and Letters* 67.4 (2014): 467–80; Schulenburg, *Forgetful of Their Sex*, 152–53.

51. Levin, "St. Frideswide and St. Uncumber," 226.

52. Blake Gutt, "Transgender Genealogy in *Tristan de Nanteuil*," *Exemplaria* 30.2 (2018): 129–46, quotation at 140.

53. Mills, *Seeing Sodomy*, 98–132; Valerie Traub, Patricia Badir, and Peggy McCracken, eds., *Ovidian Transversions: "Iphis and Ianthe," 1300–1650* (Edinburgh: Edinburgh University Press, 2019).

54. *Ovide moralisé* 9.3080–3103, translated as Appendix A in Traub, Badir, and McCracken, *Ovidian Transversions*, 283.

55. Susan Schibanoff, "True Lies: Transvestism and Idolatry in the Trial of Joan of Arc," in *Fresh Verdicts on Joan of Arc*, ed. Bonnie Wheeler and Charles T. Wood (New York: Garland, 1996), 31–60. See also Schulenburg, *Forgetful of Their Sex*, 164, reviewing an account by Hildegard of Bingen of a young female acquaintance who dresses as a schoolboy but is caught when the abbess sees through the disguise; Hildegard orders the girl to "convert to a better state."

56. For a premodern take on the limitations of "sex change" as a construct for understanding gender transitivity, see Gutt, "Transgender Genealogy," 139–40.

57. Jack Halberstam, *Trans*: A Quick and Quirky Account of Gender Variability* (Oakland: University of California Press, 2018), xiii, 24–44.

58. Halberstam, *Trans*, xiii, 4, 88.

59. At the time of writing, the tide appears to be turning against the asterisk in activist circles and popular culture. As noted by Blake Gutt and Alicia Spencer-Hall in their "Trans and Genderqueer Studies Terminology, Language, and Usage Guide," in *Trans and Genderqueer Subjects in Medieval Hagiography* (Amsterdam: Amsterdam University Press, 2021), 316: "While trans is now generally preferred to trans* when referring to individuals, trans* is frequently used in trans(*) studies to refer to broader cultural aspects of trans(*) experience, and 'trans(*)' as a discursive construct." For a recent collection of essays that harnesses the generative potential of the asterisk for historical analysis specifically, see Leah DeVun and Zeb Tortorici, eds., "Trans*Historicities," special issue of *TSQ: Transgender Studies Quarterly* 5.4 (2018).

60. For a parallel argument about the saint's "plethora of names" and the need to avoid pinning Kümmernis down to a distinct identity, see Jürgensen, "Altering the Sacred Face," 110.

CHAPTER 7

Performing and Desiring Gender Variance in the Early Modern Ottoman Empire

In his *Çenginame* (The book of *çengi* dancers), the popular Ottoman poet Enderunlu Fazıl (1757–1810) catalogues famous androgynous dancers of late eighteenth-century Istanbul.[1] This work is a supplement to two of his previous books, *Hubanname* (The book of beautiful young men, ca. 1792) and *Zenanname* (The book of beautiful women, ca. 1795), which chart beautiful men and women from different nations in Asia, Africa, Europe, and the New World. Like *Hubanname* and *Zenanname*, *Çenginame* belongs to the conventional *şehrengiz* genre, a poetic depiction of beautiful people of great cities; but it is unique in devoting an entire book to *köçeks* as objects of attraction and desire.[2] Etymologically derived from the Turkish word *küçük* (little, small) and adopted from the Persian variation *kuchak* (كوچك)—"little, young, child"—*köçek* refers to dancers assigned male at birth who were taken on at the young age of seven or eight by dancing companies and trained to perform for an exclusively male audience in attire associated with femininity.[3] What gendered work do Fazıl's *köçeks* standing next to the beautiful young men and women of the empire do? What stories about trans lives today might the *köçeks* of the past narrate?

In this essay I trace various transfigurations of *köçek* as a distinct gender category in urban settings in both Fazıl's narrative and its early modern precedents. Fazıl's inclusion of these dancers in addition to boys and women in his classification of desirable objects of adult male desire, I suggest, offers historical trans alternatives that account for the recognition of gender variant embodiments and contest the perceived stability of the two-gender system in the Ottoman Empire.[4] In my analysis I deploy a trans analytics that resists erasing historical trans potentiality in challenging gender norms by enabling us to rethink gender categories and embodiments outside binaries and further exploring frictions between older and newer gender regimes both in the past and in the present. A genealogy of these dancers presents an understanding of gender as determined by such factors as age, appearance, religion, and imperial status, and thus registers in its historical baggage intricate entanglements between imperial violence and desire in the production, objectification, and consumption of these androgynous dancers in early modernity. Accordingly, these dancers, always already in an assemblage of difference—sexual, racial, and religious—within imperial management, were sometimes celebrated and at other times condemned and oppressed, paralleling the changing norms of the empire. Fazıl's *köçeks* henceforth offer a striking example at the turn of the nineteenth century when gender plurality under the early modern imperial gaze shifted into a rigidly surveilled gender binary with the nationalistic remodeling of the Ottoman state in accordance with Western norms and regimes.

Köçeks appeared as public performers, servers in coffeehouses, participants in royal processions, and sexual partners in taverns in the Ottoman Empire between the sixteenth and the nineteenth centuries. The *köçek* was born as a gendered figure most probably as a result of gender segregation that prohibited female performers in public. As trained professionals and performers in both dance and occasionally dramatic narrative roles, *köçeks* performed at weddings, birth celebrations, circumcision festivities, celebrations after battle victories, and in public plays, as well as in taverns and at court.[5] Chosen from non-Muslim communities at a young age, these dancers lived communally (*ocak*) and formed their own guild (*kol*) with comedians and mime artists taking roles in the performing arts (*hokkabaz* [juggler], *köçek* [dancer], *cambaz* [acrobat], *atesbaz* [fire juggler], etc.).[6]

Trained at an early age, these dancers were always already in the process of shaping and performing their public genders. Scholars have long read *köçek* dancers as cross-dressing performers and as substitute for women in a gender-segregated social structure. Most prominent among them, the cultural historian Metin And, for instance, describes these dancers as simply impersonating women in both appearance and demeanor; they are of an "unnatural profession; being partly male, and partly female."[7] While their partial performance of maleness goes unexplored, their performance of femaleness is simply marked as imitative. This way of looking at the *köçek* dancers assumes the binary to be a universal and ahistorical category by assigning them to one side of the gender binary and thus erasing their gender ambiguity. By contrast, I will argue that *köçek* dancers, with their malleable, androgynous embodiments and an ability to evoke an array of performative gendered qualities, did not imitate women; nor did they temporarily travel to the other end of the gender spectrum in their performances, but freely danced in between with their own styles and gender presentations while intentionally obscuring their assigned gender. The destabilization of binary gender was typically a focal point of their performances, revealing, to borrow Simone Chess's assertion about genderqueer performance, "a queer and desirable performance of gender rather than a successful or failed disguise."[8]

These dancers, transitioning from boyhood to an androgynous expression and performance, often had two names even in their non-performance lives—one masculine, one feminine. The famous Ottoman traveler Evliya Çelebi, for example, lists some of the well-known dancers of the empire in the seventeenth century: Mazlum Şah, Küpeli Ayvaz Şah, Saçlı Ramazan Şah, Memiş Şah, Sakız Mahbubu Zalim Şah, Nazlı Yusuf. Some of these names are a combination of masculine and feminine elements, where the stereotypically feminine epithet modifies a masculine name, for example, Nazlı (coy) Yusuf, Küpeli Ayvaz (Ayvaz with earring), or Saçlı (long-hair) Ramazan.[9] (I must add that in most of these stories, it is difficult to pinpoint these dancers' genders linguistically because of the gender-neutral nature of pronouns in Turkish; the pronoun "o" is used for "he/she/it." Throughout the essay I use "he/him," "she/her," "they/them" to refer to the person, as well as to the dancing persona and to how they switch between genders, at particular moments in the narratives under analysis. Otherwise I use "they/them" to register their gender variance.)

Besides their names, their costumes and dances also blurred dichotomous gender lines. Their costumes included transparent low-neck blouses, shirts worn with short-sleeved or sleeveless velvet vests, shalwars (loose trousers) or wide trousers gathered at the ankle and worn with paneled skirts, embroidered shawls and belts encircling the waist, and elaborate shoes (figs. 7.1 and 7.2). Such stereotypically feminine items of clothing as colorful skirts and embroidered shawls and belts, as well as long hair, consolidated their androgyny. Likewise, their style of dance included slow and smooth, delicate, putatively feminine movements (belly dancing, heel-tapping, walking as if running on tiptoes, neck dance, shoulder shaking, waist dance) and more forceful masculine moves (rushing backwards, body bouncing, body shaking, and body bending). Because their gender presentations made no attempt

FIGURE 7.1. A *köçek* dancing for a young man. Illustration from Fazıl, *Hubanname*, ca. 1792. Public domain: https://en.wikipedia.org/wiki/Köçek#/media/File:Performing_Kocek.JPG.

FIGURE 7.2. *Köçeks* dancing during circumcision festivities, from *the Surname-i Vehbi*, 1720. Public domain: https://en.wikipedia.org/wiki/Köçek#/media/File:Koceks_-_Surname-i_Vehbi.jpg.

to conceal masculine elements, and because their unique dance styles deliberately mixed feminine and masculine qualities, *köçeks* offered a distinct gender performance that cannot be described as imitative cross-dressing. In fact, even dancers assigned female at birth at times themselves imitated *köçeks*, performing as *köçeks* in their shows for women, using *köçek*-specific costumes and dances.[10] *Köçek* gender evidently is not simply an approximation of femininity; rather, a *köçek* is one who disrupts and crosses lines by presenting gender as scripted, coded, and decoded.

Fazıl's *Çenginame* provides a glimpse of contemporary cultural discourses surrounding the *köçek*, who appears, along with women and boys, as a disparate gendered object of adult male desire.[11] Fazıl starts his narrative by portraying a gathering (*meclis*) where attendants discuss *köçek* dancers who are "unmatchable on earth" (*dünyada dengi bulunmaz*, 11). By creating a scene set in *meclis*, which were typically all-male gatherings where poems were produced, shared, and critiqued, and where poets built their reputation and networks, Fazıl puts androgynous figures at the center of poetic production and aesthetics.[12] Those attending Fazıl's *meclis* included poets, scholars, judges, and patrons whom Fazıl calls the "masters of love" (*ehl-i aşk*). When they ask Fazıl to shed light on these dancers (*bize çengileri kil ruşen u pak*, 29, 28), Fazıl reflects at length on forty-three dancers.[13] Among them are the Italian Todori, the Croatian Yorgaki, the Egyptian Jewish convert Şevki, the Jewish Fıstık, the Armenian Ziba, the Christian Pandeli, and the Heretic Kervan. While these names clearly evoke their ethnic, racial, religious, and geographic origins (and their difference from the Muslim population), others have non-Islamic names such as Little Andon, Antintop, or Panayot that mirror their alterity implicitly. And some other names deploy erotic and bodily metaphors: Yeni Dünya (New World), Canary Şakir, or Little Afet, or "stunner" (*afet* literally means "disaster" or "catastrophe," but it also has an erotic signification of destroying with beauty, as in "a knockout"). These names suggest that the *köçek*'s gender embodiment is perceived, as well as eroticized, in relation to their religious and racial difference.

Indeed, a history of *köçeks* reveals how imperial violence and desire are inseparably interlinked in marking their bodies as desirable sites of difference under an imperial, erotic gaze. *Köçeks*, as Refik Ahmet Sevengil reminds, were usually boys who had been captured or sold into slavery or apprenticeship, and trained in dance, music, and manners.[14] They were mostly from Greek, Armenian, Jewish, Roma, and other non-Muslim communities of the Ottoman Empire.[15] The Ottoman Empire, with different religious and ethnic communities extending to three continents, was structured around slavery.[16] Religious difference was one of the essential markers in the enslaving and managing of imperial subjects.[17] While those living within the imperial dominion were under state protection, hence unenslaveable, non-Muslim people living outside the borders of the empire (in the domain of war, *daru'l harp*) could be captured. Bearers of slave (*kul*) status, these captives did not have to assimilate or convert; they oftentimes maintained their native cultures and religions.[18] Nevertheless, despite the presumed Ottoman tolerance for all, the *kul* populations, as H. Erdem Cipa has shown, were exposed to consistent attacks as unreliable converts with an emphasis on their non-Muslim lineage.[19]

Within the imperial hierarchy, permissible and disallowed forms of gender expression were accordingly determined by religion and imperial status. What seemed appropriate for non-Muslim subjects of the empire (e.g., alcohol consumption, dancing for public entertainment) would have been unacceptable vices for Muslims, mostly as a means of preventing *fitna*, or social disturbance and disorder caused by straying from religious tenets and morality. And such imperial hierarchies and classifications based on religion and imperial status, as I discuss elsewhere, were often eroticized in abductions and enslavements within the territories ruled by the empire.[20] In particular, Euro-Christian boys, often portrayed as cup-bearing servants, were marked in this literature as objects of male desire to be abducted and possessed. Likewise, *köçeks*, mostly selected among non-Muslim boys, were forcibly transformed into a new nonconforming gender category as androgynous dancers and celebrated for adult men's pleasure and entertainment.

In an eroticized hierarchical matrix, these dancers illustrate how the production of genders intersects with imperial status; that is, gender status in this period was not marked simply by biological difference but also by a composite of differences in age, appearance, class, race, and religion and sexual role. Representations of these figures, including within Fazıl's narrative, project an imperial and erotic gaze over a gender category reserved mainly for the religious and racial Other because of its association with androgyny. Their performances, appearances, and bodies become the focus of the poetic gaze and desire that produces blazons, poetic dissections of their eyes, noses, hair, eyebrows, and facial hair. In Fazıl's account, Andon has a little mouth like his little hands (49); Ceylan (gazelle) has beautiful hazel eyes like his namesake (97); Çubukçu Güzeli (pipe-maker beauty) has "cherry lips" (85). Some have "nice waists" (85), some attractive "butts" (64, 83, 88); some are "attractive," while others become "ugly" (94). Furthermore, Fazıl notes their skin color as the source of their attraction: Tilki (fox) has darker skin (55); Pamuk (cotton) has white skin (104). Some of the most frequently described aspects of their appearance are long hair, a smooth face, fair complexion, strong muscles, and age/youth. Such features, especially youth, were celebrated, for they enabled a form of androgyny that, at least on the surface, could be manipulated to assert and reassert new gender formations and transitivity at will.

Indeed, a youthful appearance—as signified by a hairless body—is an important way for these dancers to distance themselves from any qualities that are identified as stereotypically masculine. Kervan is now old and hairy (39), but Yorgaki's and Antintop's hairless bodies shine like silver (46, 62). By contrast, Fazıl describes Todori, who is fifty-eight years old, as hairy as a "dog," writing that his barber sometimes tries to transform him into a "boy," that is, a hairless, penetrable object of love (40–42). Called a "Venetian emissary" (48), Todori is implicated in prostitution and pimping, keeps a brothel, and has syphilis (*firenk zahmeti*, 40). Fazıl ridicules other dancers as well who are now older: Andon, once putatively the Alexander the Great of the dance scene, is described as a corpse whose face is covered with flies and his mouth with ants (50). One dancer has "thorns," which seems to mean a scruff of body hair (51); another has "became wooden" in contrast to others' soft, youthful bodies (98); and one is now hairier and has darker skin like a "black cow" (kara manda, 96). While such descriptions suggest an ideal gender based on the embodied malleability of youthfulness, many köçeks retained their unique gender as they aged. In fact, as we see that while old age is reviled by the poet, the implication is that köçek is not necessarily an ephemeral category unique to youth; some of these dancers continue their dance careers as köçeks in spite of getting older.

The admiration for and celebration of youth is very much a continuation of the premodern Islamicate aesthetics and sexual economy that define the beardless boy as the epitome of beauty and erotic attractiveness.[21] The beautiful boy as the object of homoerotic desire, as Walter Andrews and Mehmet Kalpakli have shown in their study The Age of Beloveds, was not simply a literary trope but a social figure within the homonormative social structures of the early modern Ottoman Empire, in which boyhood was considered a transitional gender category. As a sign of transition from boyhood to adulthood, from the submissive to the dominant role, facial hair signified the release of the boy from his status as a legitimate object of adult male desire.[22] Yet sexual and gender ambiguity lingers for köçeks, the outsiders who transitioned from boyhood not to adult male but rather to an androgynous gender, and thus maintained their status as objects of masculine sexual desire. Most dancers in Fazıl's account are marked as sodomites (ehl-i liwat). Besides Todori, another dancer named Kız (girly) Mehmet is said to wander around seeking sex with men (75). Other dancers, such as Rubiyye, Panayot, Mısırlı Güzeli (Egyptian beauty), Altın-tob, Kanarya (canary), Kız (girl) Mehemmed, and Tûtî are also described as having sex with men. In Fazıl's narrative, these dancers remain within a non-heteronormative matrix with their attractive appearance and seductive dances.

Historically, köçeks performed and existed mostly within the realm of a masculine homoerotic space—be it in public for performance, entertainment, and festivals, or in private houses, all-"male" garden parties, taverns, and coffeehouses.[23] Almost two centuries before Fazıl, in his description of early seventeenth-century Istanbul, Evliya Çelebi depicts some popular attractive dancers. Dancers such as Can Memi Şah, Zalim Şah, and Hürrem Şah, Fitne Şah, Yusuf Şah, and Mirza Şah were so popular that, Evliya Çelebi informs us, they "performed at the court of Sultan Murad."[24] Evliya Çelebi reports that one of the guilds in particular, Baba Nazlı's, has beautiful city boys and "Gypsies"; when they put on their attire and dance, those who see them yearn with passion, exclaiming, "Oh God!" (sadâ-yi hû, 329). When some appear in their skirts and dance like peacocks in a heavenly garden, the spectators get excited and "fall in love at once" (ol dem meftûn olur, 330). Another dancer, Yavru Habib (little/baby beloved) has such beautiful eyes that his gaze and arrow-like eyelashes pierce men's hearts (330).

Similar to Evliya Çelebi's account, other literary and popular narratives also eroticize these dancers. The famous seventeenth-century court poet Nedim praises a köçek and wants to explore their body in search of "lovers' sins" hiding or revealed there:

Dancer! is the source of this appeal your dance?[25]
Are the sins of your lovers around your neck?
I can't be sated by our love union at night like a fasting man[26]
Oh silver-bodied, is the morning in your bosom?
[Rakkas, bu halet senin oynunda mıdır
Aş ıklarının günahı boynunda mıdır,
Doymam şeb-i vaslına şeb-i rûze gibi
Ey sim-beden, sabah koynunda mıdır. (363)][27]

Likewise, the court composer of Sultan Selim III, Vasdakosta Ahmet Ağa, desires to "cuddle and kiss" one of the sultan's köçeks, while Numan Ağa praises a köçek for androgynous allure in his song "Arazbarbûselik" by noting it is "not known if the köçek is girl or boy" (kız mı erkek mı bilinmez köçek).[28] The Croatian Büyük Afet, who is mentioned in Fazıl's account, emerges in Mıskalî's song as an erotic object of love with "charm" (letafet), "grace" (zarafet), golden hair (sırma saç), and a pen-like eyebrow (kalem kaşlı).[29]

Fazıl's depiction of these dancers' sexual encounters as well as the fetishization of their gender diversity is then in alignment with such long-celebrated eroticism around köçeks. In fact, Fazıl describes his own erotic relations with men and attraction to some köçeks in his works, celebrating homoeroticism in what would today be understood as a heteronormative economy that is damaging for all. In his Defter-i Aşk, which was usually bundled with Hubanname, Zenanname, and Çenginame in manuscript and print editions and where he describes his erotic life, Fazıl narrates the story of Köçek İsmail, a beautiful "Gypsy" (çingane).[30] This köçek, depicted at the age of about seventeen, is at the peak of his career and desired by all men when Fazıl sees him for the first time at a tavern in Galata. Köçek İsmail, however, stops dancing when he gets married and disappears. Years later, when Fazıl sees him performing in the streets with a bear, he hardly recognizes him because he has lost all of his alluring beauty. Marriage ruined this köçek.

While giving up their *köçek* role and assimilating into the marriage economy is destructive for the dancers in this story, in other stories it is similarly dangerous to disturb the sanctity of marriage by transgressing gender
roles. The story of Köçek Can İbo, first narrated in 1711 by Burnaz Ali in
the city of Edirne, is exemplary. Reşad Ekrem Koçu presents this story of a
child assigned female at birth, who was raised as a boy and later performed
as a *köçek* and became the most popular *köçek* in Istanbul.[31] This popularity provokes duels between men and battles among *köçek* companies. In the
meantime, İbo proceeds to have a secret love affair with their master, who
himself was a *köçek* in the past and now has his own troupe to train *köçeks*.
Their successful business and personal relationships end when the public
hears about İbo's "real" biological sex after his drunken uncle reveals the
secret in public. İbo is "a woman" disguised as a *köçek* after all. To avoid
severe punishment—a woman's cross-dressing and public performance were
unacceptable—İbo escapes to Damascus, where they refashion themself as
a female dancer with a new name, Güllü, and later marries a *köçek*, whom
she trains. Güllü becomes the most popular female dancer for women, and
her husband succeeds spectacularly as a *köçek* by using erotic moves taught
to him by his own wife. While Güllü does not become jealous of her husband
spending time with other men, her husband becomes jealous when Güllü
is desired by other women. Just as this tension is poised to ruin their happiness, her husband suddenly dies; Güllü feels liberated, moves back to Istanbul, and lives as a woman among elite women until she is eventually killed
and thrown into the sea, probably by a jealous lover. Marriage can threaten
careers and even lives when some *köçeks* transgress norms set for the marriage economy.

While Ottoman accounts celebrated these dancers and their androgyny,
European travelers to the Ottoman Empire depicted the dancers as both
gender nonconforming *and* sodomitical from a dichotomous and anti-
sexual point of view. John Hobhouse, for instance, calls them "beastly"
when he sees young dancers with Lord Byron in the Galata neighborhood
of Istanbul in 1810.[32] This echoes seventeenth-century European accounts
of *köçek*, among them John Covel's diary passage from the 1670s register-
ing that "the sight truly always was pleasant, only these *beastly* actions were
horrible."[33] Jean de Thévenot's posthumously published travel account
(1686) notes that these dancers practiced "abominable lasciviousness" and
struck the "most filthy postures imaginable" and announces, "In short, it is
horrid and incredible to see how far the impudence of the *Turks* transports
them to lust and especially to Sodomy."[34] Here we see how sodomy accusations intersect with contemporary beliefs about binary gender such that

these gender-nonconforming dancers are depicted as monstrous.[35] Such European accounts often inform the sort of scholarly work that instrumentalizes these dancers in discussions of both contemporary and early modern male homosexuality.[36] In such accounts, the *köçek* is an embodiment not only of gender inversion but also of abnormal sexual perversion. The abovementioned statement by Metin And, for instance, describing these dancers belonging to an "unnatural profession," evokes Western discourses that mark homosexuality and gender fluidity as against nature, monstrous, and outside the natural order. Yet a brief exploration of these dancers using the discourse and cultural imaginary specific to this period of Ottoman imperial history reveals that the *köçek* encapsulates gender variance that simply cannot be reduced to the modern-day hegemonic gender binary in a heteronormative matrix, which is itself a result of the changing dynamics of the nineteenth-century empire.

In the nineteenth century, the Ottomans started an energetic process of Westernization as a means to hold the empire together against the tide of nationalist independence movements (Greek, Serbian, Bulgarian) within the multi-religious, multiethnic empire. This Tanzimat (Reorganization) Period (1839–1876) initiated the Westernization of legal, educational, juridical, military, and social structures in creating a national Ottoman identity to replace the imperial hierarchization of people based on their ethnic and religious affiliation. In the process, the modernizing empire also adopted European discourses about the natural order of sexuality and gender roles and, in Deniz Kandiyoti's words, "attempted to institutionalize monogamous heterosexuality as the normative ideal."[37] Older forms of sexual and gender expressions that celebrated homoerotic love and androgyny were now associated with aberrance and shame. One account by one of the prominent leaders of the nineteenth-century reforms is telling: in his autobiographical *Maruzat* in 1850s, Cevdet Pasha reports: "With the increase of women-lovers the number of boy-beloveds decreased and the sodomites seem to have disappeared off the face of the earth. Ever since then the well-known love for and relationships with the young men of Istanbul was transferred to young women as the natural order of things."[38] In this new social order, Fazıl's *Zenanneme* was banned not solely because it was immoral but because it openly spoke out against heterosexual marriage, and his other works were censored and fell out of favor. And as Mustafa Avcı has demonstrated, such "heteronormativization took place not only on the discursive but also a practical level, with the gradually effective suppression of *köçek*."[39] In the process of suppressing homoerotic conventions and gender-queer performances, *köçek* dancers faded and went underground, whereas as recently as the beginning of the nineteenth century "there were some 600 dancing boys in the taverns of Constantinople."[40] These dancers were now seen as a source of shame, uneasiness, and social disorder; the once celebrated androgynous figures became oppressed outlaws, especially in urban settings.[41] At the same time, a strict adherence to what we might now term binary gender performance became the norm. The imposition of Western ideals of normative gender erased the visibility of gender diversity that was permissible in accordance with religious difference within a hierarchical imperial structure; now there emerged a standardized model of the gender binary under equal citizenship.

Köçek, one of many genders of the past, with its own erotic appeal, emerged under an imperial gaze and has been suppressed in favor of binary gender norms. Prior to the insistence on the binary understanding of gender, there was observable enthusiasm for these figures as well as an economy of consumption—be it theatrical, poetic, or sexual—organized around the köçek. Köçek dancers, from the sixteenth to the early nineteenth centuries, functioned as a social as well as an erotic class defined by their alluring yet stigmatized androgyny, both in public and in the poetic imagination. Fazıl's köçeks provide us with accounts of gender plurality that destabilize a contemporary binary structure that renders trans bodies unnatural. In doing so, the köçek instantiates a glimpse of trans figurations and negotiations "before trans" in early modernity.[42] Köçeks' gender-ambiguous performance and presentation force us to carefully reconsider hegemonic accounts of maleness or femaleness, and to witness instead the multiplicity of embodied categories often determined by such factors as age, religion, race, and imperial status. These categories were often also importantly constituted as legitimate objects of desire for adult men in the early modern period. In Fazıl's world, while beautiful boys were celebrated for love and women were desired for purposes of reproduction, köçeks were admired for their unmatched androgyny.

To what extent does köçek history challenge modern transphobic perspectives and attitudes in today's Turkey and other Islamicate contexts in general? Trans people are visible day and night in modern Turkey. As Rüstem Ertuğ Altınay observes, Muslim trans identities and subjectivities emerge within complex sociopolitical dynamics and develop strategies of survival in transphobic contexts.[43] Indeed, these strategies are vital when transphobia renders transgender and gender-nonconforming people vulnerable in public life. Visibly transgender people are often not allowed in hotels, college dorms, and coffee shops or on public buses. They are exposed to police brutality and public policing. They are forced to move out of their neighborhoods and homes—some of which have even been burned down. Many are physically and verbally abused, and some have been murdered. As a form of resistance against structural oppression and repressions, *köçeks* are celebrated by some trans and sexually marginalized communities, who reclaim *köçek* history as their own.[44] *Köçeks* henceforth invite us to examine genealogical ruptures and continuities in the historical as well as imperial lineages of gender variance and transgender experience. In this way we are offered a unique opportunity to reevaluate gender formations, histories, and figurations of trans lives that challenge, destabilize, and denaturalize monolithic gender norms and regimes.

Notes

I thank Selim Kuru and Colby Gordon for their generous feedback on earlier drafts of this essay.

1. *Çenginame* was a widely circulated text as evident in at least thirteen manuscript copies (ten in Turkey, three in Germany), and was often printed together with *Hubanname* and *Zenanname* in the nineteenth century. For the transcription of the text and locations of manuscripts, see Barış Karacasu, "Bize Çengileri Kıl Rûşen ü Pak" ya da "Hayra Hezlin Dahi Bir Rehberi Var," *Osmanlı Araştırmaları* 27 (2006): 133–60; and Neslihan İlknur Keskin, "Fazıl'ın Çengileri: *Çenginame* Üzerine," *Journal of Academic Social Science Studies* 6.8 (2013): 329–71. All references to Fazıl's work in this essay are to the quatrain numbers (cited parenthetically in the text) and are from Keskin, "Fazıl'ın Çengileri." All translations, unless otherwise noted, are mine.

2. For more on the *şehrengiz* genre, see Barış Karacasu, "Türk Edebiyatında Şehrengizler," *Türkiye Araştırmaları Literatür Dergisi* 5.10 (2007): 259–313; Agah Sırrı Levend, *Türk Edebiyatında Şehrengizler ve Şehrengizlerde Istanbul* (Istanbul: Fetih Cemiyeti, 1958); and Dilek Öztekin, "Şehrengizler ve Bursa: Edebiyat ve Eşcinsel Eğilim," *Kuram* 14 (1997): 37–41.

3. In his title and depictions, Fazıl uses the term *çengi*, which refers to both male and female dancers who play and dance with the *çeng*, a harp-like instrument, although it often refers to women dancers only. To avoid confusion, I use *köçek* instead of *çengi* in my references to androgynous dancers assigned male.

4. In using trans analytics and methodology, I draw on scholars who have demonstrated trans in its capaciousness as it resonates with representations of gender diversity and possible gender transitivity in premodern periods. See, for instance, Blake Gutt, "Transgender Genealogy in *Tristan de Nanteuil*," *Exemplaria* 30.2 (2018): 129–46; Ruth Mazo Karras and Tom Linkinen, "John/Eleanor Rykener Revisited," in *Founding Feminism in Medieval Studies: Essays in Honor of E. Jane Burns*, ed. Laine E. Doggett and Daniel E. O'Sullivan (Woodbridge: Boydell & Brewer, 2016), 111–22; Robert Mills, "Visibly Trans? Picturing Saint Eugenia in Medieval Art," *TSQ: Transgender Studies Quarterly* 5.4. (2018), 540–64; Robert Mills, *Seeing Sodomy in the Middle Ages* (Chicago: University of Chicago Press, 2015); and Masha Raskolnikov, "Transgendering Pride," *postmedieval: a journal of medieval studies* 1.1–2 (2010): 157–64.

5. On various public celebrations, see Metin And, *A Pictorial History of Turkish Dancing: From Folk Dancing to Whirling Dervishes, Belly Dancing to Ballet* (Ankara: Dost Yayınevi, 1976); Metin And, *Köçekler, Çengiler, Curcunabazlar, Osmanlı Şenliklerinde Turk Sanatları* (Ankara: Kültür ve Turizm Bakanlığı, 1982); Metin And, *Dances of Anatolian Turkey* (New York: Brooklyn Dance Perspectives, 1959); Suraiya Faroqhi and Arzu Öztürkmen, *Celebration, Entertainment and Theater in the Ottoman World* (New York: Seagull, 2014); Mehmet Arslan, *Osmanlı Saray Düğünleri ve Şenlikleri* (Istanbul: Sarayburnu Kitaplığı, 2009). On taverns, see Reşad Ekrem Koçu, *Eski Istanbul'da Meyhaneler ve Meyhane Köçekleri* (Istanbul: Doğan Kitap, 2002). Besides social celebrations such as weddings, circumcision celebrations, and religious holidays, the Ottoman Empire used public festivities as a form of consolidating its imperial rule. On different performances as a part of the imperial display, see Kaya Şahin, "Staging Empire: An Ottoman Circumcision Ceremony as Cultural Performance," *American Historical Review* 123.2 (2018): 463–92; Rhoads Murphey, *Exploring Ottoman Sovereignty: Tradition, Image and Practice in the Ottoman Imperial Household, 1400–1800* (London: Bloomsbury, 2008); Gülru Necipoğlu, *Architecture, Ceremonial, and Power: The Topkapı Palace in the Fifteenth and Sixteenth Centuries* (New York: Architectural History Foundation, 1991).

6. *Kol*, as Nihal Türkmen notes in *Orta Oyunu* (Istanbul: Milli Eğitim Bakanlığı Yayınları, 1991), is "a native theatrical term referring to a group of performers, team, or company. Group presentation is the sum of oral performances based on music, dancing, and miming" (8).

7. And, *Pictorial History*, 141.

8. Simone Chess, *Male-to-Female Crossdressing in Early Modern English Literature: Gender, Performance, and Queer Relations* (New York: Routledge, 2016), 8.

9. Related to the Persian word *shah*, *şah* signifies the glory attributed to their names.

10. On female dancers imitating *köçeks*, see Refik Ahmet Sevengil, *Istanbul Nasıl Eğleniyordu?* (1927; repr., Istanbul: Alfa, 2013), 130; and And, *Köçekler*.

11. By no means am I suggesting that these are the only genders organized in relation to the adult man. As I argue in my article "Early Modern Eunuchs and the Transing of Gender and Race," *Journal of Early Modern Cultural Studies* 19.4 (2019): 116–36, the black eunuch emerges as a racialized gender in the sixteenth century.

12. For more on *meclis* and its significance in the poetic imagination, see Walter Andrews and Mehmet Kalpaklı, "Osmanlı Şiirinin Yaşadığı Yer Olarak Meclis: Kökenleri ve Sosyal Uygulamalar," in *M. Ali Tanyeri'nin Anısına: Makaleler*, ed. H. Aynur, H. Koncu, and F. M. Şen (Istanbul: Ülke, 2015), 323–37. On the gender politics of *meclis*, see Didem Havlioğlu, *Mihri Hatun: Performance, Gender Bending, and Subversion in Ottoman Intellectual History* (Syracuse, NY: Syracuse University Press, 2017).

13. See Barış Karacasu, "Bize Çengileri Kıl Rûşen ü Pak," and Keskin, "Fazıl'ın Çengileri," for a list of names. For more on Fazıl's biography and other writings, see Jan Schmidt, "Fazil Beg Enderuni: Social Historian or Poet," in *Decision Making and Change in the Ottoman Empire*, ed. Caesar E. Farah (Kirksville, MO: Thomas Jefferson University Press, 1993), 183–92; and Selim S. Kuru, "Biçimin Kıskacında Bir "Tarih-i Nev-İcad: Enderunlu Fazıl Bey ve Defter-i Aşk Adlı Mesnevisi," in *Şinasi Tekin Anısına: Uygurlardan Osmanlıya*, ed. Günay Kut and Fatma Büyükkarcı Yılmaz (Istanbul: Simurg, 2005), 74–86.

14. Sevengil, *Istanbul Nasıl Eğleniyordu?*, 122.

15. Şerif Baykurt, *Anadolu Kültürleri ve Türk Halk Dansları* (Ankara: Kültür Bakanlığı Yayınları, 1997), notes that the practice of taking young boys and training them as dancers for putatively all-male audiences has a history tracing back to Central Asian, Arabic, Persian, and Byzantine influences.

16. The Ottoman Empire was one of the largest and most powerful empires in the early modern world, controlling the Mediterranean and parts of Asia, Europe, and North Africa. Empire building was the main political vision of the period, as is evident in the emergence of many competing empires, including the Spanish, Dutch, Mughal, Safavid, Russian, and Chinese, among others. In Giancarlo Casale's words, "The early modern period should be considered an Age of Empires in a truly global sense." Giancarlo Casale, "The Islamic Empires of the Early Modern World," in *The Cambridge World History*, vol. 6, *The Construction of a Global World, 1400–1800 CE*, pt. 1, *Foundations*, ed. Jerry H. Bentley, Sanjay Subrahmanyam, and Merry E. Wiesner-Hanks (Cambridge: Cambridge University Press, 2015), 323–44, quotation at 325. A focus on the management and control of both territory and different populations reveals imperial investment in colonialism, slavery, and cross-cultural encounters that shaped imperial cultures. Furthermore, as postcolonial approaches have shown, imperial practices are not simply economic but are also ideological processes. Accordingly, imperial management cannot be isolated from structures of race, gender, sexuality, class, and religion. On the Ottoman Empire, see Daniel Goffman, *The Ottomans and Early Modern Europe* (Cambridge: Cambridge University Press, 2002); Baki Tezcan, *The Second Ottoman Empire: Political and Social Transformation in the Early Modern World* (Cambridge: Cambridge University Press, 2010); Kaya Şahin, *Empire and Power in the Reign of Suleyman: Narrating the Sixteenth-Century Ottoman World* (Cambridge: Cambridge University Press, 2013); Colin Imber, *The Ottoman Empire, 1300–1650* (New York: Palgrave, 2009). On Western empires and their knotty ties with gender, sexuality, religion, and race, see Ania Loomba, *A Cultural History of Western Empires in the Renaissance*, vol. 3 (New York: Bloomsbury, 2018), 1–26. On connected histories of empires, see Joseph F. Fletcher, "Integrative History: Parallels and Interconnections," *Studies on Chinese and Islamic Inner Asia*, ed. Joseph F. Fletcher and Beatrice F. Manz (Aldershot: Variorum, 1995), 1–35; Sanjay Subrahmanyam, *Explorations in Connected History: From the Tagus to the Ganges* (Oxford: Oxford University Press, 2005); and Bentley, Subrahmanyam, and Wiesner-Hanks, *Foundations*.

17. For more on the peculiarities of Ottoman slavery, see Ehud R. Toledano, "The Concept of Slavery in Ottoman and Other Muslim Societies," in *Slave Elites in the Middle East and Africa: A Comparative Study*, ed. Miura Toru and John E. Philips (London: Kegan Paul International, 2000); Metin Kunt, *The Sultan's Servants: The Transformation of Ottoman Provincial Government, 1559–1650* (New York: Columbia University Press, 1983); Metin Kunt, "Kulların Kulları," *Boğaziçi Üniversitesi Dergisi* 3 (1975): 27–42; Hakan Erdem, *Slavery in the Ottoman Empire and Its Demise, 1800–1909* (Basingstoke: Palgrave, 1996).

18. One exception is *devşirme* (collecting), which was an institutionalized practice of capturing, converting, and assimilating boys among the non-Muslim population, who were to be brought under the authority and protection of the Islamic state. In contrast to other enslaved people, *devşirme* boys, mostly taken

from Christian Balkan populations such as the Greeks, Hungarians, Bosnians, and Albanians, underwent a process of conversion, assimilation, training, and service. These boys were raised to become the ruling bureaucrats and the elite military corps of the empire. For more on the emergence of *devşirme* practice, see Imber, *Ottoman Empire, 1300–1650*, 116–30.

19. For more on anti-*kul* sentiment and perceptions about converts, see Erdem H. ğ., "Changing Perceptions about Christian-Born Ottomans: Anti-Kul Sentiments in Ottoman Historiography," in *Disliking Others: Loathing, Hostility, and Distrust in Premodern Ottoman Lands*, ed. Hakan Karateke, H. Erdem Cipa, and Helga Anetshofer (Boston: Academic Studies Press, 2018), 1–21.

20. I discuss the eroticization of such hierarchies in abducting boys in my essay "Leander in the Ottoman Mediterranean: The Homoerotics of Abduction in the Global Renaissance," *English Literary Renaissance* 51.1 (Winter 2021): 31–62.

21. On boys as objects of homoerotic desire in the premodern period, see Walter Andrews and Mehmet Kalpaklı, *The Age of Beloveds: Love and the Beloved in Early-Modern Ottoman and European Culture and Society* (Durham, NC: Duke University Press, 2005); and Dror Ze'evi, *Producing Desire: Changing Sexual Discourse in the Ottoman Middle East, 1500–1900* (Berkeley: University of California Press, 2006). On the Iranian context, see Afsaneh Najmabadi, *Women with Mustaches and Men without Beards: Gender and Sexual Anxieties of Iranian Modernity* (Berkeley: University of California Press, 2005); and Khalid El-Rouayheb, *Before Homosexuality in the Arab-Islamic World, 1500–1800* (Chicago: University of Chicago Press, 2005).

22. For the relationship between body hair, facial hair, masculinity, and sexual availability in Islamicate societies, see El-Rouayheb, *Before Homosexuality*; Ze'evi, *Producing Desire*; and Andrews and Kalpaklı, *Age of Beloveds*.

23. On *köçek* dancers in taverns, and sexual exchanges with these dancers, see Ergun Hiçyılmaz, *Eski Istanbul Meyhaneleri ve Alemleri* (Istanbul: Pera Orient, 1992); Yener Altuntaş, "Kaybolmakta Olan Bir Kültür 'Köçeklik,'" *V. Milletlerarası Türk Halk Kültürü Kongresi Halk Müziği, Oyun, Tiyatro, Eglence Seksiyon Bildirileri* (Ankara: Kültür ve Turizm Bakanlığı, 1997), 37; and Koçu, *Eski Istanbul'da Meyhaneler ve Meyhane Köçekleri*, who notes that almost all taverns had their famous *köçeks* to attract customers.

24. Evliya Çelebi, *Evliyâ Çelebi Seyahatnâmesi*, vol. 1, *Kitap*, ed. Robert Dankoff et al. (Istanbul: Yapı Kredi Yayınları, 1996), 330.

25. The original word for dance is *oyun*, which also signifies "play;" here it connotes both dancing for and playing games with the lover.

26. The lover who yearns for their nightly union compares himself to a person who fasts all day and can only eat and enjoy himself at night.

27. Nedim, *Nedim Divanı*, ed. Abdulbaki Gölpınarlı (Istanbul: İnkılap, 2004), 363.

28. Murat Bardakçı, *Osmanlı'da Seks* (Istanbul: İnkılap, 2005), 174, 173.

29. For more on dancers in songs, see Murat Bardakçı, *Osmanlı'da Seks*, 172–81, quotation at 173.

30. For the full story of Köçek İsmail, see Kuru, "Biçimin Kıskacında"; and Koçu, *Eski Istanbul'da Meyhaneler ve Meyhane Köçekleri*, 58–60.

31. Koçu, *Eski Istanbul'da Meyhaneler ve Meyhane Köçekleri*, 65–81.

32. Marjorie Garber, *Vested Interests: Cross-Dressing and Cultural Anxiety* (New York: Routledge, 1992), 418.

33. Joseph Allen Boone, *The Homoerotics of Orientalism* (New York: Columbia University Press, 2014), 102, emphasis added.

34. Jean de Thévenot, *The Travels of Monsieur de Thevenot into the Levant. In Three Parts. Newly done out of French*, pt. 2 (London, 1687), 36.

35. For more on such travel accounts, see Boone, *The Homoerotics of Orientalism*; and Stavros Stavrou Karayanni, *Dancing Fear and Desire: Race, Sexuality, and Imperial Politics in Middle Eastern Dance* (Waterloo, ON: Wilfrid Laurier University Press, 2004), who explores male dancers in the Middle East.

36. Thijs Janssen, "Transvestites and Transsexuals in Turkey," in *Sexuality and Eroticism among Males in Moslem Societies*, ed. Arno Schmitt and Jehoeda Sofer (New York: Haworth Press, 1992), 83–90, for instance, opines that in modern Turkey, "the *transeksüel* can be seen as a modern *köçek*" (85). The oppression of transgender subjects in modern Turkey, for the critic, has a long history going back to "dishonored" *köçeks* of the early modern world; Janssen attempts to present contemporary transphobia via a history of the *köçek* by using a few Western travelogues as evidence and by conflating various different gender and sexual categories. While travel narratives are valuable sources revealing concerns of the writers and their own cultural norms, ignoring native sources or analyzing native sources solely from the perspective of travelogues uncovers more about Western assumptions—and the crisis of masculinity and sexual order implicit in travelogues—than about the native culture under observation.

37. Deniz Kandiyoti, "Some Awkward Questions on Women and Modernity in Turkey," in *Remaking Women: Feminism and Modernity in the Middle East*, ed. Lila Abu-Lughod (Princeton, NJ: Princeton University Press, 1998), 270–87, quotation at 284. On changing gender and sexual regimes in the nineteenth century, see Ze'evi, *Producing Desire*; Leslie P. Peirce, "Writing Histories of Sexuality in the Middle East," *American Historical Review* 114.5 (2009): 1325–39; Irvin Cemil Schick, "Representation of Gender and Sexuality in Ottoman and Turkish Erotic Literature," *Turkish Studies Association Journal* 28.1–2 (2007): 81–103; and Mustafa Avcı, "Shifts in Sexual Desire: Bans on Dancing Boys (Köçeks) throughout Ottoman Modernity (1800s–1920s)," *Middle Eastern Studies* 53.5 (2017): 762–81.

38. Ze'evi, *Producing Desire*, 164.

39. Avcı, "Shifts in Sexual Desire," 774.

40. And, *Dances of Anatolian Turkey*, 29–30.

41. In 1857 these androgynous dancers were banned among the Janissaries, the elite military corps, since the dancers would cause fights between soldiers. Yet as Avcı shows, it was not such fights but changing gender and sexual regimes that led to the prohibition of *köçeks*, at least in urban settings. In rural settings or inland regions, *köçek* dancers are still visible today, especially in all-male wedding celebrations; as Avcı writes, "The Istanbul *köçek* tradition disappeared in the first quarter of the nineteenth century; but of course this did not mean an end to the Anatolian *köçek* practice." Avcı, "Shifts in Sexual Desire," 775.

42. My use of "before trans" owes to Leah DeVun and Zeb Tortorici's conceptualization of "trans before trans" to refer to premodern histories of gender-variant figures as explored in articles included in the *TSQ* special issue "Trans*historicities." For more on trans, history, and historiography, see Leah DeVun and Zeb Tortorici, "Trans, Time, and History," *TSQ: Transgender Studies Quarterly* 5.4 (2018): 518–39.

On expanding the historical scope of trans studies, see the recent special issue of the *Journal for Early Modern Cultural Studies* 19.4 (2019), titled "Early Modern Trans Studies," edited by Simone Chess, Colby Gordon, and Will Fisher.

43. On complex religious negotiations among various transgender groups, see Evren Savci, "Transing Religious Studies: Beyond the Secular/Religious Binary," *Journal of Feminist Studies in Religion* 34.1 (2018): 63–68.

44. See Joanna Mansbridge, "The Zenne? Male Belly Dancers and Queer Modernity in Contemporary Turkey," *Theater Research International* 42.1 (2017): 20–36. On how young queers in Turkey subvert the hegemonic imposition of heterosexuality by adopting historical identities, see Abdulhamit Arvas, "Queers In-Between: Globalizing Sexualities, Local Resistances," in *The Postcolonial World*, ed. Jyotsna Singh and David D. Kim (New York: Routledge, 2016), 97–116.

CHAPTER 8

Without Magic or Miracle

The "Romance of Silence" and the Prehistory of Genderqueerness

Masha Raskolnikov

Medieval thought does assume that there's such a thing as a "woman" and a "man," but prior to the emergence and institutionalization of concepts like "the normal," distinctions between the two fail to map onto the gender binary as we experience it today. While history shows that people sometimes chose to live as a sex other than the one they were assigned at birth, most of the accounts that come down to us survive because their identities were challenged in court or examined in medical settings (often both). Imaginative literature, however, offers affordances to explore what the world *might be* rather than what it *is*, and can sometimes function as the space where the nature of sex and gender gets worked out in a relatively consequence-free way. There, an individual's choice to change the sex that they had been assigned at birth can be considered outside the juridical or medical frameworks that have shaped trans lives to this day. Sometimes medieval fictions conform to orthodox ideas; at other times, however, medieval works are actually able to complicate contemporary notions of gender. One such is the thirteenth-century *Roman de Silence*, a work that suggests a powerful counter-narrative about how sex and gender could be imagined otherwise.

The *Roman de Silence* has been edited twice: once by Lewis Thorpe and once by Sarah Roche-Mahdi, both from a single copy that appeared in an anthology discovered in 1911, now known as MS. Mi LM 6 in the University of Nottingham library.[1] In the romance's first lines, a narrator / authorial stand-in who names himself "master Heldris of Cornwall" promises to tell a good story and complains about the stinginess of contemporary princes, implying that he hopes to receive great rewards for telling this tale.[2] He then narrates how Ebain, king of England, came to ban women from inheriting property, and how Ebain's subjects Cador and Eufemie chose, for reasons of property inheritance, to raise their only child as a boy despite the child's "natural" sex being assigned as that of a girl. That child, named Silence, grows up excelling at all the knightly arts but worrying that their original assignment as female will be discovered, undermining their parents' plans and Silence's own life as a knight. It does not help Silence's state of mind that they are occasionally witness to a debate between the allegorical figures of Nature and Nurture, who argue whether Silence is "truly" male or "truly" female.

One key aspect of Silence's identity, then, is that they do not choose their gender; it was chosen for Silence by their parents for completely pragmatic reasons, although the romance traces the ways in which Silence reflects on and lives out this choice, at times asserting the truth of their maleness. Even so, this is not a story like so many modern stories with transgender protagonists, featuring a hero driven by inner forces to become their true self. Recognizing this can be frustrating, given that Silence is one of relatively few characters in medieval literature who *could* be understood as trans, and sometimes *is* understood that way.[3] Paying attention to ambivalences expressed both by the protagonist and by the text about what it means to "be a man" or "be a woman," however, requires reimagining them as someone whose story complicates this discourse. This article argues that the question of volition in matters of assigned versus chosen sex and gender that is raised by this romance constitutes a valuable part of what the *Roman de Silence* offers its readers.

Critics have occasionally had trouble figuring out which pronoun is the correct one to use for the character of Silence. I use "they" throughout, underlining the undecidable genderqueerness of the character rather than emphasizing their life as a male knight or their assignment as female at birth.[4] "Assignment" always manages to sound like "homework," and this valence of "gender assignment" makes it sound like being-gendered-and-sexed is a dogged, dutiful labor indeed. That useful phrase, drawn from the discourse of contemporary gender freedom activism, "assigned female at birth," becomes complicated in the case of Silence, whose body is understood to be female by their parents ("assigned" female), but has this very assignment immediately overwritten with masculinization in the name of securing a dynastic inheritance ("reassigned" as male). Silence is raised "as" a boy, in a manner that highlights the distancing structure of such a simile—to be "like" a boy is *not* to be a "real" boy, in the logic of Heldris's romance. Heldris, however, is nothing if not contradictory: despite repeatedly referencing their assigned-at-birth sex as female, the romance evinces respect for the character's own self-identification by using male pronouns when Silence is "performing" as male, and switching to female pronouns only once Silence is "revealed" as a "woman," a process described in such a way that it is not entirely clear or self-evident.[5]

Historical sources about those who lived a transgendered life in the Middle Ages support an understanding that cross-dressing was sometimes useful to those who sought work or vocational paths (monastic life, etc.) that were simply unavailable to women. It may bear saying that, under patriarchy, occupying masculinity nearly always offers more opportunities and choices than does occupying femininity, but somehow only a very small percentage of the population takes the route of correcting their assigned sex, no matter the advantages.[6] Simply by setting up a romance's main protagonist to be raised to perform successfully as a man and (therefore) repeatedly doubting that they have the ability to succeed as a woman, Heldris of Cornwall denaturalizes "male" and "female." The romance demands that we notice this: Heldris renders both "male" and "female" as things that *have to be learned*, skill sets and sets of habits that, in turn, mark the body (as when living as male renders Silence's mouth "too hard"). Even though the romance ends with "Nature's" victory, with Silence stripped bare and their body "recognized" as female, the events preceding this conclusion would surprise those who expect the European Middle Ages to stand in for conservative gender politics. While the hidden truth about Silence is clearly established as their hidden femaleness (although never femininity), this hidden truth exerts less power over Silence than one might expect.

Never explicitly stating that they desire to become "truly" male, in the course of their story Silence agonizes over whether or not they would be capable of living successfully as a woman *if* their deception were ever to be unmasked, questioning, in effect, if their life as a man has nurtured anything that might be said to be "feminine" right out of them. Without having their body changed by magic or through divine intervention, but certain that what they "are" is female because this was their assignment at birth, Silence still manages to live a gender-crossing life as a man. The question of what constitutes the "truth" of sex and gender functions as the driving force for much of the narrative, which hinges strongly on the status of "the secret," a concept that very obviously gets coded within the romance as "silence," both as the protagonist's name and as an absence of sound.[7] My own modest proposal

is to consider whether the name might actually be a sort of imperative—
"Be silent! That will relieve my anxiety!"[8] While Silence inhabits the role of
"man" impeccably, and takes a great deal of joy in their masculine accomplishments, Silence is also shown having doubts about the path that their parents had chosen for them, and—this is crucial—seems to remain male partly as an act of filial obedience rather than out of their own desires.

Can we speak of Silence as a trans or even as a genderqueer subject who is, at the same time, a subject whose intention had not at the outset been to live as male? Kendall Gerdes, writing in the inaugural "Keywords" issue of *Transgender Studies Quarterly* on the keyword "performativity," states that "transgender studies is inextricably invested in the question of intentionality: is the subject of gender in charge or not?"[9] Silence is *not*, in fact, "in charge." Their king decides that only men may inherit. Their parents decide prior to their birth that they will live their life as a man no matter how they "see" or think they see their child's sex.

Despite the documented existence of genderqueer lives during the Middle Ages, might master Heldris of Cornwall have been afraid to create a character who simply chose to live as a sex different from the one they had been assigned at birth? In other words, in order to have been written, must the *Roman de Silence* have featured gender-crossing as something being forced upon the protagonist, and might the convoluted plot forcing Silence to live as they do exist for extra-textual reasons, like the author's fear of censorship? Obviously this is speculative, but can the way in which Silence becomes male be one of the only ways available to change assigned sex, without magic or miracle, in the Middle Ages, making it seem like something that just "happens to" the individual? In what follows, I consider two aspects of the immanent, if implicit, theory of sex and gender offered in the pages of the *Roman de Silence*, examining Silence's own gender and, perhaps surprisingly, examining the gender of Silence's parents.

Defining Masculinity and Femininity

In trying to understand gender, whether in the Middle Ages or today, one usually finds oneself relying on the language of "male" and "female" (often referred to as "opposite" sexes, whatever that might mean) and their related qualities (often understood as if occupying opposing poles on a scale where each of us finds ourselves), referred to as "masculinity" and "femininity." It is notoriously impossible to define "masculinity" and "femininity": the title of this section opens itself up to your disappointment, Dear Reader. "Behaviour or qualities regarded as characteristic of a woman; feminine quality or characteristics; womanliness" and "the state or fact of being masculine; the assemblage of qualities regarded as characteristic of men; maleness, manliness," says the otherwise useful *Oxford English Dictionary*. These definitions are tautological to the point of absurdity, and yet we do no better when we consult psychoanalytic, scientific, or historical sources except to add the dimension of cultural contingency and variation to what "female" and "feminine," "male" and "masculine" qualities or characteristics might be. It is among the pleasures of studying any foreign culture to witness the contingency of gender in the encounter with cultural difference; this is certainly among the pleasures of reading the *Roman de Silence.*

What do we learn about masculinity and femininity from the *Roman de Silence*? We read the romance knowing that those categories are fictional, in the sense that Silence, King Ebain, Queen Eufemie et al. do not actually exist, and that "recognizing" that someone is male or female in a work of fiction depends on taking an author's word for it, and on accepting the gender assignments offered inside a fictional world. Of course, gender norms in a fictional world perform some measure of mimesis: they reflect prevailing attitudes of their times, with inflections and quirks drawn from a given author's "commonsense" understanding and their own history. The author says that somebody is female, and we believe them (as, indeed, we generally believe things about the sex of our interlocutors in our everyday lives). Information about Silence's "true" sex is possessed by the romance's reader— but unavailable to any person who encounters Silence before the romance's end, except their parents. The romance is steeped in dramatic irony, and one of the pleasures for readers is that of knowing something that most of the romance's protagonists do not know.

What happens to Silence? In addition to their various knightly accomplishments, Silence also runs away from home and spends some time as the world's greatest troubadour.[10] Women, including King Ebain's wife, fall in love with them, but Silence is indifferent; instead, they are occasionally witness to a debate between the allegorical figures of Nature and Nurture ("Nature" and "Noreture"), who argue whether Silence is "truly" male or "truly" female. In the end, Silence accomplishes a magical task that can be accomplished by "no man," tracking down Merlin and bringing him to court.[11] Without much discussion or Silence's consent, the king orders Silence to be stripped naked, and their identity as a "woman" is revealed through the assumption that whatever primary or secondary sex characteristics are visible to the naked eye are equivalent to the truth of this person's sex. Because King Ebain's wife had been plotting against Ebain (she has also, as it turns out, been unfaithful to him with a male knight who was living disguised as a nun in their court), and this is coincidentally discovered through Merlin's presence at court, she is put to death.[12] As a consequence, Silence, who is not only now clothed as a woman but also re-feminized by three days of labor by the allegorical personification of Nature, is forced to marry King Ebain—the same king whose ban on women inheriting property had caused Silence's gender journey to begin with.

The fact that Silence *can* be stripped naked and revealed as "actually" *female* assumes an agreement about what that means exactly; the additional detail that Nature then has to labor upon Silence's body for three days to render it *feminine*, however, introduces a measure of doubt about the possibility that Silence's femaleness is a self-evident fact.[13] This process, in the romance, occurs either passively ("Silence atornent come feme": "They dressed Silence as a woman," 6665) or with the agency of transformation attributed to Nature:

D'illuec al tierc jor que Nature	After Nature
Ot recovree sa droiture	Had recovered her rights,
Si prist Nature a repolir	She spent the next three days refinishing
Par tolt le cors et a tolir	Silence's entire body, removing every trace
Tolt quanque ot sor le cors de malle.	Of anything that being a man had left there.
Ainc n'i lassa nes point de halle:	She removed all traces of sunburn:
Remariä lués en son vis	Rose and lily were once again
Assisement le roze al lis.	Joined in conjugal harmony on her face.
	(6669–77, Roche-Mahdi)

It is hard not to marvel at the initial tail rhyme, "Nature/droiture": Nature rhymed with the law (presumably, the Law of Nature), translated by Roche-Mahdi as "rights" in this passage. That first couplet naturalizes (in a word) the victory of Nature over Nurture. And yet the work of "re-polishing" ("repolir") and the days that it requires demand acknowledgment as well; this is a work of naturalizing that, at the same time, requires some serious labor. This passage denies Silence any voice, any contribution to their own "feminization." The work is all accomplished by Nature, just as the work of "masculinization" was accomplished by Silence's father (and, to an extent, foster parents and teachers); in both cases, occupying a female or a male identity requires tutelage and hard work. The "remarriage" of "rose and lily," a symbolic wedding that immediately prefigures Silence's wedding to the king, is a product of Nature's labor. Earlier in the romance, Silence had worried, repeatedly, that their skin was too rough; now a sort of divine intervention solves their worries all at once.

Nevertheless, not all is predictable or stable even at this late, ostensibly stabilizing moment in the romance. When King Ebain marries Silence, the phrase used is "Li rois le prist a feme puis" ("Then the king took him for his wife," 6677). On the one hand, this phrase resonates with particular strength when we note that in French, as in many languages, *femme* means both wife and woman, so King Ebain is actually taking (reading, interpreting) Silence as a woman in this moment. On the other hand, and this can be hard to notice in the midst of all the work of feminization going on, the poem describes this very activity of taking Silence as a wife through the male direct object pronoun ("le"): even as they are being made into a "feme," the king is taking "him" as wife / woman. What are we to do with this odd, rebellious text? How to get our heads around its beautiful contradictions?

In a post on her blog *Transliterature: Things Transform*, M. W. Bychowski makes a claim that the *Roman de Silence* enables "a transvestite metaphysics," a term that I find enormously illuminating. For Bychowski, this metaphysics connects with the possibility of thinking about medieval science and the theory of universals that so characterizes the philosophical debates of the late Middle Ages. While I look forward to the finished version of Bychowski's reading of *Silence* as "a science of the 'tolte,'" in the important book that she is writing, we are in agreement about how Nature's work to "refinish" ("repolit," 6679) Silence's body, with a focus on their skin and on the entirety of their flesh, implies that masculinity had left permanent markings on Silence's body that could be erased only through divine intervention. The romance draws a distinction between "being female" and "being feminine": on the one hand, when King Ebain is told by Merlin that no woman could have captured the wizard and that Silence had been "desos les dras meschine. / La vesteüre, ele est de malle" ("a girl beneath his clothes. / Only the clothing is masculine," 6536–37, Roche-Mahdi), we hear the assumption that whatever is "desos" (beneath) will turn out to be "truest." In order to verify this statement, King Ebain commits an act of scopophilic violence, a convention painfully familiar to any member of a contemporary film audience who has ever watched a "reveal"—the moment of a body being stripped bare of its coverings—because what nudity displays will putatively convey an inarguable, stable "truth" that undoes any work of self-fashioning accomplished by the trans person's choice of self-presentation.[14]

Silence worries about not having been trained to be a "successful" woman, but also about being an imperfect man; when they run away from home to be a troubadour, the assumed name they use is Malduit, or "Ill-Taught." Later, when returning from years away, Silence describes themself to their father as "an inferior piece of cloth / powdered with chalk, that looks good, but isn't" ("com li malvais dras encrées / Ki samble bons, et ne l'est pas," 3643–44, Roche Mahdi). Oddly, the "inferior" piece of cloth that Silence describes is one that seems like a "bad" fabric disguised as a "good" one: a deception based in the politics of money and social class is offered as an analogy to a deception based on hidden femaleness and visible masculinity. Is masculinity, then, the false "finish" on fabric meant to disguise the "bad" material of femininity? Can such analogies even be drawn? Silence is always noble, as male and as female, and therefore this comparison is a fairly distant one; the superiority of the cloth from which they are made always seems to shine through, and, as many critics have argued, nobility "wins" over masculinity or femininity as Silence's dominant trait. But that's precisely it: this very odd romance that values social position over sex treats sex as a secondary characteristic, and therefore allows sex to be something that changes while the subject is shown to be grounded in a personhood that remains stable. Even if "Nature" and the "truth" of Silence's original female gender assignment triumph in the end, the romance expends tremendous energy in setting up a performative theory of sex that it proceeds to quash in its final lines.

Over the course of their story, Silence agonizes over whether or not they would be capable of living successfully as a woman if they ever have to revert to their assigned sex, because, in this romance's logic, life *as* a man fundamentally transforms one *into* a man: "trop dure boche ai por baisier, / Et trop rois bras por acoler. / . . . Car vallés sui et nient mescine" ("I have a mouth too hard for kisses, / and arms too rough for embraces / . . . for I'm a young man, not a girl," 2646–50, Roche-Mahdi). While this statement can seem like an avowal of authentic male identity, it doesn't quite function that way in the poem.[15] Immediately subsequent to these words, Silence states that the reason to prefer being male to being female has to do with the lower status of women (and the inheritance that they, Silence, would lose if declared female): "Ne voel perdre ma grant honor, / Ne la voel cangier a menor" ("I don't want to lose my high position; / I don't want to exchange it for a lesser," 2651–52). This sounds as though Silence's gender-crossing is ultimately somewhat pragmatic. If modern transgender identity is something assumed in the face of all disadvantages because it is urgently, psychically necessary, Silence doesn't meet that criterion—but the romance suggests that their life is no less genderqueer for that, and the criteria we use to comprehend trans and genderqueer identities must be made to expand in order to accommodate them.

While the urgency of inner necessity has been an important force in the contemporary fight for trans liberation and self-determination, it has also demanded that trans people subject themselves to the rigors of the modern confessional—not just psychological evaluation but also a sort of standardized narrative of relentless lifelong dysphoria that has to be produced on demand for various audiences.[16] Even if every particular in that narrative is true, it is a coercive and inappropriate demand for others (usually institutions) to make of trans subjects. Here, queer theory, which has been quite correctly criticized by trans scholars for having benefited enormously from figuring transgender in its critique of normativity, can actually be helpful.[17] Queer theory, working in concert with trans theory, can envision an expansive notion of gender plurality where neither gender nor sex must always be linked to the notion of an inner truth (just as, in queer theory, sexual orientation need not be essential, unchanging, and justified through recourse to psychological truths in order to be understood to exist). The *Roman de Silence* offers something like a psychology-free, internality-free version of genderqueer existence. Silence wasn't "born in the wrong body." They also weren't able to move between sexes at will, and worried volubly about whether they would be able to live a successful life as either one. What does it mean to have a work available to readers in the Middle Ages that posits gender change as seamlessly becoming the sex one chooses, as well as something that helps a person achieve financial stability (meaning, remaining their parents' heir), and as something other than purely volitional? Here, the *medieval* text actually expands the plurality of gender and sex that certain psychologizing tendencies in the modern world tend to limit.

Silence lives their life as a man, feels themself to be male, and fears that they will not know *how* to be a woman if ever they have to return to their original assignment. And yet their genderqueer, gender-crossing life is very important insofar as it offers a way of dislodging historical gender normativity as in any way a "traditional" or "historical" condition of human existence.[18]

The work of fashioning masculinity and femininity in the *Roman de Silence* is shown to require careful and difficult labor. That sheer depiction of effortful fashioning, while largely centered on the body of Silence, permeates the romance as a whole, offering a kind of "metaphysics," per Bychowski's important intervention, as well as at least a theory of sex and gender that might not fit with a routine understanding of a gender-normative Middle Ages but rather opens it up to its queer possibilities. What is femininity in this romance? It is something handmade, difficult, and so is whatever masculinity might be.

The Self-Decoding Riddles of Cador and Eufemie

The *Roman de Silence* tells the story of Silence from birth, through a youth spent in knightly derring-do and troubadour accomplishment, up to the moment of being revealed as "truly" female for the king, without ever pausing for a love story. Silence's eventual marriage to King Ebain is not foreshadowed in any way: unlike the Shakespearean version of the cross-dressed hero, neither Silence's words nor their behavior suggests a romantic motive for their loyalty to their liege lord. When Ebain's wife, Eufemie, attempts to seduce the irresistibly handsome Silence, their argument of refusal is based on the relationship of "loialté" to King Ebain and the fact that they are Ebain's relative ("Car jo sui hom vostre segnor, / et ses parens ne sais con priés," "for I am your lord's vassal, / and his blood relation, I don't know to what degree," 3806–7). Indeed, the eventual marriage of Silence and Ebain is incestuous in nature, although this never gets mentioned in the text.[19] Although the romance ends in a marriage, the love story that it tells is not that of its protagonist.

Although it is established that Silence is not romantically or sexually interested in the queen, it is not clear whether, in this case, the "nature" being referenced is Silence's loyalty and piety or Silence's knowledge that their assigned sex isn't the one that the queen expects.[20] What we know about human sexual practices notwithstanding, other genderqueer narratives from the Middle Ages—ones that do feature sexuality as a problem for a love story—are written as if it were obvious that women simply cannot have sex with women.[21] Silence, assigned male by their father but *also* assigned female, does not simply seem to assume that they cannot satisfy the queen's desires. Heldris uses the language of the natural here, as "his nature," to foreclose the very possibility of an attempt. This problematic (for a modern reader) ideological detail notwithstanding, Silence may refuse Eufeme for other reasons, including loyalty to her own future husband, Eufeme's then-current husband, King Ebain. Or lack of attraction. Or even the detail that Eufeme and Silence's mother, Eufemie, have nearly the same name, potentially invoking the incest taboo.

The story of how Silence's parents come to be married takes up fully the first third of the total length of the romance. As I indicated at the outset, the background against which Silence's gender emerges is not an entirely gender-normative one: the romance is touched throughout with genderqueerness. The extended delay involved in Silence's parents' love story is part of how Heldris of Cornwall, the poem's author, sets up a certain reading of his story as a whole. With the couple's slow courtship, the theorization of gender that governs the romance's logic is in evidence long before their future child comes into being. In that sense, the *Roman de Silence* is a self-decoding riddle where the "answer" to the questions about the subsequent events of the romance is hidden within its beginnings, and where the part clarifies the whole.

Silence is "disguised" as male though assigned female at birth in order to be able to inherit their parents' estate, a move that seems to set up a problem for the subsequent generation: if Silence is to remain male, they will presumably not be able to sire legitimate children who might in turn inherit the same estates, so the entire dynasty that their parents are trying to establish is being set up to end with Silence. Given that medieval romance is so often concerned with dynastic succession, this seems remarkably short-sighted thinking. There appears to be an implicit hope that King Ebain will either change his mind or die, permitting the law against female inheritance to change. Still, Silence's possible progeny are simply not taken into account in this plan, and the main protagonist of the *Roman de Silence* lacks a love story; this differs strikingly from how most medieval romances organize plot and action.

Cador appears in the poem as the nephew of King Ebain of England (the very king who eventually marries Silence) who becomes a hero by slaying a dragon, in some part in order to impress the daughter of the King of Cornwall, Eufemie, whom he loves. There is no doubt that Cador's and Eufemie's feelings for each other are mutual: the moment she is introduced, we immediately discover that Eufemie is in love with Cador, but well over a thousand lines are expended bringing them together. Moreover, even King Ebain wants the two to marry, and asks his counselor to help make this happen. Dilation is nothing new in romance, but the sheer length of Silence's parents' courtship is noteworthy for its level of detail, as well as for the ideas that it manages to develop over the course of its many lines. All of the symptoms of lovesickness, all of the misunderstanding between potential lovers, all of the sheer fuss that goes into the standard descriptions of medieval courtly love are present in this romance, but as the love of Silence's parents, never as Silence's own experience. In an odd way, the heterosexual love story of Silence's parents is the way in to understanding the queerness at the heart of Silence as a trans figure.

The love story of Cador and Eufemie is marked by themes that persist throughout the romance and affect their progeny. The protagonist's name, "Silence," is thought through by this romance in a complicated way, and one way it functions in the narrative is as a repeated invocation of secrecy as a driver of the romance plot (sometimes in place of love, sometimes alongside it).[22] The silence that plagues Silence's life is already present in the romance before Silence is born: the love story of Silence's parents is plagued by an unnecessary, if generically consistent, secrecy. The poem does not let readers miss this emphasis on secrecy, even as, in the context of a courtly love scenario, secrecy functions as a constitutive part of the conventional format. The literature of "fin' amors," or courtly love, requires delay before avowal, consummation, or marriage, and secrecy is a common form that delay assumes, along with misunderstanding and miscommunication. In *Silence*, Cador has "encloze" ("hid," 406, Roche-Mahdi) his love for Eufemie and suffers from all the classic symptoms of what courtly love calls "lovesickness."[23] Lovesickness thrives on secrecy, and the narrator digresses, explaining that his love is like a "fire without a flame" burning all the more brightly for being "covierte" ("covert," 411, Roche-Mahdi). Secrecy is the fuel that powers Cador, giving him the courage to defeat the dragon and sustaining him through a period of recovery from the wounds that fight causes, a period that seamlessly segues into a period of illness from wounds caused by lovesickness. The conspiracy of delay necessary to the conventions of romance is extensive and detailed, and the particular workings of that conspiracy in this poem have to do with the romance's gender politics.

Silence's genderqueer life complicates the orthodoxy that men are simply superior to women, and this is evident also in the surprising level of parity between Silence's parents. Each of them is established as having a right to ask to marry *"any* person in the land." The king grants Cador this privilege because he has killed a dragon who had menaced the king; Eufemie is granted this privilege for nursing Cador back to health after that same dragon injures him. In other words, both Eufemie and Cador are outside the typical economy of the traffic in women. Their choice of partner is a free one, and this is true of both of them. One might think that the absence of a power imbalance would simplify courtship; yet this absence, instead, silences both parties, rendering each unsure about how their intentions toward the other might be construed.

One of the major problems that prevents Cador and Eufemie from admitting their mutual love is Eufemie's excellent education, which also offers some foreshadowing about the eventual adventures of their child, Silence. Although she is introduced through Cador's love for her, and is described as "the most beautiful in the world" ("Qu'el mont n'avoit plus bele mie," 401, Roche-Madhi) she is also described, almost immediately, as "well versed in the seven arts" ("Des .vii. ars ert moult bien aprise," 403, Roche-Mahdi).[24] Eufemie is the only daughter of the fictional Count of Cornwall (Cornwall being the supposed home of Heldris, who names himself as "de Cornüälle" in the romance's very first line). It is an understatement to say that to be versed in the seven liberal arts is not a common description for a female character; female education is not generally a priority in medieval romances, and when it is, it is more like Blanchefleur's education in *Floris et Blanchefleur*, a product of two children being educated together, rather than a solitary female accomplishment.

In fact, before Silence was ever a knight who could outfight those who had been assigned maleness at birth, Eufemie was the best doctor in England: "el païs n'a si sage mie" ("the wisest doctor in the land," 594, Roche-Mahdi). According to McCracken's broad introduction, "Women and Medicine in Medieval French Narrative," the etymology of "mie" is "the Latin *medicus*, in its common usage indicating a man who practices academic medicine." McCracken describes how Eufemie's "authority as a medical practitioner is compromised by the indirect way her skill is acknowledged in the text."[25] Eufemie is twice referred to as "mie" or "mire" in a sense that is likely to have meant "doctor," both times in a somewhat negative or reversed manner: first, as we just saw, in "there was no wiser doctor," and the second time, in line 734, Eufemie is referred to as "the girl who served as his physician"—"de la meschine vus voel dire. / Esté li ot en liu de mire" ("Now I want to tell you about the girl who served as his physician," 733–34, Roche-Mahdi)—a usage repeated a second time for emphasis by Eufemie as "qu'esté vos ai en liu de mie" ("I served as your physician," 938, Roche-Mahdi). Ultimately, Eufemie's medical education is used as a plot device to bring Eufemie and Cador closer together in the small space of the sickroom, when the king asks Eufemie to care for Cador through his recovery from the wounds inflicted by his battle with the dragon.

Eufemie's status as a doctor makes use of the specialized medical vocabulary of the time. McCracken notes that Eufemie is not referred to as "miresse," the female and (therefore) more negative version of "doctor." "Sick or wounded people are often visited by 'mires' in medieval stories, but they are also treated by women with healing skills who are not called 'miresses,'" she writes.[26] While in both cases being "in place of" a doctor, Eufemie herself is not a doctor, exactly, but she is also no worse than a doctor and can serve in a doctor's stead. This logic of being "like but not quite" a doctor bears, in my estimation, a striking resemblance to the logic of how Eufemie's child, Silence, inhabits their sex, according to what they themselves say about it: they are not male, exactly, but are no worse than a man and can serve in place of a man in almost all capacities. It is almost as if Heldris of Cornwall offers us this figure, and the ultimately unnecessary detail of Eufemie's high-level doctoring skills, in order to help teach readers of the romance to understand this kind of simile-logic.

Although Eufemie essentially has no speaking role once her child is born, she seems to be an extraordinary woman. There were certainly important women physicians in the Middle Ages, including the famous Trota of Salerno and Hildegard of Bingen, who produced collections of medical writings. So is it at all strange for someone assigned female at birth to be a doctor? No more so than for someone assigned female to be a man, as Silence is repeatedly described. Both mother and child have abilities that exceed misogynist assumptions about the abilities of people who are assigned female at birth.

Silence's mother has an excellent education for yet another reason, I suspect. For Heldris, this character is also useful because it permits him to portray at least one of Silence's parents as privy to the debates in medieval medical theory about sex and gender. For medieval medical theory, "sex" (the so-called biological and physical basis of the difference between women and men) is more of a continuum than it became in later epochs. Galenic medicine relied on an index of heat: men's bodies produced more, which rendered them more intelligent, and resulted in inherent male superiority, but women's bodies produced *some*. The genitals of women were sort of the inverted-sock version of male genitalia. (Modern science, with an entirely different set of governing assumptions, sometimes seems closer to this model, given its observations of embryological development.) When male and female are understood as points on a spectrum, there is a certain amount of leeway for those who fall in the middle.[27] Later in the poem, Eufemie indicates that she knows a fair bit about pregnancy and what can and cannot be controlled about fetal sex; she seems to believe that she cannot cause the unborn fetus that will someday become her child, Silence, to be born with genitalia that conform with an assignment of maleness.[28] Eufemie's medical training plays no role in the romance's plot beyond forcing her proximity to Cador while she cares for his wounds, but it also evokes a set of discourses that, tantalizingly, we can't be *quite* sure that she or Heldris actually knew, but that *might* have made her a particularly suitable mother for a genderqueer child.

Silence's parents are brought together by Cador's injuries, by Eufemie's medical skills, and by their mutual love, and yet both still dither, each worried that they cannot know what is truly in the heart of their beloved. Eufemie is no one's reward, even though it would normally be her nature as a woman to function as an object of exchange in the consolidation of power between different houses, estates, or nations (as Eufemie's near-namesake "Eufeme," the wife of King Ebain, is used to weave peace between England and Norway in one of the romance's early passages). Cador needs to be given a free choice of wife, thinks Eufemie, pining for him. The veracity of their love demands the other's active agreement, and this seems particularly important insofar as the male character truly values his female beloved's freedom. Cador is afraid that any inquiry about Eufemie's feelings will represent undue pressure. (He fears that she will not be able to say no as a result of the king's gift to him.) In fact, in his own self-sabotaging, logic-of-romance way, Cador desires Eufemie's desire (and she his).

There are some complicated things to be said about the gender politics of such a desire. Is it "unmanly" for a medieval man to want to be a woman's free and unconstrained choice? Is it, possibly, "queer" for him to desire this? On the one hand, the characters in medieval romance (this or any other) didn't seem to be under the impression, popular in later centuries, that women were incapable of lust, so Cador must know that being desired by Eufemie is *possible*. On the other hand, relatively few of the knights of romance doubt that a woman who has been taking care of them and is of marriageable age is going to marry them, particularly when they have just done something as grand as killing a dragon. Cador's doubt about Eufemie, and Eufemie's public passivity in the face of her own narratively well-established private desire for Cador, drive the lovers' delay.

In a poem that might be about silence, one of the important silences is that of Cador and Eufemie in relation to each other. Cador's silence is clearly motivated by a fear that Eufemie might feel herself forced to love him: *He* is afraid that *she* might think that *he* might think (delightful!) that *he* is compelling *her* to love *him* back. How do these two ever escape from their quagmire of courtly uncertainty? The precipitating event that permits Silence to be engendered is actually a moment of mis-speaking.

One day, burning with a particularly unbearable desire, Eufemie speaks to Cador, and in doing so, she mis-speaks. Addressing herself to her patient, Eufemie says, "Amis, parlés, haymmi!" (883). Eufemie apparently thinks that she means to say "Speak to me, friend!" ("Dire li dut: parlés a mi," 884) but instead says something that might be translated as "Friend, speak, ah me!" or "Friend, speak [onomatopoetic representation of sigh]!" or

"Friend, speak, woe is me!"[29] The meaning of "haymmi" is intentionally and significantly unclear, and the narrator proceeds to spend more than thirty-five lines discussing what this exclamation can possibly mean. Critics have done the same (at quite a bit more length): Howard Bloch even translated the phrase as "Friend, hate me!" although many critics subsequently argued against this reading.[30] What is this "haymmi"? It seems to be parapraxis, a "Freudian slip," and encourages psychoanalytic critics to see it as a manifestation of Eufemie's unconscious. If "haymmi" is supposed to be "ami," what has been added are sounds: the breathy "h," the yelp of pain that is "i," the humming "m." The addressee himself, Cador, doesn't even know what Eufemie is saying. He is being called "amis," but being "amis" is ambiguous, and does not necessarily entail a romantic relationship. Somehow, Eufemie's exclamation has meaning precisely *because* it is nonsense; if she had simply said "speak to me, friend" (887), as Heldris tells us she had intended to do, Cador would not have taken this particular moment of speech to mean anything beyond a friendly greeting. Instead, Eufemie's "haymmi" is a mystery, a paroxysm, an emission of the body which Cador, as lovesick subject, is capable of comprehending as the injunction to speak his love.

It does not seem strange that Cador and Eufemie are ultimately brought together by parapraxis. A slip of the tongue can be full of erotic potential, and also the way that Eufemie's feelings are positioned as revealing something true underneath a false cover of silence is later echoed, in the romance's "main" narrative, by the way the "truth" of Silence's assigned sex is unwrapped from their clothes in front of the assembled court at the romance's end.

The love story of Eufemie and Cador, desiring doctor and shy dragon killer, provides the genealogy that helps make sense of Silence's genderqueer complexity. The parents do not simply foreshadow their child, although that is also a part of what they do; in this essay's climax, they merge or commingle their very selves to *become* Silence. In that process, Eufemie herself is silenced. The passage I will discuss manifests a strange alchemy, one that has received far less attention than it deserves—the one moment in the romance when a character offers an explicit theory of sex and gender, one that is neither medical nor magical but is rather theological and philosophical in nature.[31]

Once Eufemie and Cador marry and Eufemie gets pregnant, Cador expresses great concern that the child might be born female and not be allowed to inherit their considerable property. Eufemie replies to Cador's worry about the unborn child with a reasonable statement that they would love any child. Here is Cador's counterargument, with recourse to an odd attribution of the Creation to Jesus:

"Ma dolce amie," dist li cuens,	"My sweet love," said the count,
"Jhesus li pius, li vrais, li buens,	"Jesus the pious, true and good
Il fist Adan, cho est la voire,	Created Adam, this we know to be true,
Et Evain de sa coste en oire.	And right away created Eve from his rib.
Es vos l'entensiön reposte	And here is the hidden reason
Por quoi il le fist de sa coste,	Why he made her from his rib:
Qu'ensi fuscent d'une *voellance*	So that they would be of one mind [*voellance* = will]
Com il sunt fait d'une sustance.	As they are made of one substance.
Andoi eüscent un *voloir*,	Both should be of one mind
A l'esjoïr, et al doloir.	United in joy and sorrow.
Entr'ome et feme a grant commune,	There is great unity between man and woman,
Car d'als .ii. est la sustance une,	Because the two are of one substance.
Et adonques meësmement	And it is the same,
Quant il i a esposement,	When they are married,
Car el saintisme sacrement	For, with the most holy sacrament
De nostre Noviel Testament	Of our New Testament,
Met on entr'als tele aliänce,	Such an alliance is made between them
Cho sachiés vos tolt a fïance,	That you should know for certain
C'uns sans et une cars devient:	They become one flesh and blood.
Sor als est puis s'il ne se tienent.	It is upon their heads if they don't hold to this thereafter.
	Since, my sweet, our flesh is one,
Biele, quant nostre cars est une,	Let our will be one as well.
Soit nostre *volentés* commune.	Since our blood is one
Le sanc avons [nos] als commun,	Let us be of one mind" [*voloir* = to will].
Or aiens le *voloir* commun."	(1700–1724, Roche-Mahdi, emphasis added)

In his Letter to the Ephesians, Saint Paul theorizes marriage as merging, setting an important precedent for Christian discourse about male-female relations. This is the passage where the analogy is drawn that husbands are the head of their wives as Christ is the head of the church. What might be meant by "being the head of" someone or something else remains radically open to discussion, but Heldris of Cornwall understands it as a merging of the wills. In the context of this theory of sexual difference, Eve is drawn from Adam's rib so that this merging might be feasible, with the possible implication that a divine intervention was needed to reinforce the naturalness of male dominance. If gaining a male partner as one's "head" or "will" is the obligation of the woman, Silence ends up taking a long and roundabout route to this fulfillment. In context, Cador's speech is arguing that Eufemie should obey him, which, in this case, means that she needs to agree to raise Silence as a boy even if they are born with the genitals associated with women. Cador is calling upon the putative naturalness of male dominance in order to establish the condition of possibility for raising his child as a male, no matter how "un-natural" it might be to do so.[32]

The theory advanced here by Cador is that marriage creates a kind of joining of man and woman, where "the will" becomes both shared ("commune," a word repeated no fewer than four times in this relatively brief passage) and predominantly ruled by the male, turning the couple into a singular unit that combines "man" and "woman." Sarah Roche-Mahdi's translation of "voloir" as "mind," while strictly speaking inaccurate, is at the same time very helpful, because today's theories of the self are more likely to use the language of "mind" than they are of "will." Medieval theories of the will understand it to be a multiple (at least a double, often triple or more) set of forces that push against one another, demanding resolution before there can be action.[33] Cador offers Eufemie a theory of mind as well as a theory of marriage in his brief and repetitive speech. In context, this is akin to shooting pigeons with a cannon—far too much firepower deployed in order to win an argument. At the same time, in the context of the romance plot, Cador here is showing the radically different status of Eufemie as a person now that she has married him. A married couple, in this conceptualization, has a single will. Eufemie no longer has an independent will; rather, she has become a second, weaker will jostling with his stronger one inside the new person they have formed together. Do Cador and Eufemie retain their original selves in the process of commingling in this way? They might not; or, perhaps more accurately, Eufemie might not; the model of marriage that she is offered might, indeed, merit all the fears of avowal that she had expressed in earlier passages of the romance.

How does male join with female? One might imagine a literal joining, as in the ancient representations of the joining together of the nymph Salmacis with the beautiful boy whom she loved, Hermaphroditus. Here I am using

"Hermaphroditus" the character from Greek myth, to name the impossibly strange concept that Cador is expressing. The myth of Hermaphroditus participates in the intellectual history of a now obsolete and offensive term which ought not to be mistaken for the medical category of intersex. Possibly even the ancients acknowledged the offensiveness of the term: in Ovid's *Metamorphoses*, which is how it came to be famous in the medieval world, the story of Hermaphroditus is an instance of sexual violence (the nymph Salmacis rapes Hermaphroditus), a terrible joining of female with male. And yet Cador seems to understand marriage in this way, as a (now loving?) joining of two into one, with only one (the man) becoming the governing principle.

How does female join with male? Must the woman (whatever this term might reference) disappear in merging with the man? This certainly seems to be the model being invoked by Cador. While this is a spectacularly conservative view of marriage (albeit one fully reinforced by the Pauline epistles and church doctrine), in the instantiation of this particular romance, this is also, surprisingly, a genderqueer view: a married man is not "only" a man; he also contains the will of the woman he has married. This joining of selves fundamentally affirms the possibility that what is assigned female *can* become a man, that what is assigned male at birth *can* grow up to be joined with a woman. This is a conservative radicalism, a radical conservatism: this is the strange, surprising heart of Heldris of Cornwall's one romance.

When married, a woman's will is merged with that of her husband. This explanation of the gendered order of things, coming relatively early in the text, can be used to comprehend the governing theory about sex and gender that this text works through, the contribution that Heldris of Cornwall is actually making here. Within the *Roman de Silence*, other marriages might not be quite the same sort of joining into one unified two-gendered being—although it should be noted that the most discussed marriage besides that of Cador and Eufemie is that of King Ebain and his adulterous wife, Eufeme, who is put to death for her sexual transgressions. (I would maintain that adultery is the only form of literarily represented free will available to married women, even in most contemporary novels.) Even there, in this extraordinarily odd romance, it might be noted that Eufeme desires Silence, whom she understands to be male; once Silence is understood as female, King Ebain marries Silence. Eufeme's extramarital desire is fulfilled, maritally, by her husband. The question of Silence's desire is left wide open at the romance's end. I cannot answer it; I can say only that Silence had never quite consented to living life as male, and doesn't seem to quite consent to living life as female. They are sexed by figures in power (the father, the king, the magician, the husband) and live with the consequences. This is not genderqueerness as joyful play; this is, at heart, yet another tragic story (albeit about one who marries rather than one who dies at their story's end). This is also, however, a truly queer vision of gender, of love, and of language.

Silence maintains an inner monologue about their sex and gender. In the manner of a psychomachia, a dramatized allegorical conflict within a human soul, the allegorical figures of Nature and Nurture externalize Silence's self-doubt. They return again and again to debate which of them is truly in charge of Silence's identity, and this too emphasizes Silence's competence as an assigned-female person living in disguise as a man. On the one hand, if "Nature" wins out, as indeed "she" does, Silence's successful life as a man affirms the competence of those assigned female at birth, even if it is only a secret competence. The message of "Nature's" victory seems to be that if a girl is taken young and taught the martial instead of the marital arts, she can do anything a boy can do, and probably better. On the other hand, if "Nurture" were to have won the debate and triumphed in the course of the narrative, which she comes quite close to doing, *that* victory would have affirmed the changeability of sex and gender by means of the human will—indeed, through the simple application of the human will to the human body. The possibility of Nurture's win hovers over the text, tantalizing readers with the thought that the poem could be (even more of a) genderqueer work than it is now.

The *Roman de Silence* is written as if there truly is a strong counterargument to Nature's claim that a person assigned female at birth is, therefore, "truly female." *Silence* is written as if there is a valid claim to be made that a "girl" raised "as a boy" might become a boy. This claim is supported by any number of mythological and miraculous sources, such as the story of Iphis and Ianthe, familiar from Ovid, or the story of Saints Marina, Eugenia, or even Pelagia.[34] Silence is written as if there's a danger that Nurture may win the argument, in which case medieval thinkers would have had to acknowledge that sex, at least in narrative contexts, is performative—made by discourse, out of the stuff of discourse, reinforced by discourse, and in desperate need of reassuring repetition in order to remain stable in discourse. In other words, the end of *Silence*, when Nature "wins," strikes its modern readers as a potential gender-essentialist retort to the Judith Butler of *Gender Trouble* and *Bodies That Matter*. It is a retort, an argument against Butler, because its protagonist both fears and desires being unmasked as "actually" or "truly" female while, at the same time, continuing a successful career as a male knight and troubadour. In its final, silent scene when Silence is "revealed" to have been assigned female, a scene where Silence falls silent and remains so, the argument for gender essentialism seems to "win." Yet it scores a narrow enough victory that, even as it negates the discourse of gender constructionism with its conclusion, Silence deserves to be read alongside recent feminist, queer, and trans theories. In the life of Silence and of their parents that precedes the finale when Nature wins, the performativity of gender and of sex affirmed by Nurture, and the hard work of making men and making women (in fiction and in life), are all very evident.

Because *Silence* is a fiction, it is also a possible space of experimentation. As Angela Jane Weisl put it in one of the first articles surveying representations of genderqueer persons in French literature, "what happens in these poems becomes a kind of examination of potential rather than pure fantasy."[35] I take that to mean: no real person can live Silence's life, but to describe Silence's life might open up possibilities of a real person living their own differently.

This essay is not by any means the first to think of *Silence* as a trans-affirming work, although the history of the romance's reception definitely includes a period of its being read as a narrative of *female* power, while more recent publications on *Silence* have taken up Silence's gender as a question lacking a clear answer. At times this has led to readings that affirm the text as a sort of carnival of sex and gender. Katherine Terrell offers an exemplary version of this latter-day model in a 2008 article, concluding that the poem portrays both language and gender as "destabilized and destabilizing" in a way that offers "no definitive answers."[36] Such readings are important and do justice to certain aspects of the romance. One thing that such readings of textual play as intimately tied to queerness do not take into account, however, is the grave seriousness, the life-and-death quality inherent in the demand to be recognized as the sex that one truly *is*, whatever one had been assigned. The hard work of affirming sexual ontology, a work that is, in some ways, fundamentally impossible to do once and for all, is part of the labor that many contemporary trans people perform in addressing themselves to figures of authority like those who issue identity cards or medical prescriptions, or who oversee surgical interventions. Some of the labor of identifying one's true self to figures of authority resembles the sacrament of confession for Catholic Christians. The *Roman de Silence* does not require its genderqueer subject to confess a desire for another (which might seem to stabilize their gender in a certain way) or to be either male or female in any definitive sense. In that it offers some ways out of the confessional.

The *Roman de Silence* puts enormous pressure on the nature of gender *not* in order to destabilize it but to stabilize it otherwise, to open up some of its heretofore less livable possibilities. Instead of magic or miracle, instead of confession and being driven to realize one's destiny as the sex that one was not born as, the romance features a highly competent subject who lives life as male and as female, and excels at doing both, albeit with enormous effort. (The mechanisms of sex creak as Silence puts their shoulder to the wheel.) The possibility that this highly competent subject might exist is not simply foreshadowed; it is ontologically established by the material at the beginning of the romance, dealing with how Silence's parents come together as a couple that merges their manhood and womanhood into a single unit (to the detriment of the couple's female member, as always seems to happen). This is truly the alterity of medieval thinking about gender at work: conservative and radical, hopeful and hopeless all at once, it opens up onto a field of possibilities quite different from the ones that contemporary subjects might imagine or desire.

One of the things that is undecidable about the *Roman de Silence* is whether we should read it as resisting patriarchal assumptions about female incompetence, or if we should read it instead as resisting patriarchal assumptions about femaleness and maleness *as such*. I find this lack of clarity productive, perhaps even helpful to our own moment in the history of sex and gender. Another undecidable is if this romance might be asking its readers to consider whether expressed intentionality or the will to transition is or is not the sole most important component for understanding a historical person (or fiction) as part of trans history, whether or not they are recognizable to themself as trans. On the one hand, this seems like a reasonable criterion, since it resembles the psychological work required of trans subjects in the contemporary juridico-medical world. On the other hand, genderqueer persons in the past did not tend to leave us with clear confessions about their gender intentions and sometimes, like Silence, seemed to operate out of pragmatic necessity rather than psychological urgency. Perhaps the *Roman de Silence* can serve as a reminder that trans and genderqueer living constitutes a psychology-free, confession-free world of its own. However we read it, it's a text that we can understand as affirming the existence of alternatives to a monolithically patriarchal medieval England, even if these alternatives might be imaginary and secretive and, in the course of this narrative, ultimately undermined.

Notes

This essay comes out of years of productive engagement with *Silence* in the classroom, and benefited enormously from conversations with graduate and undergraduate students alike, especially Shanna Carlson and Michaela Lee. I would like to thank Kathleen Long for having organized the *Transforming Bodies* Conference at Cornell, where this was first given as a paper, and my co-editors, Greta LaFleur and Anna Kłosowska, for their incisive and helpful suggestions. I have also learned so much about writing by editing the other essays in this volume, and am grateful to my fellow contributors for their excellent work.

1. *Le Roman de Silence: A Thirteenth-Century Arthurian Verse-Romance by Heldris de Cornuälle*, ed. L. Thorpe (Cambridge: W. Heffer, 1972); *"Silence": A Thirteenth-Century French Romance*, ed. and trans. Sarah Roche-Mahdi (East Lansing, MI: Colleagues Press, 1992). There is also another translation, *Le Roman de Silence*, Regina Psaki (New York: Garland, 1991). All quotations are from the Roche-Mahdi edition, and are cited by line number.

2. I refer to Heldris of Cornwall as "he" throughout because I am not entirely convinced by the argument (much as I would like to be) proposed by Lorraine Kochanske Stock that Heldris could be either male or female. Lorraine Kochan-ske Stock, "The Importance of Being Gender 'Stable': Masculinity and Feminine Empowerment in *Le Roman de Silence*," *Arthuriana* 7.2 (Summer 1997): 28–29.

3. Caitlin Watt's article "'Car vallés sui et nient mescine': Trans Heroism and Literary Masculinity in *Le Roman de Silence*," published in "Visions of Medieval Trans Feminism," a special issue of *Medieval Feminist Forum* 55.1 (2019): 135–73, is an excellent example of reading for Silence as a heroic trans ancestor. Other important articles that work through this necessary trans reading of Silence include Karen Lurkhur, "Medieval Silence and Modern Transsexuality," *Studies in Gender and Sexuality* 11 (2010): 220–38; and Angela Jane Weisl, "'How to Be a Man, Though Female': Changing Sex in Medieval Romance," *Medieval Feminist Forum* 45.1 (2009): 110–37.

4. This is in line with works like Erin Labbie's, which claim that Silence represents what the anthropologist Gilbert Herdt (and others) terms "a third gender," meaning, in this case, not a third category added to a binary but rather "possibilities for multiple subjectivities." Erin Labbie, "The Specular Image of the Gender-Neutral Name: Naming Silence in *Le Roman de Silence*," *Arthuriana* 7.2 (Summer 1997): 63–77, quotation at 66. R. Howard Bloch agrees that "Silence represents the systematic refusal of univocal meaning." R. Howard Bloch, "Silence and Holes: The *Roman de Silence* and the Art of the Trouvère," *Yale French Studies* 70 (1986): 81–99, quotation at 88.

5. Even feminist critics sometimes forget that the point of "performative" theories of sex and gender is to break down the assumption that "sex" as biological stratum is somehow more "real" or more "inevitable" than is "gender." Heldris of Cornwall seems to be aware that, at least in this fiction, the "sex" of characters is entirely a verbal construction that, at the same time, requires labor *to construct* or *fabricate*, both verbs commonly used by Judith Butler in describing her version of what "sex" is and how it's made in discourse as well as in the material world. For example, "If the inner truth of gender is a *fabrication* and if a true gender is a fantasy *instituted* and *inscribed* on the surface of bodies, then it seems that genders can be neither true nor false, but are only *produced* as the truth effects of a discourse of primary and stable identity." Judith Butler, *Gender Trouble: Feminism and the Subversion of Identity* (New York: Routledge, 1990), 136, emphasis added. See also "Language is said *to fabricate* or to figure the body, *to produce* or *construct* it, *to constitute* or *to make* it. Thus, language is said to act, which involved a tropological understanding of language as performing and performative." Judith Butler, "How Can I Deny That These Hands and This Body

Are Mine?," in *Material Events: Paul de Man and the Afterlife of Theory* (Minneapolis: University of Minnesota Press, 2001), 258, emphasis added. When Heldris belabors, as he does, phrases such as "little was wanting for him to be a man" ("que poi en falt que il n'est malles," line 2477), he nevertheless maintains the masculine pronoun *il* after all. The "poi" or "little thing" that Heldris mentions is discussed by Watt, "Car vallés sui et nient mescine," 155.

6. For two twentieth-century examples of persons assigned female at birth living as male at least in part according to a stated desire to do work not permitted women, see the life of Denis Smith as depicted in the autobiography by Dorothy Lawrence, *Sapper Dorothy: The Only English Woman Soldier in the Royal Engineers 51st Division, 79th Tunnelling Co. during the First World War* (London: J. Lane, 1919; repr., 2010); see also the life of Billy Tipton, the famous jazz trumpet player, named Dorothy Lucille Tipton at birth, who became the subject of multiple books including the acclaimed novel *Trumpet* by Jackie Kay (London: Picador, 1998).

7. As Weisl describes it, "within the poem, *gender is silence*; it is an empty space on which meaning can be written." Weisl, "How to Be a Man," 119.

8. A great deal of ink has been spilled about the signification of Silence's name, chosen by their father because "silence relieves anxiety." Simon Gaunt has argued that the name "derives its significance from its designation of an inability to signify." Simon Gaunt, "Significance of Silence," *Paragraph* 13.2, "Displacement and Recognition," special issue on medieval literature (July 1990): 202–16, quotation at 202. In "When Silence Plays Vielle: The Metaperformance Scenes of *Le Roman de Silence* in Performance," *Mosaic* 42.1 (March 2009): 99, Linda Marie Zaerr calls the name a homonym and relates it to the "hyammi" moment in the text: "They name their child Silence, pointing out that 'silence' can take both masculine and feminine endings, 'Scilenscius' and 'Scilencia' ([lines] 2075–82). His name is thus itself a homonym. The two endings, a and us, create a further homonymic contrast: a, the feminine ending, represents the form of the name that is 'par nature [natural]' (2082), and us, the masculine ending, represents 'us,' usage or nature, which is 'contre nature [contrary to nature]' (2081)." Cador's words in naming Silence are confusing: "sel faisons apieler Scilense / El non de Sainte Paciensce, / Pro cho que silensce tolt ance"; "we will call her Silence / In the name of Saint Patience / Because Silence takes away anxiety" (2066–69). What is this patience? Is it the patience to wait until one can cease living as a man and become a woman? There is no explanation inside the text. Caroline Jewers has argued that the meaning of "relieves care / anxiety" may stem from a moment of "legal casuistry" wherein, were Cador found out to have disguised "his daughter" as "his son," he would not have directly lied because the name was ambiguous. Caroline Jewers, "The Non-Existent Knight: Adventure in 'Le Roman de Silence,'" *Arthuriana* 7.2 (Summer 1997): 94–95. While I am not convinced that this is Cador's thinking, it is the only reasonable explanation for "relieves anxiety" that I have read in the course of this research. Sarah Roche Mahdi's translation highlights the way in which silence functions as an absence of sound at the poem's end (among other places) by translating Silence's last words in the text, "jo n'ai soig mais de taisir" (6627), as "I only care to be silent," which I think provokes critics to wonder about the nature of "mysterious" feminine silence and its symmetry with "noble" masculine silence, and Silence's career as a troubadour who does not talk about themselves much, and all the other valences of silence that the poem had experimented with to that point.

I will note that Jane Tolmie translates these same words as "I will not be silent," and uses this to underline the irony of the silence that follows Silence's utterance. Jane Tolmie, "Silence in the Sewing Chamber: *Le Roman de Silence*," *French Studies* 63.1 (January 2009): 24.

9. Kendall Gerdes, "Performativity," in *TSQ: Transgender Studies Quarterly* 1 (2014): 148–50, quotation at 149.

10. More than one scholar has noted that running away to be a troubadour permits Silence to actively engage the tropes of performance by becoming a performer of musical compositions in addition to continuing to perform the maleness assigned by their parents. Interestingly, scholars have not examined the racial/social class crossing that is also required for Silence's troubadour performance: they "stain their face with nettle-juice" when they run away, which results in the other troubadours taking them for a lower-class "vilain" instead of recognizing the nobleman's son they had been playing for just hours earlier. The question of this potential combination of class-crossing with racial minstrelsy, the question of what's going on with Silence artificially darkening their skin and whether or not this needs to be considered in a racialized manner, has been remarkably underexamined by scholars of the *Roman de Silence* with the exception of Robert L. A. Clark's excellent "Queering Gender and Naturalizing Class in the *Roman de Silence*," *Arthuriana* 12.1 (Spring 2002): 50–63. Labbie mentions this passage and the fact of performance in "Naming Silence," 70.

11. The romance has some Arthurian aspects in addition to the presence of Merlin as a key figure in its climax. One such is the name of Silence's father, Cador, which is the name of a minor character in Arthurian stories going all the way back to Geoffrey of Monmouth's *History of the Kings of Britain*. There, Cador is the name of the father of Constantine, to whom King Arthur hands his crown as he dies.

12. See Kathleen Blumreich, "Lesbian Desire in the Old French 'Roman de Silence,'" *Arthuriana* 7.2 (1997): 47–62, for a discussion of how this queen bears the burden of "aberrant sexuality" in the romance. For much of its plot, her attempts to seduce Silence drive Silence to greater and greater feats of knightly accomplishment. Like Potiphar's wife of biblical fame, when rejected, the queen escalates threats to Silence and accusations to the king that Silence has attempted to seduce *her*.

13. This has been pointed out by a number of critics. See Peggy McCracken, "'The Boy Who Was a Girl': Reading Gender in the 'Roman de Silence,'" *Romanic Review* 85.4 (1994): 517–36, who writes, "It is pertinent to interrogate exactly what the king saw inscribed on Silence's body, since the 'truth' of Silence's anatomy does not appear to be self-evident at all" (532), and also "ultimately Silence's body signifies 'female' because the king says it does, not because it demonstrates an inherent truth" (534).

14. See Danielle M. Seid's incisive article "Reveal," in the "Keywords" issue of *TSQ: Transgender Studies Quarterly* 1 (2014): 176–77.

15. Here I am disagreeing with Caitlin Watt's excellent article "'Car vallés sui et nient mescine,'" in which she discusses how often Silence refers to themself or is referred to as a "mescine valet" or "valet mescine," and argues that if we consider Silence as trans-masculine, the reward will include a broader version of medieval masculinity.

16. See, for instance, Dean Spade's influential article "Mutilating Gender," which critiques the obligation for trans persons of constructing a narrative about a trans

childhood that contradicts certain lived realities of that childhood for purposes of receiving gender-confirming treatment from the hands of a medical establishment capable of accepting only certain kinds of stories as "valid." Dean Spade, "Mutilating Gender," *Transgender Studies Reader 1*, ed. Susan Stryker and Stephen Whittle (New York: Routledge, 2006), 315–32.

17. Jay Prosser's work really led the way to offering this critique; see Jay Prosser, *Second Skins: The Body Narratives of Transsexuality* (New York: Columbia University Press, 1998). Queer theory's critique of what I am calling "inner truth" is rooted in the work of Michel Foucault, and often relies on arguments made in his *History of Sexuality*, vol. 1, *An Introduction*, trans. Robert J. Hurley (New York: Pantheon Books, 1978); published in France as *La Volonté de Savoir* (Paris: Éditions Gallimard, 1976).

18. Scholarship about *Silence* is often concerned with the question of whether it is a "feminist" work or if it is a misogynist work, which medievalists tend to describe using the somewhat deceptive term "antifeminist," meaning here "anti-woman." Some of the debate about whether *Silence* is or is not *feminist*, however one might define that term, can be found in Sarah Roche-Mahdi's introduction to *Silence* (xi–xxiv). Arguments that the work is specifically antifeminist include articles by Peter Allen, "The Ambiguity of Silence: Gender, Writing, and *Le Roman de Silence*," in *Sign, Sentence, Discourse: Language in Medieval Thought and Literature*, ed. Julian N. Wasserman and Lois Roney (Syracuse, NY: Syracuse University Press, 1989), 98–112; and Gaunt "Significance of Silence."

19. Sharon Kinoshita was the first, to my knowledge, to make the argument that it is scandalous when King Ebain marries his own great-niece. Sharon Kinoshita, "Male-Order Brides: Marriage, Patriarchy, and Monarchy in the *Roman de Silence*," *Arthuriana* 12.1 (2002): 64–75. It is established early in the romance that King Ebain is worrying about Cador; the poet tells us that Cador, to the king, is one "qu'il fist norir" ("whom he brought up," 516). In Kinoshita's argument, this scandal helps explain the strange silences of the romance's ending.

20. The romance phrases the reason for Silence's rejection of the queen in a complex way: "car nel consent pas sa nature." In Roche-Mahdi's translation, these words appear as "because his nature kept him from responding" (3824), but we might note that "sa" modifies "nature" and there is no pronoun "he" in the line. Silence's sex and/or gender are not specified at this particular juncture. See also Kathleen Blumreich in "Lesbian Desire in the Old French Roman de Silence," *Arthuriana* 7.2 (Summer 1997): 47–62, for a discussion of Eufeme and her repeated claims that Silence is a queer (the word Eufeme uses, "herites" [3947], is clear in context but has roots in the word for "heretic," according to Blumreich, citing Peter Allen, "Ambiguity of Silence"). Caitlin Watt does an excellent job of listing all the ways that Heldris coyly references Silence's genitalia in her article "'Car vallés sui et nient mescine.'"

21. For thoughtful consideration of and some challenges to this view of female sexuality in another genderqueer tale from the Middle Ages (where a "girl" becomes a "boy" in order to have sex with their beloved), see the Ovidian story of Iphis and Ianthe in its repeated retellings—discussed and analyzed in Patricia Badir, Peggy McCracken, and Valerie Traub, eds., *Ovidian Transversions: Iphis and Ianthe, 1350–1650* (Edinburgh: University of Edinburgh Press, 2019).

22. Sharon Kinoshita has argued that *Silence* is actually a poem about the problems of succession rights in her article "Heldris de Cornualle's *Roman de Silence* and the Feudal Politics of Lineage," *PMLA* 110.3 (May 1995): 397–409.

23. For an extensive and magisterial discussion, see Mary F. Wack, *Lovesickness in the Middle Ages* (Philadelphia: University of Pennsylvania Press, 1990).

24. One of the odd things about this section of the poem, perhaps more so for the non-French reader, is the repetition of the rhyme "Eufemie" and "mie." "Mie" is used to mean two entirely different things when rhymed with Eufemie ("girl" and "doctor"), and while it's very clear in context which meaning seems to be intended, both words are significant ones for the poem's "plot," and the repetitiveness of the rhyme really emphasizes them both. Lewis Thorpe, the poem's first editor, notes this in an uncomplicated way: "Like all narrative poets, Heldris repeats some of his combinations too often, e.g. Eufemie: mie . . . , 401–2, 605–6, 879–80, Eufemie: mie . . . , 593–94, 937–38, enfert.: verte, 627–28, 715–16, 781–82, 949–50" (Thorpe, prefatory material, 18–33, 32).

25. Peggy McCracken, "Women and Medicine in Medieval French Narrative," *Exemplaria* 5.2 (1993): 239–62, 248, 249.

26. Ibid., 248.

27. For a venture into the fascinating subfield of medieval medical theories about sex via Ptolemy's theories of astral inclinations, which circulated widely in Latin and in translation, including one by Guillaume (or possibly Nicholas) Oresme that was dedicated to the future Charles V prior to his ascension to the throne of France, see Anna Kłosowska, "Premodern Trans and Queer in French Manuscripts and Early Printed Texts," *postmedieval: a journal of medieval cultural studies* 9.3 (2018): 349–66. For the background of this discussion, which directly informs my own thinking, see Joan Cadden's magisterial study *Meanings of Sex Difference in the Middle Ages: Medicine, Science, and Culture* (Cambridge: Cambridge University Press, 1993). Although Katherine Park's article "Cadden, Laqueur, and the 'One-Sex Body,'" *Medieval Feminist Forum* 46.1 (2010): 96–100, makes it clear that Cadden's account is more authoritative and relevant to medieval medical thought than Laqueur's, his contribution to popularizing Galenic ideas of the one-sex body in his study of the history of sexuality cannot be ignored. See Thomas Laqueur, *Making Sex: Body and Gender from the Greeks to Freud,* (Cambridge, MA: Harvard University Press, 1990). Arguing learnedly with Laqueur has been a significant pastime for those of us whose early academic lives were enormously influenced by this book; see Helen King, *The One-Sex Body on Trial: The Classical and Early Modern Evidence* (London: Routledge, 2013).

28. In fact, medieval medicine often attempted to meddle in the sex of the unborn, so Eufemie's refusal to intervene in the sex of Silence might indicate either that she belonged to a different school of medical thought or that she was choosing not to intervene in something that, after all, might need to be left up to God or chance. It is not an example of scientific neutrality that she is silent on this issue; it may in fact be an indicator of her relatively low prioritizing of male over female sex in her own child, or of some unusually poor training that she received (i.e., not being taught how to meddle in prenatal sex?), or it could mean superior "scientific" knowledge. It's hard to gauge from the little bit of information on the page.

29. "Although such translation choices are certainly justifiable, the most important feature of this term is its literal status as a signifier of disappointment or loss.

This is because the substitution of haymmi for the directive "a mi" is both a subtrac-
tion and an addition, the replacement of an intended meaning with another." Kate
Cooper discusses this in *"Elle* and *L*: Sexualized Textuality in *Le Roman de Silence,"*
Romance Notes 25 (1985): 341–60. See also Linda Zaerr's succinct analysis of the role
of the "haymmi": "Eufemie's ambiguous utterance leads ultimately to a kiss and
then a wedding. The auditory effect of homonymy is thus the foundation of their
marriage." Linda Marie Zaerr, "When Silence Plays Vielle: The Metaperformance
Scenes of *Le Roman de Silence* in Performance," *Mosaic: A Journal for the Interdisciplinary Study of Literature* 42.1 (March 2009): 99.

30. R. H. Bloch, "Silence and Holes: The *Roman de Silence* and the Art of the
Trouvère," *Yale French Studies* 70 (1986): 81–99. See, for instance, Roger Pensom's
review of Bloch's article as it was reprinted in an edited collection, *Images of Power:
Medieval History/Discourse/Literature*, ed. Kevin Brownlee and Stephen C. Nichols,
Yale French Studies 70 (New Haven, CT: Yale University Press, 1986), reviewed in
French Studies 42.2 (April 1, 1988): 198–200, where Pensom, who in this review seems
quite vehement in his opposition to deconstructive readings in general and takes
pleasure in finding errors in interpretations made by "deconstructive" critics, writes
that "the text is ruthlessly abused in the interests of his *parti pris* . . . [and of a specific
reading so that] whatever the textual problems here, this must be wrong" (199). It is
also commonly noted that some critics took Bloch's reading as the correct one, for
example: "line 886 as 'hate me' resurfacing in [Loren] Ringer, 'Exchange, Identity
and Transvestism in *Le roman de Silence*,' *Dalhousie French Studies* 28 (1994): 3–13,"
as cited in Karen Pratt, "Humor in the *Roman de Silence*," in *Arthurian Literature* 19,
Comedy in Arthurian Literature, eds. K. Busby and R. Dalrymple (Cambridge: Brewer,
2003), 87–103, quotation at 97n34. "Hate me" as a reading of "haymmi!" did not,
however, get much purchase beyond this second example.

31. M. W. Bychowski, "Transvestite Metaphysics" on the blog *Transliterature: Things Transform*, discusses this same passage as part of her consideration of
"Nature's quantum approach to gender," reading this passage in the *Roman de Silence*
as part of a philosophical/theological theory of substance being worked out in this
romance. See http://www.thingstransform.com, blog post, April 4, 2015. The blog
notes that this post is the transcription of a talk given by Bychowski titled "Transvestite Metaphysics: Quantum Entanglement and Natural Philosophy in 13th Century
Literature," delivered at the International Conference on the Fantastic in the Arts in
Orlando, March 18–22, 2015 (accessed April 18, 2018).

32. Lorraine Kochanske Stock uses this passage as an example of how Cador and
Eufemie, who had started out as relative equals despite their sexed difference, experience a "redistribution of power and authority once married. "With her mother's
complicity, Silence is consigned to a life of deceit, gender-impersonation and cross-
dressing," writes Stock in "The Importance of Being Gender 'Stable': Masculinity
and Feminine Empowerment in *Le Roman de Silence*," *Arthuriana* 7.2 (Summer 1997):
7–34, quotations at 22, 23. This perhaps does not take into account the ways in which
Silence enjoys his life as a man! In contrast, Heather Tanner argues, "Cador is clearly
the decision maker or lord, but as a good husband and lord, he always seeks his wife's
advice and consent. Her wisdom is now his, just as both are of one mind and body by
marriage. Eufemie is subsumed into Cador's persona ("the countess, his wife"), and
yet Cador never assumes her consent. He truthfully presents his ideas and plans and

seeks her agreement and counsel. By doing so, he preserves the honor of both, and the result is a productive and happy marriage as well as a peaceful county." Heather Tanner, "Lords, Wives and Vassals," *Journal of Women's History* 24.1 (Spring 2012): 150.

33. The notion of not one will but multiple wills at odds with one another is associated with Saint Augustine, who wrote of internal contradiction that "the mind orders itself to make an act of will, and it would not give this order unless it willed to do so; yet it does not carry out its own command. . . . For the will commands that an act of will should be made, and it gives this command to itself, not to some other will. The reason, then, why the command is not obeyed is that it is not given with the full will. . . . So there are two wills in us, because neither by itself is the whole will, and each possesses what the other lacks." Augustine, *Confessions*, trans. R. S. Pine-Coffin (New York: Penguin Classics, 1961), bk. 8, chap. 9, 172.

34. In the "Hagiographic Appendix" to her study *Clothes Make the Man*, Valerie Hotchkiss lists no fewer than thirty-four so-called transvestite saints, including some who had only very briefly lived their lives as a sex other than the one they had been officially assigned. Her list comprises only persons assigned female at birth who live as men ("recognition of holiness is earned primarily through the denial of womanhood." Valerie Hotchkiss, *Clothes Make the Man: Female Cross Dressing in Medieval Europe* (New York: Garland, 1996), 13.

35. Weisl, "How to Be a Man," 114.

36. In "Competing Gender Ideologies and the Limitations of Language in *Le Roman de Silence*," *Romance Quarterly* 55.1 (2008): 35–48, Katherine H. Terrell wonders why "the text lends itself to such widely divergent readings" and takes it as her objective to answer this question of, in my own words, in-between-ness. She argues that "critics disagree so fundamentally about the poem's gender politics because gender itself is a radically unstable concept in *Silence*" (36).

CHAPTER 9

Transgender Translation, Humanism, and Periodization

Vasco da Lucena's "Deeds of Alexander the Great"

ZRINKA STAHULJAK

In a copy of Vasco da Lucena's *Deeds of Alexander the Great* that is held at the Bibliothèque Nationale de France (*Les faits et gestes d'Alexandre le Grand*, Paris, BnF, Ms. fr. 20311), we find evidence of a kind of vandalism that we may wave away all too easily: the first folio of the General Prologue and the folios of the prologues to Book V and Book IX are missing. The folio that would have come just before the folio of the prologue to Book V carries, moreover, a visible trace of a cut (figs. 9.1 and 9.2). Of the four prologues in Lucena's translation, only one survived in its entirety in Ms. 20311, the prologue to Book II.[1] Often such cuts are due to a theft of precious medieval illuminations, a common occurrence since the late eighteenth century.[2] But the manuscript tradition of Vasco da Lucena's text, a translation of Quintus Curtius's *History of Alexander* that Lucena completed in 1468, is exceptionally uniform, and it points us in another direction.[3] Other better-preserved manuscripts provide evidence that the first large miniature at the beginning of the manuscript, known as the frontispiece, was commonly placed at the head of the General Prologue. This would explain the sole missing folio of the General Prologue in Ms. 20311 as theft. But in other manuscripts, miniatures do not precede the intermediary prologues to Books II, V, and IX; instead, as a rule, we find illuminations at the head of each of nine books, that is, after the prologue. More specifically, in Ms. 20311 not a single large miniature opens any of the other nine books; rather, the

FIGURE 9.1. Missing folio vii.xx.xiii. The cut is shown here between fol. 147v (fol. xii.xxi.xi verso) and fol. 148 (fol. vii.xx.xii). Vasco da Lucena, *The Deeds of Alexander the Great*. Paris, BnF, Ms. fr. 20311. Photo: Zrinka Stahuljak.

manuscript contains only single-column miniatures in semi-grisaille placed within the body of the text of the books—and none of these are missing.

If not vandalism and theft, what then could have prompted a user of this manuscript, held originally at the Collège de Navarre and transferred to the BnF sometime after 1790, to cut the non-illuminated pages of the

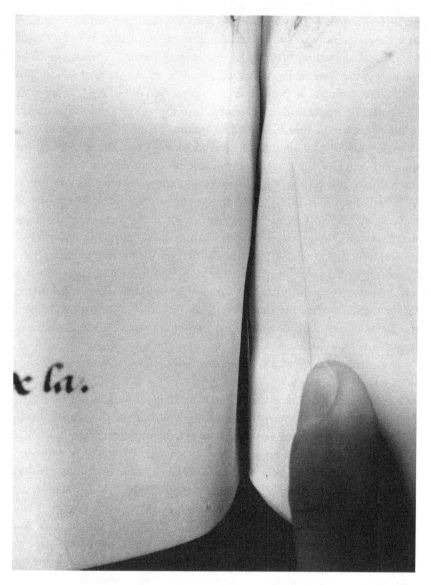

FIGURE 9.2.   Close-up of missing folio vii.xx.xiii. The cut is shown here between fol. 147v (fol. xii. xxi.xi verso) and fol. 148 (fol. vii.xx.xii). Vasco da Lucena, *The Deeds of Alexander the Great*. Paris, BnF, Ms. fr. 20311. Photo: Zrinka Stahuljak.

manuscript's two prologues to Book V and Book IX—while leaving the prologue to Book II, as well as all its images, intact? If not for precious miniatures, why cut the intermediary prologues? The manuscript tradition of Lucena's *Alexander* again provides a possible clue. Lucena glosses his own work in four prologues spread over nine books. They function as "translator's notes," as paratext to the text. They reserve the space for the translator's explanation of his task, intention, method, and duration of translation, but also for his actions and alterations of what he calls a "true history." This is especially the case in the General Prologue, preserved except for the first folio in Ms. 20311. The prologue to Book II, entirely preserved in Ms. 20311, reinforces the General Prologue with the explanation of the sources the translator used to substitute for the missing Book I of Quintus Curtius (Demosthenes, Plutarch, Flavius Josephus, and Justin) and additionally provides an apology for the inadequacy of the translation because of an insufficiency of sources. Interestingly, this prologue is often visually integrated into the conclusion of Book I, a possible reason for its preservation in Ms. 20311. The prologue to Book IX, the shortest, merely provides a list of the sections of the book that are missing in the Latin Quintus Curtius and in Lucena's supplemental sources.[4] But the content of the prologue to Book V differs significantly from the other three; while it lists the lacunae at the end of Book IV, it also explains why Lucena changed the names of certain historical characters appearing in Books V and IX. Here the translator openly acknowledges that he changed the gender, from male to female, of two of Alexander's sexual partners, Bagoas and Nicomachus.

The cuts in Ms. 20311 are interesting because they edit the translator's voice and space: along with the missing folio of the General Prologue disappears the mention of Lucena's dedicatee the Duke of Burgundy, Charles the Bold. Nevertheless, between the remaining folios of the General Prologue and the prologue to Book II, readers can still appreciate the fact that this is a translation, albeit without a specific addressee; the "mirror of prowess" ("miroir de proesse") originally intended for Duke Charles becomes a model addressed to all.[5] But the cutting of the prologue to Book V is of a different order, for, although it might have other causes, it appears to be an act of violent censorship regarding the gender of historical characters. This redaction would have occurred later, *after* the copy of Ms. 20311 was produced with its initial Roman foliation, discontinuous because of the cuts, but *before* the modern Arabic numeral refoliation of the manuscript, which is continuous.

It may not be possible to resolve the dilemma of whether Ms. 20311 was damaged because of theft or because of censorship. It is more than likely, in light of the manuscript tradition of *The Deeds of Alexander*, that the missing folio of the General Prologue was cut in Ms. 20311 because it had a large frontispiece. Scot McKendrick has established parallels between the ducal copy, Ms. fr. 22547 (BnF), and Ms. fr. 20311, based on the placement of images in the text.[6] In comparison with Ms. 22547, which has a large frontispiece, the number of missing lines in Ms. 20311 would indicate that it too may have had a large frontispiece. In addition, it is possible that miniatures preceded the manuscript's prologues to Books V and IX, given the two exceptions I have found in the manuscript tradition. I have been able to consult sixteen out of twenty-eight known illuminated manuscripts.[7] The two exceptions to the general rule—that miniatures precede books and not prologues—are Jena, Thüringer Universitäts- und Landesbibliothek, Ms. El. f. 89, where a miniature precedes the prologue to Book IX because the text of the prologue is integral to the text of the book (fol. 174), and Los Angeles, J. Paul Getty Museum, Ms. Ludwig XV 8, which integrates the prologue with Book V, and thus a miniature is placed at the head of the prologue (fol. 123). And yet if the three cuts in Ms. 20311 were of miniatures, Ms. 20311 would have been an odd exemplar of Lucena's translation with only three large miniatures (now missing), rather than the standard of a large miniature per book opening. Moreover, if Ms. 22547 is in fact closely related to Ms. 20311, it is then worth noting that it does not place large miniatures before prologues, which would bring us closer to the hypothesis of censorship.[8]

Whether theft or censorship, the excision of the folio of the prologue to Book V opens up new spaces for the writing of transgender history that I pursue in this essay. A seriously, albeit inconsistently, damaged manuscript (why leave a prologue to Book II but cut out a similar prologue to Book IX?) of a text drew my attention to its lacunae; knowledge of Lucena's text, whose textual tradition is fairly stable, prompted me to interrogate the contents of Book V and the relationship of that fragment to the whole. Together the lacuna and the evidence of the manuscript tradition brought me to the realization that Lucena's text signals something important for European history: that the translator's alteration of the characters' gender in the text of a fifteenth-century translation was not hidden in the translation's paratext, but that the translator's prologue acknowledged both his act of changing the lovers' genders and a different historical experience of sexuality. The essay thus links the history of the book and the history of sexuality. Two throughlines structure it: first, that in the period known as "humanism," in the fourteenth and fifteenth century, generally accepted as a threshold and groundswell of change between the medieval and early modern periods, translation methods changed and attitudes toward sexuality did not. In looking at humanism through its translation practices instead of its cultural practices, this essay offers, moreover, new insights about periodization from the medieval to the early modern. The second throughline holds that the actions of the humanist translator Vasco da Lucena open up the space for transgender identities. If translation has the power to change genders, might readers' imagination and identification follow? And when it comes to visualizing Lucena's translation, how do manuscript illuminators exploit the transgender potential? In short, I study a transgendering translation that in Lucena's act of changing genders offers a gender non-normative potential to its publics, its readers, and its viewers.[9]

Transgendering Translation and Humanism

So what are we to make of the seemingly contradictory fact that a translator felt the need to render Alexander's homosexual practice palatable to his fifteenth-century audiences by modifying his translation and yet did not hide but rather touted his decision to change the historical characters' gender? If there is a contradiction in the translator's actions, it may stem from our contemporary and disciplinary vantage point on the attitudes toward sexuality and gender norms of the fifteenth century, rather than from a contradiction inherent in the fifteenth century. If so, the heritage of periodization, the commonplace fifteenth-century disciplinary fissure between the European medieval and the early modern, may have obfuscated the writing of the history of sexuality.

Instead, we may posit a different periodization. There was the "invention of sodomy" in the eleventh century by the Catholic Church's Peter Damian, a term that should not be conflated with our definitions of homosexual practice, because it encompassed a far wider range of sexual behaviors: from solitary to mutual masturbation, from ejaculation between legs or thighs to anal penetration. Any non-procreative activity, whether homo- or hetero-sexual, was "against nature." The moral condemnation of what was understood to be nonconforming, because non-procreative, behavior went hand in hand with descriptions of and debates around the very behavior, as confession manuals, penitentials, and Christian theological writings amply demonstrate. There was a painful awareness, for example, that a confessor's questions might suggest sinful practice, imply that the sin is widespread, and ultimately incite kinship with other like-minded sinners.[10] Thus, Lucena's open citation of Alexander's sexual behaviors in the prologue to Book V follows the similar veiling and unveiling dynamic that is visible from the late eleventh century onward.

Accordingly, via a rereading of humanism, this essay takes aim at the stakes of re-periodization between the medieval and early modern periods. If at the time of Lucena's translation Lucena could affirm a historically viable sexual behavior, then, contrary to common assumptions, dividing attitudes toward sexuality between medieval and early modern loses its impetus. Humanist editorial and commentary practices, which we associate with progressive, "modern" critical reading practices, were like the commercials that proclaim "same formula, new look": nothing had materially changed in attitudes toward sexuality in the fourteenth and fifteenth centuries, the humanist watershed. But if humanism did not offer a new view of sexuality and gender in contrast to the eleventh century, Lucena's translation nevertheless registers something else historically: a shift toward new methods in translation. It is because of that shift that something like an alteration in sex and gender systems appears; there is a "new look" to the "same formula." Humanist translation practice introduced the method of historical distancing between antiquity and the humanist present, the notion of historicity.[11] Consequently, it introduced standards of accuracy in translation and created a gap between text and paratext; Lucena altered the historical text of his translation, but in the paratext he accurately reported this intervention. A shift in translation practice thus allows us to see clearly the veiling/unveiling dynamic of attitudes toward sexuality.

While scholarship in transgender history of the Middle Ages has dealt mainly with fictional and legendary characters in literary[12] and, more exceptionally, art works,[13] or with historical persons,[14] this essay responds to this volume's editors' aims of understanding "how normative sex and gender systems [could] have functioned" before they became as we know them today by interrogating the agency of a historical translator figure, Vasco da Lucena.[15] Lucena purposefully transgenders the historical characters of Alexander's lovers. Rather than claim that Lucena's translation reveals the emergence of normative sex and gender systems, I believe that it lets us observe instead the tension between an ongoing constitution of gender systems as we know them (text) and their continued fluidity (paratext), the gap between text and paratext, the veiling and unveiling, without this gap closing. This in turn implies that more systematic erasures and censorship of sexual behaviors considered "non-normative" may be a later development in history, beyond the humanist moment of the fourteenth and fifteenth centuries; the censorship hypothesis of Ms. 20311 would underscore this conclusion.

Instead, between text and paratext, Lucena's modification of the gender of historical characters in the text alongside the record of his translation practice in the paratext opens new pathways to transgender history and spaces of trans identification. Just as "transgender and queer theory . . . variously critique the assumption that a translator must be 'faithful' to an 'original' text or author,"[16] Lucena's translation critiques, albeit inadvertently, the assumption that gender has to be faithful to the original. Between text and paratext, humanist translation queers identities in the very attempt of the translator to foreclose them.

Humanisms

We should not let traditional notions of humanism, a moment of ostensibly greater historical accuracy and historicity compared to the earlier medieval period, obscure our sense of historical exactitude about how sexuality and gender functioned. A few words are therefore in order to explain the humanism of Vasco da Lucena at the court of the Dukes of Burgundy in the 1460s and the reasons to single out Lucena's translation as an example of the watershed moment in translation practices that allows us to see the operations of sex and gender systems on a longer time span, without claiming the humanist rupture of the medieval from the early modern.

Humanism is most often defined narrowly as an Italian phenomenon, "the study and practice of literary Latin," that is, a philological humanism directed at the recovery of Latin texts and production of new texts in Latin in fourteenth- and fifteenth-century Italy.[17] This humanist Latin had little in common with the administrative Latin of the later Middle Ages; the latter was insufficient for understanding classical Latin, for which everyone needed a translation.[18] In contrast to philological humanism, a "chivalric humanism" of classical themes and texts focused on moral precepts and was dominated by the genre of mirrors of princes (*speculum principis*), models for an ideal prince's behavior. Chivalric humanism was always in translation and concentrated in the French-speaking northwest (fourteenth- and fifteenth-century France and Burgundy, but also England). According to Nicole Oresme, translator of Aristotle for Charles V, king of France (r. 1364–1380), "the King wanted the books to be translated into French for the common good, so that he and his counselors could understand them better. The same goes for *Ethics* and *Politics*; as mentioned, the former teaches how to be a good man and the latter how to be a good king" ("le Roy voulu pour le bien commun les faire les translater en françois, affin que il et ses conseilliers et autres les puissent mieulx entendre, mesmement *Ethiques* et *Politiques*, desquelz comme dit est le premier aprent estre bon homme et l'autre prince").[19] David Aubert, the Duke of Burgundy's secretary and scribe, writes in 1463 in the prologue to the ducal copy of the *History of the Three Kings' Sons* (*Histoire de trois fils de roys*, or *Chronique de Naples*, or *Chronique royale*) that Philip the Good (r. 1419–1467) is "of all the princes the one with the richest and the most noble world library" ("le prince sur tous autres garny de la plus riche et noble librairie du monde," Paris, BnF, Ms. fr. 92, fol. 1v). The culture of the court of Burgundy was to collect an entire world of knowledge, in translation. The duke's political counselors were his cultural counselors; the collection and production of knowledge was politics.[20] And it was in following the Valois Dukes of Burgundy that the English king, Edward IV, founded the English royal library.[21]

Philological humanism introduced new attitudes toward translation, embodied in Leonardo Bruni's treatise *De interpretatione recta* (On the right way to translate, 1420): "I say that the full power of a translation resides in the fact that what is written in one language should be rightly [or correctly] translated into another" ("Dico igitur omnem interpretationis vim in eo consistere, ut, quod in altera lingua scriptum sit, id in alteram recte traducatur").[22] According to Bruni, linguistic competence must complement competence in style and form that can be acquired only through the mastery of letters, the requirement for a translator's competence and expertise in source and target languages: "The translator transforms [convertet] himself into the original author with all his mind, will, and soul, and he also ponders the problem of how to transform the shape, the stance, the gait, the style, and all the other features, and how to express them" ("interpres quidem optimus sese in primum scribendi auctorem tota mente et animo et voluntate convertet et quodammodo transformabit eiusque orationis figuram, statum, ingressum coloremque et liniamenta cuncta exprimere meditabitur").[23] A new method, "optima interpretandi ratio" (the highest rule of translation), recommends instead "that the shape of the original text should be kept as closely as possible, so that understanding does not lose the words any more than the words themselves lose brilliance and craftsmanship" ("si figura prime orationis quam optime conservetur, ut neque sensibus verba neque verbis ipsis nitor ornatusque deficiat").[24] In other words, philological humanism, with its return to the original language, imposes a new concept of translation as linguistic equivalence, and single (not multiple) translator activity, and opposes accuracy in translation to the previous relative autonomy of the text and translator(s).

In contrast, chivalric humanism was characterized by looser attitudes toward translation, summed up in the medieval concept of *translatio*. *Translatio* covers a much larger semantic field than our modern term "translation"—it is commentary (interpretation, gloss), adaptation, amplification, abbreviation—and it deploys a completely different notion of fidelity and accuracy; its goal is preservation, transmission, and "vulgarization." *Translatio* also articulates a theory of civilizational production and reproduction since, beyond linguistic translation, it stands for transfers of power (*translatio imperii*), knowledge (*translatio studii*), and physical objects or materials (such as relics in *translatio reliquiarum*).[25] But Bruni thinks that expertise should replace the basic and vital medieval concern for the transmission and preservation of knowledge that *translatio* represents: "And yet they will say that the man who publishes what he knows deserves praise, not blame, even if he is by no means well versed in those arts which require experience" ("Dicere autem: non vituperationem, sed laudem mereri eum, qui, quod habuit, in medium protulit, nequaquam rectum est in his artibus, que peritiam flagitant").[26] In other words, Bruni does not subscribe to the view of translation at any cost, even of error and inaccuracy, in the name of preservation of knowledge.

In short, scholars consider Italian humanism to be one of Latinity and identify it with the pursuit of knowledge for knowledge's sake, whereas northern humanism would be vernacular and hence "utilitarian"; translation is perceived to be driven by didacticism.[27] Nevertheless, humanism of whatever region, period, or language can be characterized as collecting knowledge. If we reduce the definition of humanism to its common definition of Italian humanism, we in fact narrow the scope of knowledge production and collection. Italian humanism was one variant of European humanisms; put another way, humanism was multi-centered, and it took on a variety of forms, some "hybrid," specifically in the Burgundian Low Countries.[28]

Vasco da Lucena came to Burgundy from Portugal via Cologne and Paris. Isabella of Portugal, Duchess of Burgundy by marriage to Philip the Good, cultivated strong relationships with Portugal, and she may have been his patron. Vasco was later the cupbearer of Margaret of York, her daughter-in-law, third wife of the young Duke Charles the Bold (r. 1467–1477), and a counselor to Charles.[29] Vasco's translation was one of the humanist manifestations at Charles's court. From a young age Charles was educated by Antoine Haneron, a humanist teacher.[30] By some accounts, he spoke excellent Italian.[31] Charles's models of rule were Rome and Caesar, and he owned many Roman histories. It was known that, during his military campaigns, "every evening [Charles] dines and has read to him of past valour, from Livy or some work on Alexander the Great or warfare, in French, and all who wish to do so can attend."[32]

Lucena was influenced by philological humanism in his choice of sources and translation method.[33] While the medieval marvelous tradition of Alexander was based on two versions of pseudo-Callisthenes, written as early as the second century BCE, Lucena derived his translation from the Italian humanist tradition based on Roman historiography, largely neglected until Petrarch. He chose the most trusted of Latin sources, Quintus Curtius's *Historiae Alexandri Magni*, which he placed in the same category of historical reliability and appreciation as the works of Titus Livy and Sallust. Lucena's choice may have been guided by the popularity Quintus Curtius enjoyed; 150 manuscripts of his Latin history still survive today.[34] Lucena declares in the General Prologue his high standard of fidelity to the original Latin: "I have labored to translate as completely and as closely to Latin that I could, without using words too mannered or too obscure. In certain places, I wasn't able to translate sentence for sentence or word for word, given the difficulty and the brevity of Latin" ("[je] me suy pene de le translater le plus entier et pres du latin que j'ay peu, sans user de termes trop haultz ne trop obscurs. En aulcuns lieux je n'ay peu translater clause a clause ne mot a mot obstant la difficulte et briefte du latin," fol. 2v).

In his choice of sources and translation method of fidelity to the source, Lucena practices the humanist double-pronged approach of linguistic and historiographic accuracy. He seeks to place antiquity in a verifiable historical chronology and to offer a history that is rational, that is, that appeals to reason rather than inciting wonder.[35] He rejects the marvelous, "the other false fables written by men ignorant of the nature of things and unaware of the falseness and the impossibility of this" ("aultres fables faintes par hommes ignorans la nature des choses, non congnoissans tout ce estre faulx et impossible," fol. 3). The highest new ideal is history without any of the mechanisms of the marvelous: "This history is therefore very useful as it teaches us the truth of how Alexander conquered all of the East . . . without flying, diving under the sea, enchantments, giants, and without the strength of Renault of Montauban, Lancelot, Tristan, or Rainouard, who could kill fifty men with one blow" ("Moult doncques est utile ceste histoire qui nous aprent au vray comment Alexandre conquist tout orient . . . sans voler en air, sans aler soubz mer, sans enchantemens, sans geans, et sans estre si fort comme Regnault de Montauban, comme Lancelot, comme Tristan, comme Raynoart qui tuoit cinquante hommes coup a coup," fol. 3). Only a "true history" is useful for a mirror of princes: "I chose a true history of Alexander in which by itself it can be made clear that, just as the enlargement and growth of kingdoms is conquered by virtue, diligence, work effort, and abstinence from pleasures, so by their contraries they are damaged and they fall" ("je me suy arreste en une vraye histoire d'Alexandre ou quel tout seul puet clerement apparoir que ainsi comme les augmentacions et croissances des royaumes se acquierent par vertu, diligence, tollerance de labeur et abstinence de delices, ainsi par leurs contraires viennent a leur detriment et a leur declin," fol. 4).

Lucena positions himself against "those histories written in French, in rhyme or prose, existing in six or seven versions . . . that are corrupted, modified, false and full of obvious lies" ("ces histoires en francoys en rime et en prose en six ou en sept manieres . . . mais corrumpues, changees, faulses et plaines de evidens mensonges," fol. 2), histories to which belongs the last marvelous version of the legend of Alexander in Jean Wauquelin's *Deeds and*

Conquests of Alexander the Great (*Les faicts et les conquestes d'Alexandre le Grand*), completed in 1448 for the Duke of Burgundy, Philip the Good, Charles's father. Wauquelin explores the full potential of the marvelous as encounters and discoveries multiply the farther Alexander advances east: the second, and last, book of Wauquelin's *Alexander* contains episodes describing the enclosure of the Gog and Magog, wild men and women, Amazons, giants, different monstrous races—hippocephalic and acephalic people, cyclopes—and Alexander's marvelous travels and abilities: his discoveries of the Perilous Valley and the Fountain of Youth, or his capacity to fly through the air and dive to the sea bottom. For centuries, European texts lingered on the marvels and luxuries that they claimed characterized the East; until Lucena, Alexander the Great was the embodiment of this European "Orientalism."

Between Text and Paratext: Transgender Spaces

The insistence on historical knowledge (that is, a return to historical sources) and linguistic accuracy (that is, deep knowledge of source and target languages) impacts European sexual normativity and gender identity because it emphasizes the variety of sexual modes of existence in historically recorded sources. Humanists who embraced Bruni's model of critical commentary de facto introduced and highlighted the existence, both in deeper history and in wider geography, of a variety of sexual and gender strategies that were not all binary or, indeed, legible through any, even the most capacious, lens of the sex and gender "norms" or methodologies circulating at the time in European Christianity. The text and paratext of Lucena's translation makes visible the tension between fluidity and normativity without settling them. It opens the transgender space before the binary or before the "gender-conforming" behavior was elaborated and policed through morality. When we compare the two translations for two Dukes of Burgundy, father and son, made twenty years apart—Wauquelin in 1448, Lucena in 1468—their translation of Alexander's sexuality tells us that humanist attitudes toward sexuality did not change; a change in translation methods just made these attitudes clear and visible.

An earlier vernacular version provides the point of comparison. The dodecasyllabic version by Thomas of Kent, written soon after 1180, offers a full biography of Alexander; in it, there is not much room for ambiguity as to Alexander's bisexuality: "If you have not had intercourse with a young man or young woman / you can continue onward to touch the [prophetic] trees [of Sun and Moon]" ("A vallet n'a meschine se tu geü nen as, / tant pués aler avant q'as arbres toucheras").[36] For the focus on sexual practices, Wauquelin substitutes the image of procreative sex: "If you and your princes are born of male and female, it is right that you should enter this place" ("Se ty et ty prince estes nez de mal et de fumelle, il te couvient entrer en ce lieu").[37] Lucena's translation is just as "moral," for he substitutes women for men. In the prologue to Book V, he openly discusses the gender "conversions" he made from the original Latin: "I converted into a young woman the character of Nicomachus who was a young man according to historical truth. I likewise transposed the character of Bagoé from a young man to a young woman" ("Je convertiz en jeune fille le personnaige de Nycomaque qui estoit ung jeune filz selon la verite de l'istoire. Ainsi que je transcrips de jouvencel en jeune fille le personnage de Bagoe," fol. 127v). Bagoé is in reality the eunuch Bagoas.[38] But Lucena's conversion comes with a difference: unlike Wauquelin, driven by the humanist translation method, Lucena explains himself. In the process, he also affirms a historically viable sexual practice.

Lucena's first justification for his translation "conversion" is "to avoid a bad example" ("pour eviter le mauvais exemple"). Lucena then affirms that the French language is actually incapable of articulating such misuses because it "does not possess terms to express such deviance" ("n'a point de termes a proferer telz abuz"). The last two reasons for the "conversion" partake of the translator's personal responsibility, which he acknowledges, passively at first: "I thank my ignorance which cannot find words for it in the French language" ("je regracie mon ignorance qui trouver ne les scet en ladite langue," fol. 127v). It is after all perhaps not the language that is to be blamed but Lucena's linguistic competences. French was not his native language; indeed, in the General Prologue, Lucena sought to justify the slowness of his translation, which he began in 1461 but finished in 1468, by begging the reader's pardon for "the imperfection and roughness of my French language, seeing that I am of Portuguese birth" ("l'imperfection et rudesse de mon langaige françois, atendu que je suy portugalois de nacion," fol. 2v). But Lucena feels compelled to offer an ever stronger justification for his decision to change the gender of protagonists and admits to an active role: "my shame cares not to look for the [right] terms in this language" ("ma honte qui ne tient cure de les cerchier en icelle"). Because of his censorship, "the noble French language remained innocent, and chaste and unsoiled by me of such crimes" ("si demourra la noble langue francoise innocent[e], de par moy, chaste et impolue de telz crimes," fol. 127v). Ultimately, the translator takes full responsibility for his agency; French, we can presume, has all the linguistic capacity necessary to describe Alexander's sexual practices, as does he.[39]

Thus the correction of historical sexuality happens without regard for the mode of translation, whether it is medieval *translatio* (Wauquelin) or humanist accuracy (Lucena). It is the humanist translation method—the gap between the text and paratext—that makes visible the fact that the production of normative sex and gender was at work already in Wauquelin. New emphasis on historical veracity and linguistic fidelity calls attention to the interventions in Lucena's translation; if anything, we can say that we see, rather than fresh attitudes toward sexuality, a tension that persisted between fluidity and normativity, between the gender plurality before the modern and the future restrictive articulations of the binary.

In the paratext, the translator acknowledges the difference between historical narrative and historical sources. Even as he corrects history in order "to avoid a bad example," by acknowledging the difference between a historically verifiable experience and the cultural production of normativity, he sets another example: the example of a character's transgendering. The gap that Lucena opens, between text and paratext, by using the power of translation to transgender characters is a space that can be filled with transgender identities, alternative histories and lives. How many readers, knowing that Bagoas and Nicomachus were men, could see the possibility of their female gender in Lucena's very transformation of Bagoas into Bagoé? The performative force of Lucena's translation cannot be denied. In his hands, translation becomes a powerful transgendering tool: a "conversion." "The translator has the power to shape transgender identity in their translations," and he does.[40] Readers can follow suit. So can, perhaps, the viewers.

Illuminating a Transgender History

The work of artists illuminating Lucena's manuscripts—twenty-eight out of thirty-five surviving manuscripts are illuminated—responds in interesting ways to this transgendering of history. Contrary to an evenness in the textual tradition, their illustration programs—the choice of themes and compositions—vary so greatly that most art historians, with the exception of Scot McKendrick, have avoided attempts at synthesis.[41] The focus in the prologue to Book V on the change of Bagoas's and Nicomachus's gender makes possible nevertheless a kind of synthesis. Two questions must be asked of illuminated manuscripts of Lucena's *Alexander*: (1) How many images does Book V have in comparison to the other eight books? (2) How do issues of sex and gender get translated visually?

Simply put, the gap Lucena created between text and paratext made the illumination of Book V problematic. In *The Deeds of Alexander* there are nine books; Book V is central, structurally and thematically. There are twenty-eight chapters in Book V; chapters 13 and 14 are thus the heart of the narrative. The beginning of the decline of Alexander occurs between chapter 13, "How the Traitor Narbazanes and Talestris, the Queen of Amazons, Came before Alexander" ("Comment Narbazanes le traytre et Talestris, royne des Amazones, vindrent devers Alexandre," fol. 138v), and chapter 14, titled "How Alexander Converted His Great Gifts into Pride and Extravagances" ("Comment Alexandre convertit en orgueil et en pompes les grans biens estans en lui," fol. 139). Chapter 13 opens with the presentation of a former concubine of King Darius. Bagoé is a "woman of singular beauty, at the peak of her youth" ("femme de singuliere beaulte et en la fleur de sa jeunesse," fol. 138v). Traitor Narbazanes, Darius's assassin, offers her to Alexander as a gift when Alexander grants him an audience to defend himself from the charge that he conspired and killed Darius: just as "once upon a time King Darius took advantage of her soon thereafter Alexander did too" ("Le roy Daire avoit jadiz use avec elle et peu apres Alexandre en usa," fol. 138v). The chapter makes an explicit link between sex and pardon, since Bagoé's entreaty will induce Alexander to forgive Narbazanes for his assassination of Darius.

After this short opening, Amazons occupy center stage in chapter 13 with their queen, Talestris.[42] Lucena calls them "barbarians" ("les barbarins," fol. 139). Talestris is "inflamed by the desire to see the king" ("emflammee par desir de veoir le roy," fol. 138v). She shamelessly confesses the reason behind her visit to Alexander's court, "that she came to converse and have children with the king" ("qu'elle venoit pour communiquier et avoir enfans avec le roy," fol. 139). Alexander unenthusiastically accepts, and "for thirteen days they devoted and applied themselves to her desire" (".xiii. iours furent despenduz et donnes a son desir," fol. 139). Lucena's translation foregrounds not only the untamed independence of Talestris, a woman who knows how to get what she wants—for "she insisted that he not let her return [to her lands] frustrated and without fulfilling her hopes" ("si perseveroit toudis a lui demander qu'il ne la soufrist retourner frustree ne vuide de son espoir," fol. 139)—but also the fact that the customs of the Amazons belong to another civilization: "One of the breasts remains intact in order to feed the children of the female sex," Lucena tells us, "but the right breast is seared so that they can bend their bows and wield their lances with ease" ("L'ung des tetins est garde sans y touchier pour nourrir les enfans du sexe femenin mais on leur brule le dextre a fin qu'elles tendent leurs arcs et brandissent leurs lances a leur aise," fol. 139). Just as the woman's desire speaks itself without shame, so is the female body laid bare.

A similar negotiation that Lucena's text and paratext undergo—revealing a historical experience and hewing closely to the historical sources in the paratext, while transgendering history and its characters in the text—can be observed in the work of the painters. In general, of the sixteen illuminated manuscripts that I have been able to consult, the central book, Book V, the one that explains the decline and fall of Alexander's empire by perversion of his good morals, is less illuminated in comparison to other books. Let me offer the example of the ducal Ms. 22547. It has only two miniatures for Book V (fol. 128 and fol. 154v), but neither depicts the women of Book V.[43] Unlike its other books, which open with half-page miniatures, the two images of Book V are much smaller and painted over one column.[44] The distribution of images is likewise disproportional: out of eighty-six miniatures, eighty-four are painted in the other eight books. This smaller number of illuminations— and there is at least one illuminated manuscript that has no miniatures for Book V[45]—is further reinforced with a sexually neutral choice of subject themes: battles, death or burial, torture. Sexuality, whether Alexander's or Talestris's, and the transgendering of Bagoas were not easily depicted.

But there exists, by all accounts, one exceptional manuscript: Los Ange-les, J. Paul Getty Museum, Ms. Ludwig XV 8.[46] The manuscript was copied by the scribe Jan du Quesne and illuminated by the Master of the Jardin de Vertueuse Consolation, in the style of Lieven van Lathem as it was developed by the Master of Margaret of York (ca. 1468–1475). Its first owner remains unknown, though likely a member of the Burgundian French-speaking upper nobility.[47] The Getty Ludwig XV 8 has fourteen miniatures, nine of which open each of the nine books. The additional five images consist of the fron-tispiece and two extra images for Books V and VI each. Thus, in the Getty Ludwig XV 8, Books V and VI each have three miniatures, one at the start of the book and then two more, whereas all other books have only one large miniature at the beginning.[48] This is against the illumination trends of all other illuminated Lucena manuscripts. The additional curiosity of the Getty manuscript is that one of the four extra images, and one of the two extra images that are in Book V, is actually a half-page miniature, the size reserved for the miniatures at the start of each book. In this image on fol. 133v, we see Bagoé on the left pleading for Alexander's mercy and, on the right, the arrival of Talestris at Alexander's court (fig. 9.3). The Master of the Jardin de Ver-tueuse Consolation paints Bagoé in sumptuous dress and in the heat of her seduction of and plea to Alexander. Narbazanes is on his knees, in a modest robe, unshaven, legs chained. For Talestris's arrival, the artist closely follows the text: "as soon as she [Talestris] saw the king, she dismounted while car-rying two lances in her hands" ("tantost qu'elle apercheut le roy descendy du cheval portant deux lances en ses mains," fol. 134). The artist is not afraid to show the alterity of the Amazons, with a small accommodation. Rather than

depicting the Amazons without the right breast, the artist chooses to represent their naked left leg.[49] In that he follows the text that explains how their
robes do not fall to the ground but stop at the knee, but he chooses specifically to render the left leg naked as a substitution for the ablated breast. The
text intends ablation of the breast as a military attribute rather than sexual
innuendo, but by choosing to show naked legs the artist manages to render
the military and the sexual in one.[50]

FIGURE 9.3. *Bagoas Pleads on Behalf of Narbazanes; Arrival of Talestris.* Master of the Jardin de Vertueuse Consolation, Lille and Bruges, ca. 1470–1475. Vasco da Lucena, *The Deeds of Alexander.* Los Angeles, J. Paul Getty Museum, Ms. Ludwig XV 8, fol. 133v. J. Paul Getty Museum is Open Source.

McKendrick identified three more manuscripts related to the Getty Ludwig XV 8: Cologny-Geneva, Fondation Martin Bodmer, Cod. Bodmer 53;
Jena, Thüringer Universitäts- und Landesbibliothek, Ms. El. f. 89; and Paris,
BnF, Ms. fr. 257. The four manuscripts of the set identified by McKendrick
were all painted in the circle of the Master of Margaret of York and are united
by the choice of illumination subject and the placement of the images.[51] But
for Book V, only one corresponds to the Getty Ludwig Ms. XV 8: Jena Ms. El.
f. 89. The Jena manuscript has half-page miniatures at the head of each of its
nine books. The miniature at the start of its Book V, on fol. 91, imitates compositionally the Getty Bagoé and Talestris miniature on fol. 133v. On the left
of the central column we see Narbazanes, disheveled, unshaven, in a modest
robe, holding out a purse of money as a pledge (Fig. 9.4). To the right of the
central column separating the image into two, Talestris has just arrived with
her entourage. The artist does not mark Talestris or her Amazons in any
special way, dressing them sumptuously but covering them completely. The
surprising thing about this image, unique to all the manuscripts that I have
consulted, is the artist's choice to show Bagoé as Bagoas: on Narbazanes's
right stands a young, well-dressed, and handsome man. This means that the
illuminator read the prologue—or had it read to him. He then chose to show
Bagoas as his historical gender, as a man, not in the least coinciding with the
in-text description of a "woman of singular beauty, at the peak of her youth"
(Jena Ms. El. f. 89, fol. 99).

While I see the Getty manuscript as enhancing the transgender potential
for readers of the prologue to Book V, because it makes visible Lucena's
transgendering translation—"I likewise transposed the character of Bagoé,
from a young man to a young woman"—the Jena miniature seems to widen
the gap between the text and paratext of Lucena's translation.[52] The gap is
so wide that it has in fact affected the ability of art historians to correctly
identify the image. McKendrick believes that the Jena miniature on fol. 91
corresponds to the opening miniature of Book V in the Getty Ludwig Ms.
XV 8 (fol. 123) and that it therefore shows Alexander and the niece of Artaxerxes III: "Even small details are repeated, such as the purse handed to the
niece of Artaxerxes (rather than the chest shown in the corresponding Getty
miniature)."[53] But the purse of money in Jena is identical to the purse in
one other of the four related manuscripts, Cologny-Geneva Ms. Bodmer 53.
Here, on fol. 82, the portrayal of Narbazanes is almost identical to Jena Ms.
El. f. 89, fol. 91; he is disheveled, unshaven, and holding out a purse of money
as a pledge. Cologny-Geneva Ms. Bodmer 53, fol. 82, thus helps us identify
the other male figure in Jena Ms. El. f. 89, fol. 91, as Bagoas.[54] Moreover, in
the Getty miniature on fol. 123, the niece of Artaxerxes is alone, without

anyone in her company, and certainly not in the company of a group of women, as is the case in the Jena manuscript. A recent catalogue entry of the Jena manuscript has taken McKendrick's misidentification even further, for it simply identifies Bagoas and Narbazanes as "zwei Männer," who are greeting the niece of Artaxerxes "mit vier Begleiterinnen steht" (standing with four

FIGURE 9.4. *Bagoas Pleads on Behalf of Narbazanes; Arrival of Talestris.* Bruges, ca. 1470–1480. Vasco da Lucena, *The Deeds of Alexander*. Jena, Thüringer Universitäts- und Landesbibliothek, Ms. El. f. 89, fol. 91. Courtesy of Friedrich Schiller University Jena.

companions), not recognizing that the group of women to the right of the central column are Amazons, and to the left of the image stands Bagoas, usually shown as Bagoé, with Narbazanes who is holding the purse of money.[55] Jena Ms. El. f. 89, fol. 91, is compositionally and thematically identical to the Getty Ludwig Ms. XV 8, fol. 133v, with one exception: Bagoé is Bagoas.

Writing a Transgender History

Writing a transgender history is an important set of stakes for a field as traditional as the history of the book. Illuminators working for the luxury book market created visual responses to the gaps revealed by transgender translation, and we must continue to pay closer attention to the interplay of text and image, or else misidentify, according to our gender-binary "norms," the characters that figure in the image. This is particularly important for studies of the northern European book market, well known for a close collaboration of scribes and illuminators in manuscript workshops; illuminators read or had read to them the text or summaries of the books that they were to illuminate.

Transgender history also changes our traditional notions of periodization. A continuity between the European medieval and humanist periods can be asserted: there is not much that distinguishes Lucena's transgendering translation from the transgender plot of the thirteenth-century *Roman de Silence*, for example, or Lucena's expression of shame and Dante's condemnation of Brunetto Latini. In his prologue to Book V, Lucena declares himself "incompetent" to describe in French the sexual behaviors of the ancients, and refuses to sully the French language. But this emergent morality is an attitude toward translation, not toward sexuality: the translator in his paratext acknowledges fully his method and intention, and the translation method forces him to highlight for his public the historical gender of Bagoas. By leaving in place what he does, Lucena hides neither what he did nor the historical truth of Alexander's sexual practices.

Humanism, then, constitutes not a rupture when the sexual binary, normativity, and morality emerged, but rather a period that highlights, because of the change in translation method that took place, the tension between fluidity and normativity (as we know it). If anything, humanism reveals one possible iteration of a transgender past; gender does not have to be faithful to its historical original; the power of words to change genders was augmented by the power of images as some illuminators exploited the gap between text and paratext. As other scholars have already shown, transgender history questions the nature of translation and the supposed (historical) necessity of the binary gender system. It is by exploring these gaps between text and paratext, and the ways in which translators and illuminators inhabit them and create spaces for gender plurality of the past, that we will continue to advance our understanding of translation studies and the history of the book, and alter the disciplinary divisions between periods that were erected by the very forces—nineteenth-century nationalist, philological, and moralist— that put in place the putatively transhistorical binary gender system and the necessity of gender conformity.

Notes

This work has been supported in part by the Research Cooperability Program of the Croatian Science Foundation funded by the European Union from the European Social Fund under the Operational Programme Efficient Human Resources 2014–2020, Project PZS—2019–02–1624—GLOHUM—Global Humanisms: New Perspectives on the Middle Ages (300–1600).

I am grateful to Charlotte Denoël, chief curator of Medieval Manuscripts at the Bibliothèque Nationale de France; Kathleen Doyle, lead curator of illuminated manuscripts at the British Library; and Elizabeth Morrison, senior curator of manuscripts at the J. Paul Getty Museum in Los Angeles, for their kind permissions to consult Vasco da Lucena's manuscripts in their respective collections.

I could not have completed this essay without the generous help of Hanno Wijsman, Elizabeth Morrison, and Anne D. Hedeman during the COVID-19 lockdown. I also wish to thank the editors of the volume, especially Greta LaFleur for her incisive questions and references and Anna Kłosowska for offering alternative frames and formulations.

1. The first folio of the General Prologue (folio iv; in modern foliation, it would have been placed between fols. 14v and 15), and the folios of the prologue to Book V (folio vii.xx.xiii; would have been placed between fols. 148v and 149) and Book IX (folios xiiii.xx.xv and xiiii.xx.xvi; would have been placed between fols. 278v and 279). The prologue to Book II is on folios 47v–48v; https://gallica.bnf.fr/ark:/12148/btv1b525081639 (last accessed April 30, 2020). Its original Roman foliation in red letters, discontinuous because of the cuts, stands in contrast to the modern (nineteenth-century) Arabic numeral refoliation of the manuscript, which is continuous. It underscores that the cuts occurred between the medieval date of production of Ms. 20311 and the date the manuscript entered the modern Bibliothèque Nationale de France collection.

2. See Roger S. Wieck, "Folia fugitiva: The Pursuit of the Illuminated Manuscript Leaf," *Journal of the Walters Art Gallery* 54 (1996): 233–54.

3. Thomas Kren and Scot McKendrick, *Illuminating the Renaissance: The Triumph of Flemish Manuscript Painting in Europe* (Los Angeles: J. Paul Getty Museum, 2003); Scot McKendrick, *The History of Alexander the Great: An Illuminated Manuscript of Vasco da Lucena's French Translation of the Ancient Text by Quintus Curtius Rufus* (Los Angeles: J. Paul Getty Museum, 1996); Scot McKendrick, "Illustrated Manuscripts of Vasco da Lucena's Translation of Curtius's *Historiae Alexandri Magni*: Nature Corrupted

by Fortune?," in *Medieval Manuscripts of the Latin Classics: Production and Use. Proceedings of the Seminar in the History of the Book to 1500 (Leiden, 1993)*, ed. Claudine Chavannes-Mazel and Margaret M. Smith (Los Altos Hills, CA: Anderson Lovelace, 1996), 131–49.

4. The four prologues would correspond to the lacunae in Quintus Curtius, according to McKendrick, *History of Alexander the Great*, 3.

5. All citations are from the ducal copy, Paris, BnF, Ms. fr. 22547, here fol. 3v; http://gallica.bnf.fr/ark:/12148/btv1b8449039t/f13.planchecontact. All translations from Middle French are mine.

6. McKendrick, *History of Alexander the Great*, 18.

7. In person: Paris, Bibliothèque nationale de France (BnF), Mss. fr. 47–49, Ms. fr. 257, Mss. fr. 708–11, Ms. fr. 6440, Ms. fr. 9738, Ms. fr. 20311, Ms. fr. 22547; London, British Library (BL), Royal 15 D IV, Royal 17. F I, Royal 20 C III, Burney 169; Los Angeles, J. Paul Getty Museum, Ms. Ludwig XV 8. Online: Geneva, Bibliothèque de Genève, Ms. fr. 76; Cologny-Geneva, Fondation Martin Bodmer, Cod. Bodmer 53; Jena, Thüringer Universitäts- und Landesbibliothek, Ms. El. f. 89; and partial online consultation of Oxford, Bodleian, Laud Misc 751.

8. On the basis of the example of Paris, BnF, Mss. fr. 708–11, it is possible to imagine censorship as a way of providing a continuous narrative without the interruptions of translator's prologues, which were not copied here.

9. My essay proposes the inverse of translating transgender experiences; see David Gramling and Aniruddha Dutta, introduction to *Translating Transgender*, a special issue of *TSQ: Transgender Studies Quarterly* 3 (2016): 333–56.

10. Mark D. Jordan, *The Invention of Sodomy in Christian Theology* (Chicago: University of Chicago Press, 1998).

11. Leah DeVun and Zeb Tortorici, "Trans, Time, and History," "Trans*Historicities," Special issue of *TSQ: Transgender Studies Quarterly* 5.4 (2018): 518–39.

12. Blake Gutt, "Medieval Trans Lives in Anamorphosis: Looking Back and Seeing Differently (Pregnant Men and Backward Birth)," *Medieval Feminist Forum* 55.1 (2019): 174–206; and Blake Gutt, "Transgender Genealogy in *Tristan de Nanteuil*," *Exemplaria* 30.2 (2018): 129–46.

13. Robert Mills, "Visibly Trans? Picturing Saint Eugenia in Medieval Art," "Trans*Historicities," special issue of *TSQ: Transgender Studies Quarterly* 5.4 (2018): 540–64.

14. Meghan Nestel, "A Space of Her Own: Genderfluidity and Negotiation in *The Life of Christina of Markyate*," *Medieval Feminist Forum* 55.1 (2019): 100–134.

15. See the introduction to this volume. I subscribe to general claims in Karma Lochrie's *Heterosyncracies: Female Sexuality When Normal Wasn't* (Minneapolis: University of Minnesota Press, 2005).

16. Emily Rose, "Keeping the Trans in Translation: Queering Early Modern Transgender Memoirs," *Translating Transgender*, special issue of *TSQ: Transgender Studies Quarterly* 3.3–4 (2016): 485–505, quotation at 488.

17. Arjo J. Vanderjagt, "Classical Learning and the Building of Power at the Fifteenth-Century Burgundian Court," in *Centres of Learning: Learning and Location in Pre-Modern Europe and the Near East*, ed. Jan Willem Drijvers and Alasdair A. MacDonald (Leiden: Brill, 1995), 267–77, quotation at 268.

18. Jacques Monfrin, "La connaissance de l'antiquité et le problème de l'humanisme en langue vulgaire dans la France du XVᵉ siècle," in *The Late Middle Ages and the Dawn of Humanism Outside of Italy: Proceedings of the International Conference, Louvain, May 11–13, 1970*, ed. M. G. Verbeke and Joseph Ijsewijn (Leuven: Leuven University Press, 1972), 131–70, quotations at 132, 161.

19. Elisabetta Barale, "'Le prologue du translateur' des *Éthiques* et des *Politiques* d'Aristote par Nicole Oresme (1370–1374)," 2013, *Corpus Eve*, https://journals.openedition.org/eve/634.

20. Zrinka Stahuljak, *Les fixeurs au Moyen Âge: Histoire et littérature connectées* (Paris: Éditions du Seuil, forthcoming 2021); and Zrinka Stahuljak, "Les langues du voyage: Le roman bourguignon et ses fixeurs méditerranéens," in *Écrire le voyage au temps des ducs de Bourgogne: Actes du colloque international organisé les 19 et 20 octobre 2017 à l'Université du Littoral—Côte d'Opale (Dunkerque)*, ed. Jean Devaux, Matthieu Marchal, and Alexandra Velissariou (Turnhout: Brepols, forthcoming 2021).

21. See https://www.bl.uk/catalogues/illuminatedmanuscripts/TourRoyalBegin.asp.

22. Leonardo Bruni, *De interpretatione recta*, ed. Charles le Blanc (Ottawa: Les Presses de l'Université d'Ottawa, 2008), 30. For the English translation, André Lefevere, ed., *Translation/History/Culture: A Sourcebook* (New York: Routledge, 1992), 82–86, quotation at 82.

23. Lefevere, *Translation/History/Culture*, 84; Bruni, *De interpretatione recta*, 44–46.

24. Lefevere, *Translation/History/Culture*, 85; Bruni, *De interpretatione recta*, 48.

25. Zrinka Stahuljak, *Bloodless Genealogies of the French Middle Ages: Translation, Kinship, and Metaphor* (Gainesville: University Press of Florida, 2005).

26. Lefevere, *Translation/History/Culture*, 84; Bruni, *De interpretatione recta*, 44.

27. Céline van Hoorebeeck, "La réception de l'humanisme dans les Pays-Bas bourguignons (XVᵉ–début XVIᵉ siècle): L'apport des bibliothèques privées," in *Matthias Corvin: Les bibliothèques princières et la genèse de l'état moderne*, ed. Jean-François Maillard, István Monok, and Donatella Nebbiai (Budapest: Országos Széchényi Könyvtár, 2009), 93–120; Monfrin, "La connaissance de l'antiquité."

28. See Hanno Wijsman, "Northern Renaissance? Burgundy and Netherlandish Art in Fifteenth-Century Europe," in *Renaissance? Perceptions of Continuity and Discontinuity in Europe, c. 1300–c. 1550*, ed. Alexander Lee, Pit Péporté, and Harry Schnitker (Leiden: Brill, 2010), 269–88; and Hanno Wijsman, "Bibliothèques princières entre Moyen Âge et humanisme: À propos des livres de Philippe le Bon et de Matthias Corvin et de l'interprétation du XVᵉ siècle," in Maillard, Monok, and Nebbiai, *Matthias Corvin*, 121–34. Both Italian and northern humanism should be distinguished from scholastic humanism, in Latin, which produced a systematic body of doctrine about God, mankind, society, and the universe and with it a large-scale unity of life and ideals; see R. W. Southern, *Scholastic Humanism and the Unification of Europe*, vol. 1, *Foundations* (Oxford: Blackwell, 1995).

29. Danielle Gallet-Guerne, *Vasque de Lucène et la Cyropédie à la cour de Bourgogne (1470): Le traité de Xénophon mis en français d'après la version latine du Pogge* (Geneva: Droz, 1974).

30. Van Hoorebeeck, "La réception de l'humanisme dans les Pays-Bas bourguignons."

31. Gallet-Guerne, *Vasque de Lucène et la Cyropédie*, 98.

32. Testimony by the Milanese ambassador Giovanni Pietro Panigarola, quoted in Scot McKendrick, "Charles the Bold and *Romuléon*: Reception, Loss, and Influence," in *Kunst und KulturTransfer zur Zeit Karls des Kühnen*, ed. Norberto Gramaccini and Marc Carel Schurr (Bern: Peter Lang, 2012), 59–84, quotation at 79.

33. We know that Leonardo Bruni was read at the court of Burgundy, in Jean Le Bègue's *La première guerre punique*, a translation of Bruni's *De bello punico*, a reconstitution of the second, missing decade of Titus Livy. Nicole Pons, "Leonardo Bruni, Jean Le Bègue et la cour: Échec d'une tentative d'humanisme à l'italienne," in *Humanisme et culture géographique au temps du concile de Constance autour de Guillaume Fillastre, actes de colloque* (Université de Reims, 1999), ed. D. Marcotte (Turnhout: Brepols, 2002), 95–105; James Hankins, "Translation Practice in the Renaissance: The Case of Leonardo Bruni," *Études classiques* 4 (1994): 154–75.

34. Copied in Italy and largely non-illuminated; McKendrick, *History of Alexander the Great*, 2, 9. Lucena's translation likewise became popular: thirty-five manuscripts survive, of which twenty-eight are illuminated.

35. Sandrine Hériché-Pradeau, "L'Alexandre de Vasque de Lucène: L'historicité en question," in *L'antiquité entre Moyen Âge et Renaissance*, ed. Chrystèle Blondeau and Marie Jacob (Paris: Presses Universitaires de Paris Ouest, 2011), 45–74. See also Catherine Gaullier-Bougassas, *Les romans d'Alexandre: Aux frontières de l'épique et du romanesque* (Paris: Honoré Champion, 1998).

36. Thomas de Kent, *Le roman d'Alexandre ou le roman de toute chevalerie*, trans. Catherine Gaullier-Bougassas and Laurence Harf-Lancner, ed. Brian Foster and Ian Short (Paris: Honoré Champion, 2003), Book III, 3793–94, my translation from Old French.

37. Jean Wauquelin, *Les faicts et les conquestes d'Alexandre le Grand*, ed. Sandrine Hériché (Geneva: Droz, 2000), 414; *The Medieval Romance of Alexander: Jehan Wauquelin's "The Deeds and Conquests of Alexander the Great*," trans. Nigel Bryant (Woodbridge: Boydell & Brewer, 2012), 222.

38. McKendrick, *History of Alexander the Great*, 5.

39. All three of the known translations by Vasco da Lucena, one into Portuguese and two into French, demonstrate the same concern with historical accuracy and decency. Gallet-Guerne, *Vasque de Lucène et la Cyropédie*, 11.

40. Rose, "Keeping the Trans in Translation," 496.

41. McKendrick, "Illustrated Manuscripts of Vasco da Lucena's Translation," 136.

42. Manuscripts vary, calling her Talestris or Calestris.

43. McKendrick, *Illuminating the Renaissance*, 227–29. The two images, fol. 128 and fol. 140v, show the events in Greece during Alexander's absence and a siege by the Macedonian army.

44. It does place large miniatures at the start of some, but not all, books: Books III–IV and VII–IX.

45. Paris, BnF, Ms. fr. 6440.

46. Zrinka Stahuljak, "D'Alexandre et de quelques Amazones: Portraits textuels et visuels," in *La femme sauvage dans les arts et les lettres*, ed. Christine Ferlampin Acher (Rennes: Presses Universitaires de Rennes, forthcoming 2021) 85–99.

47. McKendrick, *History of Alexander the Great*, 34, 62n4.

48. The second extra image in Book V (one-column miniature) is titled "Alexander Orders the Destruction of His Army's Excess Baggage," an often illustrated theme.

49. Compare this to a similar composition in BnF Ms. fr. 710, which comes out of the French tradition. Bagoé and Amazons are both in the composition, but the Amazons are represented in traditional female garb; http://gallica.bnf.fr/ark:/12148/btv1b10525303v/f1.planchecontact.

50. The Master of the Jardin de Vertueuse Consolation shows a higher level of interest in women than most illuminators, since altogether five miniatures portray women in this manuscript: in addition to Bagoas and Narbazanes with the Amazones (fol. 133v), we find Olympias, Alexander's mother (fol. 15); Sisigambis, Darius's mother (fol. 99); the niece of Antarxerxes (fol. 123; opens Book V); Bagoé and the execution of Orsines (fol. 226). All five are shown in motion, as figures with agency.

51. "The link among these four manuscripts is that they were probably based on a common pool of evolving visual models," McKendrick, *Illuminating the Renaissance*, 251; also McKendrick, *History of Alexander the Great*, 53.

52. Of the other, unrelated, manuscripts, BnF, Ms. fr. 710 (708–11) corresponds compositionally to the Getty Ludwig XV 8: Narbazanes and Bagoé, on their knees, plead for Alexander's pardon, while the Amazons approach on his right, but without any distinct traits mentioned in the text (fol. 8v). Another manuscript copied by Jan du Quesne but unrelated to his Getty manuscript shows Bagoé and Narbazanes without the Amazons (London, BL, Ms. Royal 17 F I, fol. 129v), as does a third manuscript (Paris, BnF, Ms. fr. 48, fol. 73v), by the Master of the Vienna Chroniques d'Angleterre (ca. 1470–1480).

53. McKendrick, *History of Alexander the Great*, 54; see http://www.getty.edu/art/collection/objects/1440/master-of-the-jardin-de-vertueuse-consolation-and-assistant-quintus-curtius-rufus-vasco-da-lucena-et-al-livre-des-fais-d%27alexandre-le-grant-french-and-flemish-about-1470-1475/.

54. See http://www.e-codices.unifr.ch/fr/list/one/fmb/cb-0053.

55. Joachim Ott with Hanno Wijsman, *Die Handschriften der Thüringer Universitäts- und Landesbibliothek Jena*, vol. 3, *Die mittelalterlichen französischen Handschriften der Electoralis-Gruppe; mittelalterliche Handschriften weiterer Signaturreihen (Abschluss)* (Wiesbaden: Harrassowitz Verlag, 2016), 68–74, quotation at 69.

PART III

Interventions
Critical Trans Methodologies

CHAPTER 10

Visualizing the Trans-Animal Body

The Hyena in Medieval Bestiaries

EMMA CAMPBELL

This essay critically examines transness in one
of the most significant Christian didactic traditions of the Middle Ages: the
bestiary. Works in this tradition offer moralized accounts of natural history; they comprise loosely organized groups of chapters in which various
animals, birds, and stones are described and interpreted in Christian terms.
Medieval bestiary texts ultimately derive from the Greek *Physiologus* (ten-
tatively dated to the second century CE), a work disseminated widely both
within and beyond Europe. In European contexts, late antique translations of
the Greek *Physiologus* into Latin gave rise to bestiary redactions in both Latin
and vernacular languages, notably French. The natural world depicted in the
Physiologus tradition reflects the capaciousness of God's creation, encompassing the ambiguity and even deviancy of creaturely life from a Christian
moral perspective as well as nature's reflections of the sublime. Nature as it
is represented in this tradition is therefore intentionally diverse, a diversity
that extends to these works' engagement with sex and gender.[1] Thus, despite
its temporal distance from today's understandings of sex and gender, the
medieval bestiary tradition offers an important resource for histories of gender and sexuality, including transgender histories. It also provides a means
of exploring the imbrication of animal studies, gender studies, and natural
history through a transgender prism. This essay focuses on the historical
representation of what some trans scholars refer to as "animal transex" or

"trans-animality": a form of transness that encompasses both gender and species, while demanding an analysis that also extends to sexuality, geopolitics, and race.[2] I consider the trans-animal body as part of the natural world described and allegorized in Latin and French bestiaries derived from the so-called "B-Isidore" version of the Latin *Physiologus*, a version dating from the tenth or eleventh century, which combined the late antique *Physiologus B* text with material from Isidore of Seville's *Etymologies*.[3] I concentrate most especially on how a selection of these works depicts the hyena: a creature thought to alternate between male and female sexes, or (in bestiary terms) "natures."

The hyena offers a particularly interesting point of connection between medieval engagements with the trans-animal body and more contemporary discussions of trans-animality. The medieval bestiary hyena was known for its alleged ability to switch between male and female embodiment: "There is an animal called the hyena, living in the tombs of the dead and eating their bodies. It is its nature that it is sometimes male, sometimes female, and for that reason it is an unclean animal." (Est animal quod dicitur hyaena in sepulcris mortuorum habitans, eorumque corpora vescens. Cuius natura est, ut aliquando masculus sit, aliquando femina, et ideo est immundum animal.)[4] This description of the hyena from the Latin Second Family Bestiary (ca. 1180) is embedded in a much longer history that attempts to make sense of this creature's apparent deviation from human sex and gender norms. That history stretches back at least as far as the sixth century BCE and forward to present-day discussions of the hyena as a creature that challenges binary conceptions of biological sex and gender in both scientific thinking and more popular cultural discourses. Medieval accounts of the hyena's ability to change its sex were based on textual tradition rather than observation. In drawing on earlier natural histories, these texts nonetheless pick up on an aspect of the hyena's physical makeup that continues to intrigue observers of these creatures today: the fact that the external genitalia of spotted hyenas are virtually identical in all members of the species. On the one hand, this physical particularity has made the hyena a focus of gender anxiety for those who see its body as a site where human binary gender categories are confused. On the other hand, that same body has, more recently, been positively valued as an encouragement to rethink binary conceptions of human sex and gender in both feminist and transgender studies.

The first section of this chapter briefly sketches out the longer history in which bestiary depictions of the hyena are situated and makes a case for a more comprehensive understanding of medieval bestiaries' place in that history. If the *Physiologus* has been rightly identified as the source of much of the negative symbolism subsequently associated with the hyena's sexed body, today's scholarly accounts of the tradition that flows from it are often reductive and homogenizing. Such accounts overstate the symbolic unity of the *Physiologus* tradition while overlooking its affirmation of transsex as a feature of the natural world it symbolically interprets. I argue that closer attention to the medieval bestiary tradition's treatment of the hyena not only counteracts overly simplistic historical accounts of this tradition's development but also opens up an important site from which to examine the complexities of premodern transgender formations.

My aim in so doing is not to reclaim the bestiary hyena as a positive figuration of premodern transgender or intersex embodiment. Rather, my focus is on how the multilayered mediation of this creature's supposed switching between male and female embodiment in medieval sources can be understood through a critical framework that trans studies makes possible. This bestiary creature shows how today's trans perspectives may be productively used to analyze moments where forms of sex and gender that challenge binary expectations feature in historical sources—even sources where such sex/gender formations are stigmatized and ideologically exploited in ways that are deeply distasteful. The second section of this chapter investigates the representation of the hyena's trans-animality in Latin and French bestiary texts and images. In all of the works examined, descriptions of the hyena's trans-animal body provide a substratum for a range of allegorical and moral interpretations that variously mobilize the anti-Semitic or misogynist associations of gender fluidity in medieval contexts. I consider the intricate forms of visibility to which this creature's trans-animality is subject in textual and pictorial examples, exploring how this visibility demands an approach that is attentive to the ways transness manifests itself indirectly as well as overtly, through accreted layers of bestiary representation and interpretation. This, I suggest, is an area of particularly fruitful intersection between medieval bestiary depictions and more contemporary approaches to queer and trans visibility. The troubling doubleness of the hyena's trans-animal body in these medieval sources is communicated not only through explicit forms of textual and visual description but also, more implicitly, in ways that circumvent straightforward representation. I show how the trans-animal body in these bestiary chapters endures as a literal and figural presence, irrespective of whether or not that body is represented with genital markers that make its ability to move between sexes visually explicit. The visibility of transness in these depictions requires ways of seeing that situate the hyena's nature within the particular constellation of meanings that accrue around it in any given bestiary text. In all of these respects, the optics of queer and trans visibility enable a more granular understanding of the gendering of animal bodies in medieval bestiaries. They help to foreground not only how transgender formations may be overwritten and manipulated in such sources but also how we can identify and analyze these formations through attending to the narratives and symbolic contexts that translate sex and gender in all their nonbinary complexity.

As I suggest in my conclusion, this approach to the premodern idea of nature in medieval bestiaries complements the work of transgender studies scholars by showing how modern and contemporary conceptions of "natural" sex and gender are embedded in longer cultural histories. Visualizing the trans-animal body of the hyena might, in this sense, additionally contribute to the enterprise of relativizing more contemporary visions of nature and their relationship to human gender systems in the era following the advent of modern science.

The Hyena: A Trans-Historical Overview

The hyena's association with nonbinary sex and gender has a long history, which will be summarized here only briefly. The idea that the creature alternated between male and female sexes probably originated in Aesopic lore (sixth century BCE), which suggested that this switching occurred annually.[5] In later centuries, the widespread acceptance of the hyena's sex-changing ability was challenged by Aristotle (fourth century BCE), who may have based his remarks on the observation of striped hyenas—a different species of the hyena family from the spotted hyena.[6] Refuting popular claims about the creature's alternation between male and female embodiment, Aristotle pointed out that the genitals of male and female hyenas were remarkably similar in structure.[7] Pliny the Elder (first century CE), referencing Aristotle, accordingly presented the hyena's supposed ability to change sex as popular hearsay.[8] Yet Aristotle's skepticism did not prevent other authorities from repeating the claim that the hyena changes sex, both in popular literature and in zoological treatises.[9] Aristotle's comments similarly had little impact on early Christian moralizers. The *Epistle of Barnabas* (first/second century CE) attributes the hyena's "uncleanness" (its unsuitability for consumption or sacrifice) to the creature's ability to change sex annually, combining this pronouncement with a condemnation of adultery and fornication.[10] Despite his misgivings about the legend, Clement of Alexandria (second–third century CE) also used the sex-changing hyena for the purposes of moral illustration, as a figure of instability and duplicity.[11] In the *Physiologus*, both the earlier Greek texts and the later Latin tradition claim that the hyena is an inedible animal regarded as unclean because of its switching between male and female "natures." These traditions, however, offer divergent interpretations of this characteristic. The Greek text, which may have been written shortly after the *Epistle of Barnabas* (second century CE?), makes the hyena's alternation between male and female natures the basis for a moral condemnation of male homosexuality based on apostolic authority (Romans 1:27).[12] By contrast, the late antique Latin *Physiologus* tradition associates the ambiguity of the hyena's nature with the religious indecision warned against by the Gospel of Matthew 6:24 and compares the hyena to Jews, who, it is claimed, first served God and then adored idols.[13]

Post-medieval writers continued to draw upon the hyena's earlier symbolism, while occasionally attempting to reconcile that symbolism with a more observational approach to the natural world. The creature's alleged ability to change its sex was once again called into question by the sixteenth-century Swiss professor Conrad Gessner, whose monumental *Historia animalium* (1551–1558) was further disseminated in the early seventeenth century in an edition and English translation by Edward Topsell.[14] Later seventeenth-century writers such as Sir Thomas Browne similarly dismissed the claim that hyenas (or any animals) possess both male and female natures, explaining this by reference to a "Law of their Coition" that determines the sexual position each creature adopts for copulation—a law that Browne claimed no species breaks, except humankind.[15] Such challenges to the view that hyenas change their sex were accompanied in later centuries by anatomical descriptions of the genitalia of spotted hyenas, a move that followed the identification and naming of species of hyena still recognized today.[16] Despite these more "scientific" descriptions of the creature, the negative associations of the hyena's supposed sexual instability persisted in European cultural discourses in other guises, inflecting the creature's post-medieval associations with social disorder and with sexual and racial otherness. For example, in the seventeenth and eighteenth centuries, the hyena became a metaphor for sexual disorder of a different kind: what Alan Bewell describes as "the cultural monstrosity known as the 'masculine' woman.'"[17] It also came to serve as a figure for other perceived threats to established social order among Europeans, standing for Eastern and African anarchy in the Romantic era and, from the late eighteenth century, for the unsettling alterity of new colonial environments as they were experienced by British colonizers.[18]

If the notion that the hyena alternates between male and female sexes is no longer current today, the trouble this creature causes for human sex/gender systems based on visible sexual difference has remained a source of fascination and potential unease in the present. The ways the spotted hyena confounds human binary expectations have continued to attract scientific attention and popular comment. Stephen Glickman points to the creature's "sexual ambiguity" as one of the historically significant elements ensuring the hyena's enduringly bad reputation.[19] He nonetheless emphasizes that, in contrast to the *Physiologus*'s regressive insistence on the hyena's supposedly unstable sexed body, more contemporary, scientifically informed work on the animal no longer treats its ambiguous sex as a moral concern.[20]

Modern representations of the hyena in both scientific and popular contexts nonetheless continue to be enthralled by—and occasionally anxious about—its sexual particularity. Anna Wilson has linked such responses to a more pointed discomfort with the way the female hyena is thought to deviate from human sex and gender norms.[21] Wilson argues that the fact both male and female hyenas "appear to have a penis" associates the creature with a gender "aberration" that is specifically female.[22] The female hyena's troubling of normative conceptions of gender is, Wilson emphasizes, both physical and behavioral: "The quintessential deviance of female appropriation of power is eloquently displayed both by the female hyena's deformed phallicized body and by the manifestly abhorrent behaviors of which, whether as cub or as adult, she is capable."[23] In contrast to Glickman, Wilson contends that the new methodologies and sites of hyena study in the early 2000s produced knowledges about this creature that reiterated patterns of thinking also discernible in earlier depictions of the hyena as a dangerous sex changer. Wilson makes a persuasive case for seeing scientific studies of hyena colonies as a continuation of more traditional representations of this creature dating back to antiquity. Though such studies might have moved away from seeing the hyena as a dangerous, unknowable other and toward a position that enabled the creature to be scientifically examined and understood, she points out that "the new science, almost despite itself, deploys the hyena as a warning of the consequences of deviation from sex/gender norms."[24] Instead, Wilson claims, the spotted hyena should encourage scientists to expand their thinking beyond binary conceptions of gender or unitary models for understanding gendered behavior. For the purposes of her own argument, however, the hyena is an incarnation of a type of phallic femininity that remains residually attached to a binary conception of the sexed body, rather than being a figure of intersex or transgender.[25]

Deployments of the hyena by trans scholars, activists, and artists offer a different vantage on the issues addressed in Wilson's argument. In the 1990s, queer reinterpretations of transsexuality sometimes used the hyena's apparent deviance from binary conceptions of sex and gender as an encouragement to rethink those conceptions in humans. For instance, Kate Bornstein's

Gender Outlaw: On Men, Women, and the Rest of Us (1994) mentions the female hyena in an argument that dismantles popular definitions of human maleness and femaleness, which depend either on genitals or on the supposedly "male" and "female" hormones, testosterone and estrogen. The fact that female hyenas have higher levels of testosterone than males and a kind of external vagina or clitoris resembling a penis is used to reinforce Bornstein's point "that the universal key to gender is not hormones."[26] Monika Treut's film *Gendernauts: A Journey through Shifting Identities* (1999) uses the hyena for comparable purposes. As a prelude to its examination of the lives of transgender and intersex individuals living in San Francisco, Treut's documentary opens with a sequence that draws attention to the way the hyena eliminates the human opposition of male and female.[27] The illustrative function of the hyena in these works anticipates some of the points made subsequently by scholars working within what has been termed trans-animal or tranimal studies.[28] Scholars working in this area have argued forcefully for seeing transgender as a feature of a wide variety of nonhuman organisms, a feature that calls into question the anthropocentric and transphobic idea that transness is deviant or "unnatural" when viewed from a human, biological perspective.[29] Such scholarship challenges the supposed biological inevitability of human gender binaries and simultaneously uses transness as a means of exploring the complexity of gender definitions situated between human sex/gender systems and the gendering of animals. The hyena sometimes makes an appearance in this scholarly work too. For instance, Joan Roughgarden's influential survey of sex and gender diversity in nonhuman species analyzes the spotted hyena as an example of intersex in mammals, or what she terms "intersexed plumbing."[30] Once again, the hyena in Roughgarden's argument serves to illustrate a broader point about the limitations of human gender categories: among vertebrates, from fish to mammals, binary distinctions in gamete size (which distinguish male and female in biological terms) do not translate into binary body types.[31]

Seen as part of this chronology, then, premodern descriptions of the hyena are a perfect example of "trans-historicity": they acknowledge the presence of transness in nature, albeit in a manner that fails to align with more positive contemporary assessments of the hyena's nonbinary body.[32] I am not seeking here to contest or smooth over the problematic aspects of the hyena's depiction in medieval bestiaries. There are clearly significant and troubling divergences between medieval representations of this creature and its more recent reclamations. I would nevertheless like to offer a more nuanced picture of how the bestiary tradition deals with the hyena's purported switching between male and female embodiment and to draw out what I take to be its broader significance for transgender histories and approaches. As it stands, large parts of this chronology remain unexamined or poorly understood. In today's accounts of the history of reflection on the hyena, the *Physiologus* tradition—if it features at all—primarily serves to introduce new, negative associations for the creature's supposed sexual deviance. Glickman's historical survey of depictions of the hyena is emblematic of this tendency. Glickman attributes the first negative judgments of the hyena to the *Physiologus* tradition and proposes a largely static symbolism for the creature covering the period from the second to the sixteenth century: "Early in the Christian era and continuing through the middle ages, two themes emerged: that hyenas changed sex from year to year—a morally unacceptable practice—and that they preyed upon human corpses, digging up graves. The former was linked metaphorically to the Jews and reflected the anti-semitism of this extended period, while the latter was threatening to many human traditions and persists to the present day."[33] Discussions of the *Physiologus* tradition's treatment of the hyena thus tend to homogenize an extraordinarily complex tradition. In treating the medieval bestiary as a discursive and symbolic unity, such discussions adopt an approach that has been largely abandoned in medieval scholarship on these texts.[34] They also glance over what, from a trans perspective, constitutes one of the more interesting aspects of the *Physiologus*'s insistence on the hyena's double nature, namely, *contra* Aristotle, the affirmation of transsex as a feature of the natural world.

Reclamations of the hyena as a figure of trans and nonbinary interest have understandably focused on the creature itself rather than on its more negative representation in natural histories and pre-Enlightenment scientific literature. The present essay seeks to demonstrate how premodern representations of the hyena may be examined in a way that complements the important work of transgender studies scholars by showing how our contemporary ideas of what constitutes "natural" sex and gender are themselves part of longer cultural histories. I am not, then, seeking to reclaim the bestiary hyena as an affirmative historical example of transness. Instead, I examine how this creature is, from a medieval perspective, a figure of naturally occurring sexual deviancy. The hyena exemplifies the understanding of nature in the *Physiologus* tradition as potentially aberrant as well as potentially ideal, as both meaningful and in need of interpretation. Bestiary representations thus constitute an important site from which to consider how transgender formations become visible within historical cultural discourses about nonbinary bodies, as well as through more direct forms of scientific observation. They also present us with an alternative perspective on "natural" sex and gender that may be placed in productive tension with certain conceptions of gender and of nature today.

Thick Description and Trans Visibility in Bestiary Texts

Bestiary hyenas share at least one important characteristic with their more contemporary counterparts: a nonbinary body that is a contested site for the production of meaning. This body is somewhat unusual even by bestiary standards. The hyena's double nature might be considered to echo that of hybrid creatures featured in the bestiaries, such as the siren (half woman, half fish or bird) or the centaur (half man, half ass); unlike these bestiary hybrids, however, the hyena crosses between sexes rather than species. Moreover, textual descriptions suggest the hyena metamorphoses, rather than combining within a single body the physical characteristics of creatures usually thought of as distinct—a depiction of metamorphosis that is rare in bestiary texts. Though these medieval depictions of the hyena do not explicitly encourage a rethinking of human sex/gender formations, they nonetheless affirm the nonbinary nature of the hyena's sexed body and emphasize its symbolic significance.

In so doing, bestiaries raise the question of how transness figures in these sources, in both textual and visual terms, and how we do justice to this figuration in approaching these texts today. The trans-animal body's visibility in such contexts is an area where the perspectives generated by medieval bestiaries productively intersect with the insights of queer and trans scholarship. Visibility has long been a subject of discussion in such scholarship precisely because of the problem of epistemic blindness that renders queer and transgender individuals effectively invisible in cultures structured along the lines of a binary gender order.[35] "Passing" as a cisgender, heterosexual man or woman in such contexts can be a relief or a desired aim, but may also involve the ambivalent occlusion of the individual's specific history and/or their inadvertent complicity with the existing binary gender regime. Rendering queer and transgender formations visible within dominant cultural discourses is therefore politically valuable, insofar as it offers opportunities for expanding and modifying the vocabulary and grammar of gender within those discourses. As Eveline Kilian puts it, "For queer and transgender to unfold their subversive potential they must find, or create, a space for articulation, and articulation is closely connected to visibility."[36] The flip side of the dynamic Kilian describes is the development of ways of seeing queer and transgender not only in new cultural discourses that seek to represent them as such but also within prevailing cultural discourses from which they might otherwise appear to be excluded. Such a project—in line with the theorizing of queer and trans visibility—involves modes of reading that focus not only on explicit articulations of sex and gender but also on the particular narratives in which sex and gender are embedded and through which they are translated. The bestiaries are a case in point.

A thick description of sex and gender along these lines—an attention, in other words, not only to their literal or face value presentation but also to their connections to particular contexts and histories—offers a productive way of considering the various figurations of the bestiary hyena's transanimal body. The problem for the reader of the bestiary today is not simply how we might go about "seeing" transness in or through established binary conceptions of sex and gender; this problem is also connected to the way the hyena's sexed body is used figuratively in bestiary moralizations that might appear to obscure transgender or nonbinary gender formations still further, by translating them into meanings that appear to have little to do with the sexed body per se. Yet if the hyena's sexed body gives rise to multiple interpretations, it remains present as the literal touchstone for the meanings it generates. It also inflects those interpretations in ways that exploit the anti-Semitic or misogynist associations of gender fluidity in medieval contexts. Bestiary depictions thus demand the kind of intersectional approach to trans-animality called for by Mel Y. Chen, who stresses the importance of sexuality, geopolitics, and race in more contemporary analyses of the transness of animality.[37] What I am proposing is not therefore a comfortable or politically enabling form of trans visibility such as that advocated for by Kilian. Instead, what I suggest the bestiary hyena offers us is a way of using trans perspectives to uncover and deconstruct those moments when nonbinary sex and gender or transgender feature in historical sources, as well as exposing the ways in which such sex/gender formations are exploited to particular—sometimes deeply unsavory—ideological ends.

Bestiary chapters in the B-Isidore tradition illustrate how the hyena's nature and the figurative meanings attributed to it are superimposed in a way that explains, while not erasing, the texts' literal representation of the transness of this creature. The hyena's sexed body in these works is located within a constellation of figurative meanings connected to the creature's double nature. This multiplication of meaning is quite typical of bestiary texts, which understand the natural world and the creatures that inhabit it analogically, through the so-called "senses" of biblical commentary used by medieval theologians and preachers. These include the literal and/or historical senses, the allegorical sense, the tropological (moral) sense, and the anagogic (spiritual or eschatological) sense. Any given bestiary chapter extrapolates some of these figural senses from a description of the creature (the literal or historical sense), though not necessarily all of them, and not necessarily in sequence. The figural senses frequently draw upon the literal sense in a variety of different ways, meaning that bestiary creatures and their (literal) behaviors and properties are associated with multiple symbolic values. Thus, early versions of the Latin B-Isidore text (tenth/eleventh century) begin by describing the hyena's alternation between male and female.[38] On the basis of this literal description of the creature's double nature, the text goes on to outline the allegorical meaning: like the hyena, the children of Israel switched from serving the living God to worshipping idols and indulging in riches and riotous living. To this is added a further, moral meaning (the tropological sense): those who are neither faithful nor unfaithful are also like the hyena. The hyena's double nature is thus singled out for negative comment while anchoring other, figurative meanings. The beast's literal vacillation between male and female comes, by association, to stand for more generalized forms of inconstancy that apply in the first instance to the Israelites and, by extension, to Christian readers who risk jeopardizing their souls.[39]

Later Latin bestiaries similarly demonstrate how the hyena's trans-animality is translated literally and figuratively in ways that identify the text's negative valuation of transness with anti-Semitic as well as moral messages. These versions elaborate upon the literal description of the beast found in the earlier B-Isidore text. For example, the Second Family Bestiary—a twelfth-century Latin redaction that reshapes and reorders B-Isidore—claims that, as well as moving between male and female natures, the hyena lives in the tombs of the dead and feeds on human corpses. The beast's other characteristics include a rigid spine, its nocturnal circling of sheepfolds and human domestic spaces, and its ability to imitate human voices and vomiting in order to lure men and dogs to their deaths.[40] The literal description in this later redaction thus connects the hyena's troubling of the supposed boundary between male and female natures with other forms of boundary crossing between the living and the dead, domestic and wild, human and animal. As in the earlier B-Isidore tradition, the allegorical meaning attached to the literal description of the creature connects this "unclean" boundary crossing to the children of Israel, and the tropological sense converts this allegory into a moral lesson for the Christian reader, who is advised not to emulate such double-mindedness and inconstancy. The trans-animality of the hyena in this later redaction is therefore apparent in multiple ways: not only as a property of the creature's nonbinary body and the figurative meanings associated with that body but also as a disruption of other binaries evoked in the literal description of its behavioral characteristics.

French bestiary authors who drew their material from the B-Isidore tradition further demonstrate how the hyena's trans-animal body is seen through multiple, subtly divergent translations of that body. I limit my comments here to two bestiaries written in England almost a century apart: Philippe de Thaon's *Bestiaire* (ca. 1121–1135) and Guillaume le Clerc's *Bestiaire divin* (ca. 1210/1211).[41] These two versions both rework Latin B-Isidore models, though to different effect. The interest of these versions is, in part, that they show how vernacular bestiary authors reshape their material in ways that can introduce important differences in emphasis. The fact that both texts are written in French verse rather than prose means that the degree of creative license used by these writers is much greater than that found in some other French bestiaries.[42] Another reason for focusing on these vernacular versions is that they are transmitted in illuminated copies, which enable a consideration of the visibility of the trans-animal in visual as well as textual registers, a feature of these texts that I discuss in greater detail in the final section of my argument.

The earliest bestiary written in French by Philippe de Thaon is an important example of the divergent readings that the hyena's nature sometimes produces in the vernacular development of the *Physiologus* tradition. Philippe's source was probably an early twelfth-century variant of the B-Isidore bestiary redaction, incorporating structural elements from the *Dicta Chrysostomi*.[43] His text attaches the hyena's putative sexual transformation neither to a condemnation of homosexuality (as in the Greek prototype) nor to Jewish fickleness (as in the Latin B-Isidore). Rather, Philippe's *Bestiaire* presents the creature's apparent switching between sexes as analogous to the improper adoption of female characteristics among his implicitly male target audience.[44] The opening of the chapter follows the Latin B-Isidore quite closely: Philippe claims that the hyena is a fierce creature that must not be eaten, before quoting from Jeremiah 12:8, "my inheritance is become to me as a hyena in its den" (*Bestiaire* 1177–88).[45] According to the author of the *Physiologus*, Philippe continues, the hyena is both male and female ("male e femele est," *Bestiaire* 1191) and thus considered unclean. Philippe then bypasses the allegorical meaning associating the hyena with the children of Israel and moves straight to the tropological meaning, which associates avarice, covetousness, and lecherousness with the hyena's sexual dynamism (*Bestiaire* 1193–96). Though the reference to Jeremiah might obliquely conjure up the Jewish rejection of Christ, this is not the focus of Philippe's bestiary moralization. The tropological significance identified with the hyena's osten-sible sexual transformation is in fact more misogynist than anti-Semitic: man should be stable by nature, Philippe claims, but is like a woman when he is covetous (*Bestiaire* 1197–1208). The connection in the Latin B-Isidore between the hyena's double nature and the potential doubleness and inconstancy of the male Christian reader is thus drawn out more clearly in Philippe's text, which omits other details in order to use the creature's supposed sexual transformation as the basis for a moralization focused on female (rather than Jewish) inconstancy.

In contrast to Philippe's focus on gendered bodies and behaviors, Guil-laume le Clerc's thirteenth-century *Bestiaire divin* ties the instability of the hyena's sexed body more closely to the creature's transgressive appetite while using the trans-animal as the impetus for figurative interpretations that are both misogynist and anti-Semitic. The opening of Guillaume's chapter emphasizes the hyena's association with the eating of human corpses, a char-acteristic that confirms the creature's uncleanness (*Bestiaire divin* 1580–88). In mentioning the hyena's sex changing, Guillaume again recalls that it fre-quents graves before marveling at its strange ability to change its appearance or coat ("son vestement," *Bestiaire divin.* 1599–1606)—a formulation that, in drawing on a sartorial metaphor, may already anticipate the allegorical identification of the hyena with Jews.[46] In the subsequent moralization, Guil-laume accordingly associates the feminization of Jews with their excessive lifestyle and diet, tendencies that he claims led them to abandon God and worship idols (*Bestiaire divin* 1607–18). He then suggests the hyena signifies unreliable people in general, who are neither male nor female but double and untrustworthy (*Bestiaire divin* 1619–42).

Guillaume's text thus preserves the connection between the hyena's ability to change its sex and Jewish fickleness while subtly shifting the rela-tionship between these elements in the Latin versions already examined. In Guillaume's allegory, as in his description of the hyena, the movement from male to female embodiment is inseparable from transgressive appe-tite: Jews became female "quant il furent suef norri / e as delices adenti, / a la char e a la luxure" (when they were well nourished and overcome / tamed by delights, by flesh, and by lechery; *Bestiaire divin* 1613–15). Guillaume's phrasing conflates sexual appetite (notably the cardinal sin of lust, or lech-ery) with desire for other kinds of pleasure, including food; at the same time, the satisfaction of such appetites is used as the basis for likening Jews to the corpse-devouring hyena. Such unclean nourishment links Jews not only to the hyena's sex changing, by effeminizing them, but also to the creature's ani-mality. This dehumanizing gesture is implied by Guillaume's choice of the verb *adenter* to describe Jews' feminizing submission to their appetites, a term that evokes the breaking or taming of animals as well as the experience of being overcome.[47] In Guillaume's symbolically dense rendering, then, Jews' purported effeminacy, fickleness, animality, and rejection of Christ emerge from appetites analogous to those of the hyena. This association is carried over into the tropological significance Guillaume attaches to the creature, which identifies the hyena with those duplicitous in word and deed. Neither male nor female in their double-dealing, such people, Guillaume maintains, want to serve more than one master while being faithful to neither (*Bestiaire divin* 1621–34). The doubleness of the hyena's nature is here connected to a different kind of desire, one that similarly runs counter to the Gospel's teaching that God and Mammon cannot be served simultaneously and that, in this instance, implies identification with Jews as well as with the trans-animal. Guillaume's reworking of his source thus knits the hyena's putative sexual instability more closely to its transgressive appetite while still using its trans-animal body as a crucial element—if not the foundation—for each of the figurative interpretations.

Comparison of different texts within the *Physiologus* tradition—even those within the same branch of that tradition—thus paints a more nuanced picture of the medieval bestiary hyena than that which emerges from accounts like Glickman's. Although, as we have seen, there is a large degree of consistency in the bestiaries' depiction and interpretation of the hyena's sexually dynamic nature, that nature does not have a single symbolic value; bestiary authors describe the creature in subtly different ways and place different emphases on the allegorical and moral meanings associated with its trans-animal body. Equally important for the argument I am making here is the fact that the bestiaries' interpretations of the hyena's trans-animality do not replace the literal description of the creature's nature with its associated allegorical meanings. If the French and Latin bestiarists just examined present the figurative significance of the hyena's trans-animal nature in divergent ways, that nature remains a crucial substrate connecting different layers of description and meaning. This is because bestiary chapters are constructed according to a principle of accumulation rather than substitution—a principle that underpins these works' demonstration of the richness of meaning in the created world. In this sense, what a thick description of sex and gender in chapters on the hyena reveals is how the trans-animal body persists as a literal and, sometimes, as a figural presence, regardless of whether or not that body is identified with visible genital markers. The visibility of transness here requires modes of reading that locate the hyena within the particular constellation of interpretations to which its double nature gives rise, a constellation that varies depending on the bestiary text in which it features.

Visualizing the Trans-Animal Body in Bestiary Images

The question of how we see transness within the cluster of meanings generated by bestiary chapters on the hyena poses itself in a different way when it comes to the visual images accompanying the texts. The focus on the animal in bestiary illuminations is itself historically significant: the bestiaries are among the first works to place animal subjects at the center of the image rather than using them for peripheral decoration.[48] Nevertheless, bestiary illuminations, like the chapters themselves, are less concerned with observational realism than with conventional modes of representation. The aim of bestiary images is not to provide an image of the material world drawn from life but to make the Christian symbolism of the natural world more legible to readers. In this respect, such images are not, strictly speaking, illustrations: they are neither drawn from life nor illustrations of the letter of the text they accompany. Rather, bestiary illuminations interpret, synthesize, and embellish the text. Illuminators sometimes draw attention to particular senses of interpretation in depicting animal subjects or, in some instances, encourage multidimensional modes of reading that connect the text's literal and figurative interpretations.[49] The animal in bestiary images thus often participates in the analogical thinking already observed in connection with the texts. The trans-animal body of the hyena in manuscript illuminations likewise needs to be viewed in this context.

Visual images of the hyena often draw on the bestiary chapter's literal sense, combining a depiction of the animal with characteristics included in the textual description.[50] The hyena's animal body is the focus of all of these illuminations, though its sex changing is figured in more or less overt ways. In the B-Isidore tradition, some early manuscripts represent the hyena with a forked outgrowth emerging from its mouth (e.g., London, British Library, Stowe MS 1067, fol. 3r), a visual reference to the metaphorical doubleness of its tongue in *Physiologus* as well as the doubleness of its nature.[51] In later versions, narrative images of the hyena—that is, images representing the creature in a descriptive context, as opposed to offering a portrait of it in isolation—usually represent its habit of feeding on human corpses, most often showing the beast violating a sepulchre or devouring a dead body.[52] Some of these narrative images additionally depict the hyena's switching between male and female as a kind of intersex embodiment, reinforcing the beast's association with Jews by representing it with a circumcised penis.

The intersex representation of the hyena in illuminations can be observed in several Second Family manuscripts. Aberdeen, University Library, MS 24 and Oxford, Bodleian Library, MS Ashmole 1511, two luxury manuscripts executed in the Second Family Bestiary's earliest production period (1180–1250), represent the hyena with a circumcised penis as well as a vaginal opening under its tail (figure 10.1).

A family of so-called "Transitional" bestiaries which all share textual and pictorial features with one another also show the hyena with penis and vaginal opening: New York, Morgan Library & Museum, MS M. 81 (ca. 1185); St. Petersburg, National Library of Russia, MS Lat. Q.v.V.1 (ca. 1180–1185); London, British Library, Royal MS 12 C. xix (ca. 1200–1210) (figure 10.2); and Los Angeles, J. Paul Getty Museum, MS 100 (ca. 1250–1260) (figure 10.3).[53] The elaborate belt circling the hyena's midsection in this group of Transitional bestiary images might additionally allude to the creature's doubleness by dividing its body in two.

The intersex depiction of the hyena in some Latin manuscripts appears to be a means of communicating the mobility of the creature's sexed body.

FIGURE 10.1.   The hyena attacking a corpse. The Ashmole Bestiary (Oxford, Bodleian Library, MS Ashmole 1511, fol. 17v). Photo Bodleian Libraries.

FIGURE 10.2. The hyena attacking a corpse. London, British Library, Royal MS 12 C. xix, fol. 11v. © The British Library Board.

FIGURE 10.3. The hyena attacking a corpse. The Northumberland Bestiary (Los Angeles, J. Paul Getty Museum, MS 100, fol. 12v). Digital image courtesy of the Getty's Open Content Program.

The hyena's circumcised penis encourages a multilayered reading that connects the literal and allegorical senses of the beast's nature, reinforcing the notion that what is depicted here is sexual mobility, glossed in the textual description as Jewish inconstancy. Indeed, critics have often drawn attention to images where the hyena's genitals are emphasized by illuminators in order to spotlight the anti-Semitic readings evoked by such images. Making a persuasive case for viewing images of the hyena in terms of widespread anti-Semitic sentiment in the twelfth and thirteenth centuries, Debra Strickland ventures that hyena images featuring prominent genitalia could be interpreted in light of contemporary accusations of illicit sexual relations between Jews and Christians.[54] Focusing on the image of the hyena in the Aberdeen Bestiary (Aberdeen UL, MS 24, fol. 11v), Jeffrey Cohen similarly proposes that the animal's strangeness is underscored by its depiction with an enlarged, anally positioned vagina and a circumcised penis, physical features that associate the creature with Jewish racial and sexual alterity.[55] What this suggests is that the hyena's genitals not only make its trans-animality visible in these illuminations but also connect that visibility to the legibility of its body as Jewish as well as nonbinary. The trans-animal body here is inseparable from its anti-Semitic interpretation, being identified with the ambiguously gendered, sexually threatening body of the Jew in medieval Christian thinking.

What a trans approach encourages us to consider is how the trans-animal body may appear in bestiary images that do not privilege the genital marking of sex, as well as those that do. As explained earlier, queer and trans perspectives highlight the complex ways in which sex and gender may be articulated indirectly, as well as overtly, requiring what I refer to in my readings of bestiary chapters as a thick description of sex/gender formations. Such an approach can also be applied to more conventional images of the hyena, which show the creature without visible genitalia, eating, attacking, or unearthing human corpses or body parts. This depiction of the hyena's body is in keeping with the representation of other bestiary creatures: most bestiary animals are depicted without genital markers. Yet this portrayal of the body does not necessarily amount to an absence of sex or gender. The hyena's trans-animality is equally, if differently, apparent in such illuminations. Indeed, images of the hyena without visible genitalia arguably allow for greater emphasis on the creature's vacillation between male and female natures by omitting any visible markers of its sex. In this sense, what is euphemized in images that do not explicitly feature the hyena's genitalia may be less the hyena's ambiguously sexed body than the Jewish associations of the creature's double nature. From this perspective, then, the question is less whether the hyena's body is genitally marked and more how the trans-animal body, which provides the focus for all of these images, is contexualized.

Philippe's *Bestiaire* presents a depiction of the sexually marked trans-animal that contrasts with the sexualized, anti-Semitic Latin images just mentioned. The Merton College copy of Philippe's text is one of just two illustrated manuscripts transmitting this work.[56] Like the early B-Isidore bestiary in Stowe MS 1067, this copy of Philippe's text features a portrait depiction of the hyena with penis and testicles (figure 10.4);[57] the beast is depicted in profile, without reference to any narrative or background elements.[58]

As mentioned earlier, Philippe's text omits the anti-Semitic allegory and focuses instead on a moral interpretation that encourages male readers to shun the inconstancy that, it is claimed, is typical of women. In this instance, then, although the image concentrates on the hyena's male body, that body is not designated as Jewish. Indeed, the genital markers in this image would appear to reinforce the message communicated in Philippe's moralization: the male reader, like the hyena, should cultivate properly male characteristics, even if his nature may threaten to switch the other way. The hyena thus figures the inherent fragility of male Christian identity in this text: if the trans-animal is gendered male in this image, its double nature means it is, by definition, only temporarily so.

In illuminations of Guillaume's *Bestiaire divin*, the hyena's trans-animality is most often seen in relation to its appetite for human corpses. These, mostly narrative, images conform to a common depiction of the hyena also seen in Latin manuscripts, while reinforcing the more explicit emphasis on the hyena's unclean appetite already noted in Guillaume's text. Three examples, each representing a variation on a theme, give a flavor of the imagery included alongside the chapter: in London, British Library, Cotton MS Vespasian A. VII, the hyena stands over a human body wrapped in a white shroud (fol. 15ra); in Paris, Bibliothèque Nationale de France, MS français 1444, the

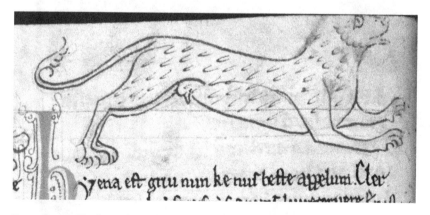

FIGURE 10.4. The hyena in profile. Philippe de Thaon's *Bestiaire* (Oxford, Merton College Library, MS 249, fol. 5v). Image courtesy of The Warden and Fellows of Merton College Oxford.

hyena runs about with a human head in its mouth (fol. 247v) (figure 10.5); and in Bibliothèque Nationale de France, MS français 14970, a dark-gray hyena with long ears is shown lurking in a cemetery (fol. 14rb).

While representing its body without genital markers, these examples all gesture at the hyena's changeable sex by associating its body with the violation of other types of boundary crossing. In one manuscript, Cambridge, Fitzwilliam Museum, MS 20 (1323), the doubleness of the hyena's nature is alluded to through the duplication of the (genitally unmarked) animal body. This codex depicts two hyenas facing in opposite directions while feeding on human heads (fol. 56ra) (figure 10.6), a doubling that also has the effect of repeating the focus on the creature's appetite.[59]

An especially complex articulation of the hyena's trans-animality in the pictorial tradition associated with Guillaume's bestiary may be seen in Paris, Bibliothèque Nationale de France, MS français 14969 (ca. 1265–1270), an Anglo-Norman manuscript believed to have been executed at St. Albans in a workshop that specialized in pictorial commentaries for other types of work, such as apocalypses.[60] BNF, MS fr. 14969 is one of only two *Bestiaire divin* manuscripts depicting the figurative or moral meanings of bestiary creatures as well as the creatures themselves, thereby introducing new iconography as well as drawing on earlier pictorial models.[61] The image program in this

FIGURE 10.5. The hyena in profile with a human head in its mouth. Guillaume Le Clerc's *Bestiaire divin* (Paris, Bibliothèque Nationale de France, MS français 1444, fol. 247v).

FIGURE 10.6. The hyena/two hyenas feeding on human heads. Guillaume Le Clerc's *Bestiaire divin* (Cambridge, Fitzwilliam Museum, MS 20, fol. 56ra). © Fitzwilliam Museum, Cambridge.

manuscript includes both allegorical and narrative illustrations for the creatures analyzed in the text; these illustrations usually invert the order of the literal and figurative descriptions in the text, placing the allegory first and the narrative illustration of the literal sense second. The allegorical illustration that introduces the chapter on the hyena in this manuscript splits into two, the top half representing the "good" Old Testament patriarchs led by Moses experiencing the vision of the burning bush and the bottom half depicting "bad" Jews worshipping the Golden Calf (fol. 29v) (figure 10.7A).[62]

The pendant image of the hyena on the next folio depicts it facing left, like the idolatrous Jews in the previous image; the creature is represented stepping over a disembodied human head to devour a male corpse (fol. 30r) (figure 10.7B). The body of the hyena represented in the image thus marks the end of the chapter, while that same body, as described in the text, provides the chapter's starting point. The trans-animal body comes into being here as part of a circular process of reading whereby the pendant image showing the hyena appears as the culmination of the textual (and visual) interpretations that make it meaningful.

C il reinemt e empert la trace
k ar il ne sec ne ne uert mie
p us ke il entre en seinte uie
d une troue il les fruz œus
c ome io dis ainz espirueus
f ei · pacience · humblire
c onciuence · e benignite
c harite · e ioie · e pes
j oie: Ke ne faudra iames
e deu k y de ioie est seignur
n us meinv a la ioie greignur
k y ne fine ne nest inuable
a mz dure tuz iurz pdurable
Ce est le sarmun del hyenne

FIGURE 10.7A. The chapter on the hyena with images showing the allegory. Guillaume Le Clerc's *Bestiaire divin* (Paris, Bibliothèque Nationale de France, MS français 14969, fol. 29v).

Ore ad adure e aretraire
Ensamples de bestiaire
Ki sunt de bestes e de oiseals
Profitables e bons e beals
Sor li tures k gt il enseigne
E n quele guise li mals remeigne
E la ueie ke deu tenir
E il k y a deu uodra uenir
E bestiare nul rewrde
D e une beste maluerse e orde
K i ad num hyenne engregeil
N e la sai nomer en franceil
a) el la ley de uie e defenir
K e lem ne la manguit nenir
N e chose ke li seit semblable
K ar ele nest mie couenable
K ar ele est cure maluerse e orz
K ar ele mangue les morz
E en lleur sepultures habite
U reskiz ceus deuore e afoibre
a k y ele pot auenir
p ur ce seu fait mut ben a tenir
d e ceste beste issi haire
d ist li propheres ieremie
l a fosse al hyaine sauuage
c e est dut il mun heritage
u ne peire porte en sun oyl
c este beste dure dire il uoil
k y desuz sa lange la re—ndreir
l em dit ke il deuinerent
l es choses ke auenir sunt
d es auentures de cest mund ·Ce est la
hyenne·

Moreover, the unsettling doubleness of the hyena's body is communicated not only through textual and visual description but also in ways that bypass direct representation. The image of the hyena on folio 30r is painted onto a ruptured folio that was stitched back together prior to the writing of the text, which is oriented around the stitching. The creature's body is consequently traversed by a visible seam in the parchment that cuts across its midsection. Medieval parchment was a material produced from specially prepared animal skins (usually those of calves, sheep, or goats). Sarah Kay has proposed that ruptured or perforated parchment in bestiary texts may produce moments when the distinction between textual content and its medium of transmission is suspended, with uncanny effect.[63] As she points out, this image offers an example of precisely such a parallel between textual content and parchment page by graphically calling attention to the hyena's double nature.[64] As well as splitting the hyena in two, the ruptured skin of this folio evokes other boundary crossings with which this creature is identified, most notably its violation of the boundary between living and dead, and between man and animal.[65] The wound in the parchment echoes the tearing of human flesh in the miniature itself, mirroring the harm inflicted by the hyena on the human corpse as the animal goes to devour it. The association of the hyena with Jews—an association that is all too clear in the allegorical image as well as in Guillaume's text—adds a further dimension to this gesture, which conjures the common medieval association of Jews with the "dead" letter of scripture. Yet even as it draws attention to the rupturing of flesh in the image, the stitching of this folio reverses the destructive gesture that satisfies the hyena's appetite. This repaired parchment is a reminder that the manuscript transmitting the text reestablishes the correct hierarchy of man and beast violated by the hyena, both as a book made by humans from slaughtered animals and as a text that instructs human beings to curb their animal appetites and cultivate a properly Christian attention to the spirit of the text.

The images examined here represent the trans-animal body in ways that draw differently on visible genital markers. The doubleness of the hyena's sex is emphasized explicitly in some illuminations through the intersex representation of the beast in some Latin manuscripts. In the Merton College copy of Philippe's text, the hyena's body is genitally marked as male in the image, although that same body, read in conjunction with the moralization, signifies in ways that encourage a more mobile conception of the animal's sexed body. In other images that omit genital markers altogether, the ambiguity of the creature's nature and the challenge that nature poses to binary thinking are communicated in less overt, though equally potent, ways. In images of this kind, the hyena's trans-animality may be communicated through the association of its body with other kinds of boundary crossing, through the duplication of its body within the image, or even by the ruptured parchment on which its body is painted. In all cases, illuminations contribute to a trans visibility that operates in conjunction with the textual descriptions and interpretations. These images, seen in terms of a thick description of sex and gender in the manuscripts that transmit them, offer ways of viewing transness as part of the cluster of interpretations that make the hyena meaningful in bestiary terms.

The Trans-Animal Body as Natural Aberration

I have argued that the bestiaries' depictions of the hyena, in contending with the creature's supposed ability to move between male and female natures, offer an uncomfortable but significant source for thinking about how transness before transgender is conceptualized through the animal body in premodern sources. This tradition affirms that transsex is part of the created world: the hyena's literal switching between male and female embodiment is precisely what makes this creature significant in figurative terms. Yet, in all their manifestations, bestiary hyenas offer negatively marked interpretations of transness, interpretations that combine transphobic, anti-Semitic, and misogynist positions. This tendency arguably makes it all the more important to examine the intricacies of how the hyena is figured in this medieval tradition. Being alert to the differences between depictions of the hyena in bestiary texts not only helps to counter the homogenizing tendencies of more contemporary historical chronologies but also, more importantly for transgender histories, exposes the ways transness was variously appropriated, maligned, and racialized in one of the most influential cultural discourses of the Middle Ages.

The engagement with the hyena's putative ability to change its sex on the part of bestiary authors and illuminators raises the important question of how we go about reading and interpreting these textual and visual figurations of transness today. I have proposed that in responding to this question, medievalists can usefully draw on queer and trans perspectives, which emphasize that sex/gender formations perceived as non-normative are often subject to complex forms of articulation and visibility within dominant cultural discourses. Seeing transness in the medieval bestiary tradition—a cultural discourse that often relies on overtly hostile presentations of fluid or nonbinary sex/gender formations—involves attending to manifestations of transness that may be more or less explicit. My analysis of the hyena illustrates how a thick description of sex and gender captures a range of ways in which trans visibility functions in the bestiaries, as well as how it varies across different texts in this tradition.[66]

Visualizing the trans-animal body of the hyena in this way is not a straightforward retrieval of an affirmative kind of trans embodiment. Rather it is an attempt to think "trans-historically" in one of the senses this collection encourages, by confronting and working with the tensions inherent in excavating a transgender past from medieval sources.[67] This approach offers a more nuanced picture of the bestiary tradition's place in the longer cultural history of the hyena—a creature with an enduring relevance to those interested in rethinking human sex/gender binaries today. In this respect, bringing the multifaceted trans-animality of the bestiary hyena more clearly into focus might enable this creature to take its place in a history of the natural world that complements the important work of trans scholars on animal transsex or trans-animality. If the medieval hyena's nonbinary nature does not fit with more inclusive arguments about sexual and gender diversity among nonhuman creatures, the bestiaries nonetheless open up sites of resistance within cultural narratives that presume the timelessness and universality of human concepts of nature, as well as concepts of sex and gender. In this regard, it is worth highlighting the fact that the hyena's supposed deviance, seen from a medieval point of view, is not identical with the notions of deviance sometimes mobilized in today's discussions of "natural" or "unnatural" sex and gender norms—notions that, as noted earlier, scholars in trans studies have vehemently challenged. Nature in these texts is potentially transgressive by definition, which is precisely why didactic works such as the bestiaries are required to intervene in disciplining the human natures of their intended audiences. Thus, if we look beyond the constellation of meanings that accrue around the hyena's trans-animal body, the bestiaries also encourage us to see how "nature" is subject to historically contingent and multilayered forms of visibility, even when that visibility is framed in terms of more objective, scientific observation. Visualizing the trans-animal body of the bestiary hyena is also an encouragement to relativize today's post-Enlightenment vision of the natural world and its reflection (or otherwise) of human sex/gender systems by situating that vision within a much longer, more complicated history.

Notes

I would like to thank Debra Strickland and Blake Gutt for their generous comments on an earlier draft of this essay. My thanks also go to the editors of this volume for encouraging me to write this piece in the first place and for invaluable suggestions on improving it. My research on the French bestiaries discussed in this article was supported by an award from the Arts and Humanities Research Council.

1. Debra Strickland [Hassig], "Sex in the Bestiaries," in *The Mark of the Beast*, ed. Debra Strickland [Hassig] (New York: Routledge, 2000), 71–97.

2. See, e.g. Myra J. Hird, "Animal Transex," *Australian Feminist Studies* 21.49 (2006): 35–50; Mel Y. Chen, "Animals without Genitals: Race and Transsubstantiation," *Women and Performance: A Journal of Feminist Theory* 20.3 (2010): 285–97.

3. The oldest manuscript transmitting the B-Isidore version is Rome, Biblioteca Apostolica Vaticana, MS Palatinus Latinus 1074, which is dated to the tenth or eleventh century.

4. Willene B. Clark, *A Medieval Book of Beasts: The Second-Family Bestiary. Commentary, Art, Text and Translation* (Woodbridge: Boydell, 2006), 131. Latin text and English translations for the Second Family Bestiary are taken from this edition.

5. Babrius and Phaedrus, *Fables*, trans. Ben Edwin Perry, Loeb Classical Library 436 (Cambridge, MA: Harvard University Press, 1965), 470, nos. 242–43.

6. There are four species in the hyena family. Aristotle's descriptions of the hyena suggest he was commenting on the striped hyena, whereas the rumors he was refuting probably originated with the spotted hyena. Stephen E. Glickman, "The Spotted Hyena from Aristotle to *The Lion King*: Reputation Is Everything," *Social Research* 62.3 (1995): 501–37, esp. 508–11.

7. Aristotle, *Historia animalium* 6.32; Aristotle, *On the Generation of Animals* 3.6; Florence McCulloch, *Mediaeval Latin and French Bestiaries* (Chapel Hill: University of North Carolina Press, 1962), 131.

8. Pliny the Elder, *Natural History*, vol. 3, *Books 8–11*, trans. H. Rackham, Loeb Classical Library 353 (Cambridge, MA: Harvard University Press, 1940), 76–77, bk. 8, nos. 105–6.

9. For example, Ovid (first century CE) used the story in *The Metamorphoses*, and the natural historian Aelian (second–third century CE) accepted it as fact. Ovid, *The Metamorphoses* 15.391–417; Aelian, *On the Characteristics of Animals*, vol. 1, *Books 1–5*, trans. A. F. Scholfield, Loeb Classical Library 446 (Cambridge, MA: Harvard University Press, 1958), 44–45, bk. 1, no. 25.

10. *The Epistle of Barnabas*, trans. J. B. Lightfoot 10.7, http://www.earlychristian writings.com/text/barnabas-lightfoot.html.

11. Clement of Alexandria, *Paedagogus*, 2.10.83 (see 85 for Clement's skepticism). John Boswell presents these developments as part of the history of Christian condemnation of homosexuality in *Christianity, Social Tolerance, and Homosexuality: Gay People in Western Europe from the Beginning of the Christian Era to the Fourteenth Century* (Chicago: University of Chicago Press, 1980), 137–41.

12. *Physiologos: Le bestiaire des bestiaires*, ed. and trans. Arnaud Zucker (Grenoble: Jérôme Millon, 2005), 163.

13. See, for example, *Physiologus Latinus: Éditions préliminaires versio B*, ed. Francis J. Carmody (Paris: Droz, 1939), 34. On this point, see also *Physiologos*, ed. and trans. Zucker, 165; McCulloch, *Medieval Latin and French Bestiaries*, 131; Debra Strickland [Hassig], *Medieval Bestiaries: Text, Image, Ideology* (Cambridge: Cambridge University Press, 1995), 145–47.

14. Conrad Gessner [Conradi Gesneri], *Historia animalium*, 4 vols. (Zurich: C. Froschauer, 1551–1558); Edward Topsell, *The History of Four-Footed Beasts and Serpents*, 2 vols. (London: William Jaggard, 1607–1608).

15. Sir Thomas Browne, *Pseudodoxia Epidemica*, in *The Works of Sir Thomas Browne*, ed. Charles Sayle, 2 vols. (London: Grant Richards, 1904), 2:40–41, quotation at 41. Browne's work first appeared in 1646. Sayle's edition is based on the sixth edition, published in 1672. See Project Gutenberg, https://www.gutenberg.org/files/39961/39961-h/39961-h.htm#CHAPTER_XVII_PE_III.

16. For a fuller account of the development of scientific literature on the hyena, see Glickman, "Spotted Hyena from Aristotle to *The Lion King*," 518–23.

17. Alan Bewell, "Hyena Trouble," *Studies in Romanticism* 53.3 (2014): 369–97, quotation at 372.

18. Bewell, "Hyena Trouble," 375–84.

19. Glickman, "Spotted Hyena from Aristotle to *The Lion King*," 508.

20. Ibid., 528.

21. Anna Wilson, "Sexing the Hyena: Intraspecies Readings of the Female Phallus," *Signs* 28.3 (2003): 755–90.

22. Ibid., 756.

23. Ibid., 785.

24. Ibid., 757.

25. Ibid., 782–85, esp. 783n51.

26. Kate Bornstein, *Gender Outlaw: On Men, Women, and the Rest of Us* (New York: Routledge, 1994), 56. For a critique of the research into hormonal influences on hyena morphology and behavior, see Wilson, "Sexing the Hyena," 766–79.

27. See also Patrick Boucher, "Le cri de la hyène: Trans, cybermedia et post-pornographie," *Rue Descartes* 79 (2013): 16–28.

28. The second *Transgender Studies Reader* includes a section titled "Transsexing Humanimality," which showcases key examples of work that had emerged in this field since the publication of the first collection in 2006. Susan Stryker and Aren Z. Aizura, eds., *The Transgender Studies Reader 2* (New York: Routledge, 2013). See also the *TSQ: Transgender Studies Quarterly* special issue "Tranimalities," 2.2 (2015).

29. Joan Roughgarden, *Evolution's Rainbow: Diversity, Gender, and Sexuality in Nature and People*, 10th ed. (Berkeley: University of California Press, 2013); Bailey Kier, "Interdependent Ecological Transsex: Notes on Re/production, "Transgender" Fish, and the Management of Populations, Species, and Resources," *Women and Performance: A Journal of Feminist Theory* 20.3 (2010): 299–319; Hird, "Animal Transex"; Chen, "Animals without Genitals".

30. Roughgarden, *Evolution's Rainbow*, 47.

31. Gamete size nonetheless continues to be evoked to support binary conceptions of "male" and "female." On the recent invocation of gamete size by TERFs (trans-exclusionary radical feminists), see this Twitter thread by Julia Serano: https://twitter.com/JuliaSerano/status/1135937130197209088. I am grateful to Blake Gutt for pointing me toward this discussion.

32. On "trans-historicity," see Stryker and Aizura, *Transgender Studies Reader 2*, 317–18; and Leah DeVun and Zeb Tortorici, "Trans, Time, and History," *TSQ: Transgender Studies Quarterly* 5.4 (2018): 518–39, esp. 522–24.

33. Glickman, "Spotted Hyena from Aristotle to *The Lion King*," 527–28 (see also 515–18). Boswell saw the *Physiologus* tradition as a hugely influential justification of prejudice against homosexuality—one that included sexual inferences about various animals, including the hyena. Boswell, *Christianity, Social Tolerance, and Homosexuality*,

141–43. Wilson speaks about the *Physiologus* as if it were a single text and proposes that it "lodges the sex-changing claim in the Western lexicon of hyenic meaning"; Wilson, "Sexing the Hyena," 760. Bewell distinguishes the bestiaries from the *Physiologus*, but somewhat misleadingly claims that "medieval bestiaries . . . routinely cast the hyena as a creature of insatiable lust and gluttony for unclean things, satisfying its appetites with a gross cross-sexing"; Bewell, "Hyena Trouble," 372.

34. Ron Baxter gives an account of this shift in *Bestiaries and Their Users in the Middle Ages* (Stroud, Gloucestershire: Sutton Publishing/Courtauld Institute, 1998), 1–28.

35. The intelligibility of queer lives and bodies has been a persistent topic in Judith Butler's work, where visibility is often tied to livability; see, for example, *Gender Trouble: Feminism and the Subversion of Identity* (New York: Routledge, 1990) and *Bodies That Matter: On the Discursive Limits of "Sex"* (New York: Routledge, 1993). Queer visibility has also been influentially explored in Eve Kosofsky Sedgwick, *Epistemology of the Closet*, 2nd ed. (Berkeley: University of California Press, 2008). Key examples of the literature on trans visibility include Sandy Stone, "The Empire Strikes Back: A Posttranssexual Manifesto," *Camera Obscura* 10.2 (1992): 150–76; Harold Garfinkel, "Passing and the Managed Achievement of Sex Status in an 'Intersexed' Person," in *The Transgender Studies Reader*, ed. Susan Stryker and Stephen Whittle (New York: Routledge, 2006), 58–93; Nan Alamilla Boyd, "Bodies in Motion: Lesbian and Transsexual Histories," in *A Queer World: The Center for Lesbian and Gay Studies Reader*, ed. Martin Duberman (New York: NYU Press, 1997), 134–52; Jamison Green, "Look! No, Don't! The Visibility Dilemma for Transsexual Men," in Stryker and Whittle, *Transgender Studies Reader*, 499–508. The visibility of transness in medieval sources has been garnering increasing attention. See, for example, Robert Mills, *Seeing Sodomy in the Middle Ages* (Chicago: University of Chicago Press, 2015), 81–132; Robert Mills, "Visibly Trans? Picturing Saint Eugenia in Medieval Art," *TSQ: Transgender Studies Quarterly* 5.4 (2018): 540–64; Blake Gutt, "Medieval Trans Lives in Anamorphosis: Looking Back and Seeing Differently (Pregnant Men and Backward Birth)," *Medieval Feminist Forum: A Journal of Gender and Sexuality* 55.1 (2019): 174–206; Dorothy Kim and M. W. Bychowski, "Visions of Medieval Trans Feminism: An Introduction," *Medieval Feminist Forum: A Journal of Gender and Sexuality* 55.1 (2019): 6–41, esp. 6–8.

36. Eveline Kilian, "Claiming Space: Transgender Visibility in the Arts," in *Transgender Experience: Place, Ethnicity, and Visibility*, ed. Chantal Zabus and David Coad (New York: Routledge, 2013), 85–100, quotation at 85–86.

37. Chen, "Animals without Genitals."

38. Luigina Morini, ed. and trans., *Bestiari medievali* (Turin: Giulio Einaudi, 1996), 44. The oldest manuscript transmitting this version is Vatican MS Pal. Lat. 1074 (tenth/eleventh century), an unillustrated Continental bestiary. The earliest English copy is contained in Oxford, Bodleian Library, MS Laud Miscellaneous 247 (ca. 1120–1150). See also Sarah Kay, *Animal Skins and the Reading Self in Medieval Latin and French Bestiaries* (Chicago: University of Chicago Press, 2017), 158; Morini, *Bestiari medievali*, 8; Baxter, *Bestiaries and Their Users*, 83. For an account of the development of this chapter in the early Latin tradition (the Y and B versions of the *Physiologus*), see Andreas Krass, "The Hyena's Cave: *Jeremiah* 12.9 in Premodern Bestiaries," *Interfaces* 5 (2018): 111–28, esp. 118–19.

39. In the *Dicta Chrysostomi* (another medieval redaction derived from *Physiologus B*), the allegorical meaning is connected to the hyena while the moral meaning is related to another transsex creature, the coot; Krass, "Hyena's Cave," 119–20.

40. These details are added from Solinus's *Collectanea*. They are also found in Pliny's account. Clark, *Medieval Book of Beasts*, 131n73.

41. Morini, *Bestiari medievali*, 112–285; Philippe de Thaon, *Bestiaire (MS BL Cotton Nero A. V)*, ed. Ian Short (Oxford: Anglo-Norman Text Society, 2018). Both of these editions share the same line numbering. Short's edition is a single manuscript edition; Morini's edition is more interventionist and does not list variants or rejected readings. Quotations and references unless otherwise indicated are from Short's edition. Guillaume le Clerc, *Le Bestiaire: Das Thierbuch des Normannischen Dichters Guillaume le Clerc zum ersten male vollständig nach den Handschriften von London, Paris und Berlin*, ed. Robert Reinsch (1890; repr., Whitefish, MT: Kessinger Publishing, n.d.). Quotations are from this edition. All translations from Old French are my own.

42. For instance, Pierre de Beauvais's bestiary is a relatively close translation of a B-Isidore model in French prose. Pierre's *Bestiaire* exists in two versions, only the first of which can be securely attributed to him: the Short Version (before 1218, possibly 1180–1206) and the Long Version (1246–1268), which incorporates the chapters from the Short Version into a much longer compilation. Only one of the manuscripts of the Short Version is illuminated.

43. Sarah Kay, "'The English Bestiary,' the Continental '*Physiologus*' and the Intersections between Them," *Medium Ævum*, 85.1 (2016): 118–42, esp. 128–32.

44. The *Bestiaire* is dedicated to at least one if not two queens: the prologue in London, British Library, Cotton Nero MS A. V. dedicates the work to Adeliza ("Aliz") of Louvain, second wife of Henry I of England; in Oxford, Merton College Library, MS 249, "Aliz" is changed to "Alienor," Henry II's queen. Nevertheless, the implied audience here is male—a feature of the work that would fit with its use as a memory book for novices.

45. This biblical quotation from the book of Jeremiah appears only in the Greek Septuagint; the reference to the hyena is in fact a distortion of the original Hebrew text. The reference may have made its way into the *Physiologus* tradition from Clement of Alexandria. See *Physiologos*, ed. and trans. Zucker, 165; Krass, "Hyena's Cave," 116–17.

46. Guillaume's poem predates by four or five years Pope Innocent III's decree that Jews be distinguishable from Christians by their dress, a decree issued following the Fourth Lateran Council of 1215. The allusion to the switching of clothing may nonetheless reflect the concerns about Jews and Muslims passing as Christians that gave rise to this decree, and which were fostered by the increasing contact among these populations within Christian Europe. The concerns articulated in canon 68 focused on the impossibility in certain provinces of differentiating Christian and non-Christian populations, leading to inadvertent and spiritually dangerous sexual relations between Christians and Jews or so-called "Saracens." Strickland [Hassig], *Medieval Bestiaries*, 147–48; Debra Higgs Strickland, "The Jews, Leviticus, and the Unclean in Medieval English Bestiaries," in *Beyond the Yellow Badge: Anti-Judaism and Antisemitism in Medieval and Early Modern Visual Culture*, ed. M. B. Merback (Leiden: Brill, 2008), 203–32, esp. 210; Nicholas Vincent, "Two Papal Letters on the Wearing of the Jewish Badge, 1221 and 1229," *Jewish Historical Studies* 34 (1994–1996): 209–24.

47. See the entry under "adanter" in the *Anglo-Norman Dictionary*, http://www. anglo-norman.net.

48. Michel Pastoureau, *Bestiaires du Moyen Âge* (Paris: Seuil, 2011), 38.

49. Strickland [Hassig], *Medieval Bestiaries*, 8–16 and 18; Pastoureau, *Bestiaires du Moyen Âge*, 39–42.

50. See my explanation of the layering of literal and figurative senses in bestiary chapters earlier in this essay, in the section "Thick Description and Trans Visibility in Bestiary Texts".

51. Kay, *Animal Skins*, 70 and 57 (fig. 5).

52. Strickland [Hassig], *Medieval Bestiaries*, 146. In bestiaries derived from the *Dicta Chrysostomi* version, the pictorial tradition includes images of two hyenas embracing. See Kay, *Animal Skins*, 70–71 and 72 (fig. 8); and Krass, "Hyena's Cave," 125.

53. Strickland [Hassig] mentions the St. Petersburg and British Library images: *Medieval Bestiaries*, figs. 151 and 152. I am grateful to Debra Strickland for discussion of other images in personal correspondence.

54. Strickland [Hassig], *Medieval Bestiaries*, 152; Strickland [Hassig], *Mark of the Beast*, 74–75.

55. Jeffrey Jerome Cohen, "Inventing with Animals in the Middle Ages," in *Engaging with Nature: Essays on the Natural World in Medieval and Early Modern Europe*, ed. Barbara A. Hanawalt and Lisa J. Kiser (Notre Dame, IN: University of Notre Dame Press, 2008), 39–62, esp. 46–48.

56. The Copenhagen manuscript transmitting Philippe's text (ca. 1300) represents the hyena as part of a narrative image that adds an association with cemeteries that is absent from Philippe's description. The beast in this illumination stands before a structure that could represent either a church or an entrance to a cemetery, holding what appears to be a spine in its mouth (Copenhagen, Kongelige Bibliotek, GKS 3466 8°, fol. 34r).

57. Though it lacks the elaborate tongue (and wings) of the hyena in Stowe MS 1067, the Merton illustration is otherwise very similar to that image. Most beasts in Merton MS 249 are represented without visible genitals. Of those creatures that are represented with a penis, the hyena's genitals are more clearly depicted than those of other beasts. Five other animals have a protuberance in the genital area that might represent a penis or testicles; the onocentaur (also on folio 5v) has three such protuberances, which look more like teats though are probably intended to represent a penis and testicles; https://digital.bodleian.ox.ac.uk/inquire/p/38f16924-e29d-4a8d-ab33-982db9db3b35.

58. On portrait images in other bestiary texts see Strickland [Hassig], *Medieval Bestiaries*, 10.

59. The codex was illuminated by a single artist known as the Ghent master. See the Fitzwilliam Museum's online record for this manuscript, "Miscellany," (2020) https://collection.beta.fitz.ms/id/object/169648 (accessed February 21, 2021). This image might be compared with that in a later, Latin bestiary (ca. 1450)—The Hague, Museum Meermanno, MS MMW 10 B 25 (fol. 7v)—where two hyenas also appear in the same frame.

60. Henri Omont, in collaboration with C. Couderc, *Bibliothèque nationale catalogue général des manuscrits français: Ancien supplément français III (n° 13091 à 15369*

du fonds français) (Paris: Ernest Leroux, 1896), 292; Paul Meyer, "Les Plus Anciens Lapidaires français," *Romania* 38.149 (1909): 44–70, esp. 54; Xénia Muratova, "Les miniatures du manuscrit fr. 14969 de la Bibliothèque nationale de Paris (le Bestiaire de Guillaume le Clerc) et la tradition iconographique franciscaine," *Marche romane* 28 (1978): 17–25; Strickland [Hassig], *Medieval Bestiaries*, 12.

61. Paris, Bibliothèque Nationale de France, MS français 24428 (ca. 1270) appears to contain two separate images representing the hyena and the moralization of its nature; the first of these may be misplaced, as it appears above a rubric announcing the chapter on the beaver. This manuscript, like BNF, MS fr. 14969, represents a hyena eating a corpse in the left-hand section of the image and Jews turning away from God on the right (fol. 64v). The second miniature on the next folio is almost identical to the first in its composition but replaces the Jews with an unidentified group of three haloed figures worshipping an idol (fol. 65r). This second image—which may have been the result of an illuminator's attempt to recover from an error in the placement of the previous image—appears to indicate that the moralization applies to Christians as well as Jews.

62. On the positioning of the Jews in this image, see Michael Camille, *The Gothic Idol: Ideology and Image-Making in Medieval Art* (Cambridge: Cambridge University Press, 1989), 166; and Strickland [Hassig], *Medieval Bestiaries*, 150–51. On the conversion imagery, see Strickland, "Jews, Leviticus, and the Unclean," 210 and 230n99.

63. Kay, *Animal Skins*, 4–7; and Sarah Kay, "Surface and Symptom on a Bestiary Page: Orifices on Folios 61v–62r of Cambridge, Fitzwilliam Museum, MS 20," *Exemplaria* 26.2–3 (2014): 127–47.

64. Kay, *Animal Skins*, 72–73.

65. On the illuminations in this manuscript, see Muratova, "Les miniatures du manuscrit fr. 14969," who suggests that moralized illuminations return to an older tradition of *Physiologus* illumination. Strickland proposes that the placing of the allegorical image first, before the depiction of the creature itself, may reflect a privileging of theological truths over the animal stories from which they are derived; Strickland [Hassig], *Medieval Bestiaries*, 151.

66. On "thick description," see my earlier discussion, in the section "Thick Description and Trans Visibility in Bestiary Texts."

67. See the introduction to this volume. This approach also chimes with other historical work in trans studies, for example, "Trans*Historicities," the special issue of *TSQ: Transgender Studies Quarterly* 5.4 (2018).

CHAPTER 11

Maimed Limbs and Biosalvation

Rehabilitation Politics in "Piers Plowman"

MICAH JAMES GOODRICH

> How is one to understand the relation of members
> and limbs to questions of gender and sexuality?
>
> —Susan Stryker and Nikki Sullivan, "King's Member,
> Queen's Body"

In the fourteenth-century allegorical dream vision *Piers Plowman*, bodies are measured according to their capacity to be productive members of a salvific collective. The poem confronts the idea of a productive body through the apparatus of salvation: to be productive is to be a "healthy" *member* of a social whole. As a medieval institution, salvation was a health-making regime, one that saw Christ's bodily suffering as an expression of spiritual redemption. *Piers Plowman* explores this paradoxical promise that bodily pain leads to spiritual health and everlasting life with Christ through the image of maimed and unmaimed bodies.

This essay considers *Piers Plowman*'s discussion of debilitated bodies and maimed limbs to critique bodily integration into a social and salvific community. I argue that when the poem focuses on broken, maimed, absent, or dismembered limbs, it links what a body can *do* to what a body *is*, and this formulation asks us to consider the limits of a system of salvation that associates spiritually *doing well* with the idealization of physically *being well*. I refer to this formulation as *biosalvation*, a technology of both harm and rehabilitation. Etymologically, salvation has its root in the Latin *salvare*, to save, heal, make safe, and preserve.[1] The work of medieval biosalvation required that some bodies be unable to work for their life's needs in order to be recipients of Christian charity. Since salvation required some bodies to be debilitated in order to be redeemed, *Piers Plowman* reveals the power of salvation to be a mediator of life, both corporeal and spiritual, earthly and divine. While some members of a Christian community were allowed refuge in anchoritic life or were part of a social elite, others were targeted for what Lauren Berlant calls "slow death."[2] As I will show in this essay, a "slow death" within a medieval salvific schematic meant that some bodies were meant to be immiserated so that others could respond with charity and thus secure their own salvation at the expense of the disenfranchised. The rehabilitation politics of the poem suggests that some bodies required maiming in order for the social body to function, for charity to work, and for the inequity of bodily physiology to reify the social politics that it represents.

Since *Piers Plowman* contemplates the legibility of debilitated bodies and their capacity to be productive members of a spiritual and social collective, transgender and disability studies offer a critical perspective to consider what kind of social collective gets to decide the authenticity of an individual body's capacity.[3] This essay puts transgender and disability studies in conversation with medieval legal theory and literature to illustrate how bodily mutilation and alteration are both created and repudiated by institutional powers.[4] Because maiming challenges the right to sovereignty over one's body, *Piers Plowman*'s meditation on the "authenticity" of maimed limbs anticipates modern legal and medical tyranny over transgender health and embodiment.

Piers Plowman challenges the work of salvation as a medieval institution since the "health" of an individual soul is contingent on the "health" of the social body of which it is a part. When the Dreamer meets Holy Church, the personification of the institutional church, he drops to his knees in supplication and asks how he might save his soul ("How Y may saue my soule," C.1.79).[5] As the first figure that the Dreamer encounters, the poem establishes Holy Church, and her representation as the Church of Christ, as the premier authority on salvation. In order to assist the Dreamer's search for the answer on how to save his soul, Holy Church advises him to remember that measure, or temperance, is medicine ("mesure is medecyne," C.1.33), that truth is the best ("treuthe is the beste," C.1.202), and that love is the remedy of life and relief of all pain ("loue is leche of lyf and lysse of alle payne," C.1.199). Through encounters with various personifications (such as Reason and Need), the Dreamer learns that some bodies, like the poor or the debilitated, are required to employ "mesure" for their medicine (forgoing basic necessities of life), while the wealthy can ensure salvation by showing those bodies charity.

Biosalvation relies on regulatory technologies that form, transform, and reform bodies in the present to secure salvation after death. This essay argues that the depiction of "fake" and "authentic" debility in *Piers Plow-man* offers not only a premodern precedent to modern biopolitics but also an unsettling genealogy of embodiment's entanglement with regimes of health.[6] By conceptualizing a medieval biopolitics through biosalvation, we can see the circuitous method in which salvation promises some people "health" only in death. Biosalvation operates by protecting the health of the many at the expense of the few. It is this biopolitical mechanism that manifests today as the legal and medical-industrial complex, which dictates the "health and wellness" of transgender people. What medieval and modern biopolitics share is a calculated control over bodies that refuse or are otherwise unable to serve the goals of a "healthy" collective and corporate body.

Piers Plowman is concerned with salvation's vise grip on embodiment, that is, how bodies ought to be maimed or debilitated only in service to salvation, like Christ's suffering on the cross. Susan Stryker and Nikki Sullivan refer to this serviceable body as the "king's member," that is, "that body part which facilitates specific uses of the biopower of the bodily remainder—it is the sovereign claim upon the body of the manually dexterous sword hand, the body of the reproductively capable genitalia, the body of the laboring limbs." Stryker and Sullivan use "queen's body" to reference "transsexual history, a particular strategy for resolving these tense negotiations over life and death between sovereignty and its subjects." In their formulation, the "queen's body" is the body that seeks "embodiment that sustains her life" but in doing so must "appeal to the sovereign power vested in the medico-juridical complex" for resources and often sanction to sustain her life.[7] This entanglement of the body's self-sovereignty with a sovereign power is, surprisingly, also the predicament of medieval salvation politics.

Before we turn to the poem's discussion of maiming, it is important to show how the poem articulates bodily sovereignty. *Piers Plowman* follows a Dreamer, sometimes referred to as Will, who tries to learn how to save his soul. In conversation with various personified figures like the virtue Patience or the personification of Need, the Dreamer works through conflicting answers to his question. It is through the image of Piers the Plowman, a laborer who represents obedience to God's law, that salvation, labor, and embodiment become intertwined. The plowman is a humble laborer, and in his obedience to God's law he submits his individual body to the redemption of the social body, the idealized Christian community, through work. In a scene often referred to as the "Ploughing of the Half-Acre," the Dreamer learns of the interdependence between the individual body and the social collective. As Piers the Plowman attempts to galvanize the social body to help him plow his half-acre, his request is met with refusal and complaint;

some decline to labor while others are unable to work because their limbs
are maimed:

> Tho were faytours aferd and fayned hem blynde
> And leyde here legges alery, as suche lorelles conneth,
> And maden here mone to Peres how thei may nat worche:
> "Ac we praye for yow, Peres, and for youre plouh bothe
> That god for his grace youre grayn multiplye
> And yelde yow of youre almesse that ye yeuen vs here.
> We may nother swynke ne swete, suche seknes vs ayleth,
> Ne haue none lymes to labory with, lord god we thonketh." (C.8.128–35)[8]

> [Those imposters were afraid and feigned to be blind
> And laid their legs backwards, as such beggars know how,
> And made their complaint to Piers about how they may not work:
> "But we pray for you, Piers, and for your plow, too,
> That God's grace will multiply your grain
> And repay you for your alms that you give us here.
> We may neither labor nor sweat, such sickness ails us,
> Nor do we have any limbs to labor with, we thank the Lord."]

Piers the Plowman, the paragon of Christian love, determines that all who
feign debility are impostors ("faytours," a Middle English term that variously
means deceiver, faker, or a beggar feigning injury)[9] and parasites in society
("wastours," C.8.139, those who waste what others reap). Yet Piers seems to
think that society can determine false from true beggars, and this determination is important because charity is at stake. Piers says he will labor and
part with his goods—both his corn and his cloth—for those who are blind or
have iron leg braces ("blind or broke-legged or bolted with yren," C.8.143).
But those who are "faytours" and "wastours" devour what true ("lele," loyal)
land-tilling men faithfully ("leely," loyally) labor for ("lele land-tilyne men
leely byswynken," C.8.140). It is for the sake of charity ("*pur charite*," C.8.169)
that Piers wants to get the "faytours" and "wastours" back to work. Numerous passages in the poem show the narrator trying to verify which bodies are
truly debilitated and which feign debility, and this process of verification is
captured in the poem's presentation of limbs.

Limbs, Members, and Salvific Bodies

Fourteenth-century Middle English recognizes that limbs and members are
interchangeable terms. Both terms, "lym" and "membre," denote extremi-
ties, organs, genitalia, and general parts of the body as well as constituent

parts of Christ. By this I mean the Christological physiology that paradoxically places extreme power in Christ's divided body as a unifying element, first outlined in the First Epistle of Saint Paul to the Corinthians:

> Just as a body, though one, has many parts, but all its many parts form one body, so it is with Christ. . . . Even so the body is not made up of one part but of many. Now if the foot should say, "Because I am not a hand, I do not belong to the body," it would not for that reason cease to be part of the body. And if the ear should say, "Because I am not an eye, I do not belong to the body," it would not for that reason cease to be part of the body. If the whole body were an eye, where would the sense of hearing be? If the whole body were an ear, where would the sense of smell be? But in fact God has placed the parts in the body, every one of them, just as he wanted them to be. If they were all one part, where would the body be? As it is, there are many parts, but one body.[10]

When variations of "lym" and "membre" crop up in *Piers Plowman*, these terms figure a person's productivity in a way that links an individual to a vision of the future crafted and sustained by parts of a social collective. When the poem presents a "lym" or "membre" as maimed, the poem asks if that maiming is excusable; in other words, the poem questions if there is a reason why a maimed member (both a limb and a member of the body of Christ) would hurt its larger social-salvific body. This question of true or false maiming is significant because the poem suggests that individuals who falsely maim their bodies to secure charity—"faytours"—are barred from salvation.[11]

Piers Plowman repeatedly describes bodies of "mishap" (misfortune), those who are physically debilitated and presented as unable or unwilling to labor. In the text's apologia—an extended pseudo-autobiographical discussion between the Dreamer (Will) and Reason, a personification of sovereignty and law—we are presented with two modalities of debility. The Dreamer's body becomes a site to deliberate his value as a productive member of a Christian community.[12] Reason questions the Dreamer about what work he is able to accomplish, asking if he can do any other kind of craft that the community needs ("eny other kynes craft þat to þe comune nedeth," C.5.20), to which the Dreamer replies that he is too weak and his limbs too pendulous to endure the work that laborers do. Yet Reason's subsequent query underscores the link between community membership and debility:

> Or thow art broke, so may be, in body or in membre
> Or ymaymed thorw som myshap, whereby thow myhte be excused?
> (C.5.33–34)

[Or are you broken, so it may be, in body or in limb

Or maimed through some mishap, whereby you might be excused?]

Here Reason outlines two possibilities for the Dreamer: Is he broken or maimed? To be broken in body or in limb is not only a genuine possibility ("so may be") but one of bodily *being*—you *are* broken ("thow art broke"). Differently, to be maimed ("ymaymed") is to be externally injured through mishap ("myshap"). We may read "myshap" here as misfortune, a mis-happening that caused one to be maimed. And under the rubric of the poem, to be "ymaymed" is to be misshapen, mis-created, altered, to be a contortion of nature or "kynde."[13] At the close of *Piers Plowman*, Conscience asks that Kynde, an allegorical representation of God as the progenitor of all things "natural," avenge him and send good fortune and health ("hap and hele," C.22.385) until he finds the figure Piers the Plowman. In order to do well ("dowel") and model life after the humble worker Piers the Plowman, one must embody "hap and hele." This formulaic request of "hap and hele" tells us, in large part, what the Dreamer is searching for throughout the poem, *salvation*, or the good fortune to be healthy in life and in salvation through death. Biosalvation shows that salvation is linked directly to the "hap and hele" of a *capacitated* body (bodies of good fortune and health, "hap and hele") in life while waiting on earth for salvation.[14]

When the poem asks if maiming or mis-shaping happens through "mishap," it suggests that to be or become debilitated is a situational and temporal event—a mis-happening. The poem's meditation on limbs, maiming, and misfortune articulates biosalvation's injustice against certain bodies within the body politic. While *Piers Plowman* does not seem to offer any resolution to determine who has falsely or truly maimed limbs, the poem does differentiate between deliberate maiming and maiming of "meschief." This word "meschief" is essential in the poem's construction of debility; it conveys misfortune and accident, a force that lives beyond the control of the body that "meschief" materializes upon.[15] The modern word "mischief" bears the same root as the word "achieve" (from medieval French *achiever*) and both have a sense of what one is able or unable to bring about in the world. The word's Middle French etymology, too, bears the shadow of the limb. It suggests a misfortune by way of a mis-heading; the "-chief" in "meschief" is from Old French *chef*, "head."[16] It also denotes the farthest extremity or end, as in the end of the town ("chef de la ville").[17] In this way, the -*chef* in "meschief" designates not only the head as part but also as extremity. The word "meschief" in medieval French means to get misdirected by way of an unfortunate event or a misunderstanding, "unfortunate event, bad fortune, misfortune, calamity" ("événement fâcheux, mauvaise fortune, malheur, calamité").[18] The word also conveys misfortune by way of wrongdoing, "harmful act, wrongdoing, mischief" (acte préjudiciable, mauvaise action, méfait). As we will see, maiming through "meschief" and maiming through "mishap" are differentiated by chance and choice.

While the valence of Middle English "meschief" attends to one's ability based on chance and misfortune, the poem's use of "mishap" focuses our attention on what a person does—a "mis-happening" or "mis-shaping" of events or bodies. According to the poem, those who are truly maimed have fallen into "meschief," and these bodies bear their mischiefs meekly and mildly at heart ("meschiefes mekeliche and myldeliche at herte," C.9.184). Limbs maimed through "meschief" are involuntarily maimed; bodies typically *fall* into "meschief." The concept of "meschief" echoes the "mishap" of the Dreamer's conversation with Reason just quoted, and the good fortune and health ("hap and hele") that Conscience begs for at the close of the poem. In this way, the poem draws a line between those who are in true need of protection from "meschief" and those who shape their own need through "mishap."

For fourteenth-century western European Christian people, salvation is an ambition fueled and funded by the power of the church, a power that controlled the resources of and access to salvation.[19] When the poem aligns productive work with salvation, the relationship between capacity and rehabilitation eliminates debilitated bodies—maimed, misshapen, and broken bodies—from its vision of the future. The productivity of the body was embedded in the design of medieval Christian salvation because Christ's return was contingent on a social collective that gave over members' bodies for the common good. In this way, each individual member was part of a social whole, which medieval political theorists, such as John of Salisbury, imagined to be divided into controllable parts. In his *Policraticus* (ca. 1159), John of Salisbury measures the body politic by the health of its parts:

The head of the body of the commonwealth is filled by the prince, who is subject only to God and to those who exercise His office and represent Him on earth, even as in the human body the head is quickened by the soul. The place of the heart is filled by the Senate, which initiates good works and ill. The duties of the eyes, ears, and tongue are claimed by the judges and governors of provinces. Officials and soldiers correspond to the hands. Those who always attend upon the prince are likened to the sides. Financial officers and keepers may be compared with the stomach and intestines, which, if they become congested through excessive avidity and retain too tenaciously their accumulations, generate innumerable and incurable diseases, so that through their ailment the whole body is threatened with destruction. The husbandmen correspond to the feet, which always cleave to the soil, and need the more especially the care and foresight of the head since, while they walk upon the earth doing service with their bodies, they are more likely than others to stumble over stones.[20]

Because of its neat and tidy model of social health and order, John of Salisbury's design of the body politic was modified and adapted by authors throughout the medieval period. Medieval theologians and political theorists believed that a productively operating body politic represented a *healthy* body politic and used wellness metaphors to describe the state of the social body. The application of the wellness metaphor to the body politic was pervasive in late medieval political writings. In the section on the Commons in Christine de Pizan's *Le corps du policie*, or *The Book of the Body Politic*, which draws heavily on the *Policraticus*, she recounts a well-known fable, perhaps popularized by Marie de France, that outlines a disagreement between the belly and its limbs. The full fable in Christine's version is as follows:

Once upon a time there was a great disagreement between the belly of a human body and its limbs. The belly complained loudly about the limbs and said that they thought badly of it and that they did not take care of it and feed as well as they should. On the other hand, the limbs complained loudly about the belly and said they were all exhausted from work, and yet despite all their labor, coming and going from working, the belly wanted to have everything and was never satisfied. The limbs then decided that they would no longer suffer such pain and labor, since nothing they did satisfied the belly. So they would stop their work and let the belly get along as best it might. The limbs stopped their work and the belly was no longer nourished. So it began to get thinner, and the limbs began to fail and weaken, and so, to spite one another, the whole body died.[21]

Christine's concern about a functioning body politic rests on the imagined health of a social collective. In the fable, she locates the dilemma of the body in the lack of reciprocal nourishment that each body part should offer. If the limbs stop working, then both belly and limbs do not live; yet the insatiable belly does not participate in the same productive labor as the limbs. In this model, the limbs die whether they work or do not work; the satiation of the belly determines the survival of the whole. She suggests that the lower parts of the body must be "maintained in health and well-being" because these limbs support the "burden of all the rest of the body." Her medical analogy cements her desire for a united social body; when Christine de Pizan writes that the human body is "defective and deformed" when it lacks any of its members, she associates the idealization of wholeness and health with productivity; a body that lacks a member, in Christine's estimation, cannot function well.[22]

Similarly, John of Salisbury saw the ruler (the head) as the medic of society. His moral duty was to restore and maintain the health of the social body.[23] Alongside the widespread Christological understanding of Christ as medic, *Christus medicus*,[24] the metaphor of a sovereign ruler as a healer is woven into medieval ideas of how the social body is constructed and maintained. As Ernst Kantorowicz's study *The King's Two Bodies* outlines, medieval social collectives—such as the Christian community under Christ, the church under the pope, or society under a king—were allegorized as a body politic.[25] The king was at once a transitory body subject to his own decrees and a divine body that symbolized the laws he created, both corruptible and corporate. His subjects made up the rest of the social body, with laborers representing the feet. Building on Kantorowicz's model, Kellie Robertson writes that "medieval legal theory demanded that incorporeal things like labor services inhere in corporeal things,"[26] and so the ideology of an ordered world, nature, and society writes itself onto the physical body.

Scholarship that discusses maiming focuses on historical accounts of corporal punishment and demonstrates the legal and bodily stakes of dismemberment, while work on medieval theological and philosophical ideas of the body illuminate the fragmented body not only as a legal but as a theological concern as well.[27] This religious landscape transformed ideas about the partition of the body, which, as Caroline Walker Bynum puts it, whether through "reunion of parts into a whole or through assertion of part *as part* to *be* the whole—was the image of paradise."[28] Depictions of Christ showed his body "fragmented by our sins," but in each fragment of Christ's body "is the whole of God."[29] These theological debates asked how a body fragmented on earth could be reassembled into a whole entity at the end of time, to reconstitute dispersed and fragmented *members* into a Christological whole.

Eschatology and the theological concern over the reunion of the partitive body into a whole on Judgment Day had enormous cultural purchase that affected legal punishments. In the fourteenth century there was an assumption that the material body required continuity across flesh and time. Bynum writes that bodily partition was so highly charged that "torturers were forbidden to effect it; they were permitted to squeeze and twist and stretch in excruciating ways, but not to sever or divide. . . . Dismemberment in capital cases . . . was reserved for only the most repulsive crimes and . . . the populace was expected to be able to read the nature of the offense from the precise way in which the criminal's body was cut apart and the pieces displayed."[30] The severing of body from body in mutilation was treated similarly to the severance of body from soul in death because theologians questioned how God would reassemble the body at resurrection. There were extensive debates on how Christ's foreskin would reassemble, and how bodily matter eaten by a cannibal would show up in the end times. All matter would eventually rise; "God's promise is that division shall finally be overcome, that ultimately there is no scattering."[31]

Even so, in the time of *Piers Plowman*, medieval Christians imagined the soul to be somatomorphic, having a body form, and theologians stressed the "wholeness" of the final person more sharply than in earlier centuries. Medieval theories of the reunion of parts appealed to ideas of natural harmony, health, and unification, and necessitated that all parts cooperate to ensure the stability of the entire social body. Maimed and altered bodies challenged the vision of wholeness—understood as non-maimed—that the social body supposedly represented and upheld. The relationship between an individual body and its social collective materializes as "bodily integration," what Stryker and Sullivan define as a sociotechnical force that "at once enables certain modes of bodily being, and denigrates or forecloses others."[32] Since embodiment is the sociotechnical tool that *integrates* or *dis-integrates* an individual into or out of a larger entity, a maimed body challenges the bodily integration that salvation requires, which articulates itself through biosalvific operations of rehabilitation.

Piers Plowman's rehabilitation politics requires that bodies labor for the community, be charitable, and conform to the law in order to attain salvation. While the poem acknowledges that not all bodies can do well ("dowel"), it recognizes that salvation is available only to those who conform to and perform for a larger Christian body. The poem is peopled by maimed, misshapen, and mutilated bodies that draw our attention to the institutional mechanisms—the church and its role in perpetuating and profiting from the uncertainty of salvation—that both create and reject such bodies. *Piers Plowman* uses maimed bodies to signal a problem with fourteenth-century ideologies of the body politic and the control it wields over the nature of humanity. The image of maimed limbs and members in *Piers Plowman* complicates the operations of capacity that salvation requires, and what consequences await bodies that do not conform.

Bodies of Mishap

Misshapen bodies are bodies that do not conform to the shape of society. When *Piers Plowman* looks to bodies of "mishap," it identifies a nonconforming body, literally a body that does not shape itself (*-form*) with a collective (*con-*), and reveals that misshapen bodies are bodies that do not conform to the law. In what Andrew Cole refers to as *Piers Plowman's* "crescendo 'lollare' passage,"[33] the poem underscores how maimed bodies challenge the apparatus of the body politic:

> Non licet vobis legem voluntati, set voluntatem coniungere legi.
> Kyndeliche, by Crist, ben suche ycald "lollares."
> As by the Engelisch of oure eldres, of olde mennes techynge,
> He that lolleth is lame or his leg out of ioynte
> Or ymaymed in som membre, for to meschief hit souneth,
> Rihte so sothly such manere ermytes
> Lollen ayen the byleue of the lawe of holy churche. (C.9.213a–18)

> [*It is not lawful for you to make the law conform to your will, but your will to the law.*
> Naturally, by Christ, such people have been called "lollers."
> As by the English of our elders, of the teaching of old men,
> He that lolls is lame or his leg is out of joint
> Or is maimed in some limb, for it sounds like mischief,
> Right so, truly, is the manner of hermits
> Who loll against the belief and the law of Holy Church.]

Just as the Dreamer was asked by Reason if he was "ymaymed," this passage uses the same language to define "lollares," that is, bodies that loll.[34] One who lolls is one who is "lame" or has a "leg out of ioynte" or is maimed in "som membre" by "meschief." The passage follows a Latin legal maxim: "It is not lawful for you to make the law conform to your will, but [rather for you to conform] your will to the law."[35] The Latin uses the verb *coniungere*, "to connect, join, yoke together, or marry," and such a word deployed in this legal maxim is significant in a passage concerned with the *shape* of bodies and the disjoining of limbs from the bodies of both people and communities. One's will, then, must join to the laws of Holy Church like a limb, shaping and connecting oneself to this institution in hope of support, assistance, charity, or salvation. To have a limb out of joint ("ioynte") is to be dislocated from the social body and salvation. The lolling, loose, or maimed body is imagined here to be physically dangling against the body of the church. Those with maimed members loll against the faith ("byleue") and law of the church. Since the church requires that bodies prove need in order to be saved, this shows that physical debility can sometimes include but often excludes membership in a salvific community.

While some bodies are maimed by falling into "meschief," the poem juxtaposes these with bodies that self-mutilate or feign mutilation and refers to these bodies as misshapen in some way. Biosalvation underscores the disciplinary techniques to which maimed and debilitated bodies are subjected. In a passage often read as a meditation on poverty, *Piers Plowman* confronts salvation's requirement that some bodies must be debilitated in order for others to offer charity (Latin *caritas*, "charity, love, care").[36] The poem uses the terms "maim," "mysshape," and "mischief" to point to bodies that have self-inflicted debility or have illicitly come into debility.[37] These are bodies—of the poor, of beggars, and of the maimed—that are unable to work because of debility. In the poem's meditation on begging, we are presented with several iterations of begging on a need-based scale of incapacitation. This debate on begging specifies that those who are granted charity and pardon from Truth, the allegorical figure of the correct, real, and true method of existence, are those who labor with their hands and live by their labor. Truth excludes beggars from this formulation. We learn of several types of beggars: the beggars with bags ("beggares with bagges," C.9.98) who fake debility, the lunatic lollers ("lunatyk lollares," C.9.107) who are healthy in body but not in mind, uneducated hermits ("lewede ermytes," C.9.140) who feign a lolling life ("lollarne lyf," C.9.140)[38] to get lodging and food, and beggars who have bastard children and break their bones to qualify for charity. These bodies are compared to those of the old, the pregnant, the bedridden, and the needy who have humbly fallen into "mischief"—the bodies that the poem holds to be truly in need of charity.

While the text recounts the variations of debilitated bodies, it gives most of its attention to those bodies who fake having maimed limbs: these bodies travel with descriptive verbs such as *faiten*, "to deceive" (C.9.100); *coveren*, "to keep secret" (C.9.139); *loken*, "to seem, appear" (C.9.141); and *mysshapen*, "to misshape" (C.9.172). *Piers Plowman* stages the problem of making one's debility legible through the figure of Truth, who seems to think there is a way to determine who is faking need. In other words, Truth believes that we should be able to discern able limbs from maimed limbs:

Ac beggares with bagges, the whiche brewhous ben here churches,
But they be blynde or tobroke or elles be syke,
Thouh he falle for defaute that fayteth for his lyflode
Reche ye neuere, ye riche, thouh suche lorelles sterue.
For alle that haen here hele and here ye-syhte
And lymes to labory with and lollares lyf vsen
Lyuen ayen goddes lawe and the lore of holi churche. (C.9.98–104)

[But beggars with bags, whose churches are the brewhouses,
If they are blind or broken or otherwise sick,
Though he collapses for lack of food, he falsely begs for his sustenance
Never reach out, you rich people, though such idle wretches starve.
For all that have their health and their eyesight
And limbs to labor with and live the life of a loller
Live against God's law and the doctrine of Holy Church.]

Bodies must prove need to merit charity, and yet the poem shows that body-based proof is still insufficient for obtaining charity and salvation. This passage underscores the dismissal of debilitated bodies who beg for sustenance ("lyflode"); a body might collapse, but if that body has its health, then charity should be withheld. The command to never reach out ("reche ye neuere") plays on the use of limbs as a tool for charity. The passage explicitly bars the wealthy from giving charity to those who fake debility ("he . . . fayteth"), encouraging their starvation. In this way, proof of need—being "blynde or tobroke or elles be syke"—is still insufficient to receive charity if the charitable giver presumes the beggar is faking need. The "riche" assume the role of the sovereign power afforded to Christ and king to determine the right of life and death, what Michel Foucault called the power to "make die, let live."[39] Jennifer Gianfalla's work on begging as disability in *Piers Plowman* suggests that both visible and invisible disability can justify begging.[40] Yet what is so unsettling about this section of the poem is that bodies are condemned for being both legible and illegible at the same time. When the poem aligns deception and secrecy with debilitated bodies, it exposes the limits of biosalvation; some bodies are deemed counterfeit and expelled from the circuit of charity that salvation requires.

Transgender individuals know all too well the violent consequences of being read as counterfeit, of supposedly "deceiving" a cisgender gaze. An individual body must make itself legible to a system that benefits from refusing its legibility. For many of us in the transgender community, the politics of making oneself legible in both social and legal registers is precisely the

process of bodily integration that Stryker and Sullivan critique. I am referring to the legal processes that require psychiatric evaluation, diagnoses of
"gender identity disorder," and regimens of hormone therapy in order to
make alterations to one's legal name, birth certificate, or legal gender, and
to obtain gender reassignment surgeries. As Elizabeth Loeb makes clear, the
legal regulations of corporeal practices specific to transgender bodies are
marred by the history of legal mayhem.[41] Maimed bodies and limbs thus
challenge the call to integration that the body politic requires but fails to
support.

Authenticating one's health and unhealth to systems of power—whether
it be the modern medical-industrial complex or the medieval institution of
salvation—is a process of verifying need. *Piers Plowman* distinguishes types of
debility through their causes: to be maimed through mishap ("mishap") or
mischief ("meschief") marks one's refusal to work as excusable. By framing
authentic debility in these terms—caused by unforeseen and uncontrollable
forces—the poem shows that charity is permitted only when debility can be
excused. Yet while some bodies are maimed by falling into "meschief," the
poem takes issue with bodies that self-mutilate or feign mutilation and refers
to these bodies as misshapen in some way. The poem shows that to be misshapen ("mysshapen") is an act of fraud by the poor:

> For they lyue in no loue ne no lawe holden
> Ne weddeth none wymmen that they with deleth;
> Bringeth forth bastardus, beggares of kynde,
> Or the bak or som bon they breke of here children
> And goen and fayten with here fauntes for eueremore aftur.
> Ther aren mo mysshape amonges suche beggares
> Then of many othere men that on this molde walken.
> And tho that lyueth thus here lyf, leue ye non other,
> Thai haue no part of pardoun ne of preyeres ne of penaunces.
> (C.9.167–75)

> [For they live in no love and hold no law
> Nor wed any women that they have dealings with;
> They bring forth bastards, beggars by nature.
> Or they break the back or some bone of their children
> And go and fake with their infants for evermore after.
> There are more misshapen people among such beggars
> Than of any other men that walk on this earth.
> And those that live their life this way, they believe in no other,
> They have no part of pardon, nor of prayer, nor of penances.]

In this passage, the breaking of children's bodies in youth allows the parents to use their maimed child in service of receiving charity. Maiming a child is abhorrent, and while the poem meditates on that abhorrence, it also shows us the desperation to make need legible in order to meet the requirements of a salvific politic. The parents have made need legible on their child's body and still, according to this last line, these bodies are not deserving of charity; they have no part of pardon, nor of prayer, nor of penances ("Thai haue no part of pardoun ne of preyeres ne of penaunces," C.9.175). This exile from pardon, prayer, and penance—technologies of salvation—leaves the poor and debilitated in a state of salvific precarity. Those who live their life in this way do so because they supposedly do not believe in any other life ("leue ye non other"). The poem suggests that these individuals resort to such violent measures to secure charity because they believe only in *this* life on earth, not the life of salvation in death. Crucially, *Piers Plowman* here focuses on which "health" is most important—that of the bodies on earth or the souls in salvation. It is on account of this that the precarious poor are removed from rehabilitation because they are maimed and deceptive. In this passage, the poor self-mutilate in order to participate in the same system that rejects them because of their "mysshapen" embodiment. The paradoxical and circular demands made by biosalvific power demonstrate that the system of salvation has no interest in the welfare of precarious bodies but rather has interest in the control of those bodies as subjects.

Bodies with lolling limbs and maimed members are designated as being out of commission. Toward the end of *Piers Plowman*, the poem offers a model of the biosalvific control of bodies and their relationship to production. The poem makes an overt reference to the Dreamer's aging and fruitless limb, often understood as his penis and its uselessness to his wife. While the medieval period did not employ the concept of reproduction as we have come to understand it since the advent of biology,[42] the late medieval English word for reproduction is "multiplicacioun," and this term recalls the primordial command to "be fertile and multiply." In other words, limbs are expected to do the work of multiplying, either through productive labor (in imitation of Piers the Plowman) or through the reproduction of bodies to restore paradise.

The scene frames the discussion of the Dreamer's unproductive and nonreproductive body by describing the aging Dreamer's hostile encounter with Elde, a personification of old age.[43] The Dreamer recounts that Elde makes him bald and bare on the crown ("baer on the crowne," C.22.184)], boxes his ears so that he may hardly hear, and strikes his mouth and knocks out the Dreamer's molars. When the Dreamer remarks that Elde shackles his body, taking away his freedom of movement, we may first understand this as the effect of an aging body. Elde's brutality toward the Dreamer's body is a moment of debilitation. Old age debilitates the Dreamer, but Elde's actions show that the violent forces against his body are external, authorial (extradiegetic), and intentional.

The Dreamer's debilitation by Elde troubles the poem's politics of bodily production and the relationship of the body to salvation. Because of Elde's violence, the Dreamer may not wander at large ("may nat go at large," C.22.192), and this recalls the poem's prologue, where the Dreamer went forth in the world to hear wonders ("wente forth in the world wondres to here," C.Prol.3). When the Dreamer looks on the fair field of folk working and wandering as the world requires ("worchyng and wandryng as this world ascuth," C.Prol.21), we must ask how Elde's debilitating effects on the Dreamer's body eliminate the Dreamer's body from productivity, from *being* and *doing* in the world. While old age would legitimate the Dreamer as a recipient of charity, the violence against the Dreamer's limb focuses our attention on the punishment of the body. Elde's violence to the Dreamer's body does not go unnoticed by the Dreamer's wife, who acknowledges the hardship of her partner's debility:

> And of the wo that Y was ynne my wyf hadde reuthe
> And wesched wel witterly that Y were in heuene.
> For the lyme that she loued me fore and leef was to fele
> A nyhtes, nameliche, when we naked were,
> Y ne myhte in none manere maken hit at her wille,
> So Elde and she hit hadde forbete. (C.22.193–98)

> [And of the woe that I was in my wife had pity
> And wished very truly that I was in heaven.
> For the limb that she loved me for and used to love to feel
> At night, namely, when we were naked,
> I might not in any manner make it do her will,
> In such a way, Elde and she had beaten it.]

Strangely, many read this scene as humorous, that the Dreamer's wife, unable to fulfill her desire, cooperates with Elde to beat the Dreamer's limb entirely out of commission. Yet much more is at stake in this brief aside, since this scene has implications for the poem's conception of the productive and reproductive body. As James Paxson shows, the Dreamer's limb-as-penis here is a "literal penile copula" as well as the reification of the Dreamer (Will, as a psychic drive of desire and volition in medieval faculty psychology).[44]

The Dreamer's "lyme" copulates (acts as a copula, in Paxson's words) by linking the Dreamer, the Dreamer's wife, and Elde into a nonproductive and nonprocreative moment. That the Dreamer's wife wishes that he were in heaven rather than unproductive on earth signals the politics of generation and rehabilitation that the poem both relies upon and critiques. The Dreamer's broken and beaten "lyme" highlights the conceptual intersection between reproduction and production in the poem: the maimed limb is severed from the body of the worker, lover, and subsequently the larger corporate, social body. The beaten and unworking "lyme" in this passage presents an uncomfortable union between reproduction and production that fictionalizes what sits at the center of biosalvation's project: to secure everlasting life with Christ in death.

This passage on Elde's maimed limb juxtaposes life and death by showing the liminal space in between that maimed bodies represent in a salvific fabric. The "lyme" that the Dreamer's wife formerly loved to feel is unable to operate productively because the Dreamer is unable to participate in the fiction of (re)production that the poem's salvific message relies upon. While the Dreamer says that he cannot in any manner make it do her will ("in none manere maken hit at here wille," 197)—the limb (described with the Middle English gender-neutral pronoun "hit") challenges the categories of volition, personified and metaphorized as the Dreamer's penis, which itself functions as a unit of production.[45] Elde, who acts here as the manifestation of temporal debility through aging, conducts and condones the violence against the Dreamer's body and makes the Dreamer's wife complicit in the act. That the violence done to the Dreamer's body is glossed by the gender-neutral pronoun "hit" is not insignificant.[46] In staging the violence against the Dreamer's penis, the poem's use of the gender-neutral Middle English pronoun suggests that the mutilation of the Dreamer's body is an action that both responds to and creates bodily debility. The Dreamer's inability to make his limb ("maken hit") perform in a normatively "healthy" way warrants violence against that very limb.[47] When Elde and the Dreamer's wife beat his limb, they punish the Dreamer's debility through debilitation. This dual debilitation—a nonworking limb and subsequently beaten limb—works to punish a body through debilitation *because* of debilitation.

Salvation works only by the exclusion of debilitated and maimed bodies, perceived as injurious to the larger social collective, and yet salvation also demands that bodies be maimed in order to control a subject's rehabilitation, shaping that body to conform to salvific visions of health, wellness, and productivity. While medieval biosalvation is contingent on bodily sacrifice—Christ is, in effect, the ultimate maimed and lolling body—it

rejects members that inflict bodily harm in order to benefit from the salvific system. This paradoxical logic affects nonconforming bodies that are
frequently denied institutional support and resources and yet require that
support to be recognized as a legitimate and productive subject by those possessing power. In this way, *Piers Plowman*'s rehabilitation politics requires a
body to be productive and conform to the same laws and political maneuvers
that debilitate those bodies.

Law of Maims and Mayhem

The exercise of control over a body's health—both individual and collective
bodies—is not a modern invention. The medieval and early modern "law
of maims," or law pertaining to the crime of mayhem, sought to control
self-amputation.[48] Maiming was punishable by law and has a long history
of enforcement. Henry Bracton's thirteenth-century *De legibus et consuetu-
dinibus Angliae* (On the Laws and Customs of England), an influential legal
text copied and circulated throughout the fourteenth-century, differentiates
punishments of maiming from wounding:

> It may be said to be mayhem when one is rendered incapable of fight-
> ing, especially by him [to] whom he is appealing, as where bones pro-
> trude from his head or a large splinter of bone projects, as was said,
> [or] a bone is broken in some part of his body, or a foot or hand, or part
> of a foot or hand, or a finger or other member is cut off, or where sin-
> ews and limb are crippled by the wound dealt, or fingers have become
> crooked, or an eye has been gouged out, or some other thing done to a
> man's body whereby he is rendered less able and effective in defending
> himself. But what shall be said of him who has his teeth broken? Ought
> the breaking of teeth to be deemed mayhem? The answer is that there
> is one kind of mayhem by which a man is rendered incapable of fight-
> ing, of which we have spoken above, and another that results in disfig-
> urement of the body. Hence, we must see whether the teeth broken
> are incisors, molars or grinders, for if molars or grinders the mayhem,
> since it is hidden, causes no great disfigurement of the body nor any
> inability to fight. But if the incisors are broken it seems that both are
> consequent thereon, for such teeth are of great assistance in winning
> a fight. Castration, though it is hidden, is deemed mayhem. There are
> also other kinds of mayhem for which, as is evident, the duel will not
> remain, as where an ear or nose is cut off, for this will be disfigurement
> of the body rather than diminishment of strength.[49]

Bracton's definition of mayhem was pervasive in medieval legal and literary writings. Mayhem is bodily mutilation that renders one's body useless to the social collective (as a laborer, soldier, and the like); wounding, however, damages the body without impairment to service. This is also evident in Bracton's formulation of physical legibility: castration is still deemed mayhem, "though it is hidden," because it incapacitates an individual's reproductive capability. Castration, like other bodily amputation, is an action that supposedly threatens one's strength and virility because it removes the possibility of reproducing or producing for the body politic. By glossing mayhem in this way, Bracton's legal code declares bodies and their alterations to be products of their position in society, where, for instance, a soldier's value is reflected in his bodily health and ability to serve. Bracton's definition of maiming shows that any damage done to an individual body also damages the larger social body, imagined as a collection of "able" and "virile" bodies.

It is clear from the medieval and early modern law of maims that this body of law was predominantly aimed at the poor. For instance, Edward Coke's *Institutes of the Laws of England* (1632), a seventeenth-century legal treatise that effectively rewrites much of Bracton's *De legibus*, declares that an individual who self-maims or "make himselfe impotent, thereby to have the more colour to begge or to be relieved without putting himselfe to any labour, caused his companion to strike off his left hand."[50] The "law of maims" suggested that the crime of mayhem, the maiming of a so-called healthy body, impaired one's capacity for self-defense. Attempts at self-maiming were efforts to escape forced labor or to authenticate one's status as a beggar, unable to work for one's livelihood.[51]

The thirteenth-century legal treatise *Fleta*, "Fleet," a possible location of where the book was written ("in Fleet it was written"),[52] considers the crime of "mayhem" a felony against the king's peace. Specifically, the law code explains that an act of mayhem includes the maiming of any body part that renders one incapable of fighting or that diminishes one's strength in performing tasks necessary for war. The crime of mayhem required retributive justice, and the maimer "should lose a member for the like member which he took away."[53] Coke's *Institutes of the Laws of England* cites Bracton directly as the authority on this issue: "Note, the life and members of every subject are under the safeguard and protection of the king; for, as *Bracton* saith, *Vita et membra sunt in potestate regis* . . . to the end that they may serve the king and their countrie, when the occasion shal be offered."[54] The safeguarding of a body's limbs is for the protection of a larger collective.

Legal and theological concerns converged in prohibitions against bodily mutilation. Religious debates were concerned with the act of maiming as transgression of the purported natural and divinely designed boundaries and thresholds (*liminal*, from Latin *limen*, "entrance, door," to which *limb* is etymologically related) of the body.[55] Robert Grosseteste, a prolific and influential thirteenth-century theologian and philosopher contemporary with Bracton, outlines the moral limits of maiming. In his *De decem mandatis*, a moral instruction on the Ten Commandments, Grosseteste delineates the relationship between body parts and the health of the soul:

> In this part of the mandate, it is a transgression to cut open any part of someone, which means it is hateful to mutilate the members of people. Since a member is living, when it is a maimed member, its life is destroyed to some degree. There is no part of the soul that can be brought back from maiming (though the soul is unaffected and cannot be cut into parts), but the active life of the limbs is truncated by maiming. For instance, an eye lives to see unless the eye is surreptitiously destroyed, and a hand lives to touch unless the hand perishes from maiming. And therefore, just as the killing of a man through murder will be punished by the law, the mutilation of the limbs of the law of retaliation which is weighed by a *tooth for a tooth, an eye for an eye, a hand for a hand, a foot for a foot*, a burning for a burning.[56]

Grosseteste suffuses body parts with life and associates the maiming of a part with the murder of a person. Maiming, in his estimation, strips the active life away from the member—both the part of the body and the member of the social community. The parts of the body—eye, hand, tooth—are open to maiming and violence, but the soul remains intact. As Masha Raskolnikov has shown regarding soul and body dualism in *Piers Plowman*, the discourse around transgender embodiment often refers to a dual nature between body and soul, citing the standard social formulation of trans identity, "'man's soul trapped in a woman's body' (or its opposite)." She writes that "this conceptualization of body and soul as sexed seems to conceive of the soul as an embodied being, and yet, simultaneously, imagines the soul as a being radically separable from its own embodiment."[57] For Grosseteste, this conceptualization imbues the body part, too, with the spirit of the soul. Maiming the body is like rendering that body part lifeless *because* it no longer functions in its productive mode: an eye can no longer see, a hand can no longer touch. This interpretation of the body reinforces the relationship between embodiment and productivity.

Within these early legal treatises and theological texts, the maimed body is punishable by law and the transgression is mitigated by the law of retaliation. Where *Fleta* states that a self-maimer "should lose a member for the like member which he took away," Grosseteste invokes the language of reciprocal punishment in Exodus 21—tooth for tooth, eye for eye. This legal punishment equalizes harm and paradoxically mutilates more of the social body in an attempt to rid it of injuring parts, that is, parts that may threaten the whole. Yet this is precisely the circuitous method of state-controlled injury: an individual must be maimed to be protected by the state, yet the maimer—regardless of intention—is punished by the same act that should have brought protection (eye for eye, tooth for tooth, body for body). Crucially, when the crime is self-inflicted maiming, mutilation, or bodily transformation, this legal logic remains. The self-maimer becomes both victim (of bodily self-injury) and perpetrator (of injuring the social body), a single body twice culpable. Since *biosalvation* requires an individual to make need legible on the body, the impulse to self-maim as proof of need both eliminates and delegitimates an individual from salvation.

While early definitions of maiming and mayhem attempted to protect individuals from assault, they also impacted an individual's personal relationship with their body. Lellia Ruggini's work on self-mutilation as protest in the late antique period reports that efforts to evade military service through self-maiming were punished by branding and imposed military service, serving as a soldier as an act of labor rather than an honor. In this way, the maimed individual would be forced to serve despite any debility. Ruggini argues that self-mutilation was a way to "assert the right to choose conditions of life which, for various reasons, were believed to be better."[58] In this scenario, an individual chooses to self-maim through body alteration for reasons of improving individual wellness and life—a self-salvation—and the state interprets that act as an act of violence against itself and the social collective it represents. The punishment of self-maiming in military service is still in effect: Article 128a in the United States *Manual for Courts-Martial* outlines the offense perpetrated by service members who intentionally or unintentionally inflict self-injury. This clause predominately addresses the maiming of limbs and attempted suicide to determine whether the conduct of the offender was "adverse to the discipline and good order" of the armed forces.[59] Punishment includes a dishonorable discharge, forfeiture of allowances and pay, and two to five years of confinement.

Even today, the "law of maims" is active in all fifty states and regards "mayhem" as a criminal offense.[60] State control over bodily maiming has real and far-reaching effects on transgender and non-normative bodies. While this legal protection aims to preserve bodies from violence, it also presupposes that bodies are both an extension and a product of the state that protects them. In July 2017, Donald Trump first tweeted about the inordinate cost that transgender military service members have "imposed" on the United States: "Our military must be focused on decisive and overwhelming . . . victory and cannot be burdened with the tremendous medical costs and disruption that transgender in the military would entail."[61] Trump's claim is that "transgender" medical costs—by which he means hormone therapy, gender-affirming surgery, and routine care—would burden the potential "victory" of the US military. This claim engages in the same paradox that medieval law of maims presents. Trump suggests that transgender individuals' alterations to their bodies are too costly for the US military to bear, and yet the US military sends troops—including transgender individuals—into war zones that have the potential to mutilate their bodies and end their lives.[62] Maiming challenges the state's sovereignty over bodies. Since the state claims the exclusive right of violence, if we do "violence" to ourselves, we are assuming the state's prerogative. Maiming in its legal valence suggests that alterations, changes, or perceived mutilations to a state-controlled body mark that body as unfit to be an integrated member in an otherwise "healthy" social community. To use Stryker and Sullivan's language: self-maiming, mutilation, or body alteration is a crime against a collective body politic. Mayhem and maiming, then, when self-inflicted, invert the disciplining strategy of salvation.[63] In other words, individuals who seek bodily transformation are perceived as injurious to a larger social collective, and because of this perception, sovereign powers reserve the right to violently remove those individuals from the social body.

Arguments against body alteration state that bodily integration (the integrity of a presumably "whole" body) is beneficial to the "health" of individual bodies and collective society. Medical ethicists claim that the request to remove so-called healthy members or limbs or remove so-called healthy body tissue through cosmetic surgery, "sex reassignment surgery," circumcision, or other procedures is a request to *maim* an otherwise healthy body.[64] David O. Cauldwell, an early twentieth-century American sexologist who contributed much to the pathologizing discourse of transgender people within the medical field, understood "sex reassignment surgery" as mutilation, claiming, "It would be criminal of a doctor to remove healthy organs."[65] Sovereignty over one's own body is pathologized because of the alleged debilitation or destruction of an otherwise "healthy" body. Yet as Jasbir Puar indicates, transgender individuals challenge "hierarchies of organ ordering" and refuse "normative attachments of capacity to various organs" in a protest against state-controlled capacitation.[66]

Just as medieval Christians were required to conform their bodies to the project of salvation, the modern medical-industrial complex, in tandem with state and national guidelines, requires transgender and disabled bodies to make their needs legible in order to access resources and be integrated into the social collective. For some transgender people, this legibility is marked by self-maiming, a process that the state both requires and rejects. On Friday, May 24, 2019, the Trump administration formally proposed to abandon a provision in the 2016 Affordable Care Act (ACA) that protects transgender, gender-nonconforming, and intersex people from discrimination in health care.[67] The 2016 ACA provision expanded the definition of "gender identity," which it defined as an "internal sense of gender, which may be male, female, neither, or a combination of male and female, and which may be different from an individual's sex assigned at birth."[68] Under the heading "Conforming to the Text of Our Laws," the 2019 proposition from the US Department of Health and Human Services (HHS) erases this definition of gender identity "to conform with the plain understanding" of gender identity that the American people purportedly recognize, that is, a fixed and finite binary of male or female. Roger Severino, director of the Office of Civil Rights under HHS, stated that Americans above all else want "vigorous protection of civil rights and faithfulness to the text of the laws."[69] The protection of civil rights and defense of law are safeguarded only for bodies presumed to belong to the American people, that is, bodies that conform to the text of law.

This excision of transgender, gender-nonconforming, and intersex bodies from health care protections in the 2019 proposition is a manifestation of governmental control over bodies which the state has, in a legal sense, created through its circuitous methods that require the transgender community to make itself legible to obtain resources. This relationship between resources, legibility, and sovereign power is expressed, albeit with wildly different stakes, in *Piers Plowman*. The rehabilitation of souls and bodies with Christ in salvation is possible only because of the system of salvation that requires some to make need legible on their own bodies. The image of the maimed limb in the poem complicates the operations that salvation requires, that is, a capacitated laborer working for the good of a Christian collective. What is crucial, in my estimation, is that in constructing a discourse of debility, the poem pushes the limits of and the requirements for salvation and the architecture of the body of the church, challenging how it is built and to whom it has allowed entry.

Health itself, as Berlant writes, can "be seen as a side effect of successful normativity"[70] in societies where the governance of the reproduction of life is organized around maintaining wellness for the prosperity of the larger community to which one belongs. The idea of health as a distinct lifesaving technique (akin to medieval salvation) is impressed upon the transgender community by the medical-industrial complex, as some of us who choose medical treatment are required to do more than prove need. In order to make our bodies legible—or even *legal*—to the medical-industrial complex and state and federal authorities, many of us who choose medical treatment do so through various types of bodily modification. While not all transgender people use this language, many might feel that they owe their lives to medical interventions performed on their bodies; in other words, that removal of breast tissue, genitoplasty, voice therapy, or hormone treatment is a work of biosalvation because it enables life where life otherwise wouldn't be livable. Yet as Dean Spade has shown, transgender body alteration is governed by diagnostic and normativizing practices that regulate the livability of transgender bodies.[71] Spade asks if illness is the appropriate interpretative model for gender variance, and in our modern period the association of trans embodiment with disability is embedded in a long history of stigmatization and pathologization.

Transgender and debilitated bodies, Puar writes, have a "thwarted connection" since the transgender subject is asked to "re-create an able body not only in terms of gender and sexuality but also in terms of economic productivity,"[72] and the debilitated subject is reliant for services on the legal apparatus of the Americans with Disabilities Act (ADA) as well as state and federally controlled health care services. For transgender and disabled people, the body is the site that the state both refuses and revives. In its desire for conforming and productive subjects, legal and medical institutions require that transgender people make our bodies legible to the larger social body. For myself as a nonbinary transgender person, I must choose "M" or "F" on my driver's license in the state where I reside—and if I want to select a gender marker that does not match the one on my birth certificate, I must present documentation confirming that my body has undergone therapy and surgery. Effectively, I must maim and train my body to be legible to a system that benefits from controlling the boundaries of my person. Just as Puar's articulation of maiming suggests that the state requires a body to be maimed in order to assist that body, the medieval church's control over bodies through biosalvation rejects maimed bodies as ineligible for a social collective and a vision of the future. As Stryker and Sullivan write, bodily mayhem "aims to preserve life itself for the body that lives it, rather than for the instrumentality that claims it—an act of resistance to being consumed, rather than becoming the victim of sovereign violence."[73] These somatechnical operations—self-maiming, mayhem, and surgery—are refusals to integrate into a controlling corporate body. For *Piers Plowman*, a body maimed in some member ("ymaymed in som membre") challenges the regime of salvific accumulation because it refuses to produce for a system that profits from its destruction.

Notes

The heart of this essay began in wonderful conversation with Bre Leake, thank you. I am grateful to the editors of this volume, Greta LaFleur, Masha Raskolnikov, and Anna M. Kłosowska, and to the anonymous readers of this essay, all of whom have added significantly to its quality and complexity.

1. See the *Oxford English Dictionary*, s.v. "salvation, n."

2. Lauren Berlant, "Slow Death (Sovereignty, Obesity, Lateral Agency)," *Critical Inquiry* 33 (2007): 754–80, quotation at 765, and *Cruel Optimism* (Durham, NC: Duke University Press, 2011), 95–120.

3. On deception, legibility, and transphobic violence, see Talia Mae Bettcher, "Evil Deceivers and Make-Believers: On Transphobic Violence and the Politics of Illusion," in *The Transgender Studies Reader*, ed. Susan Stryker and Stephen Whittle (New York: Routledge, 2006), 278–90.

4. In this essay I am concerned with the relationship between transgender body alteration and state control. I want to acknowledge that not all transgender, nonbinary, and gender-nonconforming people choose body alteration through medical transition. While this essay confronts a medieval precedent of body alteration through maiming, mutilation, and mayhem, I am not suggesting that the body alterations of transgender, nonbinary, and gender-nonconforming individuals are body mutilations—unless the subject feels affinity with that terminology, as I do as a transgender person—but rather that body alterations both medieval and modern are deemed mayhem by institutional powers such as salvation, the church, and sovereign rulers (medieval) and the medical-industrial complex, the legal system, and the state (modern).

5. There are three distinct texts of *Piers Plowman*, the A, B, and C texts. These three versions roughly follow the same narrative, but the variations between these texts engage with distinctive social and political concerns. Since the C text expands discussions of bodies and labor, all my references to *Piers Plowman* are from the C text, *Piers Plowman: A New Annotated Edition of the C-text*, ed. Derek Pearsall (Liverpool: Liverpool University Press, 2010). To compare the three versions, A, B, and C, and the Z text, see *Piers Plowman: A Parallel-Text Edition of the A, B, C and Z Versions*, ed. A. V. C. Schmidt, 2nd ed. (Kalamazoo, MI: Medieval Institute Publications, 2011).

6. Michel Foucault, *The History of Sexuality*, vol. 1, trans. Robert Hurley (New York: Pantheon Books, 1978), and *Society Must Be Defended: Lectures at the Collège de France, 1975–76*, trans. David Macey (New York: Picador, 1997).

7. Susan Stryker and Nikki Sullivan, "King's Member, Queen's Body: Transsexual Surgery, Self-Demand Amputation and the Somatechnics of Sovereign Power," in *Somatechnics: Queering the Technologisation of Bodies*, ed. Nikki Sullivan and Samantha Murray (Farnham: Ashgate, 2009), 49–64, quotation at 58–59.

8. All translations from Middle English are my own.

9. See *Middle English Dictionary*, ed. Hans Kurath et al., 13 vols. (Ann Arbor: University of Michigan Press, 1952), s.v. "faitour, n."

10. *The Writings of St. Paul*, ed. Wayne A. Meeks and John T. Fitzgerald, 2nd ed. (New York: Norton, 2007), 38. For the Latin: 1 Corinthians 12:12–20 in *Biblia Sacra: Iuxta Vulgatam Versionem*, ed. Robert Weber (Stuttgart: Deutsche Bibelgesellschaft, 1969).

11. See *Middle English Dictionary*, s.v. "faitour, n."

12. The apologia is extant only in the C text of *Piers Plowman*. On the personification of Reason in *Piers Plowman* and the larger medieval Latin concept of *ratio*, see John A. Alford, "The Idea of Reason in *Piers Plowman*," in *Medieval English Studies Presented to George Kane*, ed. Edward Donald Kennedy, Ronald Waldron, and Joseph S. Wittig (London: D. S. Brewer, 1988), 199–215.

13. See the *Middle English Dictionary* entries for "mishap," "maimen," and "kinde." The Middle English "kinde" is the root of the modern English "kind." Both words, "kind" and "kinde," have the sense of being generous and of being kindred, being of a like kind to others. The word's use in Middle English often has the meaning of "natural instincts, behaviors, forms" of a person, animal, or thing. In its adjectival form, it means "natural," "generous," "normal," or "native." *Piers Plowman* is the only poem to use the word "kynde" to mean God.

14. On the relationship between embodiment, time, and salvation, see Micah James Goodrich, "Lolling and the Suspension of Salvation in *Piers Plowman*," *Yearbook of Langland Studies* 33 (2019): 13–42.

15. See *Middle English Dictionary*, s.v. "mischef, n."

16. From the Latin *caput*, "head." See the entry on "meschief" in J. H. Baker, *Manual of Law French* (Amersham: Avebury, 1979), 150.

17. See "chef" in Robert Martin, *Dictionnaire du Moyen Français* (1330–1500), DMF2009, www.atilf.fr/dmf.

18. Ibid., "méchef."

19. Susan Wood's study *The Proprietary Church in the Medieval West* (Oxford: Oxford University Press, 2006) underscores the impact of church networks as property and argues that the legal and administrative practices of church networks in the medieval West shaped customary law. On *Piers Plowman* and institutional salvation politics, see Jill Averil Keen, *The Charters of Christ and "Piers Plowman": Documenting Salvation* (New York: Peter Lang, 2002); Emily Steiner, *Documentary Culture and the Making of Medieval English Literature* (Cambridge: Cambridge University Press, 2003), and "*Piers Plowman* and Institutional Poetry," *Études Anglaises* 66 (2013): 297–310; Hugh White, *Nature and Salvation in "Piers Plowman"* (London: D. S. Brewer, 1988).

20. John of Salisbury, *Policraticus*, trans. Cary J. Nederman (Cambridge: Cambridge University Press, 2012), 60–61.

21. Christine de Pizan, *The Book of the Body Politic*, ed. and trans. Kate Langdon Forhan (Cambridge: Cambridge University Press, 1994), 91. See also Marie de France, *Fables*, trans. Harriet Spiegel (Toronto: University of Toronto Press, 1994).

22. Christine de Pizan, *Book of the Body Politic*, 90–91.

23. John of Salisbury, *Policraticus*, bk. 4, chap. 8.

24. On the *Christus medicus* tradition in *Piers Plowman*, see David Aers, "Christ's Humanity in *Piers Plowman*: Contexts and Political Implications," *Yearbook of Langland*

Studies 8 (1994): 107–25; Rosanne Gasse, "The Practice of Medicine in *Piers Plowman*," *Chaucer Review* 39.2 (2004): 177–97; Raymond St-Jacques, "Langland's *Christus Medicus* Image and the Structure of *Piers Plowman*," *Yearbook of Langland Studies* 5 (1991): 111–27.

25. Ernst Kantorowicz, *The King's Two Bodies: A Study in Medieval Political Theology* (Princeton, NJ: Princeton University Press, 1981). See Giorgio Agamben's discussion of Kantorowicz in *Homo Sacer: Sovereign Power and Bare Life*, trans. Daniel Heller-Roazen (Stanford, CA: Stanford University Press, 1998), 91.

26. Kellie Robertson, *The Laborer's Two Bodies: Literary and Legal Productions in Britain, 1350–1500* (New York: Palgrave Macmillan, 2006), 25.

27. Rachel C. Gibbons, "'The Limbs Fail When the Head Is Removed': Reactions of the Body Politic of France to the Madness of Charles VI (1380–1422)," in *The Image and Perception of Monarchy in Medieval and Early Modern Europe*, ed. Sean McGlynn and Elena Woodacre (Newcastle upon Tyne: Cambridge Scholars, 2014), 48–67; Katherine Royer, "The Body in Parts: Reading the Execution Ritual in Late Medieval England," *Historical Reflections / Réflexions Historiques* 29.2 (2003): 319–39.

28. Caroline Walker Bynum, *Fragmentation and Redemption: Essays on Gender and the Human Body in Medieval Religion* (New York: Zone Books, 1992), 13. See also Caroline Walker Bynum, *The Resurrection of the Body in Western Christianity, 200–1336* (New York: Columbia University Press, 2017).

29. Bynum, *Fragmentation and Redemption*, 280.

30. Ibid., 272–76.

31. Ibid., 294.

32. Stryker and Sullivan, "King's Member, Queen's Body," 51.

33. Andrew Cole, *Literature and Heresy in the Age of Chaucer* (Cambridge: Cambridge University Press, 2008), 33.

34. See Goodrich, "Lolling and the Suspension of Salvation," 19–28.

35. Pearsall, *Piers Plowman: A New Annotated Edition of the C-text*, 179.

36. See Charles T. Lewis and Charles Short, eds., *A New Latin Dictionary* (Oxford: Clarendon Press, 1891), s.v. "caritas."

37. Both "maim" and "mayhem" emerge from the same Anglo-Norman root; "mayhem" was originally a variant of "maim" and became distinguishable in its legal valence. See the entry "maheme, maiheme" in Baker, *Manual of Law French*, 142. Although John Alford's *Glossary of Legal Diction* for *Piers Plowman* does not contain entries for "maim" or its lexical variant "mayhem," these terms are present throughout the poem and have a sustained legal connotation. John A. Alford, *Piers Plowman: A Glossary of Legal Diction* (London: D. S. Brewer, 1988).

38. There is a lot of debate around the Middle English term "loller" and to what kind of person this word refers. I see this expression connected with the verb "to loll" as an iteration of "to hang," and connect this to debility and temporality in Goodrich, "Lolling and the Suspension of Salvation in *Piers Plowman*," 13–42.

39. Foucault, *History of Sexuality* and *Society Must Be Defended*.

40. Jennifer M. Gianfalla, "'Ther is moore mysshapen amonges thise beggares': Discourses of Disability in *Piers Plowman*," in *Disability in the Middle Ages: Reconsiderations and Reverberations*, ed. Joshua R. Eyler (Farnham: Ashgate, 2010), 119–34, quotation at 132.

41. Elizabeth Loeb, "Cutting It Off: Bodily Integrity, Identity Disorders, and the Sovereign Stakes of Corporeal Desire in U.S. Law," *Women Studies Quarterly* 36.3–4 (2008): 44–63, esp. 46–48.

42. As Greta LaFleur and Kyla Schuller note in their introduction to the special issue of *American Quarterly* "Origins of Biopolitics in the Americas," the scientific movement from theories of "generation" to "reproduction" predominantly occurred in the eighteenth century. See Greta LaFleur and Kyla Schuller, "Technologies of Life and Architectures of Death," *American Quarterly* 71.3 (2019): 603–24. For early modern conceptions of reproduction, see Eve Foster Keller, "Embryonic Individuals: The Rhetoric of Seventeenth-Century Embryology and the Construction of Early Modern Identity," *Eighteenth-Century Studies* 33.3 (2000): 321–48, and *Generating Bodies and Gendered Selves: The Rhetoric of Reproduction in Early Modern England* (Seattle: University of Washington Press, 2007); and Staffan Müller-Wille, "Reproducing Difference: Race and Heredity from a Longue Durée Perspective," in *Race, Gender and Reproduction: Philosophy and the Early Life Sciences in Context*, ed. S. Lettow (Albany: SUNY Press, 2014), 217–36.

43. Passus 20 in the B text.

44. James J. Paxson, "Queering *Piers Plowman*: The Copula(tion)s of Figures in Medieval Allegory," *Rhetoric Society Quarterly* 29 (1999): 21–29, quotation at 25.

45. On volition, willfulness, and limbs, see Sara Ahmed, *Willful Subjects* (Durham, NC: Duke University Press, 2014).

46. See *Middle English Dictionary*, s.v. "hit, pron."

47. It is worth noting that the Middle English verb "maken" means both "to create" in a divine sense as well as a general sense of production and "to mate with"; see ibid., s.v. "maken, v. (1)" and "maken, v. (2)." The poem here suggests that the Dreamer's broken limb disallows him from production and reproduction.

48. There is more to say about the connection between medieval and early modern crimes of mayhem and the legal-literary intersection with trans embodiment that is beyond the scope of this chapter. Colby Gordon has done excellent work on the link between early modern criminal mayhem and/as trans mayhem. I thank him for letting me read a draft of his paper "Trans Mayhem in *Samson Agonistes*" for "Uncommon Bodies: Early Modern Trans x Disabilities," Macalester College, St. Paul, February 13, 2020.

49. Henry Bracton, *On the Laws and Customs of England*, vol. 1, trans. Samuel E. Thorne (Cambridge, MA: Harvard University Press, 1968), 409–10.

50. Edward Coke, *The first part of the Institutes of the laws of England*, ed. Francis Hargrave and Charles Butler (Philadelphia: Kite & Walton, 1853), 127.b.

51. Danuta Mendelson, "Historical Evolution and Modern Implications of Concepts of Consent to, and Refusal of, Medical Treatment in the Law of Trespass," *Journal of Legal Medicine* 17 (1996): 1–71; Loeb, "Cutting It Off," 44–63.

52. See the introduction in *Fleta*, vol. 4, bks. 5 and 6, ed. and trans. G. O. Sayles, Publications of the Selden Society 99 (London: Selden Society, 1983), xxii.

53. "Of Mayhems," bk. 1, chap. 38, in *Fleta*, vol. 2, bks. 1 and 2, ed. and trans. H. G. Richardson and G. O. Sayles. Publications of the Selden Society 72 (London: Selden Society, 1955), 96.

54. Coke, *First part of the Institutes of the laws of England*, 127.b.

55. See *A New Latin Dictionary*, s.v. "limen."

56. The translation is my own. Thank you to Fiona Somerset for suggestions in construing it. The Latin text is from Robert Grosseteste, *De decem mandatis* 5.7, ed. Richard C. Dales and Edward B. King (Oxford: Oxford University Press, 1987), 62. The italicized phrases mimic the italicization in the Latin edition.

57. Masha Raskolnikov, "Transgendering Pride," *postmedieval* 1.1–2 (2010): 157–64, quotations at 159.

58. Lellia Cracco Ruggini, "Mutilation of the Self: Cutting Off Fingers or Ears as Protest in Antiquity," *Rendiconti* 9.3 (1998): 375–85, esp. 382, quotation at 375.

59. See Article 128a, "Maiming," in the US *Manual for Courts-Martial*, 2019.

60. Lawrence J. Culligan and Anthony V. Amodio, eds., *Corpus Juris Secundum*, vol. 56, "Mayhem" to "Mental Health" (St. Paul: West Publishing, 1992). Loeb discusses this issue in "Cutting It Off," 50.

61. See https://twitter.com/realDonaldTrump/status/890196164313833472, July 26, 2017, 9:04 AM.

62. In 2014 the UCLA Law School's Williams Institute on Sexual Orientation and Gender Identity Law and Public Policy estimated that about 15,500 transgender individuals were on active duty or otherwise serving in the US military. See Gary J. Gates and Jody L. Herman, "Transgender Military Service in the United States," Williams Institute, UCLA School of Law, 2014.

63. Stryker and Sullivan, "King's Member, Queen's Body," 58.

64. See Arthur Caplan's statement in Randy Dotinga, "Out on a Limb," https://www.salon.com/2000/08/29/amputation/. This piece begins: "For just about everyone, losing a limb is a fate too horrible to imagine. But for New York psychoanalyst Gregg Furth, the amputation of his right leg would be a dream come true. Not that there's anything wrong with his leg. It works properly and he walks like anyone else. It's his brain that's broken." The alarming association between "defective" thinking and body alteration is all too familiar to transgender and disabled people. Transphobic and ableist language often calls intelligence into question to underscore the seeming disconnect between body alteration or accommodation and mental health.

65. Cited in Dan Irving, "Normalized Transgressions: Legitimizing the Transsexual Body as Productive," *Radical History Review* 100 (2008): 38–59, quotation at 43.

66. Jasbir Puar, *The Right to Maim: Debility, Capacity, Disability* (Durham, NC: Duke University Press, 2017), 44.

67. US Department of Health and Human Services, "HHS Proposes to Revise ACA Section 1557 Rule to Enforce Civil Rights in Healthcare, Conform to Law, and Eliminate Billions in Unnecessary Costs," May 24, 2019, https://www.hhs.gov/about/news/2019/05/24/hhs-proposes-to-revise-aca-section-1557-rule.html.

68. US Department of Health and Human Services, *Federal Register*, pt. 4, 81.96 (2016), 31467.

69. "HHS Proposes to Revise ACA Section 1557 Rule."

70. Berlant, "Slow Death," 765, and *Cruel Optimism*, 95–120. As Puar argues in *Right to Maim*, 35, the "neoliberal mandates regarding productive, capacitated bodies entrain trans bodies to re-create an able body not only in terms of gender and sexuality but also in terms of economic productivity. . . . Thus, trans relation to disability is not simply one of phobic avoidance of stigma; it is also about trans bodies being recruited, in tandem with many other bodies, for a more generalized transformation of capacitated bodies into viable neoliberal subjects."

71. Dean Spade, "Mutilating Gender," in Stryker and Whittle, *Transgender Studies Reader*, 315–32. See variously Kevin M. Barry, "Disabilityqueer: Federal Disability Rights Protection for Transgender People," *Yale Human Rights and Development Law Journal* 16.1 (2013): 1–50; Eli Clare, "Body Shame, Body Pride: Lessons from the Disability Rights Movement," in *The Transgender Studies Reader 2*, ed. Susan Stryker and Aren Z. Aizura (New York: Routledge, 2013), 261–65, and *Exile and Pride: Disability, Queerness, and Liberation* (Durham, NC: Duke University Press, 1999); Alison Kafer, *Feminist, Queer, Crip* (Bloomington: Indiana University Press, 2013); Robert McRuer and Nicole Markotić, "Leading with Your Head: On the Borders of Disability, Sexuality, and the Nation," in *Sex and Disability*, ed. Robert McRuer and Anna Mollow (Durham, NC: Duke University Press, 2012), 165–82; Jasbir K. Puar, "Disability," *TSQ: Transgender Studies Quarterly* 1.1–2 (2014): 77–81; Spade, "Mutilating Gender"; Amets Suess, Karine Espineira, and Pau Crego Walters, "Depathologization," *TSQ: Transgender Studies Quarterly* 1.1–2 (2014): 73–77.

72. Puar, *Right to Maim*, 35.

73. Stryker and Sullivan, "King's Member, Queen's Body," 57.

CHAPTER 12

Where Are All the Trans Women in Byzantium?

ROLAND BETANCOURT

From the fifth to the ninth century, there are a series of saints' lives composed in the Byzantine Empire (330–1453 CE) that detail the lives of individuals assigned female at birth, who for a variety of reasons chose to live most of their lives as monks, usually presenting as eunuchs. While masculinity was often articulated as a prized virtue for all genders, even going against official decrees and sanctions restricting the dressing of women in male-coded garments, the image of women assigned male at birth is all but absent in Byzantine sources. The question I wish to ask here is not why this is the case but rather where might we find the traces of these lives by shifting our methodological perspectives. My aim here is to focus on methodologies and modes of reading for articulating narratives and identities for women in the Byzantine Empire who had been assigned male at birth.

The answers to this question are difficult to approach, given that women and femininity were almost always seen as the lesser, imperfect sex. To become a woman or to be effeminate offered no social or spiritual gain. Therefore these women emerge only in slanderous texts and invective, more so as the imaginings of critics rather than a contouring of a specific identity. Caroline Walker Bynum understands narratives of men assigned female at birth and female masculinity as a "practical device" for these figures to avoid persecution, escape their families, and take on social roles limited to men alone. Given that they "could have gained nothing socially by it except opprobrium," as Bynum says, the archive has preserved less the lives of women assigned male at birth, whose meager accounts are short and nameless, wrapped only in accusations of immorality and depravity.[1] Bynum's views capture the prejudices of the archive as much as that of its historians, yet this perspective is by no means unique but pervasive throughout all the existing Byzantine secondary literature on the matter and related studies.[2] As Jack Halberstam critically cautioned, "female masculinity" has often been associated with "a 'natural' desire for the greater freedoms and mobility enjoyed by boys," except of course when that masculinity exceeds its bounds and challenges male identity itself.[3] This chapter aims at filling the absence of women assigned male at birth, precisely by paying attention to the sensibilities of Byzantine sources and their open and fluid handling of gender variance.[4] Here my aim is to understand the various glimmers and discussions of women who had been assigned male at birth as medieval antecedents to modern trans lives. Articulating these medieval women as trans allows us to better understand how Greek writers understood, construed, and imagined gender.

An important methodological challenge in the study and excavation of trans lives in the medieval world is that many of these stories have their origins in the Byzantine Empire.[5] While some of these narratives gained popularity in the Western medieval world in later centuries through translations, these are sources written in Greek that would have been inaccessible to the Latin-speaking West. Scholars of the Western Middle Ages have approached these issues with distinctly Western sensibilities that have a faulty understanding of Byzantine ideas about gender and sexuality. More importantly, scholars have failed to acknowledge that the corpus of ancient Greek literature on which so much discussion of premodern and early modern gender and sexuality hinges was actively preserved, commentated on, and studied in the Byzantine Empire, largely in Constantinople. This is not to say that no text of Plato, for example, was accessible in the West in translation during the Middle Ages, but rather that the corpus of classical learning preserved in its Greek original exists for us because of Byzantine learning and philosophy. Therefore these works are as much a product of antiquity as they are of the Byzantine Empire, as Byzantine scholars chose what to preserve and excerpted and compiled sources into the modern tomes we know them as today.

In this chapter I have collected a series of disparate sources across late antiquity and the medieval period, recognizing that these temporal divisions for the Byzantine Empire are deeply misleading. These selected texts describe figures assigned male at birth, yet who are said to be feminine in various capacities and whose gender identity is imputed differently across the different sources. I am approaching these various texts with distinctly Byzantine sensibilities, reading them with an attention to how Byzantium understood gender and sexuality, as well as to how these texts were transmitted and understood within Byzantine contexts. But reading through Byzantine eyes serves as a radical shift from Western scholars, including Michel Foucault.[6] Foucault, for example, read Greek texts (both ancient and late antique) on gender and sexuality as a product of the atemporal "Greeks" rather than grasping the deep and fundamental impact that the Byzantine Empire had on what we today consider Greek philosophy and literature, which was actively preserved in an empire that never referred to itself as "Byzantine" or "Byzantium" but always as "Roman" (Rōmaioi).[7]

Moving through late antique theater's impact on Constantinopolitan life, the invectives of early church writers, and the work of late antique historical chronicles, the texts in this chapter establish the foundation for how the Middle Byzantine period (843–1204 CE) understood aspects of gender and sexuality, particularly as they pertain to anxieties about effeminacy and women who were assigned male at birth. The figures discussed throughout these examples demand a revaluation of what trans identities could have looked like in late antiquity and the Byzantine Empire. My goal here is to consider an ethical proposition: if we accept that transgender persons are not a modern phenomenon but have existed in the shadows throughout history, then we must work to understand how the appearance of these figures (when presented through invective and insult) indexed the oppressed presence of medieval people who did not identify with the gender they were assigned at birth, even if their self-identification was not imagined in the same manner as it is today.

My goal is to articulate the deeply queer existence of trans women, whose identities have been all but purged from the historical record through screeds of invective. As historians, we are left to excavate these fragments from the archives, even those weakly glimmering possibilities of trans women. In the absence of clearly contoured terms in medieval sources, I use the term "trans" to refer to these figures with the goal of demonstrating a history for them and a model of "best practices" for giving representation to figures whose lives have been denied. One key commitment, however, is to resist medicalizing gender or seeing trans lives only in the representation of outward presentations of gender.[8] This chapter struggles with the absences of the archive and the potent act of grasping at lives erased and denied. "To read without a trace," as Anjali Arondekar calls it, is a way of embracing the absences of the archive, the seductions of retrieval, and the recuperative hermeneutics of accessing minoritized lives and historiographies.[9]

Much historical work in trans studies has struggled with the tension between linearity and absence, both in the archive and in how we tell our stories. In particular, I am drawn to the work of Jack Halberstam and C. Riley Snorton for their ability to balance the realities of historical subjects by seizing the complexities of our own modern experience of gender.[10] But I am more struck by the imperatives of my fellow medievalist Gabrielle M. W. Bychowski, who has been able to perceive the nuance of historical context by emplacing it within the ethical demands of our teaching and scholarship, which always requires code-switching between modern and premodern language lest we forsake the past and the present at once.[11] The ethical imperative in this chapter is to "read without a trace" in order to pry these fragments from the hands of their abusers and restore to them the dignity of a compelling historical narrative, stitched together from fragments, contradictions, and tracelessness.[12]

The Byzantine Theater and Satire

In the late antique Byzantine world, the theater is a key site for the manifestation of bodies that unsettle gender identity, particularly associated with attacks on femininity and effeminacy. One of the more controversial aspects of pantomime performances was precisely the matter of female roles played by male performers who, as Ruth Webb has argued, readily changed between roles and genders without a costume change or other narrative cues, but simply by altering their gestures, gait, and posture.[13] In an epigram preserved in the *Latin Anthology*, compiled in early sixth-century Carthage, we have a vivid depiction of such performances:

> Declining his masculine breast with a feminine inflection [mascula femineo declinans pectora flexu] and moulding his pliant torso to suit either sex, the dancer enters the stage and greets the people, promising that words will come forth from his expert hands. For when the sweet chorus pours forth its delightful song, what the singer declaims, the dancer himself confirms with his movements. He fights, he plays, he loves, he revels, he turns round, he stands still, he illuminates the truth, and imbues everything with grace. He has as many tongues as limbs, so wonderful is the art by which he can make his joints speak although his mouth is silent.[14]

Reminiscent of performances in the theaters of Constantinople in the same period, such performers drew the ire of imperial and church authorities while often being associated with sex work and other illicit sexual acts (*porneia*).[15] These attacks on performers disproportionately targeted women's sexual lives, but male performers were also included within these accusations of sex work and sexual promiscuity. In the latter cases, however, these attacks were primarily structured around the imputation of effeminacy and the desire to become a woman.[16]

In a text attributed to John Chrysostom (340/50–407 CE), the author writes that these dancers lamented the gender they were assigned at birth by their parents: "But the feminine dancers are broken men, who imitate these things against nature, grieving that they had not been born women from their parents [lypoumenos hoti mē gynē para tōn goneōn etechthē], and been assigned that desired transformation of nature."[17] This is an important text to consider, given that John Chrysostom is a central figure in Eastern Christianity, being an important Church Father, who is credited with providing the church with its key liturgical rite and whose homilies were repeatedly used in the rites of the church. The manuscript tradition's attribution of this text to John Chrysostom carried immense weight, even if modern scholars have come to question its authorship by the Church Father.

Similar suggestions are made in Amphilochius of Iconium's fourth-century iambs to Seleucus, where he describes that the twisting and turning of limbs betray the glory of male gender and destroy nature as these figures neither are male nor fully become female.[18] As Amphilochius explicitly states, they do not simply play the character but desire to become women, and that which they "so wrongly desire is not natural" (au kakōs thelousin, ouk eisin physei). The repeated notion across such texts is that if men perform as women, then they also wish to be women as well.[19] This fear and paranoia about these dancers' being both "effeminate men and masculine women" (andres gynaiki kai gynaikes andrasin), as Amphilochius puts it, are echoed in sources that address anxieties around non-normative gender expression and presentation. These concerns focused specifically around practices of dress and grooming, matters that were also codified across the Councils of Gangra and Trullo in the fourth and seventh centuries, respectively, as well as in the Theodosian Code from the mid-fifth century.[20] These restrictions generally followed the prohibition in Deuteronomy 22:5 that states that "a woman must not wear men's clothing, nor should a man dress up in women's clothing," both being an offense to God.

Since antiquity, the dress and grooming of so-called "effeminate men" is also simultaneously inscribed in sexual practices and promiscuity, primarily

ROLAND BETANCOURT

around same-gender desires.[21] In one epigram by the mid-first-century Roman poet Martial, we are graphically presented with a contemplation upon a man who practices feminine habits of depilation: "You pluck your chest and your shins and your arms, and your shaven cock is ringed with short hairs. This, Labienus, you do for your mistress' sake, as everybody knows. For whose sake, Labienus, do you depilate your arse?"[22] As this bawdy poem suggests, it would not be unexpected that a man might shave his chest, arms, legs, and pubic hair for his female lover, "as everybody knows." Yet the question is left open as to what is the extent of this alleged feminization if it applies as well to other sexual practices beyond those with his mistress. The conceit is that if the shaven pubic area welcomes a female partner, the shaven rear welcomes a male partner. Confronting male grooming practices that were seen as somehow feminine, such as coiffing, hair dyeing, or the shaving of body hair, ancient and late antique authors manifest an inherent transphobia, seemingly asking when do these "feminine" practices make men into women, where "womanhood" is understood both as an outward expression of one's gender and as implicating a man as being the receptive partner in anal sex.[23]

Also writing in the first century, the Roman satirist Juvenal confronted this problem by suggesting that men seeking a promotion in the army, for example, should endeavor to leave their hair uncombed and make sure to have untrimmed armpit and nose hair so as to emphasize their virility, manliness, and hardness.[24] Juvenal jokingly proposes the performance of an exuberant caricature of masculinity. The implication of his suggestion is not simply that a feminine man would be unsuitable for the job; this statement also contains a social critique of the fact that affectations of masculinity through a hirsute, unkempt, and rough appearance could be used to one's social advantage. Elsewhere, Juvenal reflects, "Shaggy limbs and stiff bristles all over your arms promise a spirit that's fierce, but your arsehole is smooth when the laughing doctor lances your swollen 'figs.'"[25] Here the bravado of hyper-masculine performance is foiled by the doctor who laughs while lancing hemorrhoids from the man's shaven ass, given that anal hemorrhoids were seen as a consequence of anal sex. In the instances recounted by Martial and Juvenal, we observe the enforcement of a normative masculinity that is also deeply preoccupied with a figure assigned male at birth who is allegedly concealing their femininity. At times, this femininity is understood as indicating a sexual desire to be the passive partner in same-gender relations. Repeatedly, however, this conclusion results from the observation of grooming and other bodily practices associated with women at the time.

The Early Church and Transmisogyny

By the late second century, the early Christian philosopher Clement of Alexandria (ca. 150–215 CE) would grapple with the question of femininity more broadly in his chapter on the "beautification of men" (kallōpizomenous tōn andrōn) in *The Instructor*, in which he condemns same-gender sexual desire in the service of the development of the rest of his treatise.[26] Clement describes at some length the contours of late antique Alexandria and the preponderance of "effeminate men," along with expressing in passing how to even begin to read these men who "become women" (gynaikizontai) by being "inclined toward softness" (malthakōteron). He concludes that they must be "adulterers and androgynous men" (moichous te kai androgynous).[27] He carefully details the garments and adornments they wear; the various methods they use and the street shops they frequent for depilation, hair dyeing, and coiffing; and the gestures, behaviors, movements, and habits of these "womanish creatures," while simultaneously offering sordid speculations about their sexual proclivities.[28] For Clement, this phenomenon is rooted in the "disease" of "luxury," whereby men "become effeminate, cutting their hair in an ungentlemanly and meretricious way, cloth[ing themselves] in fine and transparent garments, chewing mastic, smelling of perfume." Likewise, Clement takes aim at hair dyeing for several reasons, primarily because the bleaching and yellowing of hair was associated with women but is here offered as evidence that these are "androgynous men with a pernicious lifestyle" (androgynōn exōlōn epitēdeumata).[29]

Hair removal, however, appears to be a particular preoccupation for Clement. He begins at first by describing the various shops in town where one can go to get shaven, plucked, or waxed: the equivalent of modern waxing is "the violent tuggings of pitch-plasters." In an almost comical acrobatics of invective, he even takes issue with the process of waxing itself, condemning "the act of bending back and bending down, the violence done to nature's modesty by stepping out and bending backwards in shameful positions." What is worse is that this waxing occurs while these men are exposed to the gaze of all in these waxing shops in the middle of town, and thus "he who in the light of day denies his manhood, will prove himself manifestly a woman by night."[30] He connects the shamelessness of being publicly waxed to sexual passivity, evidenced by the need to be bent over in all sorts of positions.

This connection between hairless smoothness and sexual passivity is echoed in Clement's discussion of women who do sex work and those "boys, taught to deny their sex," who thus "act the part of women." This is understood in terms of both sexual passivity and gender performance, as he then goes on to say that these days, "men play the part of women, and women that of men, contrary to nature."[31] The misogynistic fear of men "playing" the role of women is common to early church writings. For example, in the late fourth century, John Chrysostom attacks the femininity of men who "receive women at the door, strutting as if they had been transformed into eunuchs," and also those who comport themselves with a lack of self-restraint or perform womanly tasks.[32] For Chrysostom, for a man to behave as a woman in one's actions was akin to being castrated as a eunuch. These ideas, however, reveal the tenuous manner in which gender identity was handled. Rather than understanding gender as a byproduct of a medicalized notion of sex, these comments hint at the anxieties that gender may in fact not adhere to that assigned at birth.

Furthermore, Clement of Alexandria struggles with the way these figures practice other forms of bodily adornment and garb, such as the wearing of jewelry and fine garments that are socially and legally reserved for women: "For although not allowed to wear gold, yet out of effeminate desire they enwreath their lashes and fringes with leaves of gold" or dangle gold and pearls from their ankles and necks.[33] Here we understand that the use of feminine adornments by men, while prohibited by legal decrees, was nevertheless being done quite openly. Clement ascribes this contrary-to-law practice as emerging from an inner "effeminate desire" (thēlydriōdē epithymian),[34] positing an internalized feminine identity for these men that is not exclusively associated with same-gender desire. As he goes on to say, they deny the characteristics of their sex and also spend time in women's apartments, becoming chimerical "amphibious beasts."[35] For Clement, this goes against nature, because at Creation God extracted all "smoothness and softness" from Adam when he created Eve, who was formed as his receptive partner, while Adam "remained a man, and shows himself man."[36]

While Clement might seek to connect effeminacy to same-gender desire as a trope of such earlier invective, it would seem that he is anxious about the enmeshed relationship between gender expression and sexuality. In a fanciful leap of invective, Clement tries to summarize such sexual depravity by speaking of men who engage in any form of "luxury" and father many children without their knowledge. Such men, he argues, seek out female sex workers and boys for sex, copulating unknowingly with their own progeny: these men "have intercourse with a son that has debauched himself, and daughters that are sex workers."[37] These comments clarify that for Clement of Alexandria, male "luxury" is not simply associated with men who seek out male partners but is nevertheless understood as a negative quality associated with women and femininity.[38] This is expressed earlier, when Clement grapples with the ambiguity of these effeminate men's sexuality, observing that "the embellishment of depilation . . . if it is to attract men, is the act of a womanly person, but if to attract women, is the act of an adulterer," going back to the suggestions he had made initially in The Instructor about how to read feminine men as either effeminates or adulterers.[39] Thus, while same-gender desire or sexual passivity, more broadly, might be lazily ascribed to femininity, Clement repeatedly seems to concede that this gender expression is not directly tied to sexual desire but amounts to its own category.[40] The importance of stressing this is that it attempts to make a distinction between homophobic rhetoric and transphobic rhetoric. While Clement resorts to the former, his true preoccupation is the latter.

In one instance, reflecting on men who comb, pluck, smooth, and arrange their hair, "in truth, unless you saw them naked, you would suppose them to be women."[41] While this may simply be a rhetorical exaggeration, we could also begin to read Clement as outlining a cultural understanding of a certain class of individuals that we might think of as a historical relative of something like trans identity. As he summarizes near the end of his tirade, struggling with terms to describe some of these men: "Rather we ought not to call them men [ouk andras], but lispers [batalous] and effeminates [gynnidas], whose voices are broken, and whose clothes are womanish both in feel and dye. And such creatures are manifestly shown to be what they are from their external appearance, their clothes, shoes, form, walk, cut of their hair, look."[42] While the terms batalous and gynnidas should certainly be understood as gesturing to sexualized passivity, here they are being deployed as constructions meant to articulate a different gender category, explicitly stating that these are "not men" (ouk andras) because, as he goes on to say, following Ecclesiastes 19:29–30, men should be identifiable from their dress, gait, affect, and character. Hence the implication is that these lispers and effeminates are not men but another gender altogether. This does not, however, apply wholesale to all the various figures and practices he has described throughout. Note in particular that elsewhere he does not draw attention to "broken voices" (phōnai tethrymmenai), which suggests a gender expression beyond mere grooming practices, like hair shaving, waxing, or dyeing, or the wearing of jewelry and other bodily adornments. Here we get the explicit sense not only that these figures have taken up an effeminate behavior through their "clothes, shoes, form, walk, cut of their hair, look" but also, specifically, that their dresses are those of women in "feel and dye," and that even the quality of their voices has been modified. These litanies of gender-crossed terms, like Amphilochius's "effeminate men and masculine women," are common throughout Byzantine texts, both in late antiquity and in the later Middle Ages. This struggle with language precisely demonstrates writers attempting to articulate and give voice to a reality they cannot quite name.

While there is a distracting conflation of many identities and the ways they intersect, Clement's text ultimately does offer a glimpse into what late antique authors imagined as a transgender identity. In Clement's text, we are left to understand that within a wide spectrum of practices deployed by late antique Alexandrian "effeminate men," there is a nod toward a complex spectrum of gender identities. We see here the fragments of a negatively defined identity projected onto trans women in late antiquity, shaped unwittingly and haphazardly by Clement of Alexandria's invective. Previous scholarship has all but ignored these claims, mining these texts for histories of sexuality, normative gender roles, and their ancillary prohibitions, but not as a way to see the imprints of trans women and gender-nonconforming figures. Clement's text nevertheless stages the specific challenge of naming people who, while assigned male at birth, seem to live out their lives with a female gender presentation. For Clement, this is vividly manifested by the passing comment that only their genitalia could allow them to be identified as "male," an emphasis on the genitals that echoes transphobic rhetoric to this day.[43]

Thus, to perceive any hint of transgender women's experience in the late antique and Byzantine world, we must read simultaneously along and against the grain of the archive's transmisogyny. Transmisogyny distinguishes itself from a generalized transphobic anxiety in these texts in the fact that it is trans women and trans femininity, broadly and variably conceived, that is singled out as the medium for the transphobic invective.[44] It is a disproportionate attack that singles out the figure of the trans woman as the subject of ridicule, attack, and insult based on the underlying delusion that men are better than women. It is this form of transmisogyny that we see most prominently across late antique and medieval Greek sources, effectively erasing and denying the lives of trans women and "effeminate men," except when represented as negative rhetorical figures.

Dio Cassius's Elagabalus

At the end of antiquity, we are provided with one of the most extensive narratives of a single figure who not only identified as female but also actively sought out gender-affirming surgery. This striking evidence is found in the figure of the Roman emperor Elagabalus (203–222 CE).[45] In the *Roman History*,

Elagabalus's contemporary Dio Cassius attacks the ruler's life and deeds by stressing Elagabalus's identification as a woman.[46] Dio Cassius recounts horrific and barbaric ritual sacrifices and magic associated with Elagabalus's name and offers graphic details pertaining to the ruler's various marriages and lascivious sexual conquests.[47] But of key importance here is the manner in which Elagabalus is depicted as a trans woman, that is to say, as a person who had been assigned male at birth but identified herself as female. Dio Cassius recounts precisely how Elagabalus presented her gender identity. Dio Cassius claims that Elagabalus "would go to the taverns by night, wearing a wig, and there ply the trade of a female huckster."[48] Repeatedly Elagabalus is said to behave in the manner resembling that of female sex workers, standing naked in the doorway of the palace while in a "soft and melting voice"[49] soliciting all who went by. Furthermore, Dio Cassius argues that Elagabalus took on a lover she referred to as "husband" and wished to make a co-emperor. For herself Elagabalus chose the titles of "wife, mistress, and queen." Only when she tried someone in the court of law did Elagabalus have "more or less the appearance of a man, but everywhere else he showed his affectation in his actions and in the quality of his voice." Elagabalus would shave her own face and pluck her hairs out "so as to look more like a woman," and she worked wool, wore a hairnet, and painted her eyeslids.[50]

In the figure of Elagabalus, one is confronted with an image of a ruler rooted in the tropes of classical and late antique invective, using femininity as a slanderous tactic. Yet, simultaneously, there is a careful depiction of this figure's gender expression and her quite self-conscious identification as a woman. Dio Cassius's depiction, however, often evokes Elagabalus's femininity through accusations of sexual depravity to shame the person's gender. Nevertheless, through these litanies of so-called depravities we are also offered fragments of historical evidence of a woman who had been assigned male at birth. Uniquely, the narrative states that she not only dressed in women's clothing and followed women's grooming practices but also sought gender-affirming surgical procedures, to which I now turn.

Throughout the later Byzantine sources, there is a claim that Elagabalus sought to undergo gender-affirming surgical procedures. While this is at times attributed to Dio Cassius, it is only attested across Byzantine writers.[51] In a passing yet telling comment, the twelfth-century historian John Zonaras writes that Elagabalus "carried his lewdness to such a point that he asked the physicians to contrive a woman's vagina in his body by means of an incision, promising them large sums for doing so." A similar request is found in George Kedrenos's twelfth-century *Synopsis of History*. There, Elagabalus, "according to Dio, besought his physician to employ his skill to make him bisexual [diphuē] by means of an anterior incision."[52] This detail, whose attribution to Dio Cassius by Kedrenos is plausible, captured the imagination of several other Byzantine writers. This passage is cited verbatim by both the mid-tenth-century Symeon Logothete (also referred to as Leo Grammatikos) and the twelfth-century Michael Glykas in their respective historical chronicles.[53]

Elagabalus's request stresses the desire of this figure (real or rhetorical) to undergo gender-affirming surgery in the late antique world. This point is emphasized by Dio Cassius, who leaves little uncertainty about Elagabalus's motivation. When noting that she also circumcised herself in order to lead her cult, he writes that Elagabalus "had planned, indeed, to cut off his genitals altogether, but that desire was prompted solely by his effeminacy."[54] That these details about Elagabalus's gender and desire for gender affirming surgery are often the only aspects provided about her reign in several Byzantine chronicles is immensely poignant.

Perhaps even more striking is that the late-thirteenth-century Theodore Skoutariotes presented a wholly positive image of Elagabalus, writing that she was "righteous, sharp in war, gentle, thoughtful, servicing all, and loved by all," suggesting an erroneous understanding of Elagabalus or a purposeful revision of the narrative, with the detail of her gentleness or softness (ēpios) being the only remnant of the stereotypical charges of effeminacy lodged against the trans Elagabalus.[55] His work may be partially indebted to Herodian's *History of the Empire*, which featured a more neutral approach to Elagabalus's reign while nevertheless noting Elagabalus's dressing and adornment habits.[56] Herodian's text was also known to Byzantine writers and is attested in Photius's *Bibliotheca*.[57]

The salacious details about Elgabalus's sexuality and gender identity were by no means limited to Dio Cassius's work. Similar claims are found in the works of both contemporaneous and later writers, whose dependence on Dio's *Roman History* cannot be readily assumed. For example, Philostratus of Athens tells us in the *Lives of the Sophists* that the Roman Sophist Claudius Aelianus (a contemporary of Elagabalus) composed and delivered an indignant attack against Elagabalus called the "Indictment against the Little Woman" (katēgoria tou Gynnidos).[58] Several decades later, the fourth-century anonymous author of the *Epitome de Caesaribus* wrote that Elagabalus "turned himself into a woman" (in se convertens muliebri) and also asked to be called by a female name.[59] The attack by Aelianus referring to Elagabalus as a "little woman" speaks tellingly to a widespread understanding that the ruler was a woman, beyond Dio's specific account. And while Aelianus's text was long believed to be wholly lost, Steven Smith has provocatively and convincingly suggested that fragments have in fact come down to us, preserved in the tenth-century Byzantine lexicon *The Souda*, providing further evidence that it was well known and popular in the Byzantine world.[60]

Byzantine Eunuchs and Femininity

A critical aspect in this conversation focused on Byzantium is the important role that eunuchs played in the empire, which was markedly different from the negative stereotypes that eunuchs carried in antiquity. Kathryn Ringrose has helpfully made the point that eunuchs functioned in Byzantium as a "third gender," appearing in the writings of figures like Cyril of Alexandria and Basil of Caesarea as "an accursed gender [genos] . . . neither feminine nor masculine."[61] Shaun Tougher has added to this conversation by rightly stressing that eunuchs could be considered masculine or feminine depending on the context, particularly in later centuries, when a more favorable approach to eunuchs in Byzantium replaced older cultural attitudes.[62] Byzantine authors understood castration as feminizing the body and in a sense transforming men into women. In more popular writings, this was understood potently in terms of the psychology, behavior, and appearance of eunuchs. Their character was feminine, that is, defined by their inability to control their passions, desires, and appetites. Ringrose has surveyed the manner in which eunuchs were described: accused of indulging in sexual excess, smelling of musk, weaving webs and trying to ensnare others, having soft white flesh and high shrill voices, being unable to control their emotions.[63] The eunuch served as a telling exemplar of the malleability of the body's sexes since the removal of the genitals alone, according to Aristotle, "results in such a great alteration of their old semblance, and in close approximation to the appearance of the female."[64]

Certainly it is possible that persons assigned male at birth chose to live their lives as (or become) eunuchs with a feminine gender presentation. Particularly in late antiquity, self-castration for religious purposes is evidenced in the story of Origen.[65] The topic even came up at the Council of Nicaea in 325, which in its first canon bars the person who "in sound health has castrated himself" from entering or serving in the clergy, even though those castrated for medical reasons, by barbarians, by their masters, or those who "should otherwise be found worthy" can be admitted.[66] This attack on self-castration may have been aimed at deterring any extreme ascetic drives to attempt to cut off sexual desire, but it also might have been contoured by pejorative views of the eunuch's femininity in body and character in the late antique period.

Beyond their feminine and androgynous appearance, the notion that eunuchs could operate socially as women appears in the story of the life of Matrona of Perge. At one point in the story, while she is living as the eunuch Babylas in the male monastery of Bassianos in Constantinople, she is nearly misgendered by a fellow monk while they are both gardening when he asks, "How is it, brother, that the lobes of both your ears are pierced?" After chastising the monk for not minding his own business, Babylas replies, "The woman to whom I formerly belonged was lovingly disposed toward me, maintaining me with all generosity and luxury, and she shrank not from putting gold about my ears, so that many of those who saw me said that I was a girl."[67] Here the narrative offers us an interesting example whereby a eunuch, by virtue of their garments and fine jewelry, was understood as a woman according to late antique and Byzantine associations between luxury and femininity, as we have seen earlier in Clement of Alexandria. Certainly this fits the established image of eunuchs in Constantinople, many of whom worked for the imperial court and thus would have dressed in the most exquisite finery. The fact that some eunuchs after castration could be referred to as women has precedent in the ancient Greco-Roman world.

In the *Lives of the Caesars*, Suetonius tells us that one of Nero's many depraved crimes included the fact that he "castrated the boy Sporus and actually tried to make a woman of him; and he married him with all the usual ceremonies . . . and treated him as his wife."[68] This suggests that castration could in some way be consciously understood as a surgical procedure for affirming a female identity, though there is no evidence in this case to suggest that it operated as a gender-affirming procedure for the figure being castrated. In the late Roman and Byzantine sphere, the roles that eunuchs filled were often akin to those played by women, and they had particularly privileged access to women's spaces.[69] Thus, it is likewise possible that some masters might even have had a say in the gender presentation of their eunuchs. Hence, Babylas's imaginary owner may not only have kept them in the finest clothing from Constantinople but also pierced both their ears in the style of women so as to alter their perceived gender.

As a made-up story within a saint's life, this detail must be taken lightly, yet a telling narrative from the Western medieval world sheds light on the notion that Constantinopolitan eunuchs could have served likewise as a space to maneuver for women assigned male at birth. In the *History of the Franks*, Gregory of Tours recounts the story of a eunuch who lived much of their life as a woman. As the story goes, during a revolt at a convent, various accusations are lodged against its abbess, one being that "she had a man in the monastery who wore woman's clothes and was treated as a woman although he had been very clearly shown to be a man." The figure then takes the stand, wearing the woman's clothes they were accustomed to wearing, and explains that they were "impotent" and thus took on these clothes but did not know the abbess and lived far from the convent. The accuser, frustrated with her inability to properly incriminate the abbess, states that she "makes men eunuchs" and has them live with her "as if she were an empress," drawing an allusion to stereotypes of the Byzantine capital. In the end, a doctor comes forward and reveals that he was the one who castrated the youth. As a young boy, the eunuch had suffered from a disease of the groin, and thus the doctor performed the castration procedure "in the way I had once seen physicians do in Constantinople," restoring the child's health.[70] The story is laden with the traces of Constantinople, from the comparison to the imperial presence of eunuchs associated with the empress to the fact that the physician learned the operation in the Byzantine capital, reinforcing the associations between this gender-variant figure and the Eastern empire.

In Gregory of Tours, we have an instance of a person assigned male at birth, who is castrated for medical reasons, and then chooses to live their life as a woman. The story of this figure is exceptional, appearing without challenge or judgment, given that the eunuch's revelation serves to vindicate a falsely accused religious figure. But the quality of the invective wrongly cast against the abbess demonstrates the challenge in discovering other, similar instances. As one scholar puts it, "The implication remains . . . that the only reason a man might don female garb and live in a convent was to gain sexual satisfaction from the nuns."[71] This prejudice alerts us that in order to seek out further traces of trans women in the Byzantine sphere, we require a closer scrutiny of invective against sexual depravity, seeking not simply attacks on effeminacy and same-gender desire but, more importantly, instances where figures assigned male at birth might be described as masquerading or disguising themselves as women for the sake of sexual gain. While such stories might themselves be transphobic inventions, they may well point to the presence of erased trans figures, misrepresented as sex-crazed men.

Michael Psellus and Nonbinary Gender Identity

In a culture where dressing as a woman is prohibited to individuals assigned male at birth, it is also necessary to grasp that to be and live as a gender-nonconforming individual would not always coincide with the outward manifestation of one's gender through clothing and grooming. In other words, to seek out the erased lives of both trans men and women, it is also possible to excavate these subjectivities through other practices, such as those of self-identification. For this, we can consider the gender identity of the imperial court philosopher Michael Psellus (ca. 1018–1081 CE), who in their letters repeatedly referred to themself as being feminine. In one instance Psellus writes that while they have a masculine disposition toward learning, "with regard to nature I am feminine [thēlys]," given that they are "softened [malthakizomai] with respect to natural emotions." Or, elsewhere, "my soul is indeed simply feminine [thēlys] and easily moved toward compassion."[72] While this form of feminine identification has precedent in the writings of Synesius of Cyrene, in his careful study of Psellus's gender identification, Stratis Papaioannou notes that "what is virtually unprecedented" is that Psellus "does not simply express his emotions. Nor, as it were, does he merely confess the excessively emotional sides of his personality. Rather, he identifies female affects with his unique 'nature' and 'ethos,' and these become a 'fundamental feature of the author's persona.'" Papaioannou refers to this as Psellus's "rhetorical transvestism," yet I believe this should be pushed further to recognize that what we perceive in Psellus offers the foundations of a marginalized transgender identity in Byzantium.[73]

Michael's surname Psellus does not seem to have been given to them as a patronymic, as it refers to one who lisps (*psellos*). They repeatedly not only identify as having a feminine soul or nature but also recount the ways in which they do not adhere to the masculine gender identity that they are expected to express as an imperial philosopher. Psellus states in another letter regarding their emotional states and interests that they have always been feminine, writing, "Now if this pertains to a feminine [thēleia] soul, I do not really know; at all events, my character [ēthos] has been stamped in this way all along," comparing their nature to a bit of soft, malleable wax.[74] Almost defiantly, Psellus refuses to be limited to the stereotypes of their assigned gender, saying that they will "chat with friends in a jolly spirit" and "nor will I despise the women's chamber to indulge in that quarter a bit." Thus Psellus concludes with a poetic reflection on their gender identity, comparing it to the strings of an instrument, possibly playing with notions of masculinity and femininity through the notion of low- and high-pitched voices: "I am not like the strings that are either only high-pitched or in harmony, but contain every melody, now more bright and sweet-sounding, now taut and noble."[75]

What we find in Psellus's writings about themself is a poetic reflection on gender fluidity in the Byzantine world. This highly learned figure reflects upon the sociocultural constitutions of their profession and assigned sex, which conflicts with their own self-identification as female in matters of emotion, affect, and social behavior. Psellus pushes the boundaries of what it means to perceive a transgender subjectivity in the Byzantine world, demanding that we look both at the externalization of one's gender expression through dress, grooming, and affects, and likewise at how authors perceived themselves according to the rubrics of what it meant to be male and female in the late-antique and medieval world.

Across Byzantine sources and their late antique precedents, we find a surprising distinction between gender and sexuality with a whole spectrum of gender variance. Even before Michel Foucault's *History of Sexuality*, there has been a misconception that the premodern world primarily articulated gender and sexuality as one and the same. This matter becomes all the more critical in the case of trans women and "male effeminacy," given that so much of Western rhetoric has resorted to transmisogyny to call out same-gender desire among figures assigned male at birth. While this was certainly the case in Clement of Alexandria's *The Instructor*, it was also possible to observe deeper anxieties that beyond sexuality there was an underlying "desire" among the persons described to "become women." This concern is seen centrally in Dio Cassius and Byzantine historians' fascination with the accounts of Elagabalus's gender, which, while deploying sexualized stereotypes of femininity and same-gender desire, repeatedly assert her gender identity as existing beyond sexuality alone. The nonbinary and gender-variant identification of eunuchs in the Middle Byzantine period affirms a more fluid understanding of gender over the centuries, which grappled with the malleability of the body, psychology, and social roles through the wealth of classical philosophy and medicine available to Constantinopolitan writers. This culminates in the self-identification of Michael Psellus as nonbinary, stressing how their gender identity does not adhere to cultural stereotypes and expectations but rather exists between the various categories in a harmonious unity.

While I have selected here only a very limited number of texts focused specifically on figures who identified as female or more feminine than their assigned gender, the same nuanced approach to gender variance (and attendant anxieties among critics) is extensive throughout the Middle Byzantine period. What this chapter uniquely offers is a directive to consider Byzantine authors according to the rich wealth of knowledge that the learning of the period offered, on their own terms and distinct from the models that have been created for the Western Middle Ages and early modern period. All of the lives and persons cited across this chapter are lost to us, as we confront the limits of the archive. More importantly, in attempting to liberate these lives from erasure, we are forced to re-perform and recount the violence of humiliation, misgendering, and slander that was deployed against trans women in the premodern world. As Saidiya Hartman has asked, "How does one recuperate the lives entangled with and impossible to differentiate from the terrible utterances that condemned them to death"?[76] The romanticized retrieval of such lives requires us to display the litanies of slut-shaming, misgendering, and incorrect pronouns. "The dream is to liberate them from the obscene descriptions that first introduced them to us," but as Hartman eventually goes on to say, it simply "replicates the very order of violence that it writes against by placing yet another demand upon the girl, requiring that her life be made useful or instructive." Hartman contemplates failure and restraint while at the same time having poignantly indulged in the methods she resists. Ultimately she resolves that we must seek not to absolve but to "bear what cannot be borne."[77]

In asking here, Where are all the trans women in Byzantium? I am not answering this question with a list of names nor with an answer about their locations. Instead, I am often forced to read the vitriol of male authors who have chosen to deride an imagined group—imagined because they are rhetorical tropes and argumentative foils. Unlike the records of the forgotten dead, these stories have been deemed by historians and theologians alike to bear no import on reality, that they speak no truth to a life but rather to mere inventions of the mind in the abstract. What to Hartman is the all too easy confrontation with the crimes of slavery—"It is too easy to hate a man like Thistlewood"—is a meager reckoning that Byzantine studies has not had,[78] not simply because of the erasure of trans women, but because of the fundamental refusal to consider how these transmisogynistic texts might have referred to a host of gender-variant subjects. Rather than horrors in the archive, they are simply Christian invective no different from other litanies of heresies or moralizations.

In writing this chapter, I want us to collectively confront this horror as such. Not to recuperate lost lives, restored and healed by an archive, but to simply take the attacks on those lives seriously for what they are. In this necessary process, this first step, we can simultaneously keep our eyes on the horizon to read the archive obliquely, to note the patterns and repetitions that accrue over the centuries. They suggest to us that beyond rhetorical tropes and the delusional inventions of an idiosyncratic mind, these texts are the flotsam of trans women's lives, the violences they faced and the freedoms they might have carved out for themselves in the meantime. Too often, in my reading, I have found that the wreckages of these lives are not hidden or obscure but are all around us, fragments that have continued to be left behind, denied as valid, and remained unseen. A future Byzantine trans studies must begin with a history of transphobia and transmisogyny, in order to chart out the lives those attacks reveal, and teach us new ways to creatively and fluidly seek out those lives beyond texts of shame and hate.

Notes

1. Caroline Walker Bynum, *Holy Feast and Holy Fast: The Religious Significance of Food to Medieval Women* (Berkeley: University of California Press, 1987), 291.

2. See Stephen J. Davis, "Crossed Texts, Crossed Sex: Intertextuality and Gender in Early Christian Legends of Holy Women Disguised as Men," *Journal of Early Christian Studies* 10.1 (2002): 1–36; Evelyne Patlagean, "L'histoire de la femme déguisée en moine et l'évolution de la sainteté féminine a Byzance," *Studi Medievali*, ser. 3, 17 (1976): 597–623; John Anson, "The Female Transvestite in Early Monasticism: The Origin and Development of a Motif," *Viator* 5 (1974): 1–32; Kari Vogt, "'The Woman Monk': A Theme in Byzantine Hagiography," in *Greece and Gender*, ed. Brit Berggreen and Nanno Marinatos (Bergen: Norwegian Institute at Athens, 1995), 141–48; Crystal Lynn Lubinsky, *Removing Masculine Layers to Reveal a Holy Womanhood: The Female Transvestite Monks of Late Antique Eastern Christianity* (Turnhout: Brepols, 2013); Valerie R. Hotchkiss, *Clothes Make the Man: Female Cross Dressing in Medieval Europe* (New York: Garland, 1996); Stavroula Constantinou, "Holy Actors and Actresses: Fools and Cross-Dressers as the Protagonists of Saints' Lives," in *The Ashgate Research Companion to Byzantine Hagiography*, ed. Stephanos Efthymiadis, vol. 2 (Burlington, VT: Ashgate, 2014), 343–62; Vern L. Bullough, "Transvestites in the Middle Ages," *American Journal of Sociology* 79.6 (1974): 1381–94; cf. Vern L. Bullough, "Transvestism in the Middle Ages," in *Sexual Practices and the Medieval Church*, ed. Vern L. Bullough and James Brundage (Buffalo, NY: Prometheus Books, 1982), 43–54.

3. Jack Halberstam, *Female Masculinity* (Durham, NC: Duke University Press, 1998), 6.

4. For an extensive study and further bibliography, see Roland Betancourt, *Byzantine Intersectionality: Sexuality, Gender, and Race in the Middle Ages* (Princeton, NJ: Princeton University Press, 2020).

5. As David Valentine has carefully elucidated in his ethnography on the category of "transgender" as this term came into widespread use by social actors and activists during the early 1990s, many individuals who participated in the transgender community did not always identify as transgender. The label served a key role in structuring a collective community encompassing a range of gender-variant lives and practices, even though at times not all members would have claimed it for themselves. This tension between self-identification and identification by others is critical, for—as Valentine notes—it draws attention to how the politics of identification are shaped through relations of social power. See David Valentine, *Imagining Transgender: An Ethnography of a Category* (Durham, NC: Duke University Press, 2007), esp. 1–28. In citing "best practices" for the case of representation, I also respect the power that media groups focused on representation have in promoting ever-changing guidelines for better representing modern gender-variant

communities. See "GLAAD Media Reference Guide—Transgender," www.glaad. org/reference/transgender.

6. While Foucault's *History of Sexuality* merits citing for its contribution to a long-standing discourse, viewing the premodern Greek-speaking world as a historian of the Byzantine Empire, I find it difficult to work with Foucault's generalizing observations on "the Greeks" and "Christianity." Foucault's focus on confession in Christianity (in volumes 1 and 4) has little to no function in the Eastern church. And his use of ancient Greek texts on pederasty to explore the ethics of same-gender relationality amidst other sexual relations denies the heritage and complexity of this tradition in the Greek-speaking medieval world that preserved and transmitted the texts he relies on. Authors like Kadji Amin have also rightly criticized the "attachment genealogies" of contemporary queer theory with pederastic theorizations by authors like Foucault and Genet. This Western-centric view of history, which places the Greeks and Christianity as opposed, leaves us with an impossible translation onto Byzantium, when so much of the subject formation that Foucault relies upon is oriented around "a confessing animal" and the impact of shift that occurred exclusively in Western Christianity. As the Greek Christian Empire, which also was a continuation imperially of the Roman Empire, Byzantium is a synthesis that merits a new consideration, not only because it produced or preserved the key sources Foucault relies on, but also because the cultural sensibilities of the two social and religious spheres were so markedly different. See Michel Foucault, *The History of Sexuality*, trans. Robert Hurley, 3 vols. (New York: Vintage Books, 1988–1990), quotation at 1:59. See also Michel Foucault, *Les aveux de la chair* (Paris: Gallimard, 2018); and Kadji Amin, *Disturbing Attachments: Genet, Pederasty, and Queer History* (Durham, NC: Duke University Press, 2017).

7. On the identity of the "Byzantine" Empire, see Anthony Kaldellis, *Romanland: Ethnicity and Empire in Byzantium* (Cambridge, MA: Harvard University Press, 2019).

8. On the medicalization of gender, see Dean Spade, "Resisting Medicine, Re/modeling Gender," *Berkeley Journal of Gender, Law and Justice* 18.1 (2013): 15–37.

9. Anjali Arondekar, *For the Record: On Sexuality and the Colonial Archive in India* (Durham, NC: Duke University Press, 2009), 1–25, quotation at 4.

10. See Halberstam, *Female Masculinity*; C. Riley Snorton, *Black on Both Sides: A Racial History of Trans Identity* (Minneapolis: University of Minnesota Press, 2017).

11. See Gabrielle M. W. Bychowski et al., "Trans*historicities: A Roundtable Discussion," *TSQ: Transgender Studies Quarterly* 5.4 (2018): 658–85, esp. 678–80.

12. Scholars have long struggled with the tension of using modern terms to understand past subjectivities and the complicity of sustaining the erasure of marginalized subjects in the past. See Mary Weismantel, "Towards a Transgender Archaeology: A Queer Rampage through Prehistory," in *The Transgender Studies Reader 2*, ed. Susan Stryker and Aren Z. Aizura (New York: Routledge, 2013), 319–34.

13. Ruth Webb, *Demons and Dancers: Performance in Late Antiquity* (Cambridge, MA: Harvard University Press, 2008), esp. 77–79. See also Regine May, "The Metamorphosis of Pantomime: Apuleius' *Judgment of Paris* (*Met.* 10:30–34)," in *New Directions in Ancient Pantomime*, ed. Edith Hall and Rosie Wyles (Oxford: Oxford University Press, 2008), 338–62.

14. *Latin Anthology*, 100, ed. and trans. Edith Hall and Rosie Wyles with Jonathan Powell, in "Appendix: Selected Source Texts," in Hall and Wyles, *New Directions in Ancient Pantomime*, 378–419, quotation at 402–3.

15. For a survey of the association between sex work and performance, see Webb, *Demons and Dancers*, 49–53, 152. See also Ismene Lada-Richards, *Silent Eloquence: Lucian and Pantomime Dancing* (London: Bloomsbury, 2007), esp. 56–78. These stereotypes, for example, are amply deployed in Procopius's late sixth-century *Secret History* to attack the empress Theodora as having been a mime and sex worker. See Procopius, *The Secret History* esp. 9.2–10, in *The Secret History with Related Texts*, trans. Anthony Kaldellis (Indianapolis: Hackett, 2010), 40–41. See also John Chrysostom, *Homilies on Matthew* 68, ed. Jacques-Paul Minge, *Patrologia cursus completes. Series Graeca* (Paris: Migne, 1857–1866), PG 58:644.

16. See I. Lada-Richards, "'A Worthless Feminine Thing'? Lucian and the 'Optic Intoxication' of Pantomime Dancing," *Helios* 30 (2003): 21–75.

17. Pseudo-John Chrysostom, *De paenitentia*, ed. PG 59:670.

18. Amphilochius of Iconium, *Iambi ad Seleucum* 90–99, in *Amphilochii Iconiensis iambi ad Seleucum*, ed. E. Oberg, Patristische Texte und Studien 9 (Berlin: De Gruyter, 1969), 29–40. This echoes the language used by Basil of Caesarea to describe the ambiguous and fluid gender identity of eunuchs. See Basil of Caesarea, *Letters* 115, in *Letters*, vol. 2, ed. and trans. Roy J. Deferrari, Loeb Classical Library 215 (Cambridge, MA: Harvard University Press, 1928), 230–31. Cf. Cyril of Alexandria, *Homilies* 19, ed. PG 77:1109B.

19. These charges are reiterated by Procopius of Gaza in the early fifth century in his panegyric for the emperor Anastasius I, praising the emperor's decision to exile dancers. See Procopius of Gaza, *Panegyricus in Anastasium imperatorem* 16, in *Procopio di Gaza: Panegirico per l'imperatore Anastasio*, ed. G. Matino (Naples: Accademia Pontaniana, 2005), 41–57.

20. See *Council in Trullo* 62, in *The Council in Trullo Revisited*, ed. and trans. George Nedungatt and Michael Featherstone (Rome: Pontificio Istituto Orientale, 1995), 143; *Council of Gangra* 13 and 17, trans. Henry Percival, "The Council of Gangra," in *Nicene and Post-Nicene Fathers*, 2nd ser., vol. 14, ed. Philip Schaff and Henry Wace (Buffalo, NY: Christian Literature, 1900), 89–101, esp. 97 and 99; *Theodosian Code* 16.2.27, in *The Theodosian Code*, trans. Clyde Pharr (Princeton, NJ: Princeton University Press, 1952), 445.

21. Intimately associated with these discussions of male dancers' effeminacy is the worry that these male performers also wished to become more like women by serving as receptive sexual partners in same-gender relations, popularized in part by the second-century Aelius Aristides and responses to his text. See Aelius Aristides, as preserved in Libanius, *Orationes* 64.38–40, in *Libanii opera*, vol. 4, ed. R. Foerster (Leipzig: Teubner, 1908).

22. Martial, *Epigrams* 2.62, in *Epigrams*, vol. 1, ed. and trans. D. R. Shackleton Bailey, Loeb Classical Library 94 (Cambridge, MA: Harvard University Press, 1993), 168–69. See Margaret E. Molloy, *Libanius and the Dancers* (Hildesheim: Olms-Weidmann, 1996).

23. See Craig A. Williams, *Roman Homosexuality*, 2nd ed. (Oxford: Oxford University Press, 2010), esp. 137–76.

24. Juvenal, *Satires* 14.194–95, in *Juvenal*, ed. and trans. Susanna Morton Braund, Loeb Classical Library 91 (Cambridge, MA: Harvard University Press, 2004), 472–73.

25. Juvenal, *Satires* 2.11–12, in Braund, *Juvenal*, 148–49.

26. Clement of Alexandria, *The Instructor* 3.3, trans. A. Cleveland Coxe, "The Instructor," in *The Ante-Nicene Fathers*, vol. 2, ed. Alexander Roberts and James Donaldson (Grand Rapids, MI: W. B. Eerdmanns, 1956), 207–98, esp. 275–77; *Le pédagogue*, vol. 3, ed. Claude Mondésert, Chantal Matray, and Henri-Irénée Marrou, Sources Chrétiennes 158 (Paris: Éditions du Cerf, 1970), 38–59.

27. Clement of Alexandria, *Instructor* 3.3, modified trans. Coxe, "Instructor," 275; *Le pédagogue*, 38.

28. Clement of Alexandria, *Instructor* 3.3, trans. Coxe, "Instructor," 275.

29. Clement of Alexandria, *Instructor* 3.3, modified trans. Coxe, "Instructor," 275; *Le pédagogue*, 40.

30. Clement of Alexandria, *Instructor*, 3.3, trans. Coxe, "Instructor," 275.

31. Ibid.

32. John Chrysostom, *Instruction and Refutation Directed against Those Men Cohabiting with Virgins* 10, in *Jerome, Chrysostom, and Friends: Essays and Translations*, trans. Elizabeth A. Clark (New York: Edwin Mellen, 1979), 194. See Aideen Hartney, "Manly Women and Womanly Men: The *Subintroductae* and John Chrysostom," in *Desire and Denial in Byzantium*, ed. Liz James (Burlington, VT: Ashgate, 1999), 41–48.

33. Clement of Alexandria, *Instructor* 3.3, trans. Coxe, "Instructor," 275.

34. Ibid.; *Le pédagogue*, 42.

35. Clement of Alexandria, *Instructor* 3.3, trans. Coxe, "Instructor," 275.

36. Ibid., 276.

37. Clement of Alexandria, *Instructor* 3.3, modified trans. Coxe, "Instructor," 276.

38. In attempting to find a place for male-to-female "cross-dressers" in late antiquity, Maria Doerfler has connected the tirades against effeminate men in the period to those against foreigners, pagans, and luxury. See Maria E. Doerfler, "Coming Apart at the Seams: Cross-Dressing, Masculinity, and the Social Body in Late Antiquity," in *Dressing Judeans and Christians in Antiquity*, ed. Kristi Upson-Saia, Carly Daniel-Hughes, and Alicia J. Batten (London: Routledge, 2014), 37–51.

39. Clement of Alexandria, *Instructor* 3.3, modified trans. Coxe, "Instructor," 276.

40. Robert Mills, in his study of the wide-ranging category of "sodomy" in the Western medieval world, has made the powerful suggestion that the notion of "transgender" is a better fit for the wide spectrum of queer subjectivities in the premodern world, since ancient and medieval authors often attack same-gender desire not as such but as a sign of a person's betraying their gender identity. See Robert Mills, *Seeing Sodomy in the Middle Ages* (Chicago: University of Chicago Press, 2015), esp. 81–132.

41. Clement of Alexandria, *Instructor* 3.3, trans. Coxe, "Instructor," 275.

42. Clement of Alexandria, *Instructor* 3.3, modified trans. Coxe, "Instructor," 277; *Le pédagogue*, 54.

43. Clement struggles with how precisely to characterize and categorize these bodies he identifies as men who do not simply, or at least not always, fit into the normative cultural prohibitions against same-gender desire or passivity. The active effeminates are adulterers, and the passive effeminates are "womanly" (thēlydriou).

The latter term at times implies a concurrent same-gender desire but is not necessarily limited to it. Eventually Clement realizes that the association between same-gender, passive desire and effeminacy is inadequate to describe his contemporary circumstances. See *Le pédagogue*, 46.

44. Julia Serano, *Whipping Girl: A Transsexual Woman on Sexism and the Scapegoating of Femininity* (Emeryville, CA: Seal Press, 2007), esp. 14–16.

45. On Elagabalus, see Martijn Icks, *The Crimes of Elagabalus: The Life and Legacy of Rome's Decadent Boy Emperor* (Cambridge, MA: Harvard University Press, 2012), esp. 92–122; Leonardo de Arrizabalaga y Prado, *The Emperor Elagabalus: Fact or Fiction?* (Cambridge: Cambridge University Press, 2010).

46. On trans lives in Roman antiquity, see Eva Cantarella, *Bisexuality in the Ancient World*, trans. Cormac Ó Culleanáin, 2nd ed. (New Haven, CT: Yale University Press, 2002); G. Francis, "On a Romano-British Castration Clamp Used in the Rites of Cybele," *Journal of the History of Medicine* 1 (1926): 95–110; Shelley Halles, "Looking for Eunuchs: The Galli and Attis in Roman Art," in *Eunuchs in Antiquity and Beyond*, ed. Shaun Tougher (London: Gerald Duckworth, 2002), 87–102; Cheryl Morgan, "Trans Lives in Rome," in *Introduction to Transgender Studies*, ed. Ardel Haefele-Thomas (New York: Harrington Press, 2019), 370–80; and Amy Richlin, "Not Before Homosexuality: The Materiality of the Cinaedus and the Roman Law against Love between Men," *Journal of the History of Sexuality* 3.4 (1993): 523–73.

47. Dio Cassius, *Roman History* 80.11–17, in *Roman History*, vol. 9, ed. and trans. Earnest Cary and Herbert B. Foster, Loeb Classical Library 177 (Cambridge, MA: Harvard University Press, 1927), 460–71.

48. Dio Cassius, *Roman History* 80.13, in Cary and Foster, *Roman History*, 462–63.

49. Ibid.

50. Ibid., 464–65.

51. See Fergus Millar, *A Study of Cassius Dio* (Oxford: Clarendon Press, 1964), esp. 1–4, 168–70, 195–203. See also Christopher Mallan, "The Style, Method, and Programme of Xiphilinus' *Epitome* of Cassius Dio's *Roman History*," *Greek, Roman, and Byzantine Studies* 53 (2013): 610–44; Thomas M. Banchich and Eugene N. Lane, *The History of Zonaras: From Alexander Severus to the Death of Theodosius the Great* (London: Routledge, 2009), esp. 73–75; Iordanis Grigoriadis, *Linguistic and Literary Studies in the* Epitome Historion *of John Zonaras* (Thessaloniki: Byzantine Research Center, 1998). John Xiphilinus's epitome, commissioned at the behest of Emperor Michael VII Doukas (1071–1078), specifically covered the chapters dealing with Elagabalus's reign and is preserved in a critical exemplar on Mount Athos. The Xiphilinus text is of particular importance because it attests to the enduring importance and popularity of Dio Cassius's work for Byzantine understandings of late antique Roman history. See B. C. Barmann, "The Mount Athos Epitome of Cassius Dio's Roman History," *Phoenix* 25.1 (1971): 58–67.

52. See Dio Cassius, *Roman History* 80.16, in Cary and Foster, *Roman History*, 470–71.

53. See Michael Glykas, *Chronicle* 453.6–8, in *Michaelis Glycae annals*, ed. I. Bekker, Corpus scriptorum historiae Byzantinae (Bonn: Weber, 1836), 453; Symeon Logothete [Leo Grammatikos], *Chronicle* 74:8–10, in *Leonis Grammatici chronographia*, ed. I. Bekker, Corpus scriptorum historiae Byzantinae (Bonn: Weber, 1842), 74.

54. Dio Cassius, *Roman History* 80.9, in Cary and Foster, *Roman History*, 456–57.

55. See Theodore Skoutariotes, *Chronicle* 2.40, in *Theodori Scutariotae chronica*, ed. R. Tocci, Corpus Fontium Historiae Byzantinae, Series Berolinensis 46 (Berlin: De Gruyter, 2015).

56. See also Herodian, *History of the Empire* 5, in *History of the Empire*, vol. 2, ed. and trans. C. R. Whittaker, Loeb Classical Library 455 (Cambridge, MA: Harvard University Press, 1970), 2–75.

57. Photius, *Bibliotheca* 99, in *The Library of Photius*, vol. 1, trans. J. H. Freese (New York: Macmillan, 1920), 191–93.

58. Philostratus of Athens, *Lives of the Sophists* 625, in *Lives of the Sophists*, ed. and trans. Wilmer C. Wright, Loeb Classical Library 134 (Cambridge, MA: Harvard University Press, 1921), 304–5.

59. *Epitome de Caesaribus* 23.3, in *Sextii Aurelii Victoris Liber de Caesaribus*, ed. F. Pichlmayr (Leipzig: Teubner, 1911), 157.

60. The relevant text concerns a certain Syrian mime. Evidence of a connection to Aelianus's attack on Elagabalus includes references to Elagabalus's Syrian origins, the fragment's derisive comments on the courtesan's wantonness and femininity, and the *Souda's* attribution of these quotes to Aelianus himself. See Steven D. Smith, *Man and Animal in Severan Rome: The Literary Imagination of Claudius Aelianus* (Cambridge: Cambridge University Press, 2017), esp. 274–79.

61. Kathryn M. Ringrose, "Living in the Shadows: Eunuchs and Gender in Byzantium," in *Third Sex, Third Gender: Beyond Sexual Dimorphism in Culture and History*, ed. G. Herdt (New York: Zone Books, 1994), 85–109 and 507–18. See Basil of Caesarea, *Letters* 115, in *Letters*, 2:230–31.

62. Shaun Tougher, *The Eunuch in Byzantine History and Society* (London: Routledge, 2008), 109–11.

63. Kathryn Ringrose, *The Perfect Servant: Eunuchs and the Social Construction of Gender in Byzantium* (Chicago: University of Chicago Press, 2003), esp. 35–37.

64. Aristotle, *Generation of Animals* 766a25, in *Generation of Animals*, ed. and trans. A. L. Peck, Loeb Classical Library 366 (Cambridge, MA: Harvard University Press, 1942), 390–91.

65. Tougher, *Eunuch*, 68–82.

66. *Council of Nicaea* 1, trans. Henry R. Percival, "The First Ecumenical Council," in Schaff and Wace, *Nicene and Post-Nicene Fathers*, 2nd ser., 14:1–57, quotation at 8.

67. *Life of Matrona of Perge*, 5, trans. Featherstone and Mango, "Life of St. Matrona of Perge," *Byzantine Saints' Lives in Translation*, ed. Alice-Mary Talbot (Washington, DC: Dumbarton Oaks, 1996), 23–24.

68. Suetonius, *Lives of the Caesars* 6.28, in *Suetonius*, vol. 2, ed. and trans. J. C. Rolfe, Loeb Classical Library 38 (Cambridge, MA: Harvard University Press, 1914), 127–28.

69. See Tougher, *Eunuch*, 34–35; Ringrose, *Perfect Servant*, 67–86.

70. Gregory of Tours, *History of the Franks* 10.15, in *History of the Franks*, trans. Ernest Brehaut (New York: Columbia University Press, 1916), 238–39.

71. Bullough, "Transvestism in the Middle Ages," 46.

72. Michael Psellus, *Letters* S 180, in *Michael Psellos*, ed. and trans. Stratis Papaioannou, *Michael Psellos: Rhetoric and Authorship in Byzantium* (Cambridge: Cambridge University Press, 2013), 207–8.

73. Papaioannou, *Michael Psellos*, 215 and 231.

74. Michael Psellus, *Letters* S 57, in Papaioannou, *Michael Psellos*, 196–98.

75. Ibid., 196–99.

76. Saidiya Hartman, "Venus in Two Acts," *Small Axe* 26.12–2 (June 2008): 1–14, quotation at 3.

77. Ibid., 6 and 14.

78. Ibid., 6.

CHAPTER 13

Performing Reparative Transgender Identities from *Stage Beauty* to *The King and the Clown*

ALEXA ALICE JOUBIN

What work do trans narratives do in the world? How do they impact the audiences? The early 2000s saw the emergence of some new ways of telling trans stories through film. Similar to texts in other socially engaged fields, these trans narratives often aimed for ideologically appealing messages. Transgender performances tend to be billed, or perceived, as art with a cause, as a socially reparative act leading to the amelioration of personal and social circumstances. Transgender theory has strong political and ethical implications as it seeks to remedy conditions in the world. Reparative trans performances—works in which characters see their condition improve—carry substantial affective rewards by offering optimism and emotional gratification. The call for social justice may seem universal, but the exact elements requiring reparation are malleable. The reparative arcs diverge dramatically between different works.

This chapter considers two strands of reparative performance: (1) the open-ended amelioration of injustices by enabling characters' self-realization and by calling on audiences to recognize that trans bodies do not require "reparation"; and (2) narratives that showcase directive and regressive changes organized around "restoring" trans characters to perceived norms of binary gender and heterosexuality. Both approaches seek to diagnose and correct unjust conditions, though they diverge in their interpretations of the source of trouble. The first approach empowers socially marginalized characters, while the second approach caters to (mostly) cis-heterosexual audiences' binary imaginations.

Further, both approaches are informed by the long tradition of using literature as a strategy for making sense of newly visible forms of human experience. Historically the Western canon has been given various forms of moral authority, which is why reparative performances often draw on canonical works, including, in the works I consider here, Shakespeare's plays, which are readily available reference points in popular culture. Even though Shakespeare's plays were initially performed by all-male casts, they were designed to appeal to diverse audiences. Many modern adaptations reimagine those plays through performances that explore gender nonconformity. In particular, twenty-first-century cinematic dramatizations of Renaissance cross-gender theater practices provide important commentary on transgender performance. One genre stands out in its explanatory power: films about theater-making. Depictions of gender variance and sexual fluidity in these films are enriched by gendered meanings that are simultaneously screened by cinematic devices and produced in plays-within-the-film.

Two metatheatrical films exemplify the two contrasting approaches to reparative performance. Taking the first approach to affirm its trans protagonist's right to self-determination, the South Korean blockbuster *The King and the Clown* (directed by Lee Joon-ik, Eagle Pictures, 2005) delineates the love triangle between a fifteenth-century king, a masculine jester, and his partner—a trans feminine vagabond street performer named Gong-gil. An Ophelia figure, Gong-gil presents as feminine onstage and off. Insisting that Gong-gil's trans body does not need "improvements" to fit social norms, the period drama follows an arc that carves out, sustains, and validates spaces of queerness. The reparative value of *The King and the Clown* lies in its level-headed portrayal of Gong-gil, who takes ownership of their body and social space. In contrast, other films taking the second, conservative approach, offer cis-heteronormative "corrections" of their characters. *Stage Beauty* (directed by Richard Eyre, Lions Gate, 2004), which is regarded as "a darker, bawdier version" of *Shakespeare in Love* (directed by John Madden, Universal Pictures, 1998),[1] chronicles the private life and stage career of the historical Edward (Ned) Kynaston (1640–1712), who plays exclusively female roles before taking on male roles onstage. The renowned Restoration adult "boy actor," "the last of his kind" according to the film's tagline, specializes in playing such female roles as Desdemona in *Othello*. He also presents as female in his romantic life. Eventually he "straightens up" by playing Othello onstage and by falling in love with an actress after his male lover leaves him and after King Charles II bans men from playing women.[2] The film moves toward forms of cis-heterosexual normalcy, invalidating and erasing the gender nonconformity being explored in the film.

These works have not at this writing been analyzed as transgender performances, though they have been commonly studied as texts that engage (mostly male) homosexuality. The rich history of films about theater-making provides fertile ground to examine how marginalized, embodied identities are formed and contested in the representations of trans feminine characters such as Kynaston (Desdemona) in *Stage Beauty* and Gong-gil (Ophelia) in *The King and the Clown*. Kynaston and Gong-gil have been interpreted as characters with binary gender identities in film scholarship, but this chapter demonstrates how transgender performance theories can be applied fruitfully to metatheatrical works regardless of whether they have been labeled "trans" by their producers. While these gender-variant figures are located in different cultures and historical periods, the important similarities between them can help us understand transgender performance in a global context. Like the character Gong-gil, Kynaston's life story provides a powerful framing for the idea of the artificiality of performance—of gender, of history, and of genre. The two films have one thing in common. Both Restoration English and premodern Korean appropriations of Shakespeare interpret trans feminine characters' on- and offstage lives through their sexual prowess.

Following Jack Halberstam's call for "perverse presentism,"[3] a methodology that uses history to denaturalize our contemporary articulations of gender and sexuality, my case studies reclaim as trans some narratives that have historically been interpreted as homosexual in order to expand the archive for teaching and research. As Sawyer K. Kemp has proposed, "a wider range of narratives and images" can promote a more robust understanding of "the figure of trans as both a passing and nonpassing entity, a person who may be . . . dysphoric or coherent, a body that may be content or at odds with itself, a body that may be an object of desire or ridicule."[4] *The King and the Clown* (2005) departs from the cis-normative, reparative arc in *Stage Beauty* (2004) and from most post-1990 transgender films, which tend to follow a voyeuristic, romantically motivated trajectory toward "straightening up" nonconformist characters. By reading these two films in the context of trans cinema, this chapter makes an intervention in both transgender and Shakespeare studies by demonstrating new ways to interpret gender variance beyond just a dramatic device.

Trans Femininity and *The King and the Clown*

The King and the Clown depicts the erotic entanglements between King Yeonsan (reigned 1494–1506) and two acrobatic performers in the fifteenth-century

Joseon dynasty. Following the convention of Korea's all-male vagabond street theater, Gong-gil plays feminine roles while Jang-saeng takes on macho characters. Gong-gil, however, presents as female offstage as well. Their persona during performances turns out to be much more than just a stage role. Gong-gil remains in the gored skirt and uses feminine mannerisms in their private life.

A note on pronouns before we proceed. I use gender-neutral pronouns to refer to the jester character named Gong-gil out of respect for who the character is.[5] The film takes Gong-gil's trans feminine identity at face value without question or scare quotes. Unlike other trans films that probe questions of being and becoming, *The King and the Clown* does not feature gender transformation scenes or dramatize the pains of transition. The film codes Gong-gil's relationship with the king as erotic and shrouds Gong-gil's relationship with the brother-like fellow jester in ambiguous terms. The director and actors, however, repeatedly refer to Gong-gil with masculine pronouns during interviews. Reviews and studies in English and Korean, to the best of my knowledge, also misgender Gong-gil via masculine pronouns.

When Gong-gil and Jang-saeng are recruited as the king's jesters in court, the narrative begins to evoke several of the themes and characters from Shakespeare's plays, including the revenge plot in *Hamlet*, the device of a bawdy play-within-a-play in *The Taming of the Shrew*, and the love triangle among Viola (disguised as Cesario), Duke Orsino, and Countess Olivia in *Twelfth Night*.[6] After the king hires the traveling players to help him appeal to the conscience of corrupt court officials, the film's version of the "mousetrap" play (the play-within-a-play that Hamlet designs to "catch the conscience of the king" who murdered Hamlet's father, 2.2.605) gradually supersedes the cinematic framework to become the primary and more arresting narrative. The king, long suspicious of his courtiers, investigates their involvement in his mother's deposition and mysterious death. Emboldened by the traveling players' allegorical performance of court intrigues and killing, the king finally takes action to avenge his mother.

Over time, the king, who is a composite figure of Hamlet and Claudius, becomes fond of the Ophelia-like Gong-gil. As a result, one of the king's consorts, Jang Nok-su, grows jealous of Gong-gil, who seems to be replacing her as the king's favorite subject, or *yi*. At the same time, Gong-gil's longtime street performance partner, Jang-saeng, is increasingly resentful about Gong-gil's special status at court. The king is clearly drawn to Gong-gil's appearance. King Yeon-san frequently asks Gong-gil to put on private finger puppet shows in his chamber. The king goes back and forth between his consort Nok-su and the jester Gong-gil, and the king's emotional needs are unclear.

In contrast to the scheming Nok-su, who functions as mother and lover, Gong-gil serves as an innocent figure who is not versed in court politics. The film thus focuses primarily on narrative tensions in the royal court among the king, Gong-gil, Nok-su, and Jang-saeng, with the king and Jang-saeng as contenders for Gong-gil's hand.

In what follows, I analyze the film from three perspectives: the identity of the trans feminine jester, their rejection of conservative "reparation," and the film's reception and relationship to other trans films. To watch video clips of the film, please visit the page I curated at *MIT Global Shakespeares*, https://globalshakespeares.mit.edu/the-king-and-the-clown-lee-joon-ik-2005/.

Trans Femininity

Of special interest in this chapter is how Gong-gil serves as a catalyst for the twists and turns of the plot. I suggest we read Gong-gil's role as a trans woman through thematic, visual, and narratological echoes of Ophelia. Like Ophelia, Gong-gil is objectified by what Laura Mulvey theorizes as the male gaze. As the love interests of leading male characters, both Gong-gil and Ophelia are styled by "the determining male gaze" that projects its voyeuristic fantasy onto them.[7] Similar to Ophelia, Gong-gil remains innocent of sexuality and court politics. In one scene, Gong-gil is found lying in a pool of their blood after a suicide attempt. In a scene in the royal court, Gong-gil wears a Beijing opera headdress in a protracted play-within-the-film, where the flowers on their head call to mind not only Ophelia's garland and the flowers she picks but also the figure of the androgynous flower boy in Korea, Japan, China, and Taiwan, which will be discussed in the following pages. As an Ophelia figure, Gong-gil is unable to express themself and lacks inner direction. Their path in life is determined by men around them. The innocence of Gong-gil/Ophelia contrasts with the calculations and intrigues of other characters, such as the consort Nok-su, who frames them for the crime of defaming the king and the courtier who conspires to kill Gong-gil during an imperial hunt in the woods.

The King and the Clown opens with street performer Jang-saeng (Kam Woo-sung) playing macho roles and the trans feminine Gong-gil (Lee Joon-gi) taking on *yodongmo* (queen) roles. They travel from town to town and earn a miserable living as part of an all-male troupe, as audiences enjoy their shows with nominal donations (coins thrown onto the rug on which Jang-saeng and Gong-gil perform). Jang-saeng and Gong-gil perform lewd banter on a tightrope, as bawdy jokes, acrobatics, and tightrope tricks are the staples of the all-male vagabond theater known as *namsadang nori* (a UN Intangible

Cultural Heritage). Alluding to *The Taming of the Shrew*, Gong-gil plays a rude coquette while Jang-saeng's character attempts to tame her. Walking on a tightrope to the drumbeats of the musicians, the shrewish character taunts her would-be lover with lewd and provocative postures and language. The two acrobatic actors put on this bawdy show regularly with small variations throughout the film at town squares, crossroads, and eventually at the royal court. It is fitting that a film deconstructing the gender binary should draw on the metatheatrical parody of gender roles in *The Taming of the Shrew*, an elaborate play-within-a-play designed to mock the drunken peddler Christopher Sly. Jang-saeng's manhandling of Gong-gil in their show parallels the misogynist Petruchio's psychological torment of Katharina in *Shrew*. The play within *The King and the Clown* caricatures stereotypes of heterosexual femininity and masculinity to foreshadow Gong-gil's trans femininity offstage. The camerawork (Dutch angle, close-ups of spectators' eyes) frames the rowdy lower-class audiences as the butt of the joke whose worldviews are being parodied. At this point, the film has shown Gong-gil only in their onstage persona.

The transgression of ideal femininity onstage gives way to Gong-gil's feminine identity as a restorative force offstage. There is a stark contrast between Gong-gil's onstage persona and offstage personality. Onstage, Gong-gil's character lifts her skirt, opens her legs, and speaks of checking out the manhood of Jang-saeng for size. The presence of Gong-gil's partner allows Gong-gil to present such risqué acts without being assaulted or harassed during performance. Offstage, Gong-gil is reserved, traditionally feminine, and sexually exploited. In the scene where the pair arrives jubilantly in the capital city, Hanyang (modern-day Seoul), they sample street food as they stroll along (00:17:24). A tracking shot showing Jang-saeng and Gong-gil side by side highlights the difference between their mannerisms in offstage life. Jang-saeng remains consistent with his virile onstage persona, but Gong-gil handles food in a delicate fashion. Whereas Gong-gil creates a caricature of femininity onstage (their character parodies women's desires for comedic effect), Jang-saeng walks behind random women in this scene and sways his hips in an exaggerated fashion to mock the feminine gait.

Jang-saeng harbors undefined feelings toward Gong-gil. He is clearly protective and possessive of Gong-gil. Historically, prostitution was common in the all-male vagabond troupes, but Jang-saeng uncharacteristically causes havoc when their troupe manager pimps Gong-gil out to the highest bidder, a merchant.

The scene cuts to the merchant undressing Gong-gil. In a medium close-up, the camera follows the merchant's hand down Gong-gil's naked back

My legs like wings would spread!

FIGURE 13.1.   Gong-gil on a tightrope during a street performance in *The King and the Clown*.

FIGURE 13.2.   Gong-gil reveals their face under a mask on a tightrope during a street performance in *The King and the Clown*.

toward the buttock. The erotic shot is trained on Gong-gil's curves and smooth skin. The shot is thus set up to suggest Gong-gil's feminine, embodied identity even in offstage moments. Jang-saeng breaks in just before the merchant can go any further. He rescues Gong-gil, stating he is ready for them to "die together." In stark contrast to Gong-gil's onstage persona, throughout the long sequence from the altercation to the rescue, Gong-gil is completely docile and passive, allowing themself to be handled like a doll

FIGURE 13.3.   Gong-gil's character wishes to check out the manhood of Jang-saeng during a street performance in *The King and the Clown*.

and not saying a word or making a sound. This scene of undressing teases the film audience's curiosity about anatomy-based identities without satisfying that curiosity through recourse to the idea that genitals possess some truth about gender.

Gong-gil's trans femininity is articulated in the context of the Japanese and Korean culture of flower boys. The term "flower boy," or *kkonminam*, refers to a male-identifying singer or actor whose gender is fluidly androgynous. Above all else, the flower boy subculture highlights the youthful beauty of these singers. The factor of age is part of the positively formulated but repressive stereotypes that connect youthfulness to femininity. In contemporary Japanese and South Korean flower boy subcultures, cis-female fans—some of whom are married—live vicariously through beautiful, often androgynous characters without fear of being stigmatized as being lesbian or promiscuous.[8] The figure of the flower boy fulfills female fans' fantasies about idealized male partners. The desire and sexuality of the female fans are complex. The fans may have queer feelings, or they may desire ideal heterosexual men who exist only in flower boy narratives. Jeey-oung Shin has identified these subcultures as "an alternative to the patriarchal mainstream culture," where homosexuality remains controversial and where female sexuality is confined to "the biological function of reproduction within marriage."[9] Two weeks before the film's release, a promotional interview with Lee Joon-gi,[10] who played Gong-gil, highlighted his feminine beauty and androgyny, which Ch'oe Kyŏnghúi sees as a "conscious effort to attract female audiences . . . who would willingly consume a . . . film with a stunning *kkonminam* character."[11] *The King and the Clown* emerged from such subcultures and used its connection with *kkonminam* to market itself to young female audiences.

Similar to the undressing scene, a scene in court bears further diagnostic significance. Nok-su storms in on the king and Gong-gil in an intimate moment and taunts Gong-gil about their "real" gender. Like the earlier "undressing" scene with the merchant, this scene points to voyeuristic desires that are anchored in anatomy's putative indexicality for identities. Nok-su tries to undress Gong-gil in front of the king, creating a great deal of tension. Presumably Nok-su's dramatic act of "gender revelation" is to expose Gong-gil as an abject subject with alleged physical deficiencies and thereby dissuade the king from bestowing further favors on Gong-gil. As in the previous undressing scene, Gong-gil does not say a word and seems rather docile in this moment when they are expected to respond to Nok-su's pent-up anger about Gong-gil as a competitor. The king freezes in shock. Nok-su is as frustrated by Gong-gil's version of femininity as she is jealous of the newcomer who is replacing her as the king's favorite subject. The act of peeling the dress off Gong-gil is symbolic of her desire to authenticate embodied identities, as if to up the ante in the competition. It also reveals Nok-su's anxiety about the king's sexuality. The king eventually uses brute force to throw her out of the room in order to protect Gong-gil. Such revelation scenes are a familiar trope in transgender narratives. The scene peels back the polished surface of cinema—however briefly—to reveal what Timothy Murray calls "cinematic dirt," grainy details that are best left to audiences' imaginations.[12] These scenes are part of what Danielle M. Seid has theorized as "the reveal" in trans cinema, a device of exposure that is supposed to reveal some "bodily truth."[13] Such scenes subject trans characters to, as Eliza Steinbock argues, "the pressures of a pervasive gender/sex system that seeks to make public the 'truth' of the trans person's gendered and sexed body."[14] Such revelation scenes reenact struggles over the body's meanings.

Language and the use of pronouns play equally important roles in identity politics. In a scene in Nok-su's chamber, a eunuch tells her that the king "is with her, my lady," alluding to sex as a perennial subtext in court politics. The consort is surprised by the use of feminine pronouns to refer to Gong-gil. She asks, "Her?" When forced to clarify, the eunuch slips into biological essentialism: "That clown . . . ah . . . she's a man, pardon me." Nok-su angrily presses, "What is the king doing with that girly man?" It would seem Nok-su already knows the answer but wants to hear the eunuch say it. The eunuch resorts to euphemism for the king's intimate affairs as he looks down and says, "That . . . you know, ahem." In an aside, the eunuch muses: "Man? . . . look at what he's wearing. Man, woman, it's so damn confusing." It is important to note that, despite such disparaging comments by the consort and the eunuch, unlike *Stage Beauty* and other transgender narratives, this film shows Gong-gil exclusively in an ankle-length pink gored skirt (*chima*) with a pastel *jeogori* (the traditional blouse or shirt). As Gong-gil does not change clothes for their shows, there is no identity change to speak of. The court's assumption that Gong-gil may not have been assigned female at birth would arise from troupe members' use of pronouns and the court's knowledge of the conventional setup of all-male vagabond troupes. The conflation of gender presentation and bodily sex puts Gong-gil in a double bind as an "illusory" figure according to Talia Mae Bettcher's theory.[15] If Gong-gil is perceived to be visibly trans, they would be a "pretender." If they are seen as a cis woman, they risk forced disclosure.

These interconnected scenes deploy a pornographic mode of representation by alluding to, but not showing in full, what lies beneath a character's clothes. The eroticization of Gong-gil's body in these scenes registers what Mary Ann Doane calls a "scopophiliac relation."[16] This relation, as Laura Mulvey points out, exists between the objectified character, male characters, and film viewers: "The woman displayed has functioned on two levels: as erotic object for the characters within the screen story, and as erotic object for the spectator within the auditorium, with a shifting tension between the looks on either side of the screen."[17] In Gong-gil's case, curiosity about gender nonconformity is deployed to legitimize scopophilia. The gaze focuses on bodies that are coded feminine, and the pleasure derived from looking at eroticized female bodies is enabled by the voyeuristic nature of cinema. As Stanley Cavell theorizes, films are "inherently pornographic" because of the audiences' privileged invisibility while "looking in on a private world" and "the ontological conditions of the motion picture." As an object that is dressed, the human body on-screen has the potential to be undressed. The cinema—with its nonreciprocal structure of viewing—has the power to incite and channel the desire to see a human being undressed. As a result, audiences unconsciously look for a reason for undressing "desirable human beings" in films.[18] Gender clearly plays a role in scopophilia, as feminist scholarship has astutely pointed out. As Mulvey argues, cinema as a genre facilitates the objectification of female characters and the voyeuristic conditions (gazing without being seen either by those on-screen or by other film audiences), thereby satisfying "a primordial wish for pleasurable looking."[19] Trans bodies on-screen—in comparison to cis and normative bodies—bear the additional stress of an authentication process based on the assumed indexicality of anatomical features. It doesn't help, either, that the technological apparatus of cinema tends to support normative systems of gender "that shaped its classical narrative syntax."[20]

The trans identity of Gong-gil has been overlooked by scholarship and deliberately repressed by Korean audiences, who more readily accept heterosexuality—even if practiced between a cis and a trans character—than homosexuality. The strongest evidence of Gong-gil's trans identity comes from rehearsal notes. Lee Joon-gi, who played Gong-gil, identifies as a cis man but says in interviews that he conceived his character as a trans woman. He recounted going with the film director to "special bars" to "study the attitude of trans people." Lee adopted Method acting—an immersive, emotion-oriented technique derived from Konstantin Stanislavski in which an actor identifies fully with their character. To prevent Lee from being separated from the role of Gong-gil, the film director forbade him from interacting with other actors when not on the set. He remained in his role during breaks in filming. Lee went so far as to "shut himself in a ladies' room . . . to immerse himself in his role as Gong-gil" at the studio.[21] When making choices about the character, the actor and director operated in a binary framework. Despite Lee's misconception of transgender life as superficial, adoptable behaviors in a trans bar, *The King and the Clown* does not convey such problematic views. Gong-gil, in their offstage life, does not mimic or parody stereotypical versions of femininity.

The film's construction of trans embodiment and queer space merits critical attention. Jang-saeng and Gong-gil work seamlessly as a flirtatious heterosexual couple onstage and share the same bed in their private life. The film remains ambiguous about the nature of their relationship: sharing intimate space as an act of necessity due to poverty, a sign of something beyond a brotherly bond, or both. In the historical context of the narrative, heterosexual vagabond artists would have limited opportunities and choices when it came to personal relationships on account of their poverty and low social status. Jang-saeng may be a heterosexual or bisexual cis man who forms emotional bonds with a trans feminine partner. It is debatable whether Gon-gil is a less-than-perfect but serviceable surrogate for Jang-saeng's sexual needs, or a younger sibling figure whom Jang-saeng takes under his wing. The familial setting is partly a function of Korean queer film traditions. As Chris Berry notes, East Asian queer cinema often articulates selfhood through "kinship obligations" in blood or simulated familial bonds.[22] The bonds—expressed in positive or negative terms—bring characters such as Jang-saeng and Gong-gil together in marginalized social spaces that are invisible to most members of their society. Queer films make their life and culture visible.

Rejection of Conservative "Reparation"

The film ends with Gong-gil's rejection of any fantasy the film audiences may have about reparation of trans bodies. Instead of the redemption that is more typical of other trans films, the final scene of *The King and the Clown* counteracts all the previous teasing scenes of undressing and "gender revelation." Coming full circle, the two jesters find themselves on the tightrope again in the final scene. In the preceding scene, Jang-saeng is blinded by the king's guards over false accusations of his disloyalty. A court official sympathetic to Jang-saeng releases him, but Jang-saeng cannot leave without Gong-gil. He returns to perform one final act on a tightrope in the courtyard facing the king's sleeping chamber. Jang-saeng sings that he sees worldly affairs with more clarity now that he is blind. Gong-gil—despite their position as the king's new favorite subject—abandons the king in his chamber to join Jang-saeng on the tightrope. Their performance morphs into mutual confessions in which they renew their dedication to each other. Gong-gil chooses Jang-saeng over the king, knowing that they would now be prosecuted along with Jang-saeng. As the king's soldiers approach the inner courtyard, Jang-saeng and Gong-gil—standing at opposite ends of the tightrope—prepare to die by asking each other what they would like to be in their next life. Gong-gil vows to be reborn in exactly the same body. From the character's perspective, there is nothing about their body that needs to be corrected. The film concludes with a freeze-frame of the two jesters jumping up simultaneously on the tightrope, which suggests but does not show the characters' ultimate doom.

Gong-gil's decision is an element that distinguishes *The King and the Clown* from other trans films. Gong-gil is neither in flamboyant drag nor struggling with what some films depict as gender "transition." They appear to simply live in their social role without being questioned. They are not dysphoric or in struggle to "perform" their gender. Instead they seem at ease and desirable. Unlike Gong-gil, who wishes to be reborn in exactly the same body, characters in many films featuring trans protagonists share an investment in surgical and medical interventions as an endpoint for viewers' voyeuristic pleasure. *The King and the Clown* supports the idea that social and medical transitions are not predicated upon each other. Surgery as a topic in and by itself in films with trans protagonists is not an issue, however. When accessible without "gatekeeping protocols . . . aim[ing] at restrict[ing] access to care," surgical interventions can be empowering tools and self-actualizing practices for individuals, but cinematic constructions that fetishize reconstructive surgery in imaginings of trans and queer life are problematic because, in that context, the cinematic gaze looking at the trans body is fixated on its anatomy.[23] In untangling the love triangle in its denouement, *The King and the Clown* does not privilege, as *Stage Beauty* does, heterosexual norms in romantic love as reparative of queer desires either. *The King and the Clown* enables its central trans feminine character to simply exist as themselves without justification. *The King and the Clown* does not fall into the trap of what Sara Ahmed has called "a queer politics of unhappiness," a tendency among queer films to fetishize or aestheticize the suffering of sexual minorities who are forced to "live with the consequences of being an unhappiness-cause for others."[24] Ahmed has theorized that the de rigueur unhappy endings of queer narratives—a result of social imposition and self censorship—are tolerated by queer communities for the sake of increased visibility, because "more important was the fact there was a new book about us."[25] In this light, the tragicomic *King and the Clown* succeeds as an atypical trans narrative by sustaining queer space.

Reception and Context

With a budget of $6 million, *The King and the Clown* was a box-office hit in South Korea ($85 million), where it grossed more than *Titanic* (1997) and *Avengers: Infinity Wars* (2018). It was seen by more than 12 million people—a quarter of the Korean population. The feature film's queer valences and its enthusiastic reception throughout East Asia mark a significant milestone in New Korean Wave (*hallyu*) cinema (2007–2012).[26] *Hallyu* refers to the global popularity of South Korea's music (such as K-pop), television dramas, and films.

The King and the Clown is one of the rare films with a trans protagonist to go mainstream. Interestingly, despite its high profile, the film has not been commonly identified as a trans film in East Asia. The director has made numerous public statements that *The King and the Clown* is not a gay film and kept Gon-gil an enigmatic character who does not offer any explicit statements about their gender or sexual identity.[27] While it is undeniable that the trans character Gong-gil is gendered as feminine for the king's desiring and controlling "male gaze," the film keeps fluid the sexuality of the male characters around Gong-gil.[28] Depending on what the men think Gong-gil is, the male gaze can be heterosexual, homosexual, or bisexual. It is clear, however, that the film studio sought to fulfill the fantasy of its target audience: young female filmgoers. Gong-gil's soft-spoken mannerisms, smooth pale skin, gored skirt, and hairdo with a bow exemplify "the female fantasy of the ideal gay man."[29] It is important to note that the film did draw a significant number of older audiences as well. According to Chung Jin-wan, head of Eagle Pictures, 18 percent of the audience was over forty years old.[30]

The director's use of the Korean term *gei* (gay) merits further scrutiny. Before acquiring its contemporary meaning of homosexual men, the term *gei* referred to "a male-bodied person" who wears skirts or adopts dainty mannerisms, such as covering their mouth when giggling. It also referred to transgender individuals "who did not have gender affirmation surgery," according to Han Chae-yun's study.[31] Because of its continued malleability, "gay" is an umbrella term for sexual minorities in Korea. In the United States, the UK, France, and Germany, however, *The King and the Clown* is often regarded as a gay-themed film primarily on the basis of the subdued erotic bond between the two jesters.[32] Throughout the film, heterosexual intimacy between the king and his cis consort is explicitly shown in multiple scenes, but the only potentially homoerotic scene is a brief on-screen kiss between the king and his female-presenting jester Gong-gil, who is unconscious at the time. The *Guardian* identifies these features as part of the film's "muted gay storyline."[33] In China, though, the film is banned on account of "the homosexual code" and "sexually explicit language in the film," according to the film's distributor CJ Entertainment.[34] Writing for the *New York Times*, Norimitsu Onishi compared the success of *The King and the Clown* to that of *Brokeback Mountain* (directed by Ang Lee, 2005).[35] The tendency to misread the love triangle as a gay relationship is understandable, for the film appeared one year after homosexuality was removed from the Korean Youth Protection Commission's list of socially unacceptable acts in 2004. For many viewers and critics, it can be difficult to resist the tendency to map what is uncategorizable (Gong-gil's identity) onto what one already knows (the gay rights movement). So *The King and the Clown* is misconceived as the Korean answer to the iconic *Brokeback Mountain*. The film director's capacious use of the term *gei* (gay) is lost on Western viewers. The linguistically marked transgender meanings (*gei*, gay, *kkonminam*, flower boys) are also lost in translation. The film's subtitles often gloss over nonbinary meanings, such as Gong-gil's pronouns. Subtitles are as much filtering devices as they are heuristic tools, giving the false impression that cinematic meanings are conveyed primarily through verbal messages instead of via blocking, lighting, costumes, characterization, and other elements. Both transgender narratives and translational practices are governed by the "divisions of language [and] the body . . . in ways that confound orderly linguistic categories."[36]

The film's title in both Korean (*Wang-ui namja*) and Taiwanese releases (*Wang de nanren*, The King's Man) cements the king's possession of Gong-gil not as his clown but as his male consort. Notably the English title, *The King and the Clown*, does not feature the possessive form. It puts the king and Gong-gil on equal footing, and it keeps Gong-gil's identity gender-neutral.

It is important to note that, prior to *The King and the Clown*, there had been other, more explicitly transgender-themed films from South Korea, though none of them garnered a similar level of public attention. All of them have been set in the contemporary period. *Man on High Heels* (directed by Jang Jin, 2014) is a noir film featuring a revered macho homicide detective who is a closeted trans woman. She resigns from her job in order to go through gender affirmation surgery. *Like a Virgin* (directed by Lee Hae-jun and Lee Hae-young, 2006) chronicles the life of a transgender teenage girl who takes on folk wrestling (*ssireum*) to raise money for gender affirmation surgery. Her true passion, however, lies in dancing and mimicking Madonna's singing. Set in Seoul's international district, Itaewon, *Does the American Moon Rise over Itaewon?* (directed by Yoon Sam-yuk, 1991) created a sensation for featuring a transgender striptease club performer played by Oh Yoon-hee, the country's first openly trans feminine actor. Also set in Itaewon, the gory *Mascara* (directed by Lee Hoon, 1995) follows a transgender hostess's love life and revenge on her rapists after she successfully undergoes gender affirmation surgery.[37] Notably several 1990s LGBTQ films were set in Itaewon, one of the well-known hotspots for sexual minorities in the 1990s and now home to expatriates and US military personnel.[38]

Similar to *The King and the Clown*, both *Mascara* and *Does the American Moon Rise over Itaewon?* depict the hardship faced by transgender characters who are stereotypical social outcasts doing anything for money since they do not have access to legal work. While the depictions are realistic and not judgmental, they do walk in step with stereotypes, reinforcing "a bourgeois audience's . . . view of transgender immorality."[39]

The King and the Clown, however, stands out in LGBTQ cinema for its unique nonjudgmental and atypical narrative arc. While Gong-gil may be marginalized, they are not socially alienated; they are accepted as a feminine person by characters of high and low social status. Gong-gil's gender presentation is consistently perceived as feminine in private life and onstage without any transition scenes.

Sexuality is another topic of contention in contemporary Korean films. It is coupled with positive biases about youth, such that a trans feminine person's or character's youthfulness intervenes in positive ways in societal acceptance of trans identity. In both films at issue here, age is an important vector of identity; youthfulness and femininity have become intertwined identity markers. *The King and the Clown* frames its central character Gonggil's love story as a heterosexual one. This normalization strategy makes trans identity more palatable to Korean audiences who reject homosexuality but readily accept younger, heterosexual trans women, who enjoy what the dominant culture regards as "passing" privileges. Used frequently by popular media, "passing" is a misconception, because it implies that one's identity is not authentic and that one is merely "mistaken" for something one is not.[40] The idea of "passing" is subjective and flawed.

The tendency to reject homosexuality but accept younger, heterosexual, conventionally attractive trans individuals is evident in a number of milestone events in South Korea at the turn of the millennium. In 2000, the actor Hong Suk-cheon came out as gay and lost his livelihood. All television shows and studios shunned him overnight. Amidst public uproar, the first openly gay celebrity left the entertainment industry to change careers. The 2004 "Asian hero" of *Time* magazine, Hong became—in various periods of his life—a restaurateur, a fashion arts professor, and a Democratic Labor Party candidate for public office.[41] In contrast, Harisu (punning on "Hot Issue"), the stage name of Lee Kyung-eun, has enjoyed great success and a high level of acceptance both before and after she came out as a trans woman in 2001. It is important to note that, in the context of age and societal acceptance, Harisu came out when she was twenty-six and was in a heterosexual marriage with Micky Jung from 2007 to 2017. While there are practically no openly homosexual actors, there have been several high-profile heterosexual trans feminine singers and models in the footsteps of Harisu. The year 2005 saw the debut of the first trans feminine K-pop band Lady, who cited Harisu as an inspiration. The four singers of Lady are deemed conventionally attractive. All four women, in their late teens and early twenties at the time of their debut, have openly discussed their heterosexuality and their gender affirmation surgeries. Catering to heterosexual male fans, the band even released an album featuring nude shots of its four members in the genre of *shashinshū* (photo book) popularized by Japanese pop culture. As K. S. Yoo theorizes, contemporary Korean society prioritizes sexuality over gender identity in its placement of an individual in a social hierarchy. Same-sex relationships are deemed more deviant than heterosexual ones regardless of the gender identities of the parties involved. Even a heterosexual couple consisting of a cis and a trans partner, for example, would be more acceptable than a homosexual couple of any combination of gender identities.[42] Along similar lines, Jeeyoung Shin argues that *The King and the Clown* uses subtexts such as court politics to distract audiences from what may be perceived to be a gay theme.[43] The image of Gong-gil reflects how Korean audiences seem to imagine heteronormative trans life, as in the cases just discussed, such as that of Harisu.

Trans Femininity and *Stage Beauty*

The theme of flower boys' gender nonconformity in *The King and the Clown* invokes the historical reality of early modern English boy actors. There are multiple cases of successful boy actors, such as Richard Robinson (1595–1648) and Edward Kynaston (1643–1712), who played female roles on stage and then transitioned to playing male roles when they grew up. The life stories of these actors presented boyhood as androgynous and gender fluid, but interestingly, as Simone Chess notes, they carried a "queer residue" with them into male adulthood, and they continued to perform feminine or androgynous roles.[44] Kynaston is probably the best-known example in modern times, thanks to Samuel Pepys's diary (August 1660)[45] and the 2004 feature film *Stage Beauty,* directed by Richard Eyre, a former director of the UK's National Theatre. The film depicts Edward "Ned" Kynaston as presenting as female offstage.

Based on Jeffrey Hatcher's play *Compleat Female Stage Beauty*, the film *Stage Beauty* centers on the question "Who am I?" in the career and private life of Billy Crudup's character Ned Kynaston, one of the last Restoration adult "boy actors" who exclusively played female roles.[46] The film explores the boundaries between cross-gender casting (Kynaston as Desdemona), drag (Kynaston's playful female persona in private life), proto-trans (Kynaston's male lover's statement), and transgender identities (Kynaston's statement about himself). Whereas *The King and the Clown* presents Gong-gil as they are without explanatory justification or stereotypical gender transition scenes, *Stage Beauty* recruits the audience to participate in Kynaston's affective labor toward becoming who the society thinks he "should" be. The film "redeems" Kynaston by having him straighten up through a "reparative arc" from a trans feminine person with a male lover to a cis man in love with a cis woman, Maria. Kynaston presents as both male and female on- and offstage as the narrative unfolds, and his agony and trepidation when in drag stand in stark contrast to his later, "naturalized" role as a heterosexual cis man on stage and in private life.

When Kynaston is still playing female roles, multiple scenes offer close-up shots of him applying facial makeup and fitting a wig. After the show, the camera follows Kynaston to his dressing room to witness him transforming out of drag, or "shed[ing] his skin," as he puts it. Even after he removes his wig, he continues to use practiced feminine mannerisms. Quoting the acting master who has trained him to play female parts from a young age, Kynaston states that he is told never to forget he is "a man in woman's form," but he is beginning to think perhaps it is "the other way around." Kynaston's statement about being a woman in a man's body echoes a now outdated convention of trans self-narratives about being "trapped" in the gender identity assigned at birth.

Scenes of gender transition and ambiguity in the film are designed to evoke cinematic voyeuristic pleasure. Whereas Gong-gil consistently performs female roles and presents as female offstage, Kynaston performs female parts for only half of his career. Both Gong-gil and Kynaston are actors of low social status who maintain romantic relationships with more powerful, aristocratic male characters. Kynaston is a well-known actor, and his onstage gender identity and sexuality permeate his life. He presents as female in bed with his dominant lover George Villiers, the Duke of Buckingham (Ben Chaplin). They meet regularly in the theater where Kynaston performs. As Kynaston approaches the duke, he brushes off Kynaston's affectionate feminine gestures, insisting that Kynaston wear a wig before coming to bed. Kynaston retorts playfully, "Do you ask your lady whores to wear a wig to bed?" alluding to the duke's sexually promiscuous lifestyle. Kynaston wishes to know why the duke treats his cisgender sexual partners differently from him. The duke explains that the wig is necessary to make Kynaston "more of a woman." Alluding to the destructive nature of erotic desires and the Renaissance trope relating orgasm and death, the duke says to Kynaston, "I like to see a golden flow [of hair] as I die in you." There is also a connection among sex, death, and stage performance of femininity. Once the film audience realizes that the two lovers are on Desdemona's deathbed, it becomes explicit that the duke desires Kynaston's ability to perform feminine submission in his love life. In a later scene, the duke states further, "When I did spend time with you, I always thought of you as a woman." Indeed Kynaston takes great pride in his portrayal of the murder of Desdemona ("women die beautifully"). As Sawyer Kemp observes, "male-to-female cross-casting" is often used to "downplay sexist violence."[47] Kynaston aestheticizes the masculinist killing of women in his stage performance.

There is an irony in their relationship, however. Their illicit encounters—carefully kept under wraps—always take place onstage after Kynaston's evening performance. This is parallel to Gong-gil's relationship with the king discussed earlier, in which Gong-gil is always asked to put on private shadow plays or finger puppet shows for the king. They converse in a coded manner under the guise of discussing theater works. In *Stage Beauty,* after the audiences clear the auditorium, Kynaston leaves the role of Desdemona behind only to return in the same costume to the same bed and stage set where he, as Desdemona, has just been murdered. Waiting for Kynaston in bed is the duke. The setting of the stage gives their relationship a theatrical quality. The duke's insistence on Kynaston's donning wigs and dresses further accentuates the idea that Kynaston puts on a second show each evening, a private show for an audience of one on a public stage. It is a private act in a public space. One evening there is a voyeur, Maria Hughes (Claire Danes). An admirer of Kynaston, Maria works for him as his dresser. In one scene Maria watches from the wings in horror, heartbroken, as Kynaston has sex with the duke in the bed onstage. It is clear that Maria is interested in Kynaston romantically. Maria has been an "obsessed spectator" during Kynaston's theatrical performances. Thoroughly familiar with the script and dreaming of acting, Maria watches from backstage and mouths every line Kynaston's Desdemona speaks. Now, in the second "show" of the evening, Maria steps into the role of an "illicit observer" who, like Othello, receives "ocular proof" of Kynaston's betrayal in a taboo sexual act.[48] When Maria sees that Kynaston is interested in men, her hope of attracting Kynaston is shattered. From her position of a voyeur, Maria "grossly gape[s] on, behold [Kynaston/Desdemona] topped" (*Othello* 3.3.395–96).

In fact, Kynaston maintains this secret romantic relationship as a woman only until King Charles II arranges a heterosexual marriage for the duke. Just like Desdemona and Gong-gil, Kynaston's body is gendered for the male

FIGURE 13.4.   After playing Desdemona onstage, Kynaston takes off his wig backstage in *Stage Beauty*.

FIGURE 13.5. After the audience clears the auditorium, Kynaston returns to Desdemona's bed onstage to meet the Duke of Buckingham in *Stage Beauty*.

gaze. The duke looks *through* rather than *at* Kynaston's female persona. He subsumes Kynaston within a hetero-masculinist image of female suffering. Kynaston and Gong-gil are deemed desirable objects because they fulfill male fantasies of "feminine subjugation," a notion Kynaston teaches his apprentice Maria as she learns the role of Desdemona.

Kynaston's adventures do not stop there. After another successful performance one evening, two aristocratic female fans invite him—still in makeup, petticoat, and dress—on a carriage ride. They reveal during the ride that their real purpose is to settle a wager about Kynaston's genitalia. They claim to be asking on behalf of others around them: "My father says you're much too beautiful to be a gentleman. . . . My mother's good friend, the Earl of Lauderdale, says if you're a man, you don't have a gentleman's thingy. He says you're like those Italian singers." The essentialist conversation zeroes in on Kynaston's anatomy: "The earl says they cut off your, uh, castrati, and you become a woman." Kynaston responds cheerfully and flirtatiously. Batting his eyelashes, he grasps the ladies' hands and directs them under his skirt toward his groin. Without letting them actually touch him, Kynaston assures them of his possession of a "big, bulging orb-and-scepter of a thingy." The ladies insist, "We'd have to touch it." It is unclear what happens next, but a series of reaction shots show the two gentlewomen breathless and Kynaston moaning in pleasure. In this scene, drag seems comedic because Kynaston turns it into a political act that parodies the two ladies' binary visions. The self-referentiality of drag, an imitation that Jennifer Drouin glosses as "almost but not quite" right (following Homi Bhabha's formulation), draws attention to the artifice of gendered bodies in performance. In contrast, Gong-gil's embodied identity is "neither parody nor an intentional exposure of normativity."[49] It is not an act but lived reality.

The film depicts a second attempt at a genitalia check soon afterward. Before they exit the carriage and part ways with one another, Kynaston and the two gentlewomen are confronted by Sir Charles Sedley (Richard Griffiths). Having mistaken them for three female prostitutes, Sedley approaches them for their prices. He corners Kynaston and gropes under his skirt to discover what Kynaston calls "a guardian at the gate." Gender is presented here as an artifice and a series of loosely connected symbols. Kynaston's presence disrupts binary gender categories. Kynaston does not so much "pass" as a woman (in his fans' words) as passes through the interstitial space between categories.

The duke's attachment to such gendered accessories as the wig and the two women's and Sedley's fascination with Kynaston's genitalia hark back to similar scenes of "trans revelation" in The King and the Clown. The "gender reveal" scenes in both films echo Talia Mae Bettcher's argument that the misconception of an anatomical reality of gender casts trans people as "evil . . . make-believers," locking them into being either a visible pretender or an invisible deceiver to be forcefully exposed at some point. Either way they are seen as "fundamentally illusory."[50] Will Fisher's research shows that "gendered accessories" such as codpieces and handkerchiefs and sartorial differences played key roles in early modern[51] and Galenic conception of gender.[52] Kynaston pushes back on the idea that the wig alone makes him a woman, and rejects—while humoring with a sense of playfulness—other characters' request for genital verification. Unlike the passive Gong-gil, Kynaston takes control in these "trans revelation" scenes. Despite their depiction of Kynaston's agency in self-determination, these scenes inadvertently encourage "spectators to fixate variously on the surface and on the imagined body beneath." As Elizabeth Klett theorizes, "Any attempts to fix gender on the cross-dressed . . . body are always . . . prosthetic."[53] In particular, films that depict gender variance in theater making foster a dual consciousness in their audiences: the simultaneous awareness of identities manufactured onstage and filtered by cinematic devices—an awareness that Gong-gil and Kynaston can both be themselves and be playing a role.

After King Charles II lifts the ban on actresses and bans men from performing female roles, Kynaston is bereft of both his roles and his identity. The royal decree marks a key moment "in the emergence of a new proto-Stanislavskian paradigm of acting," outlawing Kynaston's intricately stylized representation of women.[54] At a loss, he tells his protégée Maria that he does not want to play men, for they are "not beautiful" and "do nothing beautifully." He disapproves of Maria's wish to play female parts, asking, "A woman playing a woman, where's the trick in that?" Eventually Kynaston reluctantly takes Maria on as an apprentice. As he coaches Maria on "the five positions of feminine subjugation," it becomes clear that he sees femininity as a series of practiced stylized gestures. In contrast, Maria takes a naturalist-realist approach to performance, emphasizing her inalienable right to perform "more authentic" representations of women onstage simply because she is assigned female at birth. Both Maria's and Kynaston's approaches to performing female roles are reductive and essentialist. Kynaston's and Maria's contest for ownership of Desdemona becomes the backbone of the film's narrative and scopic power.

In his private life, Kynaston also goes through a very difficult period after losing his job. He is beaten by Sir Charles Sedley's henchmen, who call him a "bum boy" who is "mocking your betters." Kynaston is severely injured. As Cameron McFarlane writes, without the stage roles that have come to define him as an actor and a person, Kynaston "is reduced to a kind of gender freak."[55] Patriarchal institutions govern acceptable expressions of femininity. As has been noted by theorists such as Julia Serrano, who calls the phenomenon "scapegoating of femininity," the patriarchy focuses its energy on guarding the superiority of masculinity. Trans feminine identity devalues masculinity by rejecting it. The presence of Kynaston creates a category crisis by challenging putative binary distinctiveness of gender. Further, it poses what is known in social identity theory as distinctiveness threat. When a group sees the boundaries defining their identity as indispensable, they feel threatened when these putatively definitional boundaries are blurred.

The key event in the "straightening up" of Kynaston's gender and sexual nonconformity is his rupture with his boyfriend. Kynaston meets with the duke to ask why Buckingham has not visited him since his injury at the hands of the gang hired by Sir Charles Sedley. He attempts, as he does in the past, playful affection, but the duke rejects him. Upon learning that the duke is marrying a cis woman, Kynaston presses in a competitive tone: "What is she like in bed? What is she like to kiss?" The duke eventually acknowledges that he valued their relationship as no more than a performance, a fetish: "When we were in bed, it was always in a bed onstage. I'd think, here I am in a play, inside Desdemona, Cleopatra, poor Ophelia. You're none of them now. I don't know who you are. I doubt you do." Now that Kynaston no longer plays women onstage, the duke cannot accept him as he is: "I don't want you!

What you are now." It becomes clear that Kynaston is a temporary substitute in bed until the duke lands a cis partner.

After the breakup, Kynaston begins playing Othello in blackface and embarks on a more aggressive "therapeutic" arc. Some trans masculine characters, such as Viola in *Twelfth Night*, see their sexuality erased by circumstance. Disguised as pageboy Cesario in Illyria, Viola is forced to conceal her romantic yearning for Duke Orsino while being courted by Countess Olivia. In other cases, trans feminine characters, such as Gong-gil and Kynaston, are pressured by characters around them for binary clarifications of their sexuality. Kynaston "becomes a man" by mastering the craft of killing a woman onstage and by performing intimate acts in bed with his former dresser and current rival Maria, who now plays Desdemona. Toward the end of the film, Kynaston's "reparative" turn from the duke to Maria "looks disturbingly like the sexual conversion of a man from gay to straight."[56] The "reparation" of Kynaston follows a romantically motivated trajectory toward cis-heterosexual normalcy.

Towards a Capacious Theory

Both *The King and the Clown* and *Stage Beauty* teeter cautiously along various lines of gender expression and sexuality in their respective cultures without giving a name to gender transgressions in the narratives, commercializing queerness by introducing "narrative tension . . . without directly challenging the culture of heteronormative familialism."[57] The filmmakers have their own financial or ideological reasons for de-emphasizing, in their public statements, nonconformist aspects of their films, but it is important, from an archival point of view, to recover the trans signification of these performances that have been designated otherwise in the service of heteronormative ideologies. I treat the heterosexual trans body and non-trans sexually queer body as objects for inclusive analysis in an expanding repertoire of trans performance. By applying transgender theory to performance criticism, we can reclaim elements that have been lost to our collective trans archive. In an effort to excavate hitherto unknown trans narratives by expanding the archives we work from, I am cognizant of the risk of imposing trans as a contemporary category onto works set in Restoration England (*Stage Beauty*) or premodern Korea (*The King and the Clown*) which portray bodies that "did not yet exist under the sign of trans*."[58] The fact, however, that trans characters such as Gong-gil ("transvestitism [was] common" among pre-modern vagabond actors)[59] or Edward Kynaston (a female-presenting adult "boy actor") live under different labels does not invalidate their trans experiences.

These films and their reception reveal that transgender communities past and present have included a wide range of identities, many of which may be an inconvenient truth not only for the conservatives but also, as the case may be, for activists who may selectively focus on identities that more directly support their causes. As trans characters, Gong-gil and Kynaston re-inscribe the sexed body into social-constructivist discourses about gender while simultaneously countering the idea that anatomy is their destiny. Both narratives challenge essentialist ideas that sustain oppression based on binary models of gender. *Stage Beauty* showcases processes of gendered "becoming." *The King and the Clown* enables its central trans feminine character to simply exist as themself without justification. *The King and the Clown* registers multiple ways in which trans identities are constructed, and it participates in the "regional production of trans meanings that negotiates between local subjectivities and globalized categories."[60]

By reading narratives of flower boys (Gong-gil) and adult boy actors (Kynaston) as trans feminine and nonbinary, we build a more capacious theoretical model to elucidate not only performance histories of sexual transformation but also less explicit representations of trans identities in gender-fluid performances.

Notes

I wish to thank Simone Chess for her intellectual generosity and insightful feedback.

1. Bert Cardullo, *Screening the Stage* (Bern: Peter Lang, 2006), 254. See also Sarah Martindale, "Shakespearean Film as Art Cinema: *Stage Beauty* as a Cerebral Retort to Hollywood," in *British Art Cinema: Creativity, Experimentation and Innovation*, ed. Paul Newland and Brian Hoyle (Manchester: Manchester University Press, 2019).

2. David Alderson, "Acting Straight: Reality TV, Gender Self-Consciousness and Forms of Capital," *New Formations* 83 (2014): 7–24; John M. Clum, *Acting Gay: Male Homosexuality in Modern Drama* (New York: Columbia University Press, 1992).

3. J. Halberstam, *Female Masculinity* (Durham, NC: Duke University Press, 1998), 45–74.

4. Sawyer K. Kemp, "Transgender Shakespeare Performance: A Holistic Dramaturgy," *Journal of Early Modern Cultural Studies* 19.4 (Fall 2019): 265–83, quotation at 268.

5. While now widely accepted and used, singular gender-neutral pronouns were initially seen by some as controversial.

6. Adele Lee, Nafees Ahmed, and Antara Basu, among others, have identified key Shakespearean references in the film. Adele Lee, "The Player King and Kingly Players: Inverting *Hamlet* in Lee Joon-ik's *King and the Clown* (2005)," *Borrowers and Lenders: The Journal of Shakespeare and Appropriation* 12.1 (Fall 2018), http://www. borrowers.uga.edu/784121/show (accessed January 10, 2020); Nafees Ahmed, "The

King and the Clown (2005) Review: A Shakespearean Tragedy," *High on Films,* June 23, 2019, https://www.highonfilms.com/the-king-and-the-clown-2005-review/ (accessed April 14, 2020); Antara Basu, "Film Review: *The King and the Clown,*" *The Medium,* May 21, 2017, https://medium.com/@antarabasu/film-review-the-king-and-the-clown-2005-c76bc6816bf1 (accessed April 30, 2020).

7. Laura Mulvey, "Visual Pleasure and Narrative Cinema," *Screen* 16.3 (Autumn 1975): 6–18.

8. Mark McLelland, "The Love between 'Beautiful Boys' in Japanese Women's Comics," *Journal of Gender Studies* 9.1 (2000): 13–25.

9. Jeeyoung Shin, "Male Homosexuality in *The King and the Clown*: Hybrid Construction and Contested Meanings," *Journal of Korean Studies* 18.1 (Spring 2013): 89–114, quotation at 100.

10. The name is also spelled as Yi Chun'gi in articles using the McCune-Reischauer system of romanization.

11. Ch'oe Kyŏnghúi, "Chorong tanghal surok sesang ún chúlgŏwŏjinda" [The more ridiculed, the merrier the world becomes], www.movist.com, December 29, 2005, http://www.movist.com/article/read.asp7type=32&id=11293; quoted in English in Shin, "Male Homosexuality in *The King and the Clown,*" 101.

12. Timothy J. Murray, *Like a Film: Ideological Fantasy on Screen, Camera and Canvas* (New York: Routledge, 1993), 104, 106–7.

13. Danielle M. Seid, "Reveal," *TSQ: Transgender Studies Quarterly* 1.1–2 (2014): 176.

14. Eliza Steinbock, *Shimmering Images: Trans Cinema, Embodiment, and the Aesthetics of Change* (Durham, NC: Duke University Press, 2019), 4.

15. Talia Mae Bettcher, "Evil Deceivers and Make-Believers: On Transphobic Violence and the Politics of Illusion," *Hypatia* 22.3 (2007): 50, 59.

16. Mary Ann Doane, *The Desire to Desire: The Women's Film of the 1940s* (Bloomington: University of Indiana Press, 1987), 88.

17. Laura Mulvey, "Visual Pleasure and Narrative Cinema," *Screen* 16.3 (Autumn 1975): 6–18.

18. Stanley Cavell, *The World Viewed* (Cambridge, MA: Harvard University Press 1979), 44–45.

19. Laura Mulvey, "Visual Pleasure and Narrative Cinema," *Screen* 16.3 (Autumn 1975): 6–18.

20. Damon R. Young, *Making Sex Public and Other Cinematic Fantasies* (Durham, NC: Duke University Press, 2018), 2.

21. Interview with Lee Joon-gi, MBC Goldfish Talk Show, April 29, 2009, script published on a fandom website About My Jun, http://aboutmyjun.blogspot.com/2009/05/20090429-lee-jun-ki-mbc-goldfish_22.html?m=1 (accessed May 1, 2020).

22. Chris Berry, "Asian Values, Family Values," *Journal of Homosexuality* 40.3–4 (2001): 211–31, quotation at 213.

23. Eric Plemons and Chris Straayer, "Introduction: Reframing the Surgical," special issue of *TSQ: Transgender Studies Quarterly* 5.2 (May 2018): 164–73, quotation at 165–66.

24. Sara Ahmed, *The Promise of Happiness* (Durham, NC: Duke University Press, 2010), 89 and 109.

25. Ibid., vii.

26. Jin Dal Yong, *New Korean Wave: Transnational Cultural Power in the Age of Social Media* (Urbana: University of Illinois Press, 2016), 68–90.

27. "Bonus Features," *The King and the Clown*, directed by Joon-ik Lee (CJ Entertainment, 2006), DVD, Special Limited Edition DTS, four discs.

28. Laura Mulvey, "Visual Pleasure and Narrative Cinema," *Screen* 16.3 (Autumn 1975): 6–18.

29. Jungmin Kwon, "Spectacularizing the Homosexual Body: The Secret Rendezvous among Global Gay Media, Local Straight Women, and the Media Industry in South Korea" (PhD diss., University of Illinois at Urbana-Champaign, 2014), 136.

30. *Korea Times*, March 5, 2006.

31. Han Chae-yun, "Korean Lesbian Community History" [Hanguk rejeubieon keomyuniti-ui yeoksa], *Progressive Review [Jinbopyeongron]* 49 (2011): 100–128.

32. "South Korea Rests Oscar Hope on Gay-Themed Film," *Guardian*, September 21, 2006, https://www.theguardian.com/film/2006/sep/21/news (accessed May 10, 2020); Normitisu Onishi, "Gay-Themed Film Gives Closet Door a Tug," *New York Times*, March 31, 2006; Jan Schulz-Ojala, "Drei Farben Neon—Hollywood kann einpacken: Das südkoreanische Pusan und sein boomendes Filmfestival," *Tagesspiel*, October 24, 2006, https://www.tagesspiegel.de/kultur/drei-farben-neon/765886.html (accessed May 17, 2020). The *Tagesspiel* review does not fail to notice the homosexual subtext ("diskret angespielte homosexuelle Subtext"). Jean-François Rauger, "*Le Roi et le Clown*: Satire et pouvoir politique en Corée," *Le Monde*, January 22, 2008, https://www.lemonde.fr/cinema/article/2008/01/22/le-roi-et-le-clown-satire-et-pouvoir-politique-en-coree_1002245_3476.html (accessed May 8, 2020), examines the "unspeakable homosexuality" ("homosexualité inavouable") in the film.

33. "South Korea Rests Oscar Hope on Gay-Themed Film."

34. Benjamin Cohen, "South Korean Film Banned from China for Gay Theme," *Pink News*, July 4, 2006, https://www.pinknews.co.uk/2006/07/04/south-korean-film-banned-from-china-for-gay-theme/ (accessed May 17, 2020). See also "South Korea Rests Oscar Hope on Gay-Themed Film."

35. Onishi, "Gay-Themed Film Gives Closet Door a Tug." Onishi is an important voice in American journalism about East Asia. Fluent in Japanese and French, he was part of a team that won the Pulitzer Prize for international reporting in 2015. Despite being a subject matter specialist, however, Onishi misunderstood the film.

36. David Gramling and Aniruddha Dutta, introduction to "Translating Transgender," special issue of *TSQ: Transgender Studies Quarterly* 3.3–4 (November 2016): 333–56, quotation at 334.

37. For further details on the film, see the studio Sogang Planning's website, http://www.cine21.com/db/company/info/?company_id=168 (accessed May 15, 2020).

38. Eun Young Lee, "The Rhetorical Landscape of Itaewon: Negotiating New Transcultural Identities in South Korea" (PhD diss., Bowling Green State University, 2015), 166–67.

39. Jooran Lee, "Remembered Branches: Towards a Future of Korean Homosexual Film," in *Queer Asian Cinema: Shadows in the Shade*, ed. Andrew Grossman

(New York: Routledge, 2015), 273–82, quotation at 279. Note that I disagree with Lee's use of the male pronoun to describe the trans actor in *Does the American Moon Rise over Itaewon?*

40. Janet Mock, *Surpassing Certainty: What My Twenties Taught Me* (New York: Astra, 2017), 8.

41. Hong published a memoir titled *My Heart Still Throbs for Forgotten Love* in 2000. See also G. Kim, "Hong Suk-Cheon: 'I Lost My Job in a Day,'" *News Way*, April 28, 2010, http://www.newsway.kr/news/articleView.html?idxno=81371.

42. K. S. Yoo, "Transgender, OK! Homosexuals, NO!," *Newsen*, June 25, 2010, http://www.newsen.com/news_view.php?uid=201006030837091001.

43. Shin, "Male Homosexuality in *The King and the Clown*," 96.

44. Simone Chess, "Trans Residue: Nonbinary Affect and Boy Actors' Adult Careers," paper presented at the annual meeting of the Shakespeare Association of America, Washington, DC, April 2019.

45. Samuel Pepys, *The Diary of Samuel Pepys: A New and Complete Transcription*, 11 vols., ed. Robert Latham and William Matthews (London: Bell & Hyman, 1970–1983).

46. Richard Eyre, dir., *Stage Beauty* (Lion Gate Films, 2004); Jeffrey Hatcher, *Compleat Female Stage Beauty* (New York: Dramatists Play Service, 2006).

47. Sawyer K. Kemp, "Transgender Shakespeare Performance: A Holistic Dramaturgy," *Journal of Early Modern Cultural Studies* 19.4 (Fall 2019): 265–83, quotation at 274.

48. Elizabeth Gruber, "'No Woman Would Die Like That': *Stage Beauty* as Corrective-Counterpoint to *Othello*," in *Situating the Feminist Gaze and Spectatorship in Postwar Cinema*, ed. Marcelline Block (Newcastle: Cambridge Scholars, 2008), 226–39, quotation at 230.

49. Jennifer Drouin, "Cross-Dressing, Drag, and Passing: Slippages in Shakespearean Comedy," in *Shakespeare Re-Dressed: Cross-Gender Casting in Contemporary Performance*, ed. James C. Bulman (Madison, NJ: Fairleigh Dickinson University Press, 2008), 23.

50. Bettcher, "Evil Deceivers and Make-Believers," 50, 59.

51. Will Fisher, *Materializing Gender in Early Modern English Literature and Culture* (Cambridge: Cambridge University Press, 2006), 10.

52. Galen of Pergamon, a Greek physician, is known for his one-sex model. He writes, "Now just as the mankind is the most perfect of all the animals, so within the mankind the man is more perfect than the woman, and the reason for his perfection is his excess of heat, for heat is Nature's primary instrument." Galen, *Ut. part.: Galien, De uteri dissectione*, in *Claudii Galeni opera omni*, vol. 2, ed. Karl Gottlob Kühn (Leipzig: Libraria Car. Cnoblochii, 1821), 630; translation in Thomas Laqueur, *Making Sex: Body and Gender from the Greeks to Freud* (Cambridge, MA: Harvard University Press, 1992), 28.

53. Quoted in James C. Bulman, introduction to *Shakespeare Re-dressed*, 18.

54. Cary M. Mazer, "Sense/Memory/Sense-Memory: Reading Narratives of Shakespearian Rehearsals," *Shakespeare Survey* 62 (2009): 328–48, quotation at 334.

55. Cameron McFarlane, "'What's the Trick in That?' Performing Gender and History in *Stage Beauty*," *Journal of Popular Culture* 44.4 (2011): 179–814, quotations at 798 and 801.

56. Anna Kamaralli, "Rehearsal in Films of the Early Modern Theatre: The Erotic Art of Making Shakespeare," *Shakespeare Bulletin* 29.1 (Spring 2011): 27–41, quotation at 37.

57. John Cho believes that this commercialization of homosexuality causes "the discrepancy between the online visibility of gay men . . . and off-line invisibility." John (Song Pae) Cho, "The Three Faces of South Korea's Male Homosexuality: Pogal, Iban and Neoliberal Gay," in *Queer Korea*, ed. Todd A. Henry (Durham, NC: Duke University Press, 2020), 263–94, quotation at 290n7.

58. Rebekah Edwards, "'This Is Not a Girl': A Trans* Archival Reading," *TSQ: Transgender Studies Quarterly* 2.4 (November 2015): 650–65, quotation at 650.

59. Richard Rutt, "The Flower Boys of Silla," *Transactions of the Korean Branch of the Royal Asiatic Society* 37 (1961): 1–61, quotation at 59–60.

60. Helen Hok-Sze Leung, "Always in Translation: Trans Cinema across Languages," *TSQ: Transgender Studies Quarterly* 3.3–4 (November 2016): 433–47, quotation at 433.

CHAPTER 14

Laid Open

Examining Genders in Early America

SCOTT LARSON

> We do not call you to teach the court, but to lay open yourself.
>
> —John Winthrop at the trial of Anne Hutchinson, 1637

In 1869, officials in Monroe County, Pennsylvania, arrested the Reverend Joseph Israel Lobdell for false preaching and disturbing the local peace. His practice of begging while delivering sermons and "wild harangues" was not unusual for itinerant preachers in rural nineteenth-century America.[1] The rest of his story made national news. Lobdell had been assigned female at birth, and had once been married to a man and given birth to a child. Despite this past, he lived much of his life as a teacher, hunter, laborer, and itinerant preacher, and he had married a woman, Mary Louise Perry. He also spent portions of his life in a variety of institutions—poorhouses, jails, and asylums—and in some of these he was forced to wear women's clothes and grow his hair long. He also was one of the first incarcerated people to be clinically described as "Lesbian," following a sexological examination published by P. M. Wise in 1883.[2] This published examination placed Lobdell at a pivotal moment in the history of gender and sexuality, rendering him a specimen in a new scientific regime, one built on a long history of the public "laying open" of captive minoritarian subjects, those whose bodies were controlled by slave owners, magistrates, and doctors.[3]

Joseph Lobdell's place in the history of sexology and transgender history has been used to mark the emergence of sexological regimes at the turn of the twentieth century. But his claimed identity as *Reverend* Joseph Israel

Lobdell, his arrest while preaching, and newspaper and sexological accounts that identify Lobdell as a Methodist minister all raise questions about the place of religious identity in trans histories. Although this aspect of Lobdell's life is largely underexplored in scholarship, Lobdell's case connects to a longer history of religious gender variance in early America, particularly to forms of eighteenth- and nineteenth-century religious revivalism wherein religious participation regularly included gender-transformative practices. Lobdell's story thus exceeds its sexological framing and requires investigation of the connections between religious practice, gender variance, and "laying open" subjects for examination and judgment. This essay poses critical questions about the practice of gender examination as undertaken in three occasions: investigations of trans subjects as practiced by some contemporary scholars, the infamous Boston trial of Anne Hutchinson, and P. M. Wise's sexological examination of Joseph Lobdell.

While trans histories have been understudied, gender-variant subjects have been overexamined. Arrested, stripped, prodded, palpated, photographed, interrogated, and cross-examined, those individuals whose gender has come under scrutiny have never lacked curious audiences, particularly audiences prepared to adjudicate identity, diagnose difference, determine taxonomical belonging, or simply witness a marvelous sight. Even as many activists today call for increased visibility of trans people as a way to fight gender injustices, both historical records and contemporary critics argue that *invisibility* has never been the central problem facing trans and gender-variant people.[4] Increasing trans visibility in the current moment has indeed drawn important attention to issues of trans justice, but it has been accompanied with increasing anti-trans violence and targeted backlash, especially against trans people of color, and against those who are poor, disabled, undocumented, gender-nonconforming, engaged in sex work, and otherwise marginalized. Indeed, much of the violence and systematic injustice faced by vulnerable trans people is due not to invisibility but to exposures both spectacular and mundane.[5]

In light of the present situation, this essay considers historical examinations of trans studies as a political, methodological, and ethical problem. That is, how should trans studies work to avoid the very structures of examination, spectacle, and adjudication that unequally distribute life chances and expose visible trans subjects to disproportionate violence and necropolitical neglect? Scholars researching trans pasts now often join the long train of doctors, legislators, priests, judges, anthropologists, and photographers in demanding that gender-variant subjects disrobe and disclose all so that they might be judged and determined to be truly men or women, truly queer or straight, truly cis or trans. LGBTQ histories and queer pasts have struggled with demands from both queer-affirming and heteronormative perspectives to properly categorize historical subjects. Scholars fight and debate how *not* to fight over seemingly exclusive/overlapping sexual and gendered identity categories (lesbian/gay versus trans), and wrestle what Peter Coviello calls "vestigially prosecutorial" demands for proof that will clearly identify individuals as properly belonging to trans, gay, lesbian, or other identitarian pasts.[6]

This essay seeks a different approach by refusing contemporary demands of identity categorization and the methods of examination by which this categorization happens. Rather, this essay asks how the accounts of individuals and communities engaged in gender movement might "teach the court" of trans scholarship to attend differently to trans pasts. This means that I turn my attention here to the means of examination and argue that instead of reexamining gender-variant subjects to ascertain proof of gender identity, scholars should adopt a method of critical *trans-attendance*, which shifts the scene of inquiry to attend to alternate frameworks and articulations of power that surround the subject of examination. My methodological engagement is deeply indebted to Saidiya Hartman's critical engagements with the ethical work of doing history, and I will return to the implications of her work later in this essay.[7] Scholars must be critical of the need to categorize gender-variant subjects and challenge demands that subjects' bodies and most intimate bodily details, often extracted in moments of vulnerability and violation, be displayed and judged as part of a project of trans history. Trans-attendance seeks not to lay open gender-variant subjects but to call upon trans scholars to become teachable by the pasts they encounter.

Anne Hutchinson: Genders in Court

Anne Hutchinson achieved historical fame as a woman who challenged Boston's early Puritan theocracy and was banished from the Massachusetts Bay Colony as a result. She is often celebrated as an outspoken woman or as a religious dissenter, challenging a patriarchal order, but she is rarely considered part of transgender history, even though at Hutchinson's trial, Puritan Hugh Peters expressed her transgression explicitly as a gendered crossing: "You have stept out of your place, *you have rather bine a Husband than a Wife and a preacher rather than a Hearer; and a Magistrate than a subject.*"[8] Hutchinson's *place*, particularly as it related to the gendered power of religious teaching, was central to the case against Hutchinson in her part of the famous 1637 Boston trial, known to historians as the Antinomian

Controversy. The controversy was a doctrinal and political fight among Puritans within the colony, including Hutchinson, and it proved a major turning point for colonial Massachusetts's early theocracy. The trials punished Boston's religious dissenters and effectively entrenched the doctrinal and juridical power of Boston's Puritan leadership. Hutchinson was placed on trial for her part in supporting dissenting ministers in this controversy. She testified to receiving direct revelations from God and was ultimately found guilty of spreading religious errors. As a result, she was excommunicated and banished from the colony.

Much of Hutchinson's trial was dedicated to the question of whether or not she had engaged in teaching men when mixed groups gathered in her home to read the Bible and discuss Puritan theology. Hutchinson had been largely praised and accepted for leading groups of women in prayer and study early in her time in Massachusetts, and had acted as a midwife in the community. Even Governor John Winthrop concurred in the trial that her work in the meeting of women alone was not an offense to custom or law.[9] But the trial asked whether she had also engaged in hosting groups of men in her home and whether she had participated in dissenting theological/ political parties active in Boston theocracy. To act as a teacher, particularly as a teacher of men, and particularly in critiquing prominent Boston ministers, would mean that she had "stept out of [her] place." In her trial, Hutchinson never admitted that she taught men, and in her defense, she called upon the court to accuse her directly of doing so and to prove the accusation.

Indeed, in their courtroom exchange, both Hutchinson and Winthrop demonstrate the motility and trans-ability of gender, and in their arguments both connect gender to the practice of teaching rather than to the identity or body of the practitioner. Noting that the trial itself demanded that Hutchinson exposit truth to men on the *charged offense* of having taught men, she asked, "Do you think it not lawful for me to teach women and why do you call me to teach the court?"[10] This defense is specifically making two claims about gender. First, she claims a social and religious position as a woman by insisting that she had rightfully been performing her proper role as a Christian woman in teaching women. If it was wrong for her, as a woman, to be teaching women, she demands to know how Winthrop and the court are not forcing her out of her proper place in hierarchically gendered Boston theocracy should she proceed to "teach the court." Winthrop, in answering, rhetorically, worked to restore her proper place as woman and accused, and to assert his own as man and magistrate: "We do not call you to teach the court but to lay open yourself."[11] Teaching might make one a man, but he is not asking for teaching. He insists to Hutchinson and the court that examination is a practice of domination and submission that restores proper order. Hutchinson is not to teach but to open herself as a woman, or even as an ungendered object, before a male court.

This debate over *teaching* and laying open reveals key ways that exercising power in relation acted as a trans-ing practice—a practice that moved individuals outside of normative or expected structures of gender.[12] Certainly, gender and power have been central to most analyses of Hutchinson's history, and scholars have widely understood Hutchinson to have been transgressing gender norms. But this is significant to trans history because it is an open acknowledgment that being the teacher/object of examination was a gendered power dynamic that was enacted in social life, rather than something innate to an individual. That is, gender relations were power dynamics, and social relations across power differences were expressed as gender relations. So when Hugh Peters asserted that Anne Hutchinson had "rather bine a Husband than a Wife and a preacher rather than a Hearer, and a Magistrate than a subject," he afforded parallel gender status to the categories of wife, hearer, and subject. And while the gender/power dynamics of Hutchinson's trial is part of most analyses of this case, I want to note how Peters characterizes Hutchinson's trans-ed position. Through Hutchinson's actions, especially in criticizing and teaching men, Hutchinson *had been* a husband, preacher, and magistrate. This was not a mere metaphor on Peters's part. Hutchinson's actions were trans-actions—acting as a man— and Hutchinson's gender position and social belonging as a whole was on trial. To teach a man was to become a man. In this sense, Hutchinson is on trial not because she was an outspoken woman but because she was accused of practicing manhood.

It was not only Hutchinson's gender position at stake in the trial. Hutchinson's preaching also threatened to transform the gendered positioning of male hearers, both in her own home and in the courtroom. As Phyllis Mack argues, seventeenth-century English society understood gender, along with a range of other identity categories, as distinctly socially constructed. But the fact that gender was openly treated as a social convention did not lead to opportunities for gender-based self-expression and self-identification. Rather, the Puritan gender structure required active defense precisely because of its constructed-ness. For the Puritans of Boston, as for their associates in England:

> The decision whether to stand or sit, to become a farmer or a minister, to marry or to remain celibate, to nurse and caress an infant or to send it away, all were seen to depend more on family position, social

convention, or public policy—on an almost tangible web of social and political relationships—than on individual impulse. For these men and women, a phrase like "gender roles" would have meant precisely what it said; the adoption of the social roles or conventions of masculine or feminine behavior. And the existence of those fixed conventions, whose character was trumpeted from pulpits, thrones, and parliaments, not only gave a kind of theatricality to the actions of men and women; it implied that roles could be switched.[13]

If Hutchinson was acting as a husband, preacher, and magistrate, the men who followed her became wives through their listening. Women's preaching introduced the possibility of wholesale gender transformation that would lead to massive social and political upheaval. Critics including John Winthrop himself warned that "all things are turned upside down among us."[14] This sense of total upheaval was not merely metaphorical. As Peters's accusation clearly stated, social gender disorder threatened inversion of religious and social order more broadly.

Gender in seventeenth-century English society was not fixed or explicitly tethered to binary embodiment but rather was something crafted through the power relations of a religious theocracy. Both Winthrop and Hutchinson, in making their arguments, thus aimed to use the motility of gender in its seemingly permanent attachment to power rather than to its alienable connection to individuals. While Anne Hutchinson certainly defied the Puritan factions she opposed, she was not straightforwardly opposing the gender norms of Boston society. Hutchinson's defense "Do you think it not lawful for me to teach women and why do you call me to teach the court?"[15] calls on conventional gender order and suggests that it is in fact Winthrop who is forcing her to become a man in court in demanding her testimony.

Winthrop aims to sidestep this threat of gender disorder in his courtroom by arguing that Hutchinson's testimony is not teaching but examination. Speaking in court was a debatably gendered practice, a potentially trans-ing practice, and Winthrop works to clarify the gendered position of examination as a scene of feminine disempowerment: "lay open yourself" to the rightful power of the court, he orders her. Interpretively, readers of the court transcript may wonder how successfully Winthrop executes this demand. Despite his injunction, Hutchinson persisted in demanding that the accusations against her be proven, and then even claimed connection to a higher authority. She testified that she had received immediate revelation from God, "by the voice of his own spirit to my soul," giving her divine authority to speak.[16] In this sense, Peters's insistence that Hutchinson had been a "preacher" and "Magistrate" (and thus a "Husband") might well reflect not merely on her actions prior to the trial but also on her performance during it.

It is important, in drawing scholarly attention to this scene, and to the transitivity and motility of gender within it, not to conflate trans-ing practices of gender with gender freedom. That is, the fact that gender was connected to social power and alienable from individuals did not lead to more freedom for individuals. In fact, we might see in Hutchinson's case an explicit use of gender banishment. Hugh Peters pronounced Hutchinson a man in the order of Boston society: a husband, a preacher, and a magistrate. This pronouncement was not an acceptance of Hutchinson's actions or person but a rejection of someone who had "stept out of [her] place." As such, it constituted a sentence of removal from Boston society. I do not mean here to suggest an argument for gender essentialism, or for affixing gender designations permanently to individuals or bodies through social, bodily, or other means. Rather, I want to recall that being outside of gender or moving away from birth gender is not always an experience of freedom but can be an act of punishment, a stripping of social personhood, and an exposure to death. Hutchinson's punishment was banishment, and it did lead to her death in 1643.

Trans-ing Revival Religion

In the two and a half centuries between Hutchinson's and Lobdell's examinations, religious practices in the evangelical Atlantic world of the seventeenth and eighteenth centuries proved a robust environment for gender-transformative religious practices. Felt and expressed gender variance was central to Protestant revival cultures, especially highly emotive modes of popular religion that spread across the Atlantic world and shaped early American cultures. Seventeenth-century Puritan writers exhorted men to become "nursing fathers."[17] Eighteenth-century preachers like George Whitefield called on assembled masses to become brides of Christ, to travail and weep as laboring women and mothers. Women raised their voices to exhort public crowds, a performance that critics argued turned them into men and destroyed clear boundaries between male and female. Gender-transformative and gender-destabilizing performances were so central to early evangelical cultures that trans analyses of these practices have been largely dismissed, as scholars have insisted on the unconventional gender practices of revivals as simply convention. Yet the commonness of these gender-variant performances does not make them less relevant to

understanding trans and gender histories. Moreover, radical religious experiences and claims of divine revelation opened up theological expressions of
gender, whereby some eighteenth- and nineteenth-century individuals such
as the Publick Universal Friend claimed theological gender formulations
"away" from those assigned at birth.[18]

A trans analysis of early American religious revivalism can open up an
archive of gender-transformative accounts of desires, expressions, and trans-
ing practices that do not necessarily demand a laying open of overexamined
individuals. Interrogations of early Protestant revival cultures show how
expressive religious performance employed gender variance as a form of religious practice, as emotional "heart religion" gave theological grounding to a
range of gender identities and expressions.[19] Religion was not the only way
that individuals expressed or engaged in gender-crossing in early America,
nor was it the only realm in which gender-crossing could occur. Still, it did
offer a location where gender-crossing expressions and sensations became
widely practiced. Moreover, accounts of gender-crossing practices and gender transformation in early American religious contexts, especially in reform
Protestant contexts, help us to see how gender motion happened through a
range of practices both public and intimate that were understood to actively
construct the gender of its participants. That is, acts like praying, exhorting,
teaching, shouting, and dreaming were gendered and gender-making activities. Transforming religious practice put gender in motion, and histories of
women and gender have drawn scholarly attention to the ways that women
and femininity shaped American religious histories.[20] It is essential, however,
to understand that these histories of gender in motion are trans histories too,
and that trans studies can use religious accounts to attend anew to differently
structured gender practices of the past.

One of the major shifts in revival cultures was an embrace by some radical Protestants, among them the followers of George Fox later known as
Quakers, of the principle of spiritual equality, the idea that all people had
the same spiritual value and ability to receive inspiration from God. Theological claims of direct inspiration and spiritual equality opened up central
debates about the nature of gender, men, and women.[21] That is, if there was
no divinely ordained hierarchy that determined the difference between men
and women based on a spiritual supremacy of men over women, and all
people equally might receive divine inspiration through the inner light, what
was the difference between the sexes?[22] Phyllis Mack, in her landmark study
of Quaker women, notes that seventeenth-century Quakers "perceived the
attributes of men and women to be fluid and interchangeable. . . . Indeed,
a few women prophets actually announced to their audiences that they *were*

men; having transcended their social identities that dictated that they remain subject to their fathers and husbands, they claimed the right, with other genderless souls, to stand and speak at the very altar of the church and before the very doors of Parliament."[23]

Critics argued that spiritual equality threatened to unleash sexual and gender anarchy. In England in particular, pornographic satires accused Quakers and Methodists of engaging in a range of sexual deviance: buggery, bestiality, female sexual dominance, male impotence, same-sex sexuality, onanism, incest, and even sex with demons.[24] Henry Fielding overtly linked Methodism with gender variance and queer sexuality in *The Female Husband*, his embellished account of the famed case of Charles Hamilton. Hamilton had been assigned female at birth, but he lived as a man and, in 1746, he famously married a woman named Mary Price. Fielding claimed that Hamilton had been "susceptible enough of Enthusiasm, and ready to receive all those impressions on [Hamilton's] mind which [Hamilton's] friend the *Methodist* endeavored to make."[25] Critics in the American colonies tended to rely less on overtly pornographic representation of religious enthusiasm. But like anti-revivalists in Europe, they lambasted the public speech of women and the silence of men, considering both an effect of perverse religious enthusiasm. Women praying and speaking in assemblies, and men listening to women's exhortation, publicly performed religious gender-crossing. This trans religious practice socially transformed women into men, and men into women, and threatened to destroy gender distinctions entirely. Spiritual equality did not simply shift the relationship between two existing and historically stable categories of people. It seemed poised to eliminate distinctions of gender, as religiously inspired individuals left established gender roles and took on new forms of practice and relations. Religious practice transformed the expected relations between men and women. Men nursed and women commanded, women spoke and men listened. This was a question not simply of the liberation of women but of a larger set of trans-ing practices that were central to a range of radical and dissenting revival practices from the seventeenth to the nineteenth centuries.

The charge of enthusiasm particularly denoted forms of religious practice wherein individuals experienced divine inspiration, often in highly emotional or sensational forms: hearing voices, seeing visions, or otherwise receiving direct communication from God. Critics, including defenders of mainstream Protestantism and writers skeptical of religion broadly, used the term generally to refer to "bad" forms of religious practice. Moreover, they argued that enthusiasm was bodiliness mistaken for spirituality. They connected enthusiasm to sexual depravity, gender transgression, mental illness, Catholicism, and the criminal poor. Not only did Anne Hutchinson's trial render her a violator of gender norms, cast out of Boston society, but also through the trial she was publicly denounced as an enthusiast. In testifying that God had spoken "by the voice of his own spirit to my soul," Hutchinson claimed that her words were divinely authorized, and that she had special direct knowledge of God's will. This damned her in the eyes of her Boston judges. But her claim to direct knowledge, including her insistence that she had divinely inspired dreams, was fundamentally inextricable from the gendered power of Boston's theocracy. If God had indeed spoken directly to Hutchinson, her speech was not authorized by Puritan patriarchy; it was authorized by God. What was revealed in her being laid open was not submission but divine communication that superseded male rule.

Like Hutchinson's trial, Lobdell's 1869 encounter with the law and his subsequent gender examination began with preaching. The *Milwaukee Daily Sentinel* painted Lobdell as very much an enthusiast: "The man, who called himself Joseph Lobdell . . . delivered noisy and meaningless 'sermons,' declaring that he was a prophet of the new dispensation, and that [a] bear had been sent him by the Lord to guard him in the wilderness."[26] While newspaper accounts of Lobdell are notably exaggerated for pathetic and sensational effect (and the *Milwaukee Sentinel's* accounts more than most), they collectively emphasize Lobdell's title as the *Reverend* Joseph Lobdell, and note that his arrest came after two years of preaching and begging, which occasioned his arrest as a public nuisance. P. M. Wise's sexological examination likewise notes Lobdell's occupation as "a Methodist minister," a designation that would have carried a more pejorative connotation a century earlier, but which had become a more respectable occupation by the late nineteenth century in the United States.

Preaching and the occasion of Lobdell's 1869 arrest are largely set aside as Wise extracts a different form of gender testimony from his subject. Whereas Hutchinson's speech was demanded through court testimony—testimony that risked taking on the power of instruction and had to be proclaimed to be a subordinate "laying open" of oneself—Lobdell's speech barely appears in the sexological account. There seems no risk (or none that Wise needs to address) of Lobdell's claiming the power of teaching, as Wise clearly opens Lobdell's family history, childhood inclinations, and details of sexual relations for the edification of readers. And when Wise does quote Lobdell, it is to provide the most intimate glimpse of all: "I may be a woman in one sense, but I have particular organs that make me more a man than a woman."[27] Even this recounted testimony is superseded by Wise's own observation: "I have been unable to discover any abnormality of the genitals, except . . .," a framing that at once undermines Lobdell's own account and proceeds to offer the reader a vision of Lobdell's genitals.

In Wise's account, Lobdell's body becomes an object for instruction in sexual taxonomy. It is Wise who presumes to teach, using Lobdell's laid-open self. And indeed, it is Wise's report that is now most widely available to researchers of trans history. His case study introduces the term "Lesbian love" into the American lexicon, and in doing so, he has made Lobdell a central object lesson in the history of American sexology and a prominent if disputed figure in American trans history. Given the archival significance of Wise's text, what then is to be done with the way it violates and lays open Lobdell as an object for study? Can historians of trans pasts draw on such a text without amplifying that scene of violence and demanding once again that Lobdell be laid open to another court, for the benefit of another teacher? Here I turn to Saidiya Hartman's provocations in "Venus in Two Acts" to wrestle with the archival challenges of trans history. Wise's report, and particularly his account of his physical examination of Lobdell, acts as what Foucault calls "a register of [Lobdell's] encounter with power." Even Lobdell's own words enter the report within this encounter, and there is no straightforward way to disentangle Lobdell's statement from Wise's examination, particularly given that the only quoted testimony is a statement both defending and explaining his genitals. How, from such a record, might one engage Hartman's challenge of "listening for the unsaid, translating misconstrued, and refashioning disfigured lives . . . embody[ing] life in words and at the same time respect[ing] what we cannot know?"[28] How do we respond to lives forced open?

Critical Trans-Attendance

Joseph Lobdell, like so many other gender-variant people, entered the historical record in a moment of extreme vulnerability and violation. Gender-variant people often become visible to the public when they become less able to control or care for their bodies: when they require medical care because of injury or age, when they are arrested, when they lose jobs or housing, when they become pregnant or experience assault, when they experience disputes with partners or family members, and at other times of vulnerability. This was the case for Albert Cashier, who was assigned female at birth but who fought as a Union soldier in the Civil War and lived his life as a typical male veteran until he was injured and had to move to the Illinois Soldiers' and Sailors' Home. Even there, he was initially supported by doctors until he was transferred to an insane asylum for dementia care, where attendants forced him to assume women's clothing and made his case known. Following this revelation, Cashier had to fight to keep his soldier's pension, a court case that revealed his history to fellow soldiers, neighbors, and the national press, and which provided exceptional records for trans historians. Mary Jones likewise entered the historical record as a gender-variant person when she was arrested in 1836 for larceny while engaging in sex work and her image was sold with the caption "The Man-Monster."[29] These are just two of the many gender-variant subjects who enter trans history in the moment when they have lost the ability to control their own accounts of their lives. This raises the critical ethical question of how students of gender histories might engage these pasts without restaging these violations.

While it is not possible for scholars to undo the violence of the past, particularly the violence that has produced archival sources for histories, I propose that trans histories should aim to produce methodologies that critically attend to the histories of examination that shape gender designations. This method proposes:

1. While studies showing the presence and prevalence of gender-variant and trans people have been politically and socially powerful, the study of trans pasts should not be singularly focused on conclusively identifying or categorizing individuals as transgender. Indeed, trans history is a history of gender in motion and variation, and is not only about trans and gender-variant people. Individuals do not need to be demonstrably trans in embodiment, identity, or self-understanding to be part of trans pasts. Gender variance is not exclusive to trans people, and gender-variant people are not object lessons for how gender operates. Anne Hutchinson is significant to trans history because her story shows the ways that gender operated through relational social power in Puritan society, and because she is ultimately banished from Puritan womanhood as well as from the Massachusetts Colony. Her story shows how gender positions can move, how they can be examined, and how they can be socially revoked. And her story is a reminder that gender movement is not always gender freedom.

2. The bodies of gender-variant people should not be considered available for examination, display, or proof in ways automatically different from those of people who have not been considered gender-variant. Writing trans stories does not necessarily require detailing embodiment, particularly if those details were taken from a person by force or duress. Researchers and writers must wrestle with how and why one might include details about

embodiment in their accounts. Perhaps it is central to what a person has said about their own life, or perhaps it is the central way that this person has entered the history of gender variance. Here I wrestled with whether, and how, to include Lobdell's one statement in Wise's report. And even as I draw critically on this evidence, I remain unsure if this is something that will enhance the ethical work of trans scholarship, or if it ultimately replicates the violation I aim to critically engage. As a practice, trans-attendance means attending to the person in the historical record, and resisting the demand that gender-variant people be stripped for the satisfaction of the audience.

3. Trans-attendance treats gender-variant people as having full, and thus changeable, lives. In some cases, the focus on correctly identifying a historical subject (as trans, cisgender, lesbian, etc.) can lead to overvaluing one point in a figure's life as the moment of true identity. Often the moments of vulnerability, "discovery," or "revelation" by which gender-variant people enter the historical record are treated as evidence of identity across their entire lives. In some instances this has resulted in cisnormative histories that "celebrate" people like Albert Cashier as female soldiers and discount their lives as men.[30] But it is also the case that many gender-variant people, including Lobdell, lead lives of gender change and complexity.[31] Acknowledging multiple gender locations for individuals and change over time refuses the imperative to locate, classify, and prove a singular identity for individuals in order for them to be properly considered part of trans pasts.

Through these methodological commitments, trans-attendance works to counter juridical-diagnostic models that require gender-variant subjects to be laid open to examination. Rather, histories of the lived experience of gender as social relation, power, and performance help scholars develop a trans history that does not subject gender-variant people to yet another diagnostic gaze. This form of trans history refuses to once again expose and classify genitals, to assess the validity of sartorial representation, to measure the gait or the length of hair or the width of hips, to weigh in on the relative value of an individual's representation in the face of proclamations by kings, preachers, and asylum keepers. It is my hope that *trans* as a historical category of analysis might displace that juridical power and its diagnoses. Instead, we might ask how normative gender itself has been shaped by the ways that gender-crossing and gender variance were imagined, practiced, and policed. Gender variance does not require that an individual be displayed, examined, and categorized. Rather, this essay asks that the lives of individuals and communities engaged in gender movement might instead call a teachable court to attend differently to trans pasts.

Notes

1. "A Queer Married Couple," *St. Louis Globe-Democrat*, November 5, 1883. The most extensive historical account of Lobdell's life can be found in Jen Manion, "The Criminalized Poor," in *Female Husbands: A Trans History* (New York: Cambridge University Press, 2020), 198–230. For more on itinerant preaching and its challenges to gendered order, see Christine Leigh Heyrman, *Southern Cross: The Beginnings of the Bible Belt* (Chapel Hill: University of North Carolina Press, 1998).

2. P. M. Wise, "A Case of Sexual Perversion," *Alienist and Neurologist* 4.1 (1883): 89.

3. Joseph Lobdell's story has been explored by many different scholars, in addition to Manion, *Female Husbands*, which does not address the religious aspects of Lobdell's life. See Peter Boag, *Re-Dressing America's Frontier Past* (Berkeley: University of California Press, 2011); Emily Skidmore, *True Sex: The Lives of Trans Men at the Turn of the Twentieth Century* (New York: NYU Press, 2017). Regarding trans history of racialized medical examination, see C. Riley Snorton, *Black on Both Sides: A Racial History of Trans Identity* (Minneapolis: University of Minnesota Press, 2017).

4. See Reina Gossett, Eric A. Stanley, and Johanna Burton, eds., *Trap Door: Trans Cultural Production and the Politics of Visibility* (Cambridge, MA: MIT Press, 2017).

5. Dean Spade, *Normal Life: Administrative Violence, Critical Trans Politics, and the Limits of Law* (Durham, NC: Duke University Press, 2015).

6. Peter Coviello, *Tomorrow's Parties: Sex and the Untimely in Nineteenth-Century America* (New York: NYU Press, 2013), 6.

7. See, by Saidiya Hartman, "Venus in Two Acts," *Small Axe* 26.12–2 (June 2008): 1–14; *Scenes of Subjection: Terror, Slavery, and Self-Making in Nineteenth-Century America* (New York: Oxford University Press, 1997); *Wayward Lives, Beautiful Experiments: Intimate Histories of Riotous Black Girls, Troublesome Women, and Queer Radicals* (New York: W. W. Norton, 2020).

8. "A Report of the Trial of Mrs. Ann Hutchinson before the Church in Boston, March 1638," in *The Antinomian Controversy, 1636–1638: A Documentary History*, ed. David D. Hall, 2nd ed. (Durham, NC: Duke University Press, 1990), 382–83 (italics in the original). See also Carol F. Karlsen, *The Devil in the Shape of a Woman: Witchcraft in Colonial New England* (New York: W. W. Norton, 1987).

9. "Examination of Mrs. Anne Hutchinson," in Hall, *Antinomian Controversy*, 314.

10. Ibid.

11. Ibid.

12. On "trans-ing" analysis and practices, see Clare Sears, *Arresting Dress: Cross-Dressing, Law, and Fascination in Nineteenth-Century San Francisco* (Durham, NC: Duke University Press, 2014).

13. Phyllis Mack, *Visionary Women: Ecstatic Prophecy in Seventeenth-Century England* (Berkeley: University of California Press, 1992), 6–7.

14. John Winthrop, "A Short Story of the Rise, Reign, and Ruine of the Antinomians, Familists & Libertines," in Hall, *Antinomian Controversy*, 253.

15. "Examination of Mrs. Anne Hutchinson," 314.

16. This occasioned accusations that Hutchinson was an enthusiast, and her testimony regarding divine communication proved her undoing in this case. I will

return to the charge of enthusiasm in the latter part of this essay. "Examination of Mrs. Anne Hutchinson," 315.

17. Elizabeth Maddock Dillon, "Nursing Fathers and Brides of Christ," in *A Centre of Wonders: The Body in Early America*, ed. Janet Moore Lindeman and Michele Lise Tarter (Ithaca, NY: Cornell University Press, 2001), 129–43.

18. Scott Larson, "'Indescribable Being': Theological Performances of Genderlessness in the Society of the Publick Universal Friend, 1776–1819," *Early American Studies* 12.3 (2014): 576–600; Susan Juster, "'Neither Male nor Female': Jemima Wilkinson and the Politics of Gender in Post-Revolutionary America," in *Possible Pasts: Becoming Colonial in Early America*, ed. Robert Blair St. George (Ithaca, NY: Cornell University Press, 2000); Paul B. Moyer, *The Public Universal Friend: Jemima Wilkinson and Religious Enthusiasm in Revolutionary America* (Ithaca, NY: Cornell University Press, 2015).

19. Misty Anderson, *Imagining Methodism in Eighteenth-Century Britain: Enthusiasm, Belief, and the Borders of the Self* (Baltimore: Johns Hopkins University Press, 2012); Scott Larson, "Histrionics of the Pulpit: Trans Tonalities of Religious Enthusiasm." *TSQ: Transgender Studies Quarterly* 6.3 (August 1, 2019): 315–37.

20. Ann Braude, "Women's History Is American Religious History," in *Retelling U.S. Religious History*, ed. Thomas Tweed (Berkeley: University of California Press, 1997), 87–107; Ann Douglas, *The Feminization of American Culture* (New York: Knopf, 1978).

21. Mack, *Visionary Women*.

22. Anne Myles, "Border Crossings: The Queer Erotics of Quakerism in Seventeenth-Century New England," in *Long before Stonewall: Histories of Same-Sex Sexuality in Early America*, ed. Thomas A. Foster (New York: NYU Press, 2007).

23. Mack, *Visionary Women*, 9–10.

24. See [Ralph Jepson], *The Expounder Expounded* ([n.p.], 1742), who offers a catalogue of these accusations leveled at George Whitefield. Benjamin Franklin coyly hints at the same-sex and swindling innuendoes leveled at his friend Whitefield when he writes in his autobiography that Whitefield "had a wonderful Power over the Hearts and Purses of his Hearers, of which I myself was an Instance." Benjamin Franklin, *The Autobiography and Other Writings*, ed. Kenneth Silverman (New York: Penguin Classics, 2003), 106. Regarding accusations of Quaker buggery and bestiality, see Myles, "Border Crossings."

25. Henry Fielding, *The Female Husband: Or, The Surprising History of Mrs. Mary, Alias Mr. George Hamilton* (London, 1746). For more on Fielding and Hamilton, see Manion, *Female Husbands*; and Anderson, *Imagining Methodism*.

26. "A Wild Woman's Story," *Milwaukee Daily Sentinel*, July 27, 1876. Emily Skidmore in *True Sex* discusses the variance in local and national reporting of trans men and gender-variant people in the late nineteenth and early twentieth centuries. Lobdell marks the earlier end of this study.

27. Wise, "Case of Sexual Perversion," 90.

28. Hartman, "Venus in Two Acts," 2–3. She quotes Michel Foucault, "Lives of Infamous Men," in *The Essential Foucault*, ed. Paul Rabinow and Nikolas Rose (New York: New Press, 2003), 284.

29. See esp. Snorton, *Black on Both Sides*, 59–66.

30. DeAnne Blanton, "Women Soldiers of the Civil War," *Prologue Magazine* 25.1 (Spring 1993), National Archives, https://www.archives.gov/publications/prologue/1993/spring/women-in-the-civil-war-1.html.

31. Jen Manion's account of Lobdell's life in *Female Husbands* attends to this richness and change, and while I've here used the pronouns "he/him" for Lobdell, Manion compellingly uses "they" to reflect the multiplicity and complexity of Lobdell's life.

Epilogue
Against Consensus

Greta LaFleur

As a historian of sexuality, I have always been struck by Eve Kosofsky Sedgwick's curiosity, expressed in her masterly introduction to *Epistemology of the Closet*, about what she wryly termed "the Great Paradigm shift."[1] By this, she meant the idea that something called *sexual difference* not only made queerness what it was but also made modern sexuality *tout court*.[2] Sedgwick was interested in why one framework became, to the exclusion of all others, the defining condition of sexuality; her "Great Paradigm Shift" names the process by which "the gender of object choice emerged as sexuality's dominant grammar."[3] While this question has been only peremptorily taken up by a handful of scholars (with the exception of my colleague and collaborator Benjamin Kahan), I have always been struck by the fact that in this emergence narrative, we find not only an account of the advent of modern sexuality but an understanding of sexuality that collapses gender into something many people today call *biological sex* as well. This account of sexuality in fact turns on something that looks very much like a gender binary in order to maintain its conceptual center, and this despite the fact that historians of sexuality, and especially those of us who work on periods before 1900, have tried our best to insist on the inseparability of vocabularies for sexual preference or orientation from understandings of gendered life, performance, and embodiment.

I began working on the history and historiography of gender after draft-ing a chapter of my first book on Deborah Sampson / Robert Shurtliff, the eighteenth-century Massachusetts resident who lived as both a man and a woman, but who seems to have chosen to conclude their life—for its last several decades—as a woman.[4] Historians of sexuality have read Sampson as a lesbian, women's historians have read Sampson as a woman and a femi-nist, and trans studies scholars have read Sampson as a transcestor or trans forebear, but to me, each of these analyses has fallen just slightly short of sufficient. Each approach has ultimately been unable, on its own, to account for Shurtliff and/or Sampson and their unique and complicated life as a poor, formerly indentured white soldier; a colonial settler; a person whose mem-bership in their church was revoked after it was rumored that they might have been the lover of a free Black woman servant while they themself were living and working as a white woman servant; a spouse—a wife, in fact!—and parent; and, for some of their life, a rather visible public figure and popu-lar entertainer. The material historical realities that pressed on Sampson/Shurtliff, that both enabled and constrained them as they made decisions surrounding how they wanted to live (and who they wanted to live *as*), are very different from the realities that press on many of us today. As a scholar of eighteenth-century North America and of gender and sexuality studies, I arrived at the study of the history of gender—socially supported forms of gendered life, as well as gendered forms of being that were the target of approbation, violence, and state discipline—because I wanted to participate in the development of a more careful and rigorous set of tools for talking about the intersections of gendered and sexual experience in the past. To put it more succinctly, I came to the history of gender through the history of sexuality, in part because eighteenth-century writers neither saw embodied sex as permanent or immutable, nor understood gendered presentation as possibly distinct from the body. It seemed to me—and dozens of trans studies scholars would surely concur—that not just the history of sexuality but queer theory more broadly needed better methodologies for thinking about gen-der. Trans studies has led me, as a scholar and teacher who sits somewhere on the (often clunkily theorized) slippery transmasculine spectrum, to a height-ened awareness of the kinds of questions that queer theory and the history of sexuality have equipped us to explore, and those questions for which queer theory and the history of sexuality have proved woefully inadequate.

Since this volume opens with a discussion of Sampson/Shurtliff, it seems only right that in this brief concluding piece we return to them, mostly because I think the history of their life showcases a number of the methodological challenges and hermeneutic commitments that tend to characterize historical analyses of people who, today, might understand themselves as trans, nonbinary, genderqueer, or otherwise gender-nonconforming. The first, which has been addressed extensively elsewhere in this volume, is both extremely common and extremely important: that of terminology. How do we refer to historical people whose gendered experience clearly deviated, often quite significantly, from the social, cultural, legal, or medical expectations that we have all been burdened from birth, but who lived in times and places where current-day (and, it should be said, current-day *Anglophone*, and in the case of this volume, current-day US American and British) vocabularies for gender plurality did not obtain? This question is one with which historians of sexuality have extensive experience, but it is also a question on which scholars from all fields come down very differently—a matter of taste, politics, ethics, commitments.

Consider, for example, the term *nonbinary*. Readers versed in contemporary vocabularies that designate the scope of gendered experience will notice that this term appears unevenly in this volume. This is not the result of any sort of unwillingness or refusal on the part of the editorial team or contributors to imagine that there may have been figures in the distant past who could have been described by this term. The reluctance, and I can only speak for myself here, to describe pre- and early modern historical people as "nonbinary" derives from the fact that the gender binary—the idea that the categories *male* and *female* existed on a polarized dimorphous spectrum—has a history, and it is one that scholars such as Beans Velocci have argued is a product of late-nineteenth and early-twentieth-century human and animal sciences.[5] To categorize a figure as "nonbinary" before the gender binary in fact existed sits uncomfortably with me, as a historian; my scholarly, and indeed my personal and political, preference (although all of these impulses are, of course, ineluctably entwined) would be to sit with the terms that these figures developed for themselves, and to use them. Indeed, trans people have always been ingenious and, furthermore, often very stylish authors of vocabularies for their own experiences, and then and now, I think it is of the utmost importance that we listen to them rather than assume that present-day vocabularies would automatically take some sort of Whiggish, progressive priority over past ways of being and naming.[6] At a moment when so-called feminist philosophers refuse to acknowledge the womanhood of trans women; when for four years a presidential administration seemed hellbent on refusing trans people access to basic medical care (not that medicine has ever been an advocate of trans lives and bodies); and when conservative pundits of all stripes seem to understand trans experience as something to be debated—yea or nay!—why would we assume that our current ways of understanding trans experience are better, or that the many present social, cultural, and political contexts that forge the conditions for trans life have been an improvement on those of the distant past? For a field that loves a takedown of so-called Enlightenment logic, this might be a moment when it behooves us to take a hard look inward.

This is not to say that I am skeptical about the possibility or reality of *longue durée* trans histories; indeed, what I always tell my students is that a trans-centered analysis allows us to understand all sorts of figures, moments, and people—even those who explicitly claimed inclusion in traditional gendered forms—as not merely part of trans history but *teachers* of it. Think, for example, of Sojourner Truth's famous, and possibly apocryphal, speech at the 1851 Women's Rights Conference in Akron, Ohio. Truth, who had been born into enslavement in 1797, gave a speech that would be reported and re-reported in many of the major urban newspapers of the United States and settler territories at the time.[7] Retroactively titled "Ain't I a Woman?" Truth's speech remains to this day one of the most widely read "first-wave" women's rights movement texts taught in high schools and undergraduate seminars, in part because of the way that Truth openly challenges the categorical coherence of the experience of womanhood. In her speech, Truth calls attention to how her status as a Black woman in the United States—remember that slavery was still a flourishing and legal system of labor in most states and territories in 1851—effectively rendered her experiences and priorities unrecognizable to the primarily white women and men who planned, organized, and ran the conference. Truth explains:

> That man over there says that women need to be helped into carriages, and lifted over ditches, and to have the best place everywhere. Nobody ever helps me into carriages, or over mud-puddles, or gives me any best place! And ain't I a woman? Look at me! Look at my arm! I have ploughed and planted, and gathered into barns, and no man could head me! And ain't I a woman? I could work as much and eat as much as a man—when I could get it—and bear the lash as well! And ain't I a woman? I have borne thirteen children, and seen most all sold off to slavery, and when I cried out with my mother's grief, none but Jesus heard me! And ain't I a woman?[8]

What Truth is gesturing to here—especially in the first line, "that man over there says that women need to be helped into carriages, and lifted over

ditches"—is one man's response to the claims that the ostensibly white organizers and primarily white speakers were making for equality in marriage,
representation (the vote, also known as the franchise), and property ownership, rights that had generally been unavailable to most propertied white
women prior to 1839 with the advent of the passage of the Married Women's
Property Acts in many states.[9] These demands, however, were radically out
of sync with the realities of Black women in the United States at the time;
in states and territories in which slavery was still legal and operative, the
majority of Black women lived under conditions of enslavement, and even
free Black women in states that had abolished slavery were subject to intense
legal and other limitations on their ability to own property, register a complaint in court, or even claim autonomy over their own bodies.[10] The con-
descending remark that Truth purportedly registered from the man in the
audience—that women needed the social protection of men because they
were ostensibly the weaker sex—must have seemed laughable to Truth, who
had been doing what many wealthy white people would have considered
"men's" work, without pay, since she was a child.[11] Because she was Black,
she was not eligible for even the everyday legal and social paternalisms that
so galled white women. Her refrain "Ain't I a Woman?" effectively names
how the vision of "womanhood" at the center of the 1851 Women's Rights
Conference in Akron was not a vision of *all* women but a vision of white
women—and generally propertied white women at that. Truth's demand
"Look at me! Look at my arm! I have ploughed and planted, and gathered
into barns, and no man could head me! And ain't I a woman? I could work as
much and eat as much as a man—when I could get it—and bear the lash as
well!" claims a kind of masculinization that is the direct result of the labor
she was forced to perform under bondage. Here Truth names how her Black-
ness and status as an enslaved person have relegated her to the margins of
womanhood, as the category was understood by the nineteenth-century
women's suffrage movement. Is this not part of trans history, not *despite* but
because of Truth's repeated claim to her own womanhood—which, today, we
would probably term cis?[12]

While some historians might laud the approach to trans history that I am
describing here as the oft-cited ideal of doing history "on its own terms,"
I want to be clear that I am patently uninterested in that idea as a guiding historiographical principle, and furthermore am actively committed to doing
history only in the service of the present. Why, then, eschew contemporary
vocabularies for describing trans histories? Because, I would argue, it makes
it harder to perceive some of the unique and, at times, long-gone ways of
making sense of gender plurality that existed in the centuries before us. It

also tends to circumscribe and even delimit what we are able to imagine, recognize, or identify as trans history. Following C. Riley Snorton, think, for example, about conversations surrounding the relationship between histories of bondage, exploitation, racialized violence, and gender that have emerged from the intersections of scholarship on the history of slavery and Black studies.[13] Scholars such as Hortense Spillers and Saidiya Hartman have each developed enormously influential analyses of how "woman" as a category of the human, and "gender" as a category of social experience, have been definitionally wrought, especially for Black women and feminine people, by the massive historical harms that have maintained their staying power in the form of anti-Black racism into the present moment. In *Scenes of Subjection*, Hartman's landmark 1997 study, for example, she insists on the critical importance of continuing to historicize the category of "woman," "not as a foundational category with given characteristics, attributes, or circumstances but within a particular racial economy of property that intensified its control over the object of property through the deployment of sexuality."[14] Rather than allow the category of woman or the study of gender to be collapsed into whiteness or cis womanhood, Hartman insists upon the importance of a continued and careful attention to gender as vector of racialization, arguing that "what is at stake here is not maintaining gender as an identitarian category but rather examining gender formation in relation to property relations, the sexual economy of slavery, and the calculation of injury."[15] This, as Snorton has taught us, is undoubtedly trans history, even as these insights have emerged in the context of a discussion about a form of womanhood that some might describe as cis.

Assuming the preeminence of the highly delimited vocabularies for current-day transness over those that existed in earlier times also, on occasion, encourages a heavy-handed refusal to attend to historical terms that are today understood to be offensive. Readers who have perused this volume in its entirety will notice how often the term "hermaphrodite," distasteful and even violent to many ears today, appears in the primary texts that are examined in a number of the essays collected here.[16] As editors, we discussed at length how we wanted to handle the term; Do we ask the contributors to put it in scare quotes? To not use the term except when it was absolutely necessary to elaborate a point? We ultimately decided to ask contributors to explain—in the text of their essay itself instead of the endnotes—the historical context of the use of the term and how it relates to their argument. But refusing to use or consider the term altogether, offensive as it is today, would allow us to ignore ways of understanding gendered experience that transcended dominant understandings of womanhood or manhood and, furthermore, would obscure some of what to my mind are among the most fascinating and potentially instructive logics surrounding gender that proliferated in the pre- and early modern periods but have not maintained their staying power.

In the undergraduate introduction to trans studies course that I have been teaching every year since 2014, I typically assign a range of works that theorize the intersections and divergences between trans and intersex politics and experience. A growing conversation among scholars such as Hil Malatino has come to elaborate that it is not only gender—something that women's studies scholars have spent several decades painstakingly insisting to be "social" or "constructed"—that is plural; Malatino and others assert that gendered morphology, sometimes imagined as "biological sex," is plural, or nonbinary, too.[17] This point has been contentious to many, and especially to those "gender critical" so-called feminists who have built something of a political platform organized entirely around denying the reality of trans people and experience.[18] But as Kathleen Perry Long points out in her essay on the seventeenth-century case of Marin le Marcis, the idea that something called *biological sex* is limited to a dimorphous, binary relation comprehended by the poles of *man* and *woman* is a profoundly modern idea, and one deeply at odds with ways of understanding human sexual morphology that have flourished in prior centuries. And one of the terms under which discussions of gendered morphological diversity flourished, not only in medical and philosophical texts but also in texts written by people who might today identify as trans and/or intersex *themselves*, was "hermaphrodite." While Marin le Marcis might well have identified as trans in our own moment, I worry that simply to stop there is to refuse to listen to something that this person could teach us some four centuries later: that there are as many distinct gendered bodily morphologies as there are trans and nonbinary identities, whether the people who live in those bodies identify at odds with social and cultural expectations surrounding womanhood or manhood, or not.

To return to Sampson/Shurtliff, merely naming a figure as trans in our own moment often imports to the eighteenth century a series of twenty-first-century assumptions about what trans experience is or is not. Jen Manion, in their *Female Husbands: A Trans History*, makes a point of referring to this figure simply as Robert Shurtliff, chiding readers, "Allow me to remind you that this transition and this name was their choice, and of their own doing."[19] While this is, of course, Manion voicing their laudable political and ethical commitment to referring to this figure by using their own name and pronoun (although Sampson/Shurtliff referred to themself neither as trans nor as a female husband), and an effort to pull Sampson/Shurtliff's story out of the women's history in which it was primarily entrenched in the 1990s and early 2000s, there is more to Sampson/Shurtliff's story than their life as Robert Shurtliff. Sampson/Shurtliff lived as Shurtliff for a few years, both during and after their time serving in the military in the Revolutionary War. They eventually married, living again as Deborah Sampson (but taking their husband's name, and thus living as Deborah Sampson Gannett) and having several children, and coming into the public eye when they enlisted a series of well-known writers and printers, including Philip Freneau, to take up their cause as they petitioned for an invalid's pension from the new United States government. While I do not take issue with Manion's reading of Sampson/Shurtliff as a trancestor or figure populating the field of trans history—indeed, I read them the same way in my first book—I do worry that Manion participates in the same sort of flattening reading practice as that of which they implicitly accuse women's historians, who have tended to read Sampson/Shurtliff as a feminist forebear and have generally ignored or explained away their decision to live as Shurtliff. Indeed, women's historians, queer studies critics, and trans historians alike all seem reluctant to approach Sampson/Shurtliff in their uncertain complexity, preferring instead to collapse Sampson/Shurtliff's fascinating and at times contradictory life into a singular narrative about their womanhood, their manhood, or their queerness. If we are truly committed to respecting Sampson/Shurtliff's "own doing" relative to the way they occupied the world as a gendered person, then I think we owe Sampson/Shurtliff an analysis of their life that attends to the fact that they lived as a woman and as a man. Their trans life included their time as Deborah Sampson, whose possible sexual intimacy with a Black woman servant lost them membership in their church congregation; as Robert Shurtliff, a soldier whose military fame derived, at least in part, from the murder of Native people on military scouting missions; and as Deborah Sampson Gannett, a poor person who chose, for whatever reason, to marry and have children. We, as very late arrivals to the history of Sampson/Shurtliff's life and times, truly have no idea what Sampson/Shurtliff thought about their body, their gender, or the life chances available to them as a man or as a woman. And even if we could somehow know for certain that Sampson/Shurtliff was trans, we would still lack any insight whatsoever into what that meant to them: whether they experienced it in terms akin to our present-day "identity" frameworks, whether it was expedient or pragmatic, or whether it represented their lived truth.

While I do not believe in the radical alterity of distant historical periods, I do believe in the total and fundamental unknowability of history and think there is value in not trying to "lay open," as Scott Larson puts it, what a historical personage "really" was.[20] Would Sampson/Shurtliff not be includable in trans history if they had lived as Shurtliff simply because they were poor and needed the enlistment bonus that would come with signing up for the Continental Army? Would Sampson/Shurtliff not be eligible to be a trans ancestor if they only truly identified as a man for two or three years? Would Sampson/Shurtliff not constitute a part of trans history if they identified as a woman but chose to live as a man for access to greater financial stability, social mobility, and a broader range of sexual options? Must past trans people announce that their gender presentation bears some sort of relationship to inner truth in order for us to identify or recognize them as part of trans history? Must transness be *permanent*, or *forever*, in order for it to be real? Among my wonderful group of friends and chosen family are individuals who have transitioned, in some cases, multiple times; might this not also be true of people who lived centuries before us? Considering that the many strains of anti-trans sentiment in the United States and England consistently revert to the rhetoric of permanence—the permanent "damage" supposedly incurred by children who transition, the supposed trendiness or faddishness of trans identities that critics read as an indictment of the realness of trans experience, and so on—I think we would do well to make as much room as we can, especially in histories as distant as that of Sampson/Shurtliff, for the ephemeral or the fleeting.

I ask these questions not to initiate some sort of takedown of trans historians or historians of gender, but rather to mark the fact that there is not, and probably will never be, consensus regarding what trans history is or means, how to recognize it, or how to practice it. And this is, in fact, a strength of this burgeoning field, rather than a weakness; it requires that we be attentive to not only historical sources but historical methods as well, and to the cissexist heteropatriarchies that usually inform them.[21] The essays that appear in this volume alone evince a wide range of stances relative to trans history, some insisting on establishing the correct reading of trans figures such as Eleanor Rykener, whom scholars have historically refused to acknowledge as trans in favor of claiming her for queer history, and some deploying the logics of trans studies scholarship to craft exciting new observations about human-animal relations or medieval theories of bodily integrity. All of these insights are important, all of these arguments eminently portable for the production of what Lillian Faderman once called a "usable past," and what some of the most interesting historians I know today are calling an "abusable" one.[22] Ultimately, I hope the lack of consensus that I invoke here will eventually (and probably sooner than later) provide just the kind of fertile rot that will render fecund ground for new, more nuanced, and more creative inquiry. I can't wait.

Notes

1. Eve Kosofsky Sedgwick, *Epistemology of the Closet* (Berkeley: University of California Press, 1990), 44.

2. Benjamin Kahan, introduction to *The Book of Minor Perverts: Sexology, Etiology, and the Emergence of Sexuality* (Chicago: University of Chicago Press, 2019), 1–25.

3. Kahan, *Book of Minor Perverts*, 4. Kahan argues that this inattention to how "sexuality" came to be defined along a homo/hetero binary is the result of queer theory's studied refusal of questions of etiology, but I would argue that queer theory's storied early inattention to both race and ethnicity *and* to trans experience also enabled this inattention.

4. Greta LaFleur, *The Natural History of Sexuality in Early America* (Baltimore: Johns Hopkins University Press, 2018), esp. chap. 4; Greta LaFleur, "Sex and Unsex," *Early American Studies* 12.3 (Fall 2014): 469–99. Sampson lived as Sampson until they were in their late teens or early twenties, then lived as Robert Shurtliff for two years after joining the Continental Army—and continued to live as Shurtliff for a year once they were discharged—and then they lived again as Sampson, marrying a man and having several children while also petitioning the United States for an "Invalid's Pension" (effectively veteran's pay).

5. See Beans Velocci, "Binary Logic: Race, Expertise, and the Persistence of Uncertainty in American Sex Research" (PhD diss., Yale University, forthcoming). My thanks to Velocci for all of their insight; I've learned a great deal from their dissertation work, which will undoubtedly become a very important book.

6. "Whiggish" is an adjective that generally describes a historiographical style that understands history as progressive, and the past as a steppingstone toward a better, freer, more democratic, and more enlightened future.

7. There have been significant debates among scholars of African American and women's history over the general accuracy of newspaper transcriptions of Truth's "Ain't I a Woman?" speech, but for the purposes of this discussion, it is the cultural circulation of the speech, apocryphal or not, that concerns me, and especially its inclusion in almost all introductory gender and sexuality studies courses.

8. See, for example, the National Park Service website account of the speech, which acknowledges the plurality of transcriptions of Truth's speech; https://www.nps.gov/articles/sojourner-truth.htm. See also the comparative view of the two speeches from The Sojourner Truth Project, https://www.thesojournertruthproject.com/compare-the-speeches/.

9. Many scholars consider the Married Women's Property Acts to be the end of the power of the legal doctrine of *couverture*, which describes how a woman's legal status was subsumed under that of her husband (and, previously, her father) when she married. The first Married Women's Property Act was passed in Mississippi in 1839.

10. Remember, of course, that the Thirteenth (1865), Fourteenth (1868), and Fifteenth (1870) Amendments to the Constitution (which, respectively, abolished

slavery, made formerly enslaved persons citizens, and bestowed upon Black and brown men the right to vote) would not be passed until almost twenty years after Truth made her famous speech.

11. My reading of this speech is indebted to the writing and thinking of my former undergraduate student Hanuel Sim, who reads Truth's speech as an iteration of the way that racialized forms of labor can reconfigure the physical body in a manner that makes the body itself at odds with conventional understandings of womanhood or manhood. Sim thus reads this moment through trans studies frameworks as well and considers Truth's speech a piece of trans history. At this writing Sim is a PhD student working at the intersections of histories of gender, labor, and race in the Department of History at Princeton University.

12. On this point, also see Omise'eke Natasha Tinsley's *Ezili's Mirrors: Imagining Black Queer Genders* (Durham, NC: Duke University Press, 2018).

13. C. Riley Snorton, *Black on Both Sides: A Racial History of Trans Identity* (Minneapolis: University of Minnesota Press, 2017).

14. Saidiya Hartman, *Scenes of Subjection* (New York: Oxford University Press, 1997), 101.

15. Ibid., 97. Hartman is responding in part to Hortense Spillers's field-defining 1987 essay "Mama's Baby, Papa's Maybe," *Diacritics* 17.2 (Summer 1987): 64–81. Trans studies scholars are increasingly engaging these works.

16. While today this term is generally understood to be an offensive way of speaking about intersex individuals, in prior times, as the essays in this collection detail, it was a term that indexed a wide array of gender experiences that transcended hard (or even soft!) divisions between manhood and womanhood, masculinity and femininity.

17. See also the forthcoming special issue of *Transgender Studies Quarterly*, "Intersex and Trans Studies," *TSQ* 9.2 (2022), edited by Michelle Wolff, David Rubin, and Amanda Lock Swarr, and Hil Malatino's *Queer Embodiment: Monstrosity, Medical Violence, and Intersex Experience* (Omaha: University of Nebraska Press, 2019). See also Anne Fausto-Sterling. "Why Sex Is Not Binary," *New York Times*, October 25, 2018.

18. On this, see the forthcoming special issue of *Transgender Studies Quarterly*, "Trans-Exclusionary Feminism and the Rise of the New Right," edited by myself (Greta LaFleur) and Serena Bassi: "Trans-Exclusionary Feminisms and the Global New Right," *Transgender Studies Quarterly* 9.2 (May 2022).

19. Jen Manion, *Female Husbands: A Trans History* (Cambridge: Cambridge University Press, 2019), 95. See also chap. 4 of LaFleur, *Natural History of Sexuality in Early America*, esp. 155–58, on Sampson/Shurtliff's participation in settler colonial violence as a condition for the expression of their transness. For my prior discussions of Sampson, and queer and trans readings of Sampson, see LaFleur, "Precipitous Sensations: Herman Mann's *The Female Review*, Botanical Sexuality, and the Challenge of Queer Historiography," *Early American Literature* 48.1 (2013): 93–123.

20. Here I am invoking Scott Larson's intervention in "Laid Open: Examining Genders in Early America," the essay preceding this one in this collection.

21. See M. W. Bychowski and Dorothy Kim's special issue "Visions of Medieval Trans Feminism," *Medieval Feminist Forum* 55.1 (2019); and Simone Chess and Colby

Gordon's special issue "Early Modern Trans Studies," *Journal of Early Modern Cultural Studies* 19.4 (Fall 2020).

22. See Lillian Faderman, "A Usable Past?," in *The Lesbian Premodern: The New Middle Ages*, ed. Noreen Giffney, Michelle M. Sauer, and Diane Watt (New York: Palgrave Macmillan, 2011), 171–78. See also *The Abusable Past*, a blog sponsored and hosted by the *Radical History Review*, https://www.radicalhistoryreview.org/abus ablepast/about/, which refers to Friedrich Nietzsche, "On the Use and Abuse of History for Life," trans. Ian C. Johnston, http://la.utexas.edu/users/hcleaver/330T/ 350kPEENietzscheAbuseTableAll.pdf.

CONTRIBUTORS

Abdulhamit Arvas is assistant professor of English at the University of Pennsylvania. His work on early modern sexualities, genders, race, cross-cultural encounters, and sexual politics in modern Turkey has appeared in journals including *English Literary Renaissance, Journal of Early Modern Cultural Studies, Shakespeare Survey*, and *GLQ: A Journal of Lesbian and Gay Studies*, and in edited collections such as *The Postcolonial World, The Cambridge History of Gay and Lesbian Literature, England's Asian Renaissance*, and *A Companion to Global Shakespeares*. He has co-edited the tenth-anniversary issue of *postmedieval: a journal of medieval cultural studies*. His book project explores English and Ottoman sexualities with a focus on abductions of beautiful boys in the Mediterranean during the sixteenth and early seventeenth centuries.

Roland Betancourt is professor of art history and Chancellor's Fellow at the University of California, Irvine. They are the author of *Sight, Touch, and Imagination in Byzantium* (2018), *Byzantine Intersectionality: Sexuality, Gender, and Race in the Middle Ages* (2020), and *Performing the Gospels in Byzantium: Sight, Sound, and Space in the Divine Liturgy* (2021). Betancourt's ongoing work looks at issues of temporality and simulacral spaces across the medieval and modern worlds, considering how ideas of technology, sexuality, and historical referentiality intersect.

M. W. Bychowski is full-time English faculty at Case Western Reserve University. She received her PhD in English literature from the George Washington University. As the Anisfield-Wolf SAGES Fellow, Bychowski teaches courses on diversity and social justice, including seminars on transgender literature, queer Christianity, women of the civil rights movement, disability studies, and intersectional traditions of feminism. Her scholarship appears in *TSQ* ("Trans*Historicities" and "On Genesis"), *postmedieval* ("Trans Textuality" and "The Isle of Hermaphrodites"), *Accessus* ("Unconfessing Transgender"), the *Medieval Disability Sourcebook*, and the *Ashgate Research Companion to Medieval Disability Studies*. Together with Dorothy Kim, she edited the "Medieval Trans Feminism" special issue collection for *Medieval Feminist Forum*, for which she contributed a piece on medieval transgender suicide ("The Necropolitics of

Narcissus") and co-wrote the introduction. Additionally, she maintains Trans-literature Online (www.ThingsTransform.com), a center for digital scholarship on transgender and disability studies, medieval and post-medieval.

Emma Campbell is associate professor/reader in the School of Modern Languages and Cultures at Warwick University. She has published on a broad range of medieval French texts prior to the fourteenth century, including major traditions such as saints' lives and bestiaries. She is particularly interested in theoretically oriented approaches to medieval literature and manuscript studies, notably in relation to feminism and queer theory, anthropology, postcolonial theory, and translation studies. She is the author of *Medieval Saints' Lives: The Gift, Kinship and Community in Old French Hagiography* and co-editor of *Rethinking Medieval Translation: Ethics, Politics, Theory* and of *Troubled Vision: Gender, Sexuality and Sight in Medieval Text and Image*.

Igor H. De Souza is a lecturer in gender studies and in Spanish and Portuguese at Yale University. He is also an Associate Research Fellow in Judaic studies at Yale. He received his PhD in Jewish studies from the University of Chicago, and he was the Flegg Post-Doctoral Fellow in the Department of Jewish Studies at McGill University in Montreal. De Souza teaches seminars in the history of sexuality and in intellectual history. They include "Race, Religion, and Sex in the Inquisition," "Sexual Minorities from Plato to the Enlightenment," and "Persecution and Deviance in the West." He is currently preparing a seminar on Foucault's *History of Sexuality*. He has published research on medieval Jewish thought, including a book, *Rewriting Maimonides*, as well as essays in edited volumes. His work in progress is a book on the history of sodomy in Jewish tradition.

Leah DeVun is an associate professor of history at Rutgers University. She is the author of *Prophecy, Alchemy, and the End of Time* (2009) and *The Shape of Sex: Nonbinary Gender from Genesis to the Renaissance* (2021). She is co-editor (with Zeb Tortorici) of "Trans*Historicities," a special issue of *TSQ: Transgender Studies Quarterly*. She has also published articles in *GLQ, Radical History Review, Osiris, Journal of the History of Ideas, WSQ: Women's Studies Quarterly*, and *postmedieval*.

Micah James Goodrich earned his PhD in the English Department, Medieval Studies Program, at the University of Connecticut. He works on Middle English literature, the literary history of gender, sexuality, and embodiment, transgender studies, disability studies, and queer/trans ecologies. Goodrich has published on animacy and species division in *Early Middle English*, and on chrononormative salvation and queer labor in the *Yearbook of Langland Studies*, and he has a forthcoming essay in *Medieval Futurity: Essays for the Future of a Queer Medieval Studies*. Alongside Mary Rambaran-Olm and M. Breann Leake, Micah has been co-editing a special tenth-anniversary issue of *postmedieval* on race and revolution in medieval studies.

Alexa Alice Joubin is professor of English, women's, gender, and sexuality studies, theater, international affairs, and East Asian languages and cultures at George Washington University in Washington, DC, where she is founding co-director of the Digital Humanities Institute. At MIT she is co-founder and co-director of the open access Global Shakespeares digital performance archive (https://globalshakespeares.mit.edu/). Her latest books include *Shakespeare and East Asia* (2021), *Race* (with Martin Orkin), *Local and Global Myths in Shakespearean Performance* (co-editor, 2018), and *Shakespeare and the Ethics of Appropriation* (co-editor, 2014). She is co–general editor of *The Shakespearean International Yearbook* and editor of the Global Shakespeares series published by Palgrave Macmillan.

Anna Kłosowska is professor of French literature at Miami University. Her recent publications include *Disturbing Times: Medieval Pasts, Reimagined Futures*, co-edited with Catherine Karkov and Vincent W. J. van Gerven Oei (2020). She is the author of *Queer Love in the Middle Ages* (2005). She edited and translated Madeleine de l'Aubepine's *Selected Poems* (2007) and has published forty articles and six co-edited journal issues or collections. Her current book-in-progress, *Remarkable Objects: Silk, Metal, Ceramics, Paper, Ivory*, examines medieval France in the light of five exceptional objects from Nishapur, Damascus, North Africa, and Al-Andalus.

Greta LaFleur is an associate professor of American studies at Yale University. She is the author of *The Natural History of Sexuality in Early America* (2018) and the co-editor (with Kyla Schuller) of "The Origins of Biopolitics in the Americas," a 2019 special issue of *American Quarterly*, and the forthcoming "The Science of Sex 'Itself'" (co-edited with Benjamin Kahan), a special issue of *GLQ*. Her writing has also appeared in *Early American Studies*, *Early American Literature*, *American Literature*, *Criticism*, and the *New Republic*, and on *Public Books* and *BLARB: The Blog of the Los Angeles Review of Books*.

Scott Larson is a Lecturer IV in the Department of American Culture at the University of Michigan, Ann Arbor. He is a scholar of transgender history and culture, with a particular focus on early American culture and religion. His scholarship investigates the ways that radical religious experience in the eighteenth-century Atlantic world transformed gender, sexuality, disability, and racial formations in early America. His work has appeared in the *Journal of Early American Studies* and the *Transgender Studies Quarterly*. He received an MA in theology from Yale Divinity School and received his PhD in American studies from George Washington University.

Kathleen Perry Long is professor of French in the Department of Romance Studies at Cornell University. She is the author of two books, *Another Reality: Metamorphosis and the Imagination in the Poetry of Ovid, Petrarch, and Ronsard* and *Hermaphrodites in Renaissance Europe*, and editor of the volumes *High Anxiety: Masculinity in Crisis in Early Modern France, Religious Differences in France*, and *Gender and Scientific Discourse in Early Modern Europe*. She has written numerous articles on the work of Théodore Agrippa d'Aubigné, on gender, and on monsters. She is preparing a translation into English of *L'isle des hermaphrodites* (*The Island of Hermaphrodites*), a book on literature in the wake of the Wars of Religion, and a book on early modern discourses of monstrosity and modern discourses of disability. She is the co-editor of the series *Monsters and Marvels: Alterity in the Medieval and Early Modern Worlds*.

Robert Mills is professor of Medieval studies and head of the History of Art Department at University College London. Previously he directed the Queer@King's research center at King's College London between 2008 and 2012 and the qUCL research network at UCL between 2015 and 2018. Author of *Suspended Animation: Pain, Pleasure and Punishment in Medieval Culture* (2005), *Seeing Sodomy in the Middle Ages* (2015), and *Derek Jarman's Medieval Modern* (2018), Mills also contributed the medieval section to *A Gay History of Britain* (2007). Other recent publications include a study of images of Saint Eugenia in medieval art in *Transgender Studies Quarterly* (2018) and an article on Hieronymus Bosch's *Visions of the Hereafter* series in a volume on medieval abstraction (2021).

Masha Raskolnikov is associate professor of English at Cornell University. She is primarily interested in critical theory as a project of unmaking "common sense," and working with medieval literature as a means of doing so; she also teaches, works, and publishes in feminist, lesbian, gay, and transgender/transsexual studies. The author of *Body against Soul: Gender and Sowlehele in Middle English Allegory* (2009), she is currently working on a book on the rhetorical mode of the apology and has published articles in *postmedieval*, the

Yearbook of Langland Studies, and *GLQ* as well as Blackwell's *New Companion to Chaucer* and *Literature Compass*.

Zrinka Stahuljak, professor of comparative literature and French at the University of California, Los Angeles (UCLA), has written widely on medieval vernacular literature, historiography, and contemporary translation studies. She is the author of *Les fixeurs au Moyen Âge: Histoire et littérature connectées* (2021), *Médiéval contemporain: Pour une littérature connectée*, *Pornographic Archaeology: Medicine, Medievalism, and the Invention of the French Nation* (2013; French translation 2018), *Bloodless Genealogies of the French Middle Ages* (2005), and co-author of *The Adventures of Gillion de Trazegnies: Chivalry and Romance in the Medieval East* (2015) and *Thinking through Chrétien de Troyes* (2011). She is currently preparing *Medieval Fixers: Translation across the Mediterranean, 1250–1500*, on interlingual mediators in the medieval Mediterranean. Her work has been recognized, among others, with a visiting professorship at the Collège de France (2018), and fellowships from the Guggenheim (2016), Fulbright (2012–13), and the IAS Princeton (2005–6).

INDEX

Page numbers in italics refer to figures.

Printed in the USA
CPSIA information can be obtained
at www.ICGtesting.com
CBHW020335121224
18869CB00008BA/186